Betwixt and Between
Liminality and Marginality

Betwixt and Between Liminality and Marginality

Mind the Gap

Edited by
Zohar Hadromi-Allouche and
Michael Hubbard MacKay

LEXINGTON BOOKS
Lanham • Boulder • New York • London

Published by Lexington Books
An imprint of The Rowman & Littlefield Publishing Group, Inc.
4501 Forbes Boulevard, Suite 200, Lanham, Maryland 20706
www.rowman.com

86-90 Paul Street, London EC2A 4NE

British Library Cataloguing in Publication Information Available

Library of Congress Cataloging-in-Publication Data

Names: Hadromi-Allouche, Zohar, editor. | MacKay, Michael Hubbard, editor.
Title: Betwixt and between liminality and marginality : mind the gap / Edited by Zohar
    Hadromi-Allouche and Michael Hubbard MacKay.
Description: Lanham : Lexington Books, [2023] | Includes bibliographical references
    and index.
Identifiers: LCCN 2023000196 (print) | LCCN 2023000197 (ebook) |
    ISBN 9781793644893 (cloth) | ISBN 9781793644909 (ebook)
Subjects: LCSH: Marginality, Social. | Liminality. | Turner, Victor W. (Victor Witter),
    1920-1983 | Ethnology—Philosophy.
Classification: LCC GN367 .B48 2023 (print) | LCC GN367 (ebook) |
    DDC 305.5/68—dc23/eng/20230109
LC record available at https://lccn.loc.gov/2023000196
LC ebook record available at https://lccn.loc.gov/2023000197

Contents

v

Introduction

Mind the Gap

Betwixt and between Liminality and Marginality

Michael Hubbard MacKay and
Zohar Hadromi-Allouche

Anyone riding the trains in the United Kingdom has heard the warning call to "mind the gap" as you carefully step over the space between the train's carriage and the platform. "Your train is arriving. Please mind the gap." This idiom draws attention to the space that is in between the train and the train station. The phrase is tiled on the walls and platforms of London's underground, and the idiom has found its way onto bumper stickers and t-shirts across the world. How does a space betwixt and between the platform and the train garner so much attention?

Like the movement from the train to the platform, we are constantly moving from one space to another (like the capital building to the parking lot),[1] one social context to another (like board meetings to football games),[2] and one time to another (like Christmas day to boxing day).[3] Liminality—the gap between the worlds—articulates, shapes, defines, or serves the development of individuals, societies, and cultures in manifold ways.[4] This volume explores the liminal world of history, race, religion, class, communities, discourse, theology, and politics to develop the academic notion of liminality in multiple disciplines, a generation removed from its original instantiation. It uses a supple notion of liminality to challenge and extend Victor Turner's symbolic anthropology into a kind of liminality that goes beyond social structure and demands an interdisciplinary landscape of ideas and examples to articulate.

This volume does not revive Turner's work, it challenges it as the authors of this volume use it to theorize within their own contemporary scholarship, but it also celebrates its continued influence and recasting into disciplines

1

outside of anthropology. Even after a generation of academic scrutiny his work is still relevant in a completely different setting and under new theoretical constraints. Though Turner's liminality was quickly challenged by the early 1980s, this volume represents the sustained interest, expansion, contests, and encounters with his work across the disciplines. In particular, the authors examine marginalized people like African Hebrew Israelites and Mormon women ritually practicing polygamy. It explores the dialogic relationship of space and agency, to recognize marginal groups and people within society, literature, theology, and history. Making marginality a central focus in this volume, it emphasizes the important relationship between marginal groups and work that occurs within liminal states. In its simplest forms, liminality provides language for meaningful approaches to articulate transition and change, while also representing complex social theories beyond Turner's classical symbolic approach. Though Turner's symbolic anthropology is not in vogue and critical reframing has occurred, this volume compliments recent work adapting and using his earlier notions of liminality in scholarship about Modernity, organizational studies, literary studies, borderlands in American Studies, and travel, geography, and space.[5] This volume demonstrates that Turner's language for expressing transition and the work that is done in transition is still relevant for even complex scholarship across disciplines examining contemporary social issues. Yet, it also suggests that theorizing with Turner's work requires updating and even abandonment of some of his primary ideas. In this way, it is a challenge to the pedestrian simplifications of Turner's work, and a realistic approach to using classical social theory in contemporary scholarship.

CRITICAL LIMINALITY

A brief examination of Turner's work and the challenges to it will help establish the value of the chapters in this volume. Let's start with the idea of liminality. This term was first introduced by the French folklorist Arnold van Gennep in 1909.[6] In his studies of rites of passage in many societies, van Gennep argued that each such rite combined three phases: separation, margin (or *limen*), and reaggregation. Of these, the first phase (separating the ritual subjects from their old place in society) and the last one (returning them after their transformation to new places) are clear, whereas the middle phase is ambiguous. During this stage, the subjects of the rite are no longer part of their old place in society, nor do they yet belong to their new one. Van Gennep, therefore, defines this middle phase as liminal, whereas liminality he regards as an intermediate, ambivalent social reality.

Since the mid-1970s, this concept has been reinvented in the work of the anthropologist Victor Turner,[7] who defines liminal as the movement "between the formerly familiar and stable and the not-yet familiar and stable," in the context of "passages from one state of society or mind to another."[8] He regards liminality as characteristic of inter-structural, "betwixt and between" situations, of ambiguity and transition, and the "liminaries" as those who cannot be classified in the ordinary classification for they are neither here nor there, neither one thing nor the other.

Turner trained under Max Gluckman who emphasized a Marxian form of British structural-functionalism. For Turner, society is defined by conflict and disagreement, in which its parts are disparate and in contrast to each other. His project gave answers to how the normal state of society was maintained despite its inconsistencies and disputes. He gave rise to important terminology that is still used across disciplines, developing the words and phrases, "liminaility," "communitas," "social drama," "rite of passage," and "anti-structure." Categorized as a symbolic anthropologist, he uniquely used symbol as a guide through social processes, like in his linear use of a rite of passage, instead of Arnold van Gennep's cyclical use of rite of passage. Symbols produced social transformation, like the rites of maturation or marriage. The movement from one social status to another became a bastion of his research. He focused on the ritual mechanism that left individuals in between normal states of society, using terms like "communitas," "liminality," and "marginality."

Since Turner died on the cusp of theoretical change in anthropology and philosophy, critiques waged at his work are primarily from the theories that became highly influential after his death.[9] Facing the impact of the culture wars in the United States during the 1990s and the robust development of post-structuralism, there were many critiques of his form of symbolic anthropology. Sherry Ortner explains that much of the critique became part of the theoretical agenda of the next schools of thought, making his work a transition from one theoretical approach to the next in anthropology. She notes that Turner and symbolic anthropology lacked "a systematic sociology . . . [an] underdeveloped sense of the politics of culture; and [a] lack of curiosity concerning the production and maintenance of symbolic systems." It also appeared mystical and ambiguous to the scientifically oriented ecological anthropologists.[10] But, maybe the most potent critique came from Renato Rosaldo who argues that Turner's explanation of the way of passage or reintegration into society is utopian and ahistorical since it idealizes normal society and individuals' desire to reaggregate.[11] Reintegration is not always possible nor desirable. Demonstrable values and norms do not always find themselves moving downstream again in a flow comparable to communitas.

In fact, as the chapters in this book demonstrate, reaggregation may include swimming upstream for women in Islam or for Christians in Algeria's Islamic culture.

Marginals tend to avoid the ritual consensus, described as communitas. As Turner argued, "Marginals like liminars are also betwixt and between, but unlike ritual liminars they have no cultural assurance of a final stable resolution of their ambiguity."[12] Turner's recognition of this issue has left an important thinking space for scholarship in this volume that also supports others who have valued his work by critiquing it and finding what parts of his work continue to aid in social theory. Donald Weber emphasizes this by analyzing borders in American Studies and associating theoretical thought surrounding them with liminality and its relationship with marginal figures.[13] Ideas that Turner explored are still relevant and so is much of his analysis. We continue to ask, without a harmonious resolution, what happens to the marginals? And has race, class, gender, and sexual orientation now become the space for thinking about reintegration and communitas? While Turnerian models of social analysis are not followed with exactness, the language he developed to describe change and movement has lasted into the twenty-first century, invoking disregard for his work by some, but thoughtful engagement with it has enlightened its replacements and found its influence in the most contemporary theories today.

This is not a book about Turner nor is it limited to anthropological theory. Instead, by using Turner and the critiques of his work as a framework for interdisciplinary thinking, this volume focuses on "the marginal" within society. Each chapter examines marginal groups or liminal spaces and ideas not only with an eye toward the validity of the critiques against Turner but also hopeful to find the value of Turner's ideas as a "classical" theorist. It develops the value of Turner's descriptive language and conceptual framework while finding meaning in individual examples of how marginal groups destabilize, shape, and effect the dominant culture. Liminality has since been applied in a variety of contexts in multiple disciplines in the humanities and the social sciences.

This volume aims at expanding this discourse and following the research across disciplines in each chapter's individual path. For one, its claim for an interdisciplinary approach that emerges from both the diverse fields it covers, as well as its organization along thematic (rather than disciplinary) lines. Second, the chapters apply liminality to concepts that are beyond the immediate association of this term and examine the diverse implications of liminality in regard to topics such as polygamy, dance, coppersmith, leadership, and the porches of churches. Engaging with a broad variety of perspectives, such as religion, anthropology, arts and craft, and literature and philosophy, it explores the ambivalent potential of the liminal condition in fulfilling an interactive and dialogical role within, and between, groups and communities, as well as an agent of social change. The "betwixt and between" position emerges as perpetual, ambivalent, and challenging, as well as potentially helpful for promoting change and dialogue. By approaching liminality as a form of interaction, both within and between groups (and individuals) and relating to binary opposites such as live/digital, strange/familiar, master/apprentice, individual/institution, or leader/follower, it examines the extent to which liminality as a permanent position makes a preferable choice.

The volume consists of thirteen chapters. The introductory chapter, which provides a theoretical background, is followed by four more sections: (1) *Liminality without: Marginalized Communities*; (2) *Liminality within: Group Interaction within the Liminal Space;* (3) *Within and without: Liminality and Dialogue*; and (4) *Liminality as an Agent of Change.*

LIMINALITY WITHOUT: MARGINALIZED COMMUNITIES

Chapters in this section emphasize the liminality of minority communities that live in an environment where they are marginalized due to their identity—religious, ethnic, racial, cultural, or all at once. This liminality, however, is experienced differently by each of these communities.

"Layers of Liminality and Marginality in the African Hebrew Israelite Community" by Michael T. Miller examines how the Hebrew Israelites have utilized this narrative of liminal marginalization in their quest for identity and self-determination. The African Hebrew Israelites are an expatriate black American group who have lived in Israel since 1969. Drawing on a long tradition in the black American church that self-identified as the biblical Israelites, the Hebrew Israelites inhabit a doubly or triply liminal space: Americans were not fully Americans, Judeans were not Jews, and (for forty years until they were finally granted citizenship), Israelis were not Israelis. Crossing the physical and conceptual borders in the search for identity and the right to define themselves, the Hebrews help demonstrate the inherent theology of marginalization which has been a part of the construction of both Judaism and early Christianity in competition with hostile majorities.

Patrick J. S. Brittenden uses liminality in order to understand the identity and development of the Muslim-background Church of Algeria. In "Liberating Liminality in the Contemporary Church of Algeria," he examines the four main axes along which this liminality is visible. These are the dialectics of centers and margins; particularity and universality; East and West; and the pedagogical liminality of knowing, being, and doing. While possessing uncomfortable liminality, this multidimensional drama of Algerian liminality does not have to be a tragedy. The paradox of liminality can be viewed as a positive state pregnant with potential for all Algerians and for Algerian Christians, in particular. An examination of how the liminal transitions in personal and corporate identities among Christian converts from a Muslim background is followed by considering how the Algerian Christian experience of liminality can be transformed into a context of liberation. "Liberating liminality" thus becomes a means of transforming the ontology and teleology of this subordinate religious minority.

This section concludes with "Neither here nor there": Border-crossing and Liminal States in Rose Tremain's *The Road Home."* Maria Antonietta Struzziero highlights the liminality and marginalization of work migrants, as reflected in Rose Tremain's 2008 novel. This is the story of Lev who, after the death of his wife, migrated from Ukraine to London, in search of a better future for himself and the young daughter he leaves behind. Struzziero highlights how the novel articulates the condition of liminality and its ritual tripartite structure and ambivalent potential. This is evident in the overall narrative trajectory of the novel, as well as in single episodes, and in the protagonist's psychological awakening to a new sense of self. Lev, who alternates psychologically and emotionally between two states, split betwixt and between home and the host country, manifests those attributes that Turner identified as typical of liminal *personae.* When he finally returns to his native community, Lev is a transformed person.

LIMINALITY WITHIN: GROUP INTERACTION WITHIN THE LIMINAL SPACE

This section examines examples of liminal spaces and times and the link between these dimensions. In particular, it emphasizes the role of the liminal gap as a space of communication, interactions, and development within a specific group.

In "Liminal Space and Liminal Place: The Medieval Church Porch" Jamie Ingram establishes the multiple uses and mixed function of the porch of the medieval parish church. These multiple uses transformed the medieval church porch from a mere door into a ritual space and liminal place. A noisy, messy space, it is located between the ontological worlds of the secular and the divine, as historical graffiti depositions reveal. Exploring the survey data of archaeological recording and interpretation of historical graffiti within medieval churches of England, Ingram highlights the connection between the space as a point of ritual interface and a place created by the ritual empowerment.

Michele Avis Feder-Nadoff in "Hammering in-between: Liminality and Contingency in Artisanal Practice, Santa Clara del Cobre, Michoacán,

Mexico" examines the liminality of artisan agency. In light of Turner's own application of theories of liminality into an anthropology of performance, Feder-Nadoff applies these theories to craft. Turner argued for a performative engaged methodology of ethnographic practice and analysis via theatrical reenactment. He realized that ambiguity was a necessary principle of the liminal and that agency was only expressed through contingency. Using Turner as a leaving point, Feder-Nadoff examines the ethnography of artisanal-skilled practice as based in performative apprenticeship. By looking at the limen joining master-apprentice, ethnographer-subject, artisan-(craft)work, (craft)work-receivers, (craft)work-materia prima, and ordinary-extraordinary artisan performance, she addresses the states of between and betwixt that are encountered by the coppersmith in performance, as well as the "as-is" contingencies of the coppersmiths' lives that are transformed into "as if's."

"Liminality in Time: The Taipei Dance Circle as a Process" by Yu-Chun Chen examines the liminality across bodies, space, and time in a dance troupe, which lost its leader. The Taipei Dance Circle (TDC), founded by Shaw-Lu Liu, created the baby-oil dance as an avant-garde genre. This special material has both changed the relationship between the floor and dancers and developed new kinesthesia, alternative aesthetics, and a process of professional socialization. The death of Shaw-Lu Liu's in 2014 not only led the TDC into a transitional phase of uncertainty but also created a space for other choreographers' collaborations to emerge. This chapter examines how this collaborative choreography, combined with training and improvization, transformed the kinesthesia and aesthetics of the troupe, changing its ways of dancing as well as the relationship between individuals and the institution.

This section concludes with Michael MacKay's chapter "Mormon Polygamy: Liminal or Normative?" in which he examines Mormon polygamy as a normative religious practice to challenge previous interpretations of polygamy as a liminal practice. Though Turner's theories have benefited Mormon Studies in their ability to theorize about ritual and liminality, it has also narrowed its focus by assuming reaggregation of liminars into "normal" society. This chapter examines Mormon polygamy as a rite and broadens the analysis to make sense of secularism and religion for understanding normative discourses in religion.

WITHIN AND WITHOUT: LIMINALITY AND DIALOGUE

Chapters in this section explore the dialogical role of liminality. Such dialogues occur, for example, between minority and majority groups; human and environment; or artists and audience, as well as artists among themselves.

Eric Ziolkowski discusses in "Liminal Dialogue: Solomon Ibn Verga's Tale of Ephraim Ibn Sanjo and King Pedro I of Aragon" liminality within the context of court dialogues. Focusing on the renown motif of the wise and righteous Jew summoned for questioning to the court of a foreign king (typically Christian or Muslim), he uses as a case study the dialogue from the anecdote in Solomon Ibn Verga's *Shevet Yehudah*. This dialogue involves a Jewish interviewee in King Pedro of Aragon's court. This chapter analyzes the interviewee's situation before Pedro within a Turnerian framework of ritual drama as an example of precarious liminality, in this case, an intensely liminal predicament.

This section concludes with Pauline Brooks, who discusses the process of "Intermediality: Performing the Liminal in the Dance Work Falling." Brooks examines in this chapter the space created when a work of art combines live and digital images moving in and out of the stage and the liminal interactions of these images among themselves, as well as such interactions among the media of live performance and digital images.

LIMINALITY AS AN AGENT OF CHANGE

Finally, section IV explores the transformative agency of liminality and its role as an agent of change. The philosophical aspect of this function, which contrasts the traditional role of liminality, is followed by two examples that highlight the application of such a change and the rejection that such a change might evoke among those benefiting from the existing structures.

In "The Pedagogics of Liminality: Ivan Illich and the Critique of Institutional Ritualization," Jose R. Irizarry discusses the argument made by Austrian philosopher and priest Ivan Illich for giving the liminal experience a status of recurrent permanence. At the time Victor Turner resurrected van Gennep's concept of liminality, Illich was analyzing the rituals of industrial society that transferred communities' traditional tools of subsistence into the hands of certified professionals. He contended that when modern institutions exercise this professional monopoly *beyond a certain threshold* their impact on people's life is, rather than intended development, *counterproductivity*. Illich seeks to demonstrate how the professionalization of schooling is detrimental to learning, mass transportation with accelerated vehicles impedes mobility, and technology obstructs communication. This chapter reintroduces Illich's work to expand the application of *liminality* to the larger question of social relationships in an industrial and technological culture. It also contrasts Turner's idea of *communitas* as dialectically affirming existing social structures, with Illich's idea of *conviviality* as the arrival state for restoring a productive and generative social order, centered in new tools rather than preestablished structures.

Keren Abbou Hershkovits demonstrates in "Agents of Conversion, Agency of Women in Early Islam" the linkage between liminality and change, as she examines the role of Muslim women in Late Antiquity as agents of conversion. Despite the limited status of women at that time, several cases are documented of women who were active agents of conversion into Islam, either for the sake of faith, or, in some cases, with the intention of improving their social stand. By highlighting several case studies, this chapter demonstrates the liminal characteristics of these women, who were both agents of transition and becoming. By being such agents, these women also altered their own position in society.

Finally, in "Wife and Leader: Khadījah as a First Follower," Zohar Hadromi-Allouche explores a specific example of such an agent, through examining the activity of Khadījah through the combined prism of liminality and leadership studies. The theory of the "first follower" that is often discussed within the contexts of business, marketing or even pedagogy, is here applied to female leadership in Islam and, in particular, the character of Khadījah. Often referred to as the first wife of prophet Muhammad, Khadījah has a crucial role in the emergence of Islam. Through her position as the first convert to Islam and the first follower of Muhammad, her support of Muhammad and the new movement was decisive in the new religious movement coming into being. The leadership of a first follower is, however, liminal by essence, and this chapter examines how this liminality, combined with the *perceived* gender-related liminality of Khadījah, affects her portrayal in classical and modern sources alike.

NOTES

1. A. Cook-Sather, "Newly betwixt and between: Revising liminality in the context of a teacher preparation program," *Anthropology & Education Quarterly* 37, no. 2 (2006): 110–127; P. Wood, "Blogs as liminal space: Student teachers at the threshold," *Technology, Pedagogy and Education* 21, no. 1 (2021): 85–99; C. Tansley & S. Tietze, "Rites of passage through talent management progression stages: An identity work perspective," *The International Journal of Human Resource Management* 24, no. 9 (2013): 1799–1815; I. Winkler & M. K. Mahmood, "The liminality of temporary agency work: Exploring the dimensions of Danish temporary agency workers' liminal experience," *Old Site of Nordic Journal of Working Life Studies* 5, no. 1 (2015): 51–68.

2. G. Adorno, "Between two worlds: Liminality and late-stage cancer-directed therapy," *OMEGA-Journal of Death and Dying* 71, no. 2 (2015): 99–125; E. S. Cohn, "From waiting to relating: Parents' experiences in the waiting room of an occupational therapy clinic," *American Journal of Occupational Therapy* 55, no. 2 (2001): 167–174.

3. S. Bigger, "Victor Turner, liminality, and cultural performance," *Journal of Beliefs & Values* 30, no. 2 (2009): 209–212; A. Szakolczai, "Liminality and

experience: Structuring transitory situations and transformative events," *International Political Anthropology* 2, no. 1 (2009): 141–172; B. Thomassen, "The uses and meanings of liminality," *International Political Anthropology* 2, no. 1 (2009): 5–27; M. Bamber, J. Allen-Collinson, & J. McCormack, "Occupational limbo, transitional liminality and permanent liminality: New conceptual distinctions," *Human Relations* 70, no. 12 (2017): 1514–1537.

4. M. Kornberger, L. Justesen, & J. Mouritsen, "'When you make manager, we put a big mountain in front of you': An ethnography of managers in a Big 4 accounting firm," *Accounting, Organizations and Society* 36, no. 8 (2011): 514–533; A. G. Sleight, "Liminality and ritual in biographical work: A theoretical framework for cancer survivorship," *International Journal of Transpersonal Studies* 35, no. 1 (2016): 52–61; Szakolczai, "Liminality and experience," 141–172.

5. Bjørn Thomassen, *Liminality and the Modern: Living Through the In-Between* (Ashgate, 2014); Maria Rita Tagliaventi, *Liminality in Organization Studies: Theory and Method* (Routledge, 2020); C. N. Van der Merwe, *Beyond the Threshold: Explorations of Liminality in Literature* (Peter Lang, 2007); Hazel Andrews & Les Roberts (eds.), *Liminal Landscapes: Travel, Experience and Spaces In-between* (Routledge, 2012); Cook-Sather, "Newly betwixt and between," 110–127; Donald Weber, "From Limin to border: A meditation on the legacy of Victor Turner for American cultural studies," *American Quarterly* 47, no. 3 (1995): 525–536.

6. Arnold van Gennep, *The Rites of Passage*, trans. Monika B. Vizedom and Gabrielle L. Caffee, ed. Solon T. Kimball (Chicago: University of Chicago Press, 1965, c1960 [1909]).

7. Victor Turner, *Blazing the Trail: Way Marks in the Exploration of Symbols*, ed. Edith Turner (Tuscon and London: University of Arizona Press, 1992), 48–52, 132–136.

8. Ibid., 132.

9. See, for example, Marshall Sahlins, *Islands of History* (Chicago, IL: University of Chicago Press, 1985); Louis Dumont, *Essays on Individualism: Modern Ideology in Anthropological Perspective* (Chicago, IL: University of Chicago Press, 1986).

10. Sherry B. Ortner, "Theory in anthropology since the sixties," *Comparative Studies in Society and History* 26, no. 1 (1984): 126–166.

11. Renato Rosaldo, *Culture and Truth: The Remaking of Social Analysis* (Boston: Beacon Press, 1993), 96–97.

12. Victor Turner, *Dramas, Fields, and Metaphors: Symbolic Action in Human Society* (Ithaca, NY and London: Cornell University Press, 1974), 232–33.

13. Weber, "From Limin to Border," 532.

BIBLIOGRAPHY

Adorno, G. "Between Two Worlds: Liminality and Late-Stage Cancer-Directed Therapy." *OMEGA-Journal of Death and Dying* 71, no. 2 (2015): 99–125.
Andrews, Hazel and Les Roberts, eds. *Liminal Landscapes: Travel, Experience and Spaces In-Between*. Routledge, 2012.

Bamber, M., J. Allen-Collinson, and J. McCormack. "Occupational Limbo, Transitional Liminality and Permanent Liminality: New Conceptual Distinctions." *Human Relations* 70, no. 12 (2017): 1514–1537.

Bigger, S. "Victor Turner, Liminality, and Cultural Performance." *Journal of Beliefs & Values* 30, no. 2 (2009): 209–212.

Cohn, E. S. "From Waiting to Relating: Parents' Experiences in the Waiting Room of an Occupational Therapy Clinic." *American Journal of Occupational Therapy* 55, no. 2 (2001): 167–174.

Cook-Sather, A. "Newly Betwixt and Between: Revising Liminality in the Context of a Teacher Preparation Program." *Anthropology & Education Quarterly* 37, no. 2 (2006): 110–127.

Dumont, Louis. *Essays on Individualism: Modern Ideology in Anthropological Perspective*. Chicago, IL: University of Chicago Press, 1986.

Kornberger, M., L. Justesen, and J. Mouritsen. "'When You Make Manager, We Put a Big Mountain in Front of You': An Ethnography of Managers in a Big 4 Accounting Firm." *Accounting, Organizations and Society* 36, no. 8 (2011): 514–533.

Ortner, Sherry B. "Theory in Anthropology since the Sixties." *Comparative Studies in Society and History* 26, no. 1 (1984): 126–166.

Renato, Rosaldo. *Culture and Truth: The Remaking of Social Analysis*. Boston: Beacon Press, 1993.

Sahlins, Marshall. *Islands of History*. Chicago, IL: University of Chicago Press, 1985.

Sleight, A. G. "Liminality and Ritual in Biographical Work: A Theoretical Framework for Cancer Survivorship." *International Journal of Transpersonal Studies*, 35 no. 1 (2016): 52–61.

Szakolczai, A. "Liminality and Experience: Structuring Transitory Situations and Transformative Events." *International Political Anthropology* 2, no. 1 (2009): 141–172.

Tagliaventi, Maria Rita. *Liminality in Organization Studies: Theory and Method*. Routledge: 2020.

Tansley, C. and S. Tietze. "Rites of Passage Through Talent Management Progression Stages: An Identity Work Perspective." *The International Journal of human Resource Management* 24, no. 9 (2013): 1799–1815.

Thomassen, B. "The Uses and Meanings of Liminality." *International Political Anthropology* 2, no. 1 (2009): 5–27.

Thomassen, Bjørn. *Liminality and the Modern: Living Through the In-Between*. Ashgate: 2014.

Turner, Victor. *Blazing the Trail: Way Marks in the Exploration of Symbols*, edited by Edith Turner. Tuscon, AZ and London: University of Arizona Press, 1992.

Turner, Victor. *Dramas, Fields, and Metaphors: Symbolic Action in Human Society*. Ithaca, NY and London: Cornell University Press, 1974.

van der Merwe, C. N. *Beyond the Threshold: Explorations of Liminality in Literature*. Peter Lang, 2007.

van Gennep, Arnold. *The Rites of Passage*. Translated by Monika B. Vizedom and Gabrielle L. Caffee; introduction by Solon T. Kimball. Chicago, IL: University of Chicago Press, 1965, c1960 [1909].

Weber, Donald. "From Limin to Border: A Meditation on the Legacy of Victor Turner for American Cultural Studies." *American Quarterly* 47, no. 3 (1995): 525–536.

Winkler, I. and M. K. Mahmood. "The Liminality of Temporary Agency Work: Exploring the Dimensions of Danish Temporary Agency Workers' Liminal Experience." *Old Site of Nordic Journal of Working Life Studies* 5, no. 1 (2015): 51–68.

Wood, P. "Blogs as Liminal Space: Student Teachers at the Threshold." *Technology, Pedagogy and Education* 21, no. 1 (2021): 85–99.

LIMINALITY WITHOUT

MARGINALIZED COMMUNITIES

Chapter 1

Layers of Liminality and Marginality in the African Hebrew Israelite Community

Michael T. Miller

The African Hebrew Israelites are an expatriate black American group who have lived in Israel since 1969 when their spiritual leader Ben Ammi received a revelation from the angel Gabriel to take his people back to the promised land. Drawing on a long tradition in the black American church that self-identified as the biblical Israelites, the Hebrew Israelites are both a marginal and liminal group, having been Americans who were not fully Americans, they believe themselves to be Judeans, who are not Jews, and in the forty-year struggle with the state of Israel prior to the granting of citizenship they were Israelis who were not Israelis. Arguing that their forty-year "wilderness" period was a liminal state that allowed them to create themselves a new, I will show how the Hebrews crossed physical and conceptual borders in the search for identity and to demonstrate the inherent theology of marginalization, which has been a part of the construction of both Judaism and early Christianity in competition with hostile majorities. This chapter will look at the way the Hebrew Israelites have utilized this narrative of marginalization in their own quest for identity and self-determination.

The African Hebrew Israelites of Jerusalem (hereafter AHIJ) are an expatriate African American group who have been living in Israel for more than fifty years, who live by biblical but not rabbinic precepts. At around 3,000 people[1] constitute the largest community of African Americans outside of the USA, and have been called "The most successful African American utopian separatist project in history."[2]

The AHIJ emerged against the background of 1960s black America, the civil rights struggle, and the growing influence of its more militant cousin, the Black Power movement. The community are interesting partly because they succeeded where (arguably) most others failed. While Marcus Garvey,

Malcolm X, and Martin Luther King fought and won some battles for their people, the situation for many black Americans today is still far from ideal: the recent emergence of the Black Lives Matter movement highlights just one area of ongoing concern (police brutality) among many. But this community stepped outside of the concepts provided by white America's power structures and claimed the right to define their own identity and place in the world. Their community is now a prospering example of a people who have achieved self-sufficiency, know their priorities, and, having escaped a precipitous situation themselves, see their role as helping to lead the rest of humankind out of the abyss we currently inhabit.

The AHIJ are both a marginal and liminal community:[3] they were Americans who were not fully Americans; they claim to be Judean Israelites but not Jews; and in the forty-year struggle with the state of Israel prior to the granting of citizenship they were Israelis who were not Israelis. They exist in the nexus between African American and Jewish, without fitting comfortably into either category. But in van Gennep and Turner's terms, they existed for decades between the stages of separation and integration, having abandoned the USA and their American identities (in many cases even renouncing their citizenship) but had not yet achieved acceptance and legal status in Israel. This extended liminal period, during which they existed on the fringes of Israeli society, subject to frequent deportations and without the rights or responsibilities of citizenship, constituted the disorienting and pressurized environment in which they matured, forming their theology, values, and communal structure. I will argue that this very liminality has been used by them to develop a new theology founded on the dialectic of oppression and liberation which is an oft-cited theme of the Hebrew Bible, the New Testament, and the Qur'an.

THE HISTORY OF THE COMMUNITY

Since the end of the nineteenth century, some black-led churches and preachers in the USA have held the belief that African Americans were descendants of the Ancient Israelites. Scholars are still untangling the prehistory but it likely originated in a perceived similarity between the struggles of the biblical Israelites against Egyptian and Babylonian slavery, and the conditions of enslaved blacks in the USA, which mixed with multiracial black and Jewish migrants from the Caribbean and descendants of slaves from Jewish households.[4] There are nowadays many Hebrew Israelite groups in the USA, some are militant, separatist, and antisemitic and some viewing themselves as siblings to rabbinic Judaism. Generally they prefer to be called Israelites, Hebrews, or Hebrew Israelites rather than Jews, as a way of asserting identification with the people of the Bible in distinction to the people of the Bible and the Talmud, although not infrequently they're referred to simply as "Black Jews" (something which has caused annoyance for some black practitioners of normative rabbinic Judaism). The AHIJ is just one sect of this broad movement.

In 1963,[5] a Chicago steel worker named Ben Carter, having been given the Hebrew name Ben Ammi ("Son of my People") by one of his teachers, helped to found the A-Beta Hebrew Culture Center, an organization to unify the diverse black Jewish groups in the city. In 1966—a time of extreme strain upon the black American community, Jim Crow segregation having only just been repealed and the gains of the Civil Rights movement facing increasing pushback from white Americans[6]—he received a vision (putatively from the angel Gabriel) commanding him to take his people home to the promised land. By 1967, he had accumulated up to 300 people willing to make such a journey and the money necessary to fly them halfway across the world. They spent two years in Liberia before entering the young state of Israel, under the Law of Return, which allows for Jews to claim Israeli citizenship, in three separate groups. The first group of five were granted citizenship with the understanding that they would undergo conversion to mainstream Judaism but the Israeli government grew increasingly dubious as two more groups, of thirty-nine and forty-nine, successively entered and refused to convert, claiming that they were not Jews but *the* authentic Israelites. This led to some two decades of tension as the state made several attempts to encourage them to leave, to the extent of deporting members, and persistently refused basic citizen rights such as work permits or schooling. The group were living crammed into the apartments granted to the first two groups in the development towns of Dimona, Arad, and Mitzpe Ramon on the edge of the Negev desert, struggling with internal power disputes and trying to figure themselves and their way of life out. They frequently made aggressively antisemitic statements, casting Jews as colonial usurpers of authentic Israelite identity which was in fact black African and even threatened the imminent arrival of two million black Americans who would "drive out the Europeans"[7] while actively engaging in surreptitious illegal immigration of new recruits. Israel for its part would have liked to expel all of them but feared international condemnation and was particularly concerned about provoking black-Jewish tensions in America.[8]

The last two decades however have seen a progressive thawing to the extent that most of the community now have citizenship or permanent resident status and the youth perform military service. Negotiations began in 1990 and saw the progressive awarding of temporary then permanent resident status and finally the possibility of citizenship upon application in 2009. They are now a vibrant and well-liked part of Israeli society numbering some 3,000 individuals, members regularly write editorials in HaAretz, run a vegan food factory and Israel's first vegan restaurant, and have represented Israel in the Eurovision song contest (twice: in 1999 and 2006). They are particularly fond of pointing out that former prime minister Shimon Peres celebrated his eighty-fifth birthday with the community in 2008. They've also been involved in mediation between American black and Jewish groups, between Chicago street gangs, and—less successfully—between the Israelis and Palestinians. They were even featured by popular Palestinian-American vlogger Nas Daily in 2018.[9]

Their success is not limited to the political realm. The community boasts an impressive longevity and absence of disease,[10] a socially cohesive and happy society, zero drug abuse, smoking or alcoholism, and in general a complete turnaround from the previous black American inner-city life of, as they see it, crime, violence, suffering, bigotry, disease, and mortality, all within a society that didn't respect or accept them.[11]

Ben Ammi died in December 2014, but the community appears to be thriving. Still, his theology and his many writings and speeches inform every aspect of the community; referred to as Abba (father), his picture hangs in all members' apartments along with his quotes, and his books (of which there are eleven, between 1982 and 2011) are considered a new revelation by members.

The three phases that van Gennep described in ritual—separation, margin, aggregation[12]—are evidenced in the AHIJ history, as (1) their exodus to Liberia, literally separating themselves from American society and from their own past as is suggested by their own claims that this was a period intended to cleanse themselves of the attributes developed/imposed on them during their enslavement in America; (2) the wilderness years of no status in Israel; and (3) the slow acceptance into Israeli society and legal structure since 1990.

The community themselves have claimed that they retraced their ancestors' path *out* of the land of Israel in their return, identifying Liberia as symbolic of the west coast locations at which their ancestors were captured and transported to America. This symbolic identification can be contrasted with a clear replication of the earlier, biblical journey of the Israelites from Egypt through the desert wilderness of Sinai (symbolized by Liberia) into the promised land, preceded by a unit of spies sent to investigate conditions (Num.13). In 1968, Ben Ammi and Hezekiyahu (Charles Blackwell) appear to have replicated this when they flew from Liberia to Israel in order to investigate the state and its apparatuses. Ben Ammi returned to Liberia but Hezekiyahu remained in Israel, learning the process of citizenship and becoming fluent in modern Hebrew while working at a kibbutz, he was the welcoming party and guide for subsequent arrivals. In this dual mimetic replication and inverted retracing, we can see a nod toward the imitative and the reversal aspects of the liminal stage.[13]

Bjørn Thomassen suggests that liminal peoples

challenge social order by setting themselves apart from any normally accepted social rules from their "betwixt and between" position; they become nameless, timeless and socially "unstructured," existing in a floating state of being, even as they acquire throughout the liminal period the necessary knowledge and experience in order that their transformed beings may eventually re-enter society and take up their new roles, which are recognized and stamped onto them in the re-aggregation ritual.[14]

I will argue that the AHIJ did precisely this. There are several ways in which we can interpret liminal zones or stages during their history. Most potently perhaps, in extracting themselves from American society, they for forty years inhabited a liminal zone, and it was in this space that they elaborated and developed their theology and sense of identity, growing into a community that could finally be integrated by their new home, Israel.

Having stepped out of the social structure of the USA, they inhabited a *voluntarily* liminal space in Liberia, and in their move to Israel in 1969 they found that they could neither continue their existence as they had in Liberia nor integrate into Israel's social structure—so began the long *involuntary* liminal zone of their non-citizenship. It was only in 1990 that this began to thaw and the process of integration, with legal status, rights and responsibilities, began. Interestingly, Israel did attempt to perform a kind of aggregation/incorporation rite as soon as they arrived—which was articulated as religious conversion. If completed, this would have incorporated the community into Israeli society without complaint. The rejection of this rite and form of incorporation meant that the liminal stage was prolonged indefinitely, resolving itself only by a tenuous process of negotiations which culminated in the new rite of incorporation into the society which did not conflict with the identity claim of the AHIJ—making them Israelis but not Jews.

During the liminal period, the community exhibited several features of *communitas* as outlined by Turner[15]—they lived communally without private property and in an egalitarian structure. There was a strict social order, although it may not have been as clear at the beginning as it became in later times. Indeed, Turner writes that

like the neophytes in the African circumcision lodge, or the Benedictine monks, or the members of a millenarian movement, those living in community seem to require, sooner or later, an absolute authority, whether this be a religious commandment, a divinely inspired leader, or a dictator.[16]

Ben Ammi became this when he instigated a new order in 1973, transitioning from presumptive leader to total ruler. Diet was also changed, the community became vegan at this point. Sexuality was controlled, but its boundaries were changed from those of American society, permitting no premarital sex but more than one marriage per male,[17] and clothing was regulated in a way that made members visibly distinct from all other Israelis.

A key motif of the liminal is the paradoxical "power of the weak," where those who find themselves outside the structure of society are, because of that fact, able to act in new and creative ways, manifesting an innovative energy which can change their environment once they are reintegrated.[18] They also hold a certain pseudo-magical power which is both threatening and holy to broader society. Van Gennep writes:

> An individual or group that does not have an immediate right, by birth or through specially acquired attributes to enter a particular house and to become established in one of its sections is in a state of isolation. This isolation has two aspects, which may be found separately or in combination: such a person is weak, because he is outside a given group or society, but he is also strong since he is in the sacred realm with respect to the group's members for whom their society constitutes the secular world. In consequence some peoples kill, strip, and mistreat a stranger without ceremony, while others fear him, take great care of him, treat him as a powerful being, or take magico-religious protective measures against him.[19]

The AHIJ's liminal stage when they were without legal status in Israel evokes several of these qualities—while no member was killed by the broader community, their treatment by the state and employers was often very negative, abusive even—the state invaded their homes to detain members for deportation and often those who employed members illegally would refuse to pay once work was complete; however, this contrasts with the care and protection offered them by neighbors and local residents, who helped them to survive.

Related to this paradoxical power of the weak, one of the key tools that allowed them to survive and prosper during this period (when despite their persecution by the state, they grew tenfold) was the trope of marginalization which is central in all Abrahamic religions.

MARGINALISM AND THE "POWER OF THE WEAK" AS A RELIGIOUS TROPE IN ABRAHAMIC SCRIPTURE

One of the recurring features of Abrahamic religion is an emphasis on marginalism, on the paradoxical power of the weak, and the significance of those who exist outside the conventional power structures. This is repeated throughout the Hebrew Bible, in which kings, empires, and apparently "alpha" types are given very little respect. Rulers are often unjust and their fate is unpleasant whereas the central historical figures are usually nobodies who rise from positions hidden in the shadows: Abraham was not a great man from an important family, simply someone who had a vision (son of an idol-maker, a sculptor according to rabbinic legend[20]). Joseph was abused by his brothers in an act of peculiarly jock-like bullying. Moses was an adoptee of slave descent, with a speech impediment. The Israelites generally are a wandering people, enslaved and beaten, finally inhabiting a tiny land constantly overrun by the powerful empires of the day, lacking in any political power, laying the foundation for Isaiah's motif of the suffering servant as the key to redemption. Indeed, there is an inherent liminality to the ancient Israelite narrative too: the word Hebrew is related to the root עבר, to pass over, and to transition, just as Abraham traveled from Mesopotamia to Canaan and Moses (the liminal Egyptian-Israelite) led his people across Sinai into the new-old land of Canaan-Israel. Rabbinic tradition continues this emphasis, with the Talmuds's knowledge of the Jews as everywhere a minority community existing under the thumb of foreign powers, and the lowly status of the Messiah was an established Jewish tradition: the Talmud states that the Messiah, born on the day of the Jerusalem Temple's destruction by Rome, would be found among the poor and lepers.[21]

In the New Testament, the Messiah is the son of a craftsman from Galilee who opposes the ruling elite of Judea and chooses the company of simple folk and outsiders, prostitutes and fishermen, over the austere Pharisaic or Sadduccean elites. And in the Qur'an, Mohammad is an orphan and perhaps illiterate.[22] In more recent times, we can think of the sixteenth-century Lurianic Kabbalah wherein the Messiah is described as arising from the lowest level of humanity, from the metaphorical foot of the primordial human archetype,[23] and of twentieth-century Liberation Theology which draws on the Old and New Testaments to develop a new theology privileging the underprivileged, arguing that the poor and destitute have an intrinsically closer relationship to God, and that it is the insights of poverty which should guide humanity in matters theological.[24]

Because of this, Abrahamic monotheism has often carried this notion of liberation, of setting-free and lifting up the downtrodden, and of the special place that they inhabit in the grand scheme. This has often been interpreted metaphorically, as freeing oneself from the world and from the self-oppressive mindset which accompanies life without God, being freed into the metaphysical realm of truth. But it has also been interpreted literally as the liberation of a community or people from oppression such as that of the Judaeans under Rome or the Latin Americans via Liberation Theology.[25]

For any oppressed group, the recognition of oneself in the monotheistic narrative and its promise of release offers a potent way out. We can think here of the enthusiastic uptake among Indian Dalits of any flavor of Abrahamism to free them from the Hindu caste system.[26] Arguably it is these mechanisms which initially encouraged Black American preachers and congregations more than 100 years ago to perceive a kinship between their life experiences and those of the Israelites, to the point of thinking "this is talking about us."

One original member of the community even drew an explicit parallel between Jesus as "an outcast, rebel and reject by the established religious and political order of his day" and Ben Ammi as "a member of the reject 'negro' race . . . despised by this world's rulers."[27] This marginalization of the African American people was a crucial part of Ben Ammi's theology and the marginalization/extended liminality which the community experienced in Israel not only provided the ground for them to develop a radically new theology, one based on the Hebrew Bible and their inherited interpretations of it but also expanded far beyond the limited horizons of previous generations of Hebrew Israelites.

Ben Ammi utilized the liminal stage of their existence, during which they were withdrawn from the normalizing effect of participation in society, developing his theology and historical narrative as a radical critique of Western civilization from the outside. This would not have been possible had they been warmly welcomed into the fold of Israeli society; the outsider perspective, the marginal and liminal position they inhabited, contributed the possibility of looking at the prevailing norms of Western society from outside, free to critique it.

MARGINALIZATION AS A TOOL OF POWER
FOR THE AFRICAN HEBREW ISRAELITES

Ben Ammi's narrative describes the descent of the Black African Israelites from their unique, chosen status as "Sons of God" into "a non-people (negroes)."[28] His version of events is identical with the accepted history, up until the Roman sacking of Jerusalem in the first and second centuries of the Common Era; at this point, however, the expelled Judeans did not disperse into the Roman Empire and further east into Babylonia but moved south and west, migrating through Africa where, over the course of 1,600 years they forgot their identity, their language, their God, and His laws.[29] This forgetting then triggered a curse described in the book of Deuteronomy:

> If you do not obey the LORD your God to observe faithfully all His commandments and laws which I enjoin upon you this day, all these curses shall come

upon you and take effect: [. . .] A people you do not know shall eat up the produce of your soil and all your gains; you shall be abused and downtrodden continually, [. . .] The LORD will drive you, and the king you have set over you, to a nation unknown to you or your fathers, where you shall serve other gods, of wood and stone. [. . .] Because you would not serve the LORD your God in joy and gladness over the abundance of everything, you shall have to serve—in hunger and thirst, naked and lacking everything—the enemies whom the LORD will let loose against you. He will put an iron yoke upon your neck until He has wiped you out. [. . .] The LORD will bring a nation against you from afar, from the end of the earth, which will swoop down like the eagle—a nation whose language you do not understand, a ruthless nation, that will show the old no regard and the young no mercy. [. . .] The LORD will send you back to Egypt in galleys, by a route which I told you you should not see again.[30]

These verses have commonly been seen by Hebrew Israelite thinkers as describing the humiliations of American slavery, which is understood as a punishment for the loss of identity and righteousness which took place after the biblical period, the missing chapter in between recorded biblical history and the modern realization of Hebrew identity and return to the law.[31]

According to Ben Ammi, the Israelites (those today called African Americans) were originally the central people, those chosen by God; but they had been progressively marginalized and pushed out of the spotlight:

Black people were initially chosen by God to guide the world out of its state of ignorance, but instead they chose to join the world of iniquity. Because of their provocation of God, Black people are not only abhorred by all nations but are foolishly out of step with the rhythms and patterns established by God for perfection in each of their lives.[32]

The African Hebrews had a special destiny, but they preferred to follow their own desires and interests, and so, God let them go. Now they, who had once been at the forefront of righteousness, have become "negroes." Even the name "negro" is one determined by others, from a European language and perspective: a way of dehumanizing and deracinating the Israelites along with other Africans, until "the people who were once rulers of advanced civilizations like Songhai, Egypt and Mali have descended into the pits of the most barbaric societies." And now they are "the laughing stock of the world, disrespected by all people."[33]

The movement out of the center and onto the peripheries, although precipitated by the Israelites' choices, was actioned by God through an intermediary European people. Just as the Hebrew Bible describes attacks and conquest by other nations as a method of punishment for Israel's sins, Ben Ammi understands the history of colonization, slavery, and discrimination as part of God's justice.

The Euro-gentiles,[34] although themselves mired in an evil mindset, were ultimately doing God's work in the oppression of black Americans. These most brutal exemplars, from the Roman Empire through to twentieth-century USA, have carried out a 2,000-year plan, the "Era of the Great Deception."[35] During this time the scriptures were carried into Europe, reinterpreted into pagan ideology (now known as Christianity, with the commandments and way of life of the Torah dismissed in favor of the worship of a picturesque white man with a Latin-Greek name, "Jesus Christ"), and the Israelites were redacted as white Europeans. This was a process of concealing which would fundamentally reorient the world around the ideals of pagan Europe rather than around the ideals of righteousness as revealed to the Hebrews. The Hebrews had a mission of leadership and redemption of humanity after the fall of Adam and Eve, but they had so far proved that they wouldn't live up to the task.

A conspiracy on the part of the Euro-gentiles had played out over millennia in order to push the Israelites off of center stage and keep them in the margins.[36] The Euro-gentiles had spread a false history, wherein the African has no relation to the Israelite; the people of the Bible and of the covenant were white Europeans not black Africans; and the African is nothing more than a slave. Through this narrative, the African was self-alienated, unable to find their way back to their God, and desired to be something else than what they were (i.e., they wished to be white). The Hebrews had entered a liminal state, unrooted and without an authentic identity, wishing only to mimic the slavemaster. This situation had endured for the prophesied 400 years (from 1555, the year that the first African slave entered America, until the lifting of the Jim Crow segregation laws in 1965[37]) and only in the mid-1960s were the Hebrews beginning the process of redemption, when Ben Ammi and his group began proceedings to leave America.

Thus began the final stages of the liberation from American bondage that began with the emancipation proclamation of 1863. But, true freedom is not this simple: for any oppressed people, there are at least two struggles which must be fought. The first is the external, the structure and system of oppression which presses down upon them, and the second is the internal, that is, the derogatory self-perception inculcated by the system of oppression. This latter is arguably the more difficult to fully overcome: The question of how people became oppressed, of how and why they found themselves at the bottom of the hierarchy, is a delicate one. Some will always be tempted to adopt the narrative of the oppressors and affirm that the fact they lost this battle indicates their inferiority. Therefore, in the pursuit of liberation, the natural course would be to emulate the victors, to mimic their abilities and capacities and grow in strength such as to be their equals, if this is possible. As the Civil Rights Movement did, they would demand formal equality and then try to advance within the existing power structures of education, employment, and social mobility. Following Civil Rights and acknowledging its shortcomings, the Black Power movement took a more radical approach to liberation, arguing that the US society was rotten to the core and structurally racist. One could not achieve equality within a system built on inequality and oppression and so the system must be destroyed and replaced.

Ben Ammi's narrative borrowed much from Black Power but still took a unique approach: one which asserts that African Americans were oppressed because they are *more* important and because they had a responsibility that they didn't meet. The (temporary) victors in this struggle, the Euro-gentile nations, were victorious only because they were being used by God to punish the Hebrews for their sins: "The Euro-gentile world is our rod of correction in the Plan of Redemption of God Almighty."[38] The Hebrews had forgotten their God, their language, His laws, and His revelation. Therefore the responsibility for their predicament was upon them. In this way, Ben Ammi successfully reclaims a sense of agency for his people in their historical plight: they are no longer merely passive victims but were the active cause of their misfortune and can therefore be the agents of their own redemption. Their suffering can be permanently overcome by making the choice to return to God and righteousness. Their imminent redemption explains and justifies their oppression: not only was the suffering meaningful, it was their responsibility, a deserved punishment which is now being annulled.

These are the three components to this network of ideas. The basic idea, "We have been oppressed and are now freeing ourselves" is explained by

- We were victims of a satanic conspiracy to conceal our true identity.
- We were being punished for forgetting our God and His commandments.
- And therefore, living righteously is the key to redemption and failure will mean a return to slavery.

The final statement, the conclusion to this syllogism, sums up the sense of responsibility and necessity of staying true to their calling; if this is accepted, then it is imperative that they do not allow themselves to fall back into old habits or allow themselves to be discouraged by temporary failures.

There is a further element to Ben Ammi's thought which sits atop this structure. Because the Israelites are God's Chosen People, they have a special role in the world. Their forsaking of this was what led to their punishment, but now they are reclaiming that identity, they can take their place at the forefront of humanity, as a "light to the gentiles" (Is.49:6):

Because the Children of Israel dodged their responsibility to be Godly leaders and pacesetters, and failed to show others the benefits of righteous living, all men were denied the glory of a world where governments were headed by men governed by God.[39]

And now, "The priority of the Messianic nation is to show forth the Glory of God in their lifestyles and morality, that they may bear witness to the benefits of a people living under the laws (instructions) of God."[40]

This heightened sense of responsibility with which Ben Ammi imbues his community serves to inspire dignity and a determination to live up to these expectations. The humiliations of slavery and segregation now become not signifiers of weakness but the inspiration for strength and self-discipline. Taking the central role in the cosmic drama, Ben Ammi argues that his people have the highest responsibility to themselves, to other humans, and to God to fulfil their potential and rectify the world. In doing this, they are aligning themselves with the order of creation and the will of God and so victory is assured.

While Ben Ammi is certainly a theologian rather than simply a social reformer and makes no qualms about the validity of his message for all people across the world, he never strays far from his prime concern, which is his own people: the Hebrew Israelites/African Americans who were enslaved in the USA. As such, identity is a prime factor in Ben Ammi's thought and that of the African Hebrew Israelites generally. Ben Ammi talks constantly in his books about the humiliations of American bondage and the necessity of orienting themselves again toward God and righteousness as the only means of liberation. Failing to fulfill this role once again will lead to a repeat of those experiences.

This focus on precisely the identity which was cast outside the mainstream value system of Western society therefore was ripe for inversion: in this case, Ben Ammi transformed the indignities foisted upon black America up until the twentieth century into a central role in the history of salvation—the people were God's chosen, and their current circumstance was simply punishment for their straying for not living up to their calling. If the people could reclaim their prior righteousness and live according to the rules that God had provided three millennia ago, they could once again ascend to the pinnacle of humanity as an example for all. The marginalized status then was not a result of weakness but a curse which indicated their higher responsibility.

It is particularly interesting that a portion of African Americans effectively chose to empower themselves through the adoption of a marginal identity which straddled two minorities: blacks and Jews. While the Jewish community has established a social capital in the USA, it is still subject to discrimination and often still conceived as being outside the normative "white" category. This would not normally (and especially during the first half of the twentieth century) create an appealing identity to claim as one's own, the "model minority" arguments and assertions of luminaries such as Booker T. Washington aside.[41] Yet we can see with Ben Ammi's theological narrative, this additional marginalizing aspect has actually been leveraged in support of identifying African Americans not with modern-day Jews as some Hebrew Israelites did but with the biblical narrative of an enslaved and persecuted people who had gone on to achieve greatness and logically would do so again.

During Ben Ammi's life, the world changed immensely: from the civil rights era post-Jim Crow where black leaders were being assassinated by the American state to the election of Barack Obama; from the "curse of Ham" to the recognition of Africa as the birthplace of humanity; and from disrespected American underclass to the establishment and gradual acceptance of the successful autonomous community in Israel. These events were all taken as indicative of the emerging messianic age which was being brought about as a result of the return of the Israelites to righteousness and, to no small extent, the return of the Holy people to the Holy Land.

In this sense then the Israelites had been marginalized by history but were always *really* at the center of the narrative. Their marginalization was only apparent, an illusion to be swept away by the truth.

African Americans had lived in the margins of society for a long time: the underclass for 400 years, landless and history-less. Just like the biblical Israelites, whose sojourns in Egypt and Babylon represented humiliations that would be overcome and lead to a greater role on the world-historical stage, as God's favored people, black Americans would soon rise up, open their eyes, and fulfil their potential.

As I have already hinted, it is possible to read the American period as a liminal stage in the salvation history of the Hebrew Israelites. The 400 years during which African Americans were enslaved in America constituted a period when they were outside of a traditional social framework—they became non-persons, nameless/renamed, stripped of their individual identities, owners of nothing, and their familial ties disintegrated forcibly by both the dislocation from their past and the splitting of families in the system of slavery. Their identity went into an abeyance during which they were subject to manifold abuses, insulted, attacked, and killed at will and without justice. This period was prophesied, but so was their emergence from it, with a renewed sense of self and mission in the world. Only at the end of the gentile domination, the Era of the Great Deception, are they now reemerging as the newly reconstituted Israelite nation. At this point, the "the real, but secularly secret, names of the deities or spirits believed to preside over the rites,"[42] that is, the Hebrew Divine Name YHWH which is elided from Christian Bibles was revealed again to them.

Of course, as they imagined it, in their mythology, it was Liberia that was the liminal zone—the two years spent there have been compared to the forty years the Israelites spent in the Sinai desert before their initial entry to the promised land and Turner acknowledges that "the wilderness" is a frequent cognate of liminality.[43] It was there that they cleansed themselves of their slave identities, reforming themselves in order to take their place once again (the fact that only a few hundred—300 max—endured Liberia, and many left the group during this time, to be replaced by new recruits who moved directly to Israel or remained in the USA, is not seen as significant: *the group* experienced this time, and it is part of their shared history).

In fact, if we think of the beginning of Ben Ammi's Abeta Center in 1963 as the assertion of a non-American identity for the group, it was a forty-year stay in the wilderness that culminated in 2003s granting of permanent resident status to the community, or we could likewise argue that their liminal phase went from their entry to Israel in 1969 to 2009, when the first member was granted citizenship.

THE POWER TO DEFINE

But in another sense, we can argue that Ben Ammi and his community have spent fifty years actively recalibrating the compass of themselves and those around them. A central feature of Ben Ammi's writing and outlook is "the Power to Define." This principle directly empowers the community, by placing in their hands the right to critically analyze the concepts and values which America has instilled in them and to redefine as they see fit based on their own assessment of what is correct, what is meaningful, and what is useful to them and their mission.

According to Ben Ammi, "The Power to Define—the ability to discern and the will to interpret and implement ideas and philosophies in order to be totally victorious in battle against one's enemy—is the essentiality of spiritual warfare."[44] It is the right and the ability to impose an interpretation upon the world and to determine the meaning and value of objects, places, events, and procedures. It is the ability to break free from concepts designed by others, especially by those who are not sympathetic to one's community, to one's well-being, to one's priorities or values, and to decide for oneself according to one's own criteria what the hierarchy of values are and what the best way of life is. As such it is a crucial tool in self-determination and in the construction of a healthy and self-beneficial society.

At this stage of the Kingdom of Yah (the community's alternative title for itself), Ben Ammi asserts that all that has gone before, all the assumptions that were inculcated into the people during the American bondage must be reassessed: "We must question every facet of existence under Euro-gentile domination. All things must be brought to the Sons of God as they were brought to Adam, for naming and renaming."[45] And now, much that was absorbed and taken for granted will be shown to be unrighteous and detrimental to good living:

> As we start the journey back, we will find our people clothed with ungodly lifestyles, symbols and perverted Euro-gentile wisdom. There has to be an undressing piece by piece until we arrive in Genesis naked (innocent) and pristine before God, that He may redress us in Holiness.[46]

So they redefine the Israelites as black Africans; well-being as living a righteous life; holiness as healthiness; spirituality as living as God intends in *this* world rather than concentrating on the next world; marriage as being not necessarily monogamous; and Israel as being Northeast Africa.[47] In so doing, they actually orient the world and its values around themselves; the black American outlook which has been marginalized, degraded and ignored then is no longer being effaced and replaced but is being held as the gold standard by which the world should live that which is provided by God. They have redefined the margins as the center.

The AHIJ clearly displays the "Power of the Weak" in their claiming the Power to Define. While Israeli and American officials bickered over how to handle this small, almost insignificant presence, the community were slowly growing, building institutions, and laying claim to concepts that would help them in the future. They expanded more than tenfold in forty years and won important allies.

CONCLUSION: ESCHATOLOGICAL IMPLICATIONS (WHAT HAPPENS TO THOSE IN-BETWEEN?)

Any theology which foregrounds liberation as the goal, as the outcome of its own process, must presume and grow from a state of oppression; one must be oppressed first in order to benefit from liberation. But it is less obvious that a theology grounded in marginalization must require an eschatology of mainstreaming; that is to say, does theological liberation necessitate the incorporation of the marginal into the central and the diffusion of liminal status?

Many of the biblical prophets emphasize that in the end of days the unrighteous will face destruction: the nations, those who have persecuted Israel as well as Israel's own unrighteous members will be annihilated from the face of the earth. In this case all else will be removed so that there are no longer margins nor center. But sometimes a different view is taken, such that "all flesh shall come to worship [God]" (Is.66:23), who "will make the peoples pure of speech, so that they all invoke YHWH by name and serve Him with one accord" (Zeph.3:9) and "all the children of men will become righteous, and all the peoples will serve and bless [God]" (1En.10:21).[48] In this tradition, the splitting of humanity from Noah's sons (Gen.10) and via the confusion of languages and peoples that took place at Babel (Gen.11) will be reversed, and all will worship the one God through the same language. Thus the mainstream is absorbed into the marginal, which was always secretly the central current. Ben Ammi is an eschatological thinker but one who prefers the later motif: spiritual evil will be destroyed, and all humans will have their eyes opened to the truth that previously was the preserve of Israel (although even they forgot it for many centuries). His third book *The Messiah and the End of This World* (1991) details his eschatological concepts with a clear narrative about the overturning of the present order and Euro-gentile domination, so that humanity will emerge into a new golden age led by the Hebrew Israelite people who have shown the rest of the world how a good life really should be led.

In conclusion, the African Hebrew Israelites—a community of extreme marginality, existing on the shared margins of four different communities (American, Israeli, Black, and Jewish), present a theology which has based itself in historical marginalization and liminality, interpreting this in line with the biblical text, and making liberation the prime goal. Their exit from the final stage of liminality, when they were accepted as Israeli citizens, represents their ultimate *secular* liberation. Theologically, the sacred liberation—the end of their liminal phase in America—was the divine destiny of the people, who because of their world-historical role are now set to liberate all of humanity from their blinkered vision, such that the world order can be overturned, and the existing separation of center and margins are redrawn when everyone else accepts the Hebrew Israelite outlook.

NOTES

1. The community number roughly 3,000 in Israel, but they have large satellite communities in the USA, UK, the Caribbean, and Ghana.
2. Armin Rosen, "African. Hebrew. Israelite," *Tablet,* March 28, 2019. https://www.tabletmag.com/jewish-arts-and-culture/282261/african-hebrew-israelite.

3. While Turner uses marginal and liminal interchangeably, the academic concepts of marginality and liminality are distinct; the former is most usually a permanent state of in-betweenness, the latter a temporary state of transition.

4. The most comprehensive histories have been given in James E. Landing, *Black Judaism: Story of an American Movement* (Durham: Carolina Academic Press, 2002) and Jacob S. Dorman, *Chosen People: The Rise of American Black Israelite Religions* (Oxford: Oxford University Press, 2013). I will not herein be addressing the validity of their narrative but for an alternative assessment of the history—one which favors the Hebrew Israelite perception that they *are* authentically descended from both Israelites and Jews, see Walter Isaac, "Locating Afro-American Judaism: A Critique of White Normativity," in *The Companion to African American Studies*, ed. Lewis R. Gordon and Jane Anna Gordon (Malden, MA: Blackwell, 2006), 512–542. My own summation of the debates can be found in Michael Miller, "Black Judaism(s) and the Hebrew Israelites," *Religion Compass* 13, no. 11 (2019): e12346.

5. This history is collated from the many accounts given in scholarly literature, as well as conversations with members. A very good overview is provided by Merrill Singer, "Symbolic Identity Formation in an African American Religious Sect: The Black Hebrew Israelites," and Ethan Michaeli, "Another Exodus: The Hebrew Israelites from Chicago to Dimona," both in *Black Zion: African American Religious Encounters with Judaism*, ed. Yvonne Chireau and Nathaniel Deutsch (New York: Oxford University Press, 2000), 55–72 and 73–90, respectively. The most recent monograph on the AHIJ is John L. Jackson, Jr., *Thin Description: Ethnography and the African Hebrew Israelites of Jerusalem* (Cambridge, MA: Harvard University Press, 2013).

6. For a close-up perspective, see Robert B. McKersie, *A Decisive Decade: An Insider's View of the Chicago Civil Rights Movement During the 1960s* (Carbondale: Southern Illinois University Press, 2013).

7. See Merrill Charles Singer, "Saints of the Kingdom: Group Emergence, Individual Affiliation, and Social Change among the Black Hebrews of Israel" (Doctoral dissertation, University of Utah, Salt Lake City, 1979), 186.

8. On this history and the vacillating Israeli perceptions, see Michael T. Miller, "The African Hebrew Israelites of Jerusalem: A Borderline Case," in *Jewish Perspectives on The Stranger in Early Modern and Modern Jewish Tradition*, ed. Catherine Bartlett and Joachim Schlör (Leiden: Brill, 2021), 28–46.

9. Nas Daily, "The Shocking Vegan Village," https://www.facebook.com/watch/?v=735022803608306. Accessed 4th June 2020.

10. Shelley Elkayam, "'Food for Peace': The Vegan Religion of the Hebrews of Jerusalem," *Idea* 26 (2014): 317–340, esp. n. 22 (p. 322). According to Ben Ammi, there have been no cases of cancer, diabetes, or kidney failure in the community: "The Prophecy," *Essence* 26, no. 10 (February 1996): 54.

11. "[R]ampant disease, drug abuse, sexual abuse, corruption, ecological destruction, disintegration of the family unity" is how the Western world is typified at the About Us: Why Israel? Section of the community's website http://africanhebrewisraelitesofjerusalem.com/?page_id=2 (accessed 5 March 2019). Jackson also discusses the perceived pathology of African American culture, *Thin Description*, 71–73.

12. Arnold van Gennep, *The Rites of Passage* (Chicago: University of Chicago Press, 1960), 21.

13. Bjørn Thomassen, *Liminality and the Modern: Living Through the In-Between* (Surrey: Ashgate, 2014), 102.

14. Ibid., 92.

15. Victor Turner, *The Ritual Process: Structure and Anti-Structure* (Ithaca: Cornell University Press, 1977), 94–130.

16. Ibid., 129.

17. The community are polygynous, meaning that each male may take up to seven wives, if he is able to support them. This has been a point of critique, but the community has always defended its right and its reasoning that, at least in the early stages, there were many more women in the community than men, meaning that without polygyny many women would be forcibly single. In recent years, the practice has become rarer as the new generations integrate into Israeli culture and norms. On this and related issues, see Fran Markowitz, "Millenarian Motherhood: Motives, Meanings and Practices among African Hebrew Israelite Women," *Nashim: A Journal of Jewish Women's Studies & Gender Issues* 3 (2000): 106–138.

18. Turner, *Ritual Process*, 108–111.

19. van Gennep, *Rites of Passage,* 26.

20. Genesis Rabba 38:13.

21. b.Sanhedrin 98a.

22. This was one traditional interpretation, although the original meaning is subject to debate. See, for example, Sebastian Günther, "Muḥammad, the Illiterate Prophet: An Islamic Creed in the Qur'an and Qur'anic Exegesis," *Journal of Qur'anic Studies* 4, no. 1 (2002): 1–26.

23. Traditionally kabbalists have believed the Messiah's soul would originate from the lowest *sefirah* of the *Etz Chaim* (Tree of Life), likely based on the Talmudic passage mentioned previously. On the evolution of this into Chaim Vital's belief that the Messiah would be a *converso*, see Shaul Magid, *From Metaphysics to Midrash: Myth, History, and the Interpretation of Scripture in Lurianic Kabbalah* (Bloomington: Indiana University Press, 2008), 75–110.

24. On the use of the Bible in liberation theologies, see Gerald West, "The Bible and the Poor: A New Way of Doing Theology," in *The Cambridge Companion to Liberation Theology*, 2nd edition, ed. Christopher Rowland (Cambridge: Cambridge University Press, 2007), 159–182.

25. The Puebla conference in Mexico 1968 articulated two strands to Christian liberation: from socioeconomic factors (external) and from sin (internal).

26. About 70 percent of Indian Christians are of Dalit origin. S. M. Michael, ed., *Dalits in Modern India: Vision and Values* (New Delhi: Sage Publications, 2007), 82.

27. Gavriel haGadol, "Foreword" in Ammi's *The Messiah and the End of this World,* iii.

28. Ben Ammi, *God, the Black Man and Truth* (2nd revised ed) (Washington, DC: Communicators Press, 1990), 152.

29. While Ben Ammi's writings maintain that only some Africans are descended from the Israelites, since the 1980s and the mutual peacebuilding efforts with Israel,

publicly the community have asserted that modern Jews also descend from Judean Israelites, who migrated north and west at this point. While this is the public-facing narrative, my own conversations with members suggest that it is a matter of individual preference but many retain the original concept of exclusively African American lineage, while arguing that the most important aspects are behavior and outlook; the community has welcomed white and Jewish members. Worth noting is former American representative Prince Asiel's statement in 2018, "The things that I've experienced and the welcome that we've received and the growth that we've developed in Israel is because the people of God that's in Israel that knew us have always been there supporting us and guiding us. Even when they did not really understand that we understood who they were and who we were. But we've grown in those fifty years that we now see it as one family, not black and not white but the people of God that have been scattered over the world and all that suffered; whether you was a white Jew or black Jew, whether you was Sephardic or Ashkenazi, there was no rest as we know." *Voice out of Zion—Prince Asiel Ben Israel: How it All Began,* December 23, 2018. https://www.youtube.com/watch?v=NbfVoEQOAO8 accessed 4th June 2020.

30. Deut. 28:15–68

31. Andre Key has analyzed the use of this passage in several Hebrew Israelite texts: Andre E. Key, "If Thou Do Not Hearken Unto the Voice of the Lord thy God: A Critique of Theodicy in Black Judaism," *Black Theology* 12, no. 3 (2014): 267–288.

32. Ammi, *God, the Black Man and Truth,* 181.

33. Ibid., 152.

34. All Ben Ammi's books begin with an explanation of terminology including the compound term "Euro-gentile" as "a people or nation that is without the knowledge of the True and Living God of Creation" and specifically "the entire European family of nations" from America to New Zealand.

35. Ibid., 30.

36. This theme of concealing is found also in the Nation of Islam (NOI). See Eric C. Lincoln, *The Black Muslims in America* (Boston: Beacon Press, 1973). Other similarities include the focus on diet and health and the banning of alcohol and tobacco, although in the case of NOI these ultimately descend from Noble Drew Ali's Moorish Science Temple, which was part of the matrix out of which the early Hebrew Israelite movement was developing in the first quarter of the twentieth century (Landing, *Black Judaism,* 438).

37. Ammi, *God, the Black Man and Truth,* 29. The calculation of the precise start and end points of the 400 years has been attempted in various ways by different thinkers. Another original member of the community, Shaleak Ben Yehuda, located the beginning at 1445 when African slaves entered Portugal and ending with Frederick Douglass; see Morris Lounds, Jr., *Israel's Black Hebrews: Black Americans in Search of Identity* (Washington, DC: University Press of America, 1981), 54 and Prince Asiel calculated it from 1619, meaning that 2019 was the pivotal point.

38. Ammi, *God, the Black Man and Truth,* 164.

39. Ben Ammi, *The Messiah and the End of this World* (Washington, DC: Communicators Press, 1991), 17.

40. Ibid., 30.

41. "We have a very bright and striking example in the history of the Jews in this and other countries. There is, perhaps, no race that has suffered so much, not so much in America as in some of the countries in Europe. But these people have clung together. They have had a certain amount of unity, pride, and love of race, and, as the years go on, they will be more and more influential in this country—a country where they were once despised, and looked upon with scorn and derision. It is largely because the Jewish race has had faith in itself. Unless the Negro learns more and more to imitate the Jew in these matters, to have faith in himself, he cannot expect to have any high degree of success." Booker T. Washington, *The Future of the American Negro* (Boston: Small, Maynard, 1899), 182–183.

42. Victor Turner, *The Forest of Symbols: Aspects of Ndembu Ritual* (London: Cornell University Press, 1967), 103.

43. Turner, *Ritual Process*, 95.

44. Ammi, *God, the Black Man and Truth,* 57.

45. Ibid., 61.

46. Ibid., 31.

47. They reason that until the Suez Canal was dug out in the 1860s, Israel was connected by land to the continent. The Middle East they understand as a colonial fiction coined in order to make people think that this region is not essentially African. See Fran Markowitz, "Israel as Africa, Africa as Israel: 'Divine Geography' in the Personal Narratives and Community Identity of the Black Hebrew Israelites," *Anthropological Quarterly* 69 (1996): 193–205.

48. On this persistent theme in late Second Temple apocalyptic literature, see Loren T. Stuckenbruck, "The Eschatological Worship of God by the Nations: An Enquiry into the Early Enoch Tradition," in *With Wisdom as a Robe: Qumran and Other Jewish Studies in Honor of Ida Frölich*, ed. Károly Dániel Dobos and Miklós Köszeghy (Sheffield: Sheffield Phoenix Press, 2009), 189–206. He explains that "the motif of the nations' worship of God expresses hope for a reversal of the conditions of subjugation which . . . Israel presently suffers" (192).

BIBLIOGRAPHY

About Us: Why Israel? Accessed March 5, 2019. http://africanhebrewisraelitesofje rusalem.com/?page_id=2.

Ben, Ammi Ben Israel. "The Prophecy." *Essence* 26, no. 10 (1996): 54.

Ammi Ben Israel, Ben and Ammi, Ben. *God, the Black Man and Truth* (2nd revised ed). Washington, DC: Communicators Press, 1990.

Ben, Ammi. *The Messiah and the End of this World.* Washington, DC: Communicators Press, 1991.

Daily, Nas. "The Shocking Vegan Village." Accessed June 4, 2020. https://www .facebook.com/watch/?v=735022803608306.

Dorman, Jacob S. *Chosen People: The Rise of American Black Israelite Religions.* Oxford: Oxford University Press, 2013.

Elkayam, Shelley. "'Food for Peace': The Vegan Religion of the Hebrews of Jerusalem." *Idea* 26 (2014): 317–340.

Günther, Sebastian. "Muḥammad, the illiterate Prophet: An Islamic Creed in the Qur'an and Qur'anic Exegesis." *Journal of Qur'anic Studies* 4, no. 1 (2002): 1–26.

Isaac, Walter. "Locating Afro-American Judaism: A Critique of White Normativity." In *The Companion to African American Studies*, edited by Lewis R. Gordon and Jane Anna Gordon, 512–542. Malden, MA: Blackwell, 2006.

Jackson, John L. Jr. *Thin Description: Ethnography and the African Hebrew Israelites of Jerusalem.* Cambridge, MA: Harvard University Press, 2013.

Key, Andre E. "If Thou Do Not Hearken Unto the Voice of the Lord thy God: A Critique of Theodicy in Black Judaism." *Black Theology* 12, no. 3 (2014): 267–288.

Landing, James E. *Black Judaism: Story of an American Movement.* Durham, NC: Carolina Academic Press, 2002.

Lincoln, Eric C. *The Black Muslims in America.* Boston, MA: Beacon Press, 1973.

Lounds, Morris Jr. *Israel's Black Hebrews: Black Americans in Search of Identity.* Washington, DC: University Press of America, 1981.

Magid, Shaul. *From Metaphysics to Midrash: Myth, History, and the Interpretation of Scripture in Lurianic Kabbalah.* Bloomington, IN: Indiana University Press, 2008.

Markowitz, Fran. "Israel as Africa, Africa as Israel: 'Divine Geography' in the Personal Narratives and Community Identity of the Black Hebrew Israelites." *Anthropological Quarterly* 69 (1996): 193–205.

Markowitz, Fran. "Millenarian Motherhood: Motives, Meanings and Practices among African Hebrew Israelite Women." *Nashim: A Journal of Jewish Women's Studies & Gender Issues* 3 (2000): 106–138.

McKersie, Robert B. *A Decisive Decade: An Insider's View of the Chicago Civil Rights Movement During the 1960s.* Carbondale, IL: Southern Illinois University Press, 2013.

Michael, S. M., ed. *Dalits in Modern India: Vision and Values.* New Delhi: Sage Publications, 2007.

Michaeli, Ethan. "Another Exodus: The Hebrew Israelites from Chicago to Dimona." In *Black Zion: African American Religious Encounters with* Judaism, edited by Yvonne Chireau and Nathaniel Deutsch, 73–90. New York: Oxford University Press, 2000.

Miller, Michael T. "Black Judaism(s) and the Hebrew Israelites." *Religion Compass* 13, no. 11 (2019): e12346.

Miller, Michael T. "The African Hebrew Israelites of Jerusalem: A Borderline Case." In *The Stranger in Early Modern and Modern Jewish Tradition*, edited by Catherine Bartlett and Joachim Schlör, 28–46. Leiden: Brill, 2021.

Rosen, Armin. "African. Hebrew. Israelite." *Tablet*, March 28, 2019. Accessed June 4, 2020. https://www.tabletmag.com/jewish-arts-and-culture/282261/african -hebrew-israelite.

Singer, Merrill Charles. "Saints of the Kingdom: Group Emergence, Individual Affiliation, and Social Change among the Black Hebrews of Israel." Doctoral dissertation, University of Utah, Salt Lake City, 1979.

Singer, Merrill. "Symbolic Identity Formation in an African American Religious Sect: The Black Hebrew Israelites." In *Black Zion: African American Religious Encounters with Judaism*, edited by Yvonne Chireau and Nathaniel Deutsch, 55–72. New York: Oxford University Press, 2000.

Stuckenbruck, Loren T. "The Eschatological Worship of God by the Nations: An Enquiry into the Early Enoch Tradition." In *With Wisdom as a Robe: Qumran and Other Jewish Studies in Honor of Ida Frölich*, edited by Károly Dániel Dobos and Miklós Köszeghy, 189–206. Sheffield: Sheffield Phoenix Press, 2009.

Thomassen, Bjørn. *Liminality and the Modern: Living Through the In-Between*. Surrey: Ashgate, 2014.

Turner, Victor. *The Ritual Process: Structure and Anti-Structure*. Ithaca, NY: Cornell University Press, 1977.

van Gennep, Arnold. *The Rites of Passage*. Chicago, IL: University of Chicago Press, 1960.

Voice Out of Zion. *Voice Out of Zion—Prince Asiel Ben Israel: How it All Began*. December 23, 2018. Accessed June 4, 2020. https://www.youtube.com/watch?v=NbfVoEQOAO8.

Washington, Booker T. *The Future of the American Negro*. Boston, MA: Small, Maynard, 1899.

West, Gerald. "The Bible and the Poor: A New Way of Doing Theology." In *The Cambridge Companion to Liberation Theology*, 2nd edition, edited by Christopher Rowland, 159–182. Cambridge: Cambridge University Press, 2007.

Chapter 2

Liberating Liminality in the Contemporary Church of Algeria

Patrick J. S. Brittenden

The growth of the indigenous—largely Kabyle—contemporary church of Algeria in the past thirty-five years, though documented, is a relatively little known social phenomenon. Unsurprisingly, this convert "apostate" church has met with opposition and in some cases persecution, though until very recently, this has not been a state-sponsored oppression.[1] Its presence and growth, seemingly unaffected by any discernible foreign missionary activity, can be seen as a feature of Algeria's fledgling tentative emerging pluralism.[2] Unique, not just in the Maghreb but in the majority Muslim world, the Algerian Church is the only expression of indigenous Christianity to have been officially recognized by the state. While this does not discernibly alter the "statut personnelle" (individual civic status) of Algerian citizens—still viewed as indelibly Muslim—nonetheless, the status of Algerian Christians has been recognized via the law on associations. In 2011, the process of "mise en conformité" (reregistration) of all non-Muslim religious associations resulted in the Église Protestante d'Algérie (EPA),[3] hitherto a bilateral foreign Algerian association, being constituted as a fully Algerian organization, with the requirement that it be totally self-governed, self-led, and self-financed.[4]

Though its growth as a liminoid *communitas* predates 2010, the Algerian Church might well be viewed as a feature of popular reforms involving the "full participation of all citizens, women, men, from all social classes and religious and cultural backgrounds" that have occurred with mixed results across the majority Muslim nations of North Africa and the Middle East since the Arab Awakening over a decade ago.[5] In Tariq Ramadan's discerning of a new *wisatiya*—a "middle way"—distinct from the polarized dialectic of "theocracy-loving Islamists" versus "secularist Western puppets," where religious references begin to influence a vision of social justice there may be a place for this convert *communitas*. Ramadan writes:

> The principle of "no compulsion in religion" must inform the state, as must human rights, which must apply to all without distinction. At the heart of social reality, the management of religious pluralism is strengthened by the internal dynamics of religions themselves. They can only exist and flourish—and even spread—in a space free of constraint, through the strength of coherence and persuasion, never by imposition or prohibition.[6]

Though Ramadan refers to the role of historic Christians and other minorities in post-Arab Awakening majority Muslim countries, he makes no reference to convert communities such as the Algerian Church. However, might this Kabyle Christian "spontaneous *communitas*"[7] be able to "exist and even spread" and therefore contribute to the kind of majority-Muslim pluralistic state that Ramadan describes? For now, it is too early to discern. In the majority Muslim context of Algeria relations between the EPA and the Algerian government operate within a discourse in which Algerian culture is viewed as a bounded entity and, in Robert Jackson's terms, Algerian Christianity is a "subordinate culture functioning in their own private space and dependent on the values of the dominant culture for their continued existence."[8] Muslim-Christian relations in Algeria also inhabit a paradigm, which, from the perspective of Algerian Muslims, assume that Christianity is foreign at best or colonial at worst. Nonetheless, the presence and growth of the contemporary Algerian Church are challenging the discourse that Algeria is irreducibly Muslim and that Christianity is primarily Western.

My recent doctoral study—a theological reflection on the place of teaching and learning in the development of the contemporary church of Algeria—points to several polarities along which the liminality of the Algerian Church is visible. At least three of these are the polarity between *centers* (Arabism and east-facing Islam) and *margins* (Kabyle and Christian) and *particularity* (of Algeria's fledgling tentative emerging cultural, linguistic, and religious pluralism) and *universality* (of Algeria's "official" national identity) and the *East-West* polarity. Like a repeated motif, these are visible in the three lenses through which my doctoral research explores the story of the Algerian Church. These are the ethnographic lens of Berber-Kabyle culture, the lens of Algerian Islam and the lens of state education.[9] This multidimensional social drama of Algerian, Kabyle and Christian liminality is pregnant with possibilities for what Carson et al. describe as,

> understanding and employing the power of "edge" experiences and "in-between" places in relation to the deeper processes of transformation they midwife.[10]

This chapter aims to highlight some of these liminal processes and by so doing hopefully to contribute not just to our understanding of social transformation in Algeria but also to liminality as a hermeneutical key to understanding this social drama. This will be achieved by first discussing the appropriateness and rationale for the use of liminality as a heuristic concept then by briefly considering how liminality relates to identity transition among Algerian Christians from a Muslim background. Having justified how and why this concept of liminality is so relevant to the experience of this particular community, it will explore how the Algerian Christians' experience of liminality seems to be transforming from its current ambiguity and de-humanizing marginality to become a context for liberation. From this point in the margins, it will present the notion of what I have called "liberating liminality" as a way of viewing the development of this Christian *communitas* and her contribution to Algeria's ontological quest for an authentic and increasingly pluralist national identity.

WHY LIMINALITY?

There are four reasons why this concept has been so helpful. First, the usefulness of liminality to me as a practical theologian trying to understand the social drama of the corporate life and practices of the Algerian Church in context. As Marcel Barnard points out, liminality works for the theologian as a heuristic "hands-on" concept enabling theologians to use it as a hermeneutical key or even a pastoral method.[11] Liminality has provided me with a hermeneutical key to understanding the multidimensional transitions and transformations in Algerian Christians betwixt and between the world of Algerian Islam and Western Christianity. As Carson et al. explain,

> This is indeed what we are learning about liminality in our current age after van Gennep and Turner—it arises from experience which is now tested over several decades. It is absolutely not a "theory of everything" and yet it is a useful way of viewing the process of change in persons, organizations and human society.[12]

If liminality is fundamentally concerned with how human beings experience and react to change,[13] then, as Carson et al. ask, how can we discern whether such processes of change are properly liminal as opposed to simply transitional or even how they "make someone marginal, leaving them stuck on the edge or genuinely transformative"?[14] The polarity created in the experience of converts in a Muslim context gives rise to precisely this question. What moves their experience of liminality from one of being perpetually on the edge, what might be called "dehumanizing marginality," to being genuinely transformative, and what we might call "liberating marginality"?

A further appeal in my work as a practical theologian is Victor Turner's engagement with the transcendent at the heart of the *communitas* in the world of anti-structure which he describes in his *The Ritual Process* (1970). Building on the work of Arnold van Gennep in *Rites of Passage* (1909), Turner developed his understanding of the three stages of the *limen* by exploring movement from the "world of structure" through "anti-structure" back to a world of structure again. His interpretation of the van Gennep's three stages in the rites of passage in tribal cultures focuses on the undefined, chaotic anti-structure of the liminal stage. While the whole process can be described as liminal, Turner's articulation of the three stages as *pre-liminal rites*, separation from the old way of life; *liminal*, entry into the undefined chaotic period; and *post-liminal rites*, reaggregation into society with a changed role focusses on the engagement with the transcendent and the community of those sharing this transitional world of "anti-structure." He describes the relationality of this society of the liminal as *communitas*.[15] As Carson et al. observe, although Turner was not writing from a wholly Christian perspective—his primary research was on human behavior in the Ndembu Tribe of Zambia and subsequently applied to many other cultures—nonetheless, he was able to identify human behavior in relation to transition and the transcendent, which can be recognized widely within the Christian tradition.[16] Turner's use of liminality provides a helpful way to understand and interpret engagement with the transcendent in the Algerian convert *communitas*.

The second reason I was drawn to this concept was van Gennep's countercultural resistance to the essentializing of religious rites and customs so characteristic of the scientific positivism of Emile Durkheim and other leading lights of early twentieth-century French anthropology.[17] While van Gennep conceived of liminality as a "fact of existence" in a universe governed by transition and movements, his first use of the term "liminality" is associated with the publication of his *Rites de Passage* in 1909. In it van Gennep uses the term "liminality" to analyze the "middle stage" in ritual passages within tribal societies. Liminality is a way of describing a period of margin, what Victor Turner calls an "interstructural situation" between "states."[18] In his *Rites de Passage*, van Gennep explores how "rites" indicate transitions *between* "states." A "state" in this context describes a relatively fixed condition rather than a "status" or "office." Such a state is culturally recognizable like being married, single, or the state of infancy.[19] Liminality describes the "world of contingency" in-between states in which reality can be carried off in different directions and in which the outcome of the liminal period is not certain. There are three stages in van Gennep's "rites of transition": first "separation," second "margin" (or transition), and third, "incorporation."[20]

The first stage involves the detachment of the person from the previous fixed point within the social structure. The second stage is the liminal period in which the "state" of the person, what Turner describes as the "passenger,"[21] is ambiguous, belonging neither to the place where they have come from or their destination. The third stage is the consummation where the traveler is once again in a clearly defined and structurally stable state and because of this is expected to behave according to certain customary norms and ethical standards.[22]

Van Gennep's foundational concept has of course come to be recognized by contemporary anthropologists as a fundamental device applicable to all societies. However, while this interpretation is widely embraced in our postmodern context, this was not the case during his lifetime. This is mainly because he was trying to establish himself during the heyday of early twentieth-century scientific positivism and he clashed with that movement's leading light, Emile Durkheim.[23] The powerful French Academy saw in van Gennep a competitor to its own very different approach to anthropological research. Van Gennep's approach was inspired by what he called *une biologie scientifique'*; namely the direct observation of "living facts."[24] This was in contrast to dead abstract social "facts" and in opposition to the essentializing tendency seen in Durkheim's reliance on "a priori" categories that he used as units in his well-known taxonomy.[25] For van Gennep, Durkheim's claim to find foundations of society from a single religious institution (totemism) reduced rituals to a timeless consolidation of society and reflected an epistemology, consistent with much postenlightenment rationalism, which misrepresented social "facts."[26] For van Gennep, society was not a monocellular organism and its foundations were based not on scientific positivism but on human experiences and responses to liminality.

It is this same scientifically positivist—thoroughly modernist—approach which is behind the conceptualizations of the modern nation-state and society as a monocultural organism. The influence of this in Algeria can be seen in both the nineteenth-century French colonial ethnographies of Algeria and in the subsequent counter-ethnographies of the early twentieth-century Salafist architects of Algeria. The proselytizing rationalism of these reformist "ulemā" with their driving centrist claim to a unity of Islam and the Algerian self is another instance of what Jacques Berque refers as an "Islam Jacobin,"[27] that is, a Jacobean renaissance template of nations as entities united by a single (centralizing) claim of unity (one language, one ethnicity, one religion).

Third, this notion of liminality is also of interest to me because of the significance of personal narrative in the exploration of this concept. It's worth noting that Victor Turner's own discovery—as it were "by accident"—of van Gennep's concept, which resulted in his highly influential "Betwixt and Between"[28] chapter occurred when he was himself experiencing the liminality of a prolonged move from the United Kingdom to the United States as he awaited his US visa.[29] My own sense of "perpetual liminality" has been a significant factor in my exploration of this concept and its application to the identity transition and broader development of the Algerian Church. My research methodology acknowledges the unavoidable reality that I am an "outsider."[30] However, my own hybridity makes me an a-typical Western "outsider," and this has undoubtedly colored my methodological approach. My research therefore arises from a lifelong sense of hybridity. Observations of the double marginalization of Algerian Christians in both the Algerian nation-state and the world church are linked through my own reflexivity as a hybrid. My own liminal identity as an "homme frontière"[31] has contributed to my desire to inhabit the divisions between different worlds, seeing these as challenges somehow to be navigated. This narrative as a French- and Arabic-speaking "adopted son" of Algeria have been a significant tool in the cocreation of the mode and content of this research.

Fourth and final, it is of interest to me that van Gennep did some of his best original anthropological fieldwork among the Kabyles in Algeria in the first decade of the twentieth century.[32] A century later I find myself having conducted my own field research among the Kabyles in Algeria inspired by the "world of contingency" that van Gennep discovered in his concept of liminality. Notably, my use of liminality is not only or primarily to describe "in-between" periods but as a way to understand the performance of new a social drama and—in Turner's terms—in order to better understand human reactions to liminal experiences and how personality and society are shaped by liminality.[33]

LIMINALITY AND IDENTITY TRANSITION AMONG ALGERIAN CONVERTS

While Carson et al. are right in pointing out that the transformations, changes, and encounters with the transcendent defy categories and the liminal process cannot be controlled or "produced on demand"[34] nonetheless the concept of liminality can help us to understand periods of personal and social transition. Social anthropologists Ybema, Beech, and Ellis propose that to be liminal is "to be caught up in intense 'boundary' or 'identity' work."[35] It is a discursive activity undertaken to understand and construct the self. The drama of the Algerian Church's development is one such site of personal and corporate identity reconstruction.

Timothy Green's doctoral research explores precisely such identity reconstruction in adult converts from Islam to Christianity in Pakistan.[36] His sociological study examines the consequences of conversion and issues of "life development," liminal identity, and the transmission of Christian faith to the next generation via three levels of identity: the "collective identity," the "social identity," and the "ego-identity."[37] Not surprisingly, in majority-Muslim cultures, each of these levels is affected by conversion. The religious "collective identity" is held together by powerful rituals of loyalty and belonging, which categorize the Muslim individual whether or not he or she believes in them personally.[38] Traditionally, Islam has functioned as a collective identity label. At a "social identity" level, Islam is assumed more than chosen. As Green explains,

> To be Muslim is automatic unless deliberate apostasy is chosen . . . it is this "glue" of Muslim social identity which marks one of the biggest barriers and sharpest costs for conversion out of Islam[39]

In this sense the religious social identity is adopted through birth and a socialization process.[40] However, Islam also functions at an "ego-identity" level. The "ego-identity" is the sense of self that enables a person to conceive of who they are in a way that provides continuity to the self through transition and change in life. This is especially the case for converts to Islam or those born Muslim who question their beliefs. With reference to Beit-Hallahmi's *Prolegomena to the Psychological Study of Religion* (1989), Green argues that "ego-identity" is therefore central to the conversion process. Observations from my research confirm the centrality of the ego-identity in the growth and development of Algerian Christians, especially when this "ego-identity'" unavoidably clashes with their Muslim "social" and "collective" identities.

One of the concepts that Green uses to evaluate the pain of these clashes between the converted "ego-identity" and an unresponsive or hostile "social identity" in Muslim society is the phenomenon of "passing." This term is used in at least two distinct ways: "passing into" or joining a new community, such as the convert from Islam joining a traditional Christian church (which unlike Algeria exists in Pakistan) and "passing as," such as when a convert acts a role so convincingly as to be considered "original" to that community.[41] This is visible when the convert "passes as" a Muslim through fear of being rejected by the wider Muslim social group because of who they have become. "Passing" therefore creates a space for "self-determination and agency." However, crucially, this self-determination is only possible when and where society tolerates it. So, while the transformation of the ego-identity is vital to the convert subsequent navigation of both social and collective identities in majority Muslim societies, at present this type of liminality resembles more of a survival strategy for converts. In Turner's terms, therefore, the convert community is still a "spontaneous *communitas*" that has yet to become a "normative *communitas*."[42]

This ambiguity in the experience of converts "passing" from one identity to a range of others is visible in the contemporary Church of Algeria. At present, this is an ambiguous, painful, and sometimes destructive experience in the "border-zones" of liminality[43] in the marginality between structure and anti-structure of majority Muslim societies.

FROM DEHUMANIZING TO LIBERATING MARGINALITY

The concept of "marginality" is of course closely linked to—though not synonymous with—liminality." It is mostly viewed as a negative term describing an existence *in* the margins, cut-off from the mainstream. This might be through: disability, sexism, poverty, religious discrimination, persecution, and so forth. We might call this dehumanizing marginality. However, "marginality" also describes an existence *between* realities. In sociology, a marginal person is someone who exists in-between worlds, cultures, races, or classes neither one thing nor the other. In his treatment of marginality as the context and method of multicultural theology, Korean-American theologian Jung Young Lee challenges the classical "self-negating" definition of marginality, which assumes a structural separation between a dominant and a subordinate group in society—advocated by Stonequist, *The Marginal Man*, (1961)—by introducing a "self-affirming" conception of marginality not defined by the dominant group.[44] Lee suggests that marginality is

> a nexus where two or three worlds are interconnected . . . an open-ended and unfolding horizon where the others come to meet and go away.[45]

For Lee, Jesus Christ is the ultimate marginal person and true Christian formation and flourishing only occurs through "self-affirming" marginality.

In Lee's terms, the Algerian Church is highly marginal. Algerian converts are Christians but until now, unlike the historic churches of the Middle East, they have no "centre." They exist as an existential or spontaneous *communitas* in a world of anti-structure. As Christians of a predominantly Berber (Kabyle) ethnicity, they experience the double marginalization of being non-Arab and non-Muslim in a modern nation-state that has been predicated on an "irreducible" formula of being Muslim and Arab. This formula for "authentic" Algerian identity was itself consciously developed in the context of years of colonial repression in which both Islam and Arabic were minimized. It was the success of the early twentieth-century "Salafiyya" reform movement, led by the charismatic figure of Abd al-Hamid Ibn Badis (1889–1940), which resulted in the irreducible three-fold formula for *the* national identity (Algérienneté)—'Islam is our religion, Algeria our nation (homeland) and Arabic our language.' However, despite the success of this Arab-Islamic centrism, more than fifty years after independence, this irreducible three-fold "structure" seems to many Algerians—Muslims, Christians, and those of all faiths and none—to be a formula that has kept Algerians, to use Abdallah Mazouni's phrase, from a long overdue "rendezvous avec nous mêmes"—a rendezvous with ourselves.[46] This imagined "authentic" changelessness forced on it by colonialism has therefore become a context for the marginalization of the Algerian Christian community.

Lee describes the way in which this kind of marginalization can dehumanize.

> To be in-between two worlds means to be fully in neither. The marginal person who is placed between this two-world boundary feels like a non-being. This existential "nothingness" caused by the perspective of two (or more) dominant worlds is the root of dehumanization.[47]

Algerian Christians are seeking to develop their own identity and purpose in the context of a modern nation-state created within a post-Enlightenment monocultural vision of society. Liminality is hermeneutically useful here not only as a heuristic concept but also because of van Gennep's core challenge to the scientific positivism of his time. As we have seen, he challenged the tendency to essentialism with his argument for an interpretation of social data that is much more dynamic and performative and that views social data as a narrative in progress. This kind of liminality in the experience of Algerian converts is visible not only in the polarity of structure and anti-structure in their majority Muslim context but also betwixt and between the centers (or centrisms) and margins of the World Christian Movement.

Hence, several features of Victor Turner's expanded interpretation of liminality have resonance with the liminoid experience that I have observed among Algerian Christians. Turner's description of the invisible liminal personae as a kind of structurally indefinable "transitional being" with a classification focusing on being "in-between" rather than "in-both" is similar to the experience of Algerian Christians.[48] The idea that the liminal persona is "no longer" a Muslim and "not yet" fully or properly "Christian" in the eyes of some "traditional" Christians is also familiar. Certainly, for Algerian Christians who have been declared as "Harkis" (traitors),[49] denounced, and disowned, the idea that liminals are treated as dead and stripped of their names also had resonances for converts who experience the liminality being neither fully living within their new Christian family nor fully dead to their previous Muslim family. The ambiguity of this liminal condition therefore resonates with the experience of Algerian Christians in the margins "betwixt and between" and without a socially recognizable or culturally acceptable classification in Algeria. While the ambiguity of this "statelessness"[50] is dehumanizing for Algerian Christians it also appears to be a context for transformation and liberation.

LIBERAT*ED* AND LIBERAT*ING* LIMINALITY

The paradigm shift in Lee's thesis on marginality is a conceptual move from a destructive to a creative conception of the border zones of marginality. This move might provide a hermeneutical key interpreting how Algerian Christians seem to be able to move from a situation of destructive and dehumanizing liminality to a "liberat*ed*" and "liberat*ing* liminality." The margins created by the liminal situation are pregnant with potential and possibilities that might transform both those in the centers and those in the margins. Viewed this way, liminality is a heuristic device for understanding social change and the interplay between structure and anti-structure and potential of this for social change not just in the *communitas* of the Algerian Church but also for social change in wider Algerian society.

Lee suggests that the idea of being "in-between" can lead to a positive self-affirming understanding of marginality that both recognizes this tension but moves toward being "in-both" rather than "in-between." In his terms the "in-both" conception complements the "in-between."[51] To stress the "in-both" identity requires the affirmation of the realities and roots of each. This conception looks at margins as a potentially "creative core" rather than those defined by one or more "centrisms" that create them; whether—as in the Algerian context—those are Arab, Berber, Islamist, Western Christian, or any other. This in turn leads to the potential of becoming a "new marginal person" not only "in-between" "in-both" but also "in-beyond" a series of margins.[52] Lee's "in-between," "in-both," and "in-beyond" concept is a kind of polarity in which the liminoid live with and dances between structure and anti-structure. So, what might have been viewed as a problem to be solved or a binary dialectic to be resolved instead becomes for the *communitas* of the Algerian Church a liberated and liberating dance. In Carson et al.'s words,

> The movement between the two poles has energy and power for good or ill and both sides interpenetrate one another so that it is not always easy to distinguish separate periods or elements of structure and communitas.[53]

Although Lee doesn't interact specifically with the literature on liminality,[54] his methodological move from "self-negating" to "self-affirming" marginality through a theological reevaluation of margins as a positive and creative nexus is particularly helpful. It opens the way to reimagine how the Algerian Church's liminality might be viewed not as a binary dialectic between structure and anti-structure but rather a context for transformation; "in-between" and "in-both" and "in-beyond" these polarities. This is what I have called "liberated" and "liberating liminality." This concept is inspired by the "pure possibility" of liminality described by Turner.

> Liminality may perhaps be regarded as the nay to all positive structural assertions, but it is in some sense the source of all of them, and more than that, is a realm of pure possibility whence novel configurations of ideas and relations may arise.[55]

This is the potential for the Algerian Church that I have observed. From Algerian converts "nay" to various "'positive structural assertions"—whether Arab-Nationalist, Islamist, colonial, or even neo-colonial Western Christian structures—to the source of new pluralistic structural assertions. In this way, as Algerian converts engage with the transcendent in communitas, it seems to be giving rise to a process not just of personal transformation within their "anti-structure" but also an experience of "liberated" and "liberating liminality" which is contributing to "novel configurations" in development of Algerian society and in the movement of World Christianity.

Illustrating some dimensions of the liberated liminal "dance," Naim, an Algerian Church leader, spoke to me about the paradox of being part of a worldwide Christian community on pilgrimage and yet fully present in his local Muslim family and culture. With a series of powerful metaphors, he described both the liminality of his experience and his resulting struggle as an Algerian Christian in this way,

> The first thing that I must do, the first on my list of responsibility as a Christian among all my responsibilities, is to liberate the Algerian. I free him; I need to become one with him. Because you know today, I am his enemy. I am Christian so I am his enemy . . . I've two faces, two rooms, one opposite the other, which can be opposed one to the other. I've this natural connection, brother with brother, whatever his nationality; but I've also another brother who I need to recover. The presence of one makes the other uncomfortable. I walk on a tight rope... and I don't want it to break . . . At present I am concerned with the big connection with the large family of Christ but I have a problem with the local home connection "in my kitchen." It's the connection with my fellow (Muslim) citizen.[56]

His words graphically express the liminality of the Algerian Church. However, the idea of being "in-between" while paradoxical and painful can become a positive self-affirming understanding that both recognizes this tension but moves toward being "in-both" rather than merely "in-between." Following Lee's "'self-affirming" conception of marginality, this liminal space becomes a "creative core" in which the liminoid encounter with the transcendent opens the way to go "in-beyond"' both centers and margins, structure and anti-structure. Naim describes it like this,

> Once I am connected to Christ I'm sort of connected to everybody. It's true I'm a pilgrim, only a lodger here. I say jokingly that "I'm not a local; I'm just waiting for the bus." However, while waiting, I have things to do. The first thing that I must do, the first on my list of responsibility as a Christian among all my responsibilities, is to liberate the Algerian. I free him; I need to become one with him.[57]

Central to the Church's potential liberating role in the development of this emerging pluralistic civil society will be perceptions of its minority status. One of the respondents in my doctoral research was insistent that the Church not be described as a "minority" but rather as an "entity." In part this was to distance the Church from the accusation that its development has been implanted as an aegis for foreign (especially American) involvement in Algeria's internal affairs. However, more positively it seems to be linked to an affirmation of an emerging pluralistic vision of Algerian citizenship, one that recognizes Algeria's de facto multiethic, multilinguistic, and increasingly multireligious character. He explained it this way,

> The Algerian Christian is a citizen, or the citizen is a Christian. I think that it's thanks to the existence of the Church that this notion of citizenship is going to change, that it's going to change with time at a level, or towards the model of a new notion of citizenship.[58]

CONCLUSION

Algeria's ontological quest is a struggle with its own liminality as a nation from being a department of France under the French colonial administration to an independent nation fashioned in shape of the single-party socialist Arab and Muslim nation and to today's tentative expression of a modern reformed Muslim pluralist civil society. Both French colonial (West-facing) and Arab-Salafist (East-facing) factors have shaped the national identity of Algeria. For over fifty years since its independence, the only official narrative binding Algeria's collective national identity has been the mantra of the FLNs "glorious liberation struggle." Today, the unwillingness of most Algerians to accept the legitimacy of this official narrative is one of the factors behind the recent *Hirak* protest movement across Algeria.[59] Additionally, the imposed and problematic "non-negotiable" Arab-Islamic centrism upon which the nation's ontology and teleology were founded, is today, being resisted by numerous different elements of Algerian society.

The presence and growth of the Algerian Church, primarily though not exclusively among Kabyles, are challenging the Arab-Islamist formulae of national identity and contributing to the struggle to redefine it. Whilst this formula (or centrism) has been an obstacle to the Church, I have observed that it is also proving to be an opportunity for the development of both the Church and the nation. The liminality of Kabyle's self-expression in the margins of Algeria's "official" national identity has mirrored the particularity of contemporary Algerian Christianity in the margins of the Universal Church. Algerian believers clearly articulate their sense of belonging to a universal Christian Church called to a worldwide mission. However, they are also aware of the particularity of their place as Algerian Christians. Kabyle believers talk about the concept of being "chosen"' for a universal mission in and beyond Algeria. Some also speak of the sense in which this mission is also linked to their sense of responsibility to transform the structures of Algerian national identity not by being a self-defensive "minority" (a self-negating particularity) but rather as an Algerian "entity" (a liberat*ed* and liberat*ing* particularity). The Algerian Church is demonstrating this by avoiding the association with Western neo-colonialisms (a harmful universalism) and equally avoiding association with the Kabyle autonomy movement (a potentially harmful particularity). By its presence and engagement, it is provoking Algerians to re-define old publicly affirmed solidarities and in so doing is taking its place in the liminality of Algeria's ontological and teleological quest.

NOTES

1. Despite having a legal statute as a 100% Algerian organization, in the past four years (2018–2022) at least seventeen churches have been ordered to close with the Algerian police forcibly removing worshipers from these well-established places of worship.

2. Boutheina Cheriet, "The Evaluation of the Higher Education System in Algeria," in *The Evaluation of Higher Education Systems. World Yearbook of Education,* ed. Robert Cowen (London: Kogan Page Limited, 1996), 4–5.

3. The Église Protestant d'Algérie—EPA (The Protestant Church of Algeria) is a legally recognised Algerian association.

4. Patrick Brittenden, "Towards an Appropriate Pedagogy for the Development of the Muslim-Background Church of Algeria" (Doctoral dissertation, University of Oxford, 2018), 9–13.

5. Tariq Ramadan, *The Arab Awakening: Islam and the New Middle East* (London: Penguin, 2012), xii.

6. Ramadan, 126.

7. Victor Turner, *The Ritual Process: Structure and Anti-Structure,* new edition (London: Aldine Transaction, 2009 [1969]), 132.

8. Robert Victor Jackson, *International Perspectives on Citizenship, Education and Religious Diversity* (London: Routledge, 2002), 11.

9. Brittenden, 88–124, 125–174 and 174–226.

10. T. Carson, R. Fairhurst, N. Rooms & L. R. Withrow, eds., *Crossing Thresholds: A Practical Theology of Liminality* (Cambridge: The Lutterworth Press, 2021), xx.

11. Marcel Barnard, "Flows of Worship in the Network Society: Liminality as Heuristic Concept in Practical Theology beyond Action Theory," *In die Skriflig* 44, no. 1 (2010): 67–84.

12. Carson *et al.*, 23.

13. Bjorn Thomassen, "The Uses and Meanings of Liminality," *International Political Anthropology* 2, no. 1 (2009): 1.

14. Carson *et al.*, xx.

15. Turner [1969], 97.

16. Carson *et al.*, 3.

17. Thomassen, 7–12.

18. Victor Turner, *The Forest of Symbols: Aspects of Ndembu Ritual* (London: Cornell University Press, 1970), 93.

19. Turner [1970], 93–94.

20. Arnold van Gennep, *The Rites of Passage* (Chicago: University of Chicago Press, 1960).

21. Turner [1970], 94.

22. Brittenden, 231.

23. Arpad Szakolczai, "Liminality and Experience: Structuring Transitory Situations and Transformative Events," *International Political Anthropology* 2, no. 1 (2009): 142.

24. Thomassen, 9–10.

25. Émile Durkheim, *The Elementary Forms of the Religious Life* (New York: Free Press, 1965).

26. Thomassen, 12.

27. Jacques Berque, *Le Maghreb Entre les Deux Guerres* (Paris: Editions du Seuil, 1979), 67–72.

28. Turner [1970], 93–111.

29. Thomassen, 14.

30. Am originally from New Zealand, was born in the UK, and then grew up from the age of two in Algeria.

31. Alec G. Hargreaves & Michael J. Hefferman, eds., *France and Algeria. Identities from Colonial Times to the Present: A Century of Interactions* (Lewiston: Edwin Mellen Press, 1993), 9.

32. Emmanuelle Sibeud, "Une Ethnographie face a la Colonialisation: Arnold van Gennep en Algerie (1911–1912)," *Revue d'Histoire des Sciences Humaines* 10 (2004): 73–103.

33. Turner [1970], 98–110.

34. Carson *et al.*, 6.

35. S. Ybema, N. Beech & N. Ellis, eds., "Transitional and Perpetual Liminality: An Identity Practice Perspective," *Anthropology Southern Africa* 34, nos. 1–2 (2011): 23–24.

36. Timothy Green, "Issues of Identity for Christians of a Muslim Background in Pakistan" (Doctoral dissertation, SOAS, 2014).

37. Green, 19–20.

38. Green, 25–26.

39. Green, 36.

40. Green, 32.

41. Green, 37–38.

42. Turner [1969], 132.

43. Jens Barnett, "Longing for Community: Church, Ummah, or Somewhere in Between?," in *Longing for Community: Church, Ummah, or Somewhere in Between?*, ed. David Greenlee (Littleton: William Carey Library, 2013), 34.

44. Jung Young Lee, *Marginality: The Key to Multicultural Theology* (Minneapolis: Fortress Press, 1995), 43–49.

45. Lee, 47.

46. Abdallah Mazouni, *Culture et enseignement en Algérie et au Maghreb* (Paris: Maspero, 1969), 80.

47. Lee, 45.

48. Turner [1970], 95–97.

49. Originating from the Arabic adjective "warring" (as in warring party or movement), this is a term that was used in Algeria to describe indigenous Algerians who served the French Army during the Algerian war of independence. See also Guemriche's treatment of this term in the context of Christian converts in Algeria.

Salah Guemriche, *Le Christ s'est arrêté à Tizi-Ouzou: Enquête sur conversions les en terre d'islam* (Paris: Editions Denoël, Salah, 2011), 43–55, 56–58, and 91–99.

50. Turner [1969], 97.

51. Lee, 43–49.

52. Lee, 55–76.

53. Carson *et al.*, 25.

54. With the exception of some references to Victor Turner's concept of the *communitas* in *The Ritual Process* (1969), Lee, 152–157.

55. Turner [1970], 97.

56. Brittenden, Loc 80.

57. Brittenden, Loc 81.

58. Brittenden, Loc 62.

59. The *Hirak* Movement, sometimes referred to as the "Revolution of smiles" because of unprecedented peaceful way in which they have been conducted, was a movement of weekly mass demonstrations cutting across all sectors of society unhappy with the military-backed elite running the country that have taken place in major cities across Algeria from February 16, 2019, to March 20, 2020.

BIBLIOGRAPHY

Barnard, Marcel. "Flows of Worship in the Network Society: Liminality as Heuristic Concept in Practical Theology beyond Action Theory." *In die Skriflig* 44, no. 1, (2010) 67–84.

Barnett, Jens. "Longing for Community: Church, Ummah, or Somewhere in Between?" in *Longing for ,Community: Church, Ummah, or Somewhere In Between*, edited by David Greenlee. Littleton, CO: William Carey Library, (2013): 69–78.

Beit-Hallahmi, Benjamin. *Prolegomena to the Psychological Study of Religion.* Lewisburg, PA: Bucknell University Press, 1989.

Berque, Jacques. *Le Maghreb Entre les Deux Guerres.* Paris: Editions du Seuil, 1979.

Brittenden, Patrick. "Christianity in the Maghrib." In *The Handbook of the Maghreb,* edited by George Joffe. London: Routledge, Expected 2023, Ch18.

Brittenden, Patrick. "Towards an Appropriate Pedagogy for the Development of the Muslim-Background Church of Algeria." Doctoral dissertation, University of Oxford 1, 2018.

Carson, T., R. Fairhurst, N. Rooms, and L. R. Withrow, eds. *Crossing Thresholds: A Practical Theology of Liminality.* Cambridge: The Lutterworth Press, 2021.

Cheriet, Boutheina. "The Evaluation of the Higher Education System in Algeria." In *The Evaluation of Higher Education Systems: World Yearbook of Education,* edited by Robert Cowen. London: Kogan Page Limited, (1996): 4–5.

Durkheim, Émile. *The Elementary Forms of the Religious Life.* New York: Free Press, 1965.

Green, Timothy. "Issues of Identity for Christians of a Muslim Background in Pakistan." Doctoral dissertation, SOAS, 2014.

Guemriche, Salah. *Le Christ s'est arrêté à Tizi-Ouzou: Enquête sur conversions les en terre d'islam.* Paris: Editions Denoël, 2011.

Hargreaves, Alec G. and Michael J. Hefferman, eds. *France and Algeria. Identities from Colonial Times to the Present: A Century of Interactions.* Lewiston: Edwin Mellen Press, 1993.

Jackson, Robert Victor. *International Perspectives on Citizenship, Education and Religious Diversity.* London: Routledge, 2002.

Lee, Jung Young. *Marginality: The Key to Multicultural Theology.* Minneapolis, MN: Fortress Press, 1995.

Mazouni, Abdallah. *Culture et enseignement en Algérie et au Maghreb.* Paris: Maspero, 1969.

Ramadan, Tariq. *The Arab Awakening: Islam and the New Middle East.* London: Penguin, 2012.

Said, Edward. *Orientalism.* London: Routledge and Kegan, 1978.

Sibeud, Emmanuelle. "Une Ethnographie face a la Colonialisation: Arnold van Gennep en Algerie (1911–1912). *Revue d'Histoire des Sciences Humaines* 10, (2004): 79–103.

Stonequist, Everett V. *The Marginal Man: A Study in Personality and Culture Conflict.* New York: Russell & Russell, 1961.

Szakolczai, Arpad. "Liminality and Experience: Structuring Transitory Situations and Transformative Events." *International Political Anthropology* 2, no. 1 (2009): 141–167.

Thomassen, Bjorn. "The Uses and Meanings of Liminality." *International Political Anthropology* 2, no. 1 (2009): 5–24.

Turner, Victor. *The Forest of Symbols: Aspects of Ndembu Ritual*. London: Cornell University Press, 1970.

Turner, Victor. *The Ritual Process: Steructure and Anti-Structure,* New edition. London: Aldine Transaction, 2009 [1969].

van Gennep, Arnold. *The Rites of Passage*. Chicago, IL: University of Chicago Press, 1960.

Ybema, S., N. Beech, and N. Ellis, eds. "Transitional and Perpetual Liminality: An Identity Practice Perspective." *Anthropology Southern Africa* 34, no. 1–2 (2011): 21–29.

Chapter 3

"Neither here nor there"

Border-Crossing and Liminal States in Rose Tremain's The Road Home

Maria Antonietta Struzziero

Thou shalt leave each thing
Beloved most dearly: This is the first shaft
Shot from the bow of exile. Thou shalt prove
How salt the savour is of other's bread;
How hard the passage, to descend and climb
By other's stairs
> —Dante Alighieri, *Divine Comedy, Paradiso*, Canto XVII, ll. 55–60

These are the terms describing Dante's future lifelong exile from Florence, his native city, and the exilic afflictions he would have to bear, prophesized by his great-great-grandfather Cacciaguida during their encounter in Paradise. These words resonate with great emotional impact on the poet and conjure up the dire condition of exile poignantly in each image. The metaphor of exile as a "bow" shooting a piercing "shaft," a wound that tears apart his whole self; the loss of whatever is "beloved most dearly," home, country, family affections; and a demeaning dependence on others, having to savor the bitter, salty taste of "other's bread" and "to descend and climb/ By other's stairs," so to rely on their benevolent hospitality.

A "hard [. . .] passage" indeed for the poet who, actually, was already an exile, banished from Florence. In the *Divine Comedy*, a pilgrim in the afterworld, Dante, explores and negotiates threshold experiences and voices his anguish while imaginatively facing unique tests and crossing boundaries in a succession of inherently liminal places.

The poem begins and ends in spaces that can be described as the ultimate threshold of human existence, places of shadows and obscure meanings, where the poet ascends from one system of belief to another and is transformed in the process. In his underworld descent, "one of the most profound models for the exilic experience in literature,"[1] the poet himself is a liminal figure, in transition between spiritual and psychological states, a figure voyaging out from darkness, across nightmarish landscapes, toward the light.

The cluster of powerful images that the Italian poet compresses in these few lines encapsulates the predicament of all the people who, for whatever reason, experience the fractured condition of exile, having to leave their own country and family. It is an all too common painful state for the many migrants who move across borders all over the world, facing difficult, harrowing conditions, and who meet our eyes while walking the streets of our cities, all too often constrained to depend on someone's help.

The compelling emotional atmosphere evoked by the Italian poet resonates, albeit with all due differences, in the psychological portrait of Lev, the protagonist of Rose Tremain's *The Road Home* (2008), and his experience as a modern economic migrant.

MOVING FORWARD, WHILE STILL LOOKING BACKWARD

Rose Tremain's *The Road Home* (2008) hinges on the story of Lev, a man in his early forties who, driven away from home by both bereavement and lack of employment, migrates to England in search of a better future for himself and the five-year-old daughter whom he leaves behind in the care of his old mother, carrying a heavy load of memories with him.

The novel charts Lev's journey from his small village in an unidentified former Communist country in Eastern Europe (one of the new EU member states) to London and back home. When he arrives in London, the narrative follows his initial hesitant steps through the city, determined to work his way up. As he is uprooted from both place and community, this "beyond" space becomes itself a frontier that begets "yet more crossing points, to proliferate into thresholds of other kinds,"[2] sometimes barely perceptible: psychological, cultural, and linguistic, a space whose parameters must be constantly redefined, while he tries to adjust to the new sociocultural reality. He moves inside this "alien" territory as a liminal being, haunted by the ruins of his former self and by fossil memories welling up from deep within his psyche, recollections of a "lost woman—lost land, lost language."[3] He appears to be a subject-in-crisis who fears that his identity and psychological integrity might be under threat and he might lose himself.

From the moment he sets foot in this foreign territory, he is plunged into a period of inner conflict and disorientation. He realizes that he inhabits a marginal position between two worlds, a psychological condition commonly experienced by border crossers, be they migrants or exiles, diasporic subjects "who make and re-make themselves in relation to new sociocultural environments."[4]

Lev starts from the bottom rung, initially sleeping rough and earning a meagre wage; then, he gradually moves from being a dishwasher to becoming an accomplished chef in a chic restaurant, with an interval as a farm laborer in Suffolk. Along the way he meets and is helped by other economic migrants, among them Lydia, his good-hearted traveling companion, a former teacher of English and translator, who is instrumental in helping him in his quest for self-fulfillment. Acting as the traditional "helper," one of the roles identified by A.-J. Greimas in his actantial model, she will assist Lev in finding a job at G. K. Ashe and a room lodging with the lonely Christy Slane, a divorced Irishman, who will be not only another helper but a good friend and a kindred spirit. From their first meeting, Lev "recognis[es] something of himself"[5] in Christy, being both foreigners, marginalized and emotionally wounded by similar painful losses. Theirs is the encounter and mutual recognition of two othernesses that, at least for some time, balances Lev's wandering and puts an end to it. Christy instinctively welcomes him, because he senses that, in opening his home to a stranger, his own loneliness is shared with, and eased by, Lev's presence. Together with a number of other variously displaced migrant characters Lev crosses paths with, they will construct a sense of *communitas* inside which there is not "a structure of hierarchically arrayed positions"[6] and they can be their authentic selves. He establishes with them a feeling of comradership and belonging that "transcends distinctions of rank, age, kinship position."[7] In the end, having acquired experience and skills, and saved some money, he decides to return back home, completing the circular movement the novel's title hints at.

RITES OF PASSAGE

The narrative trajectory of the protagonist's life, this chapter argues, articulates the conditions of liminality, first investigated by the French anthropologist Arnold van Gennep, then developed and applied to modern Western societies by the British anthropologist Victor Turner, now considered a master concept in the social and political sciences.

Van Gennep studied the underlying characteristic patterns and ritual dynamics that "accompany every change of place, state, social position and age,"[8] pervasively expressed throughout the life of an individual despite societal variation and that he defined *rites of passage*. He identified three phases in such rites: separation (preliminal), transition (liminal), and incorporation (postliminal). This tripartite structure is sometimes reduplicated when "the transitional period is sufficiently elaborated to constitute an independent state."[9]

The first phase—involving a journey and a sacrifice—is activated by events, either positive or negative, that signal the end of a stage in a person's life, as in Lev's case, and her/his detachment from an earlier position in the social structure or from a set of cultural conditions.

Separation is followed by liminality, a period "that has few or none of the attributes of the past or the coming state; [. . .] a realm of pure possibility whence novel configurations of ideas and relations may arise,"[10] that enable the subject to experiment with alternative social relations. It is a special condition that may last for a certain length of time, during which one "wavers between two worlds. [. . .] This symbolic and spatial area of transition may be found in more or less pronounced form in all ceremonies which accompany the passage from one social [. . .] position to another."[11]

In *The Forest of Symbols*, in Chapter IV, "Betwixt and Between: The Liminal Period in *Rites de Passage*," Turner focused his attention on a detailed analysis of the phase of liminality and the symbolism attached to and surrounding the liminal *persona*. Building upon van Gennep's observation that rites of passage and other rituals are liminal in that they temporarily extricate participants from their social statuses, Turner argued that these rites are antithetical to existing social structure and "subjunctive" because they invite new possibilities. Homi Bhabha holds a similar view in *The Location of Culture* (1994): he discusses the importance of borders and maintains that "'in-between' spaces provide the terrain for elaborating strategies of self-hood- singular or communal- that initiate new signs of identity,"[12] so processes that have a truly transformative power for identity formation.

The third phase of incorporation or aggregation completes the cycle, a process punctuated by a number of trials, set at critical points of transition that societies ritualize publicly.

BORDER-CROSSING AND LIMINALITY

The in-depth reading of *The Road Home* shows that the basic components of this framework constitute the fabric of the plot and that the attributes associated with the liminal persona reverberate through the text in Lev's psychological profile, giving "an outward and visible form to an inward and conceptual process."[13]

The analysis of the novel will focus on some of the symbolic elements and motifs that recur at key moments and will discuss how each stage marks a fracture that has an epiphanic function for the protagonist. Indeed, the whole process contributes to a profound cultural and psychological metamorphosis, personal development, and acquisition of new knowledge for Lev that will re-orient his world view and allow him, in the end, to articulate his cultural difference, even though with some unresolved ambivalence at the end of his quest for self-realization that will be observed and discussed in the conclusive remarks.

The rite of passage process is encapsulated at a micronarrative level in the novel's first chapter where Tremain introduces a set of tropes and symbols typical of the discourse of liminality, a cluster of images that will recur over and over again in the novel. Their metaphorical value hints at an unbearable rift that cannot be articulated in literal terms because in excess of the suffering experienced. Lev is in the traumatic condition of moving across liminal spaces, a frontier that is "a site of unexpected and sudden openness and transformations"[14] uprooted from family and community, fragmented between different places and selves, and a sort of disseminated self racked by nostalgia and melancholia.

Using a third-person heterodiegetic narrator who adopts the protagonist's privileged point of observation to give the reader an in-depth view of his thoughts, perceptions, and emotions, the chapter follows the protagonist's fifty-hour-long coach journey from his village to London, a movement that for Lev acquires the form of a restless interrogation. The narrative of the actual journey in this section intersects with the thread of Lev's meandering mind shifting between the present—with its emotional burden of doubts, fears, and expectations—and the past—with the haunting presence of shards of memories, regrets, and losses that weight him down. It is a compulsive retrospection tendency that already starts when he boards the coach and continues to surface at various moments, with a different degree of intensity, throughout his stay in England. All the flashbacks are essential to provide valuable insights into the key motivations behind his decision to leave his country: his wife's untimely death of leukemia; the loss of his job in the Baryn sawmill which was closed down; and his responsibility for his five-year-old daughter Maya and his aging mother. All these events persuade Lev not to indulge in a nostalgic cult of the past, as his father used to do when he was still alive, but move forward and migrate to London, defying "the longing of his father's to resist change" (29), a movement that stems from the fear of being engulfed in existential paralysis.

It is a journey that demands a sacrifice of him, the temporary separation from his beloved daughter, on top of his other losses. So, this chapter is an interesting narrative segment and an effective epistemological key to access the fictional world of the whole novel. It foregrounds the idea of border-crossing and epitomizes the protagonist's in-between state, a psychological and existential condition that is a dominant motif in the text.

The journey itself is a liminal experience, indeed *the* central symbol of any process of transition, and the images connected with this semantic area are scattered throughout the novel. Lev's coach journey is both literal and metaphorical. It is a territorial passage during which he crosses borders and countries and transit spaces across Europe on the way to Britain, a floating world that he observes from the coach window, a symbolic threshold introduced in the very first sentence of the novel, "he sat huddled against the window" (1), repeated a few paragraphs on, and found at several key moments in the rest of the novel. His head leans against its cold-framed space, like "an impermeable membrane."[15] On the one hand, the window shields him against the darkness "falling outside" (4), a darkness that is the signifier of his present psychological condition; on the other, the window relates the outside world to the interior and the self. So, it may signify both seclusion and exclusion, as well as connection, permeability.

At the same time, the journey, driven by the secret wound of a loss and the desire to explore the possibility of renewal of life, also marks a symbolic separation from his old mourning self, a sort of "ritual death" before entering the "liminal." It is a lonely journey of the psyche, a movement from the known into the unknown, which he pictures as the "infernal luck" (6), an oxymoron that enucleates the ambivalent expectations he has about his near future.

The coach on which Lev travels is a small microcosm crowded with migrant people like him, a non-place between destinations, and the "long agony" (1) of the journey seems to be taking place outside time. For Lev, it is the beginning of a revisionary phase, the initial segment of a gradual readjustment of the self, an ongoing process that "demands an encounter with 'newness' that is not part of the continuum of past and present. It creates a sense of the new as an insurgent act of cultural translation."[16]

Even at this early stage, Lev already betrays some of the ambiguous features of threshold people. He no longer belongs to his old world and is not yet part of the new, caught on linguistic and cultural frontiers, between words and worlds, at the intersection of histories and memories, in a psychological and mental liminality in which anxiety and hope coexist.

Still "in transit and uncertain what time [his] watch [. . .] should be telling" (9), his mind follows the paths of memory and fluctuates between fragments of the past, the lack he holds on to, that is still very much alive for him; the present in abeyance; and the beckoning of an elusive, unimaginable future with its unexplored routes. These temporal shifts are formally reflected in the novel's dense narrative texture.

He feels "adrift on an ocean that had no limits and never broke on any human shore" (15), in an existential gap, "neither here nor there", suspended in the "betwixt and between"[17] that Turner mentions as a trait of the "transitional being"—which he aptly calls the "passenger"[18]who crosses a threshold that can be both informative and potentially transformative, moments of processes when, indeed, new subjectivities are produced and cultural differences are articulated.

During the intervening liminal period, Lev is structurally, if not physically, invisible. He is surrounded by "a deep, impenetrable darkness" (9), an obscurity that he will experience anytime the new culture becomes opaque, impregnable to his attempts at decoding its signs and entering its discourses, or at connecting with it, and he feels marginalized. Actually, the new space is so radically unlike the ordinary for him that, at times, it can be described only using metaphors like death, dissolution, going underground, images that signal the gradual dissolution of his old self to allow the new self to surface, the paradigm of a subject in constant transformation.

Divested of his sociocultural constituents, Lev alternates psychologically and emotionally between two states, a subject split between home and host country, living in the tension and dislocation generated by the rift between the self and its true home. It is a characteristic common to both émigré and exilic conditions, as also the exile inhabits one place and remembers or projects the reality of another. Constantly torn between the here and now and a past elsewhere he experiences the process of migration as "both discontinuity and continuity."[19] The writer André Aciman voices this condition with emotional intensity, having experienced the same condition himself: "When exiles see one place they're also seeing—or looking for—another behind it. Everything bears two faces, everything is shifty because everything is mobile, the point being that exile, like love, is not just a condition of pain, it's a condition of deceit."[20]

This dichotomy is foregrounded, on the one hand, by Lev's habit of daydreaming—a nostalgia saturated with images, voices, and fragrances of his past that make him, to quote Julia Kristeva, "a dreamer making love with absence."[21] On the other, by the frequent need to call his best friend Rudi, the thread connecting him with his home country, the native territory re-created by a heightened and sharpened memory, that helps provide continuity within dislocation.

Throughout his stay in London, he manifests some of the typical aspects of liminal *personae,* identified by Victor Turner as entities whose conditions "elude or slip through the network of classifications that normally locate states and positions in cultural space."[22] So he straddles between visibility and invisibility, integration and interstitial survival, in a precarious balance on the threshold between the two modalities, a position that appears to foreclose the relief of stopping as well as the possibility of taking roots.

At one point, after some months in London, he even experiences a deep inner fracture. Cut off from his roots, he feels that the Lev who left his home country is actually inhabiting not only another space but another body,

harboring a disturbing uncanny foreign *other* inside "*that* Lev had been a different man" whereas now he is "an old, sorrowful, anxious man" (178) who
is a stranger to himself. It is a hidden presence that lingers on, that cannot
be erased or silenced and that problematizes his present. Lev's perception
of having aged in a short time is common among people who experience
similar conditions. "The difficulties the foreigner will necessarily encounter,"
Kristeva argues, "wound him severely [and] make him turn gray, impercep-
tibly, [. . .] always ready to resume his infinite journey, farther, elsewhere",[23]
as actually Lev does.

LIVING WITH THE OTHERS, *AS OTHER*

On his arrival at Victoria station, left to himself by Lydia who goes to her
"separate future in the unknown city" (17) and "devoid of any plan for the
next few days and hours of his life" (20), Lev looks for a washroom, longing to rub himself clean of his old muddy self that "stank" (17). It is almost
a purification ritual, an attempt to wash off his Easterness, with a symbolic
function quite similar to the rites observed by van Gennep during transition
periods, a ritual performed to signify a person's separation from previous
surroundings.

From there, he begins to look for work and a place to sleep. So, still disori-
entated and "with no known ending or destination" (25) in mind, he sets out
on a new journey through London, a motif that Tremain uses to illustrate the
novel's central themes: traumatic displacement; the yearning for attachment
and belonging; the pathos implicit in the loss of community and identity; and
what it feels like to be dependent on others.

This quest inevitably entails facing obstacles, stepping across thresholds
to enter another semantic field and undergoing trials. Barriers take different
forms in the novel. Some are real, physical barriers that he must learn either
to identify as such or to decode and translate as signifiers of other, more subtle sociocultural boundaries and sources of culture clashes at different levels,
behind which people are firmly entrenched, deploying legal, psychological,
and linguistic mechanisms to reaffirm and protect them.

He already meets, and clashes with, a few such barriers during the first
two days after his arrival, in combination with psychological and linguistic
obstacles, due to his scanty knowledge of English, a discourse through which
he hopes to constitute his new self by entering the available linguistic and
discursive practices devised by and contained within the new sociocultural
reality.

The first is an iron grating against which, shortly after his arrival, still
exhausted from the long journey, he sits down and falls asleep. He is

brusquely woken up by an unfriendly, bullying policeman who misinterprets Lev's movement to reach for his passport and seizes his wrist "with fearsome force" (22), pinioning him against a tree to search his body. Then, the policeman checks his passport and bag and questions him about his status and address in London, a point on which Lev's inaccurate pronunciation of "B&B" generates further misunderstanding and warns Lev against sleeping in the street, informing him that it is considered "anti-social behaviour and liable to a heavy fine" (24).

It is a micronarrative segment that on a small, but significant, scale exemplifies a pattern that will be found at other moments in the novel: the dual *hierarchized* opposition superior/inferior, in which someone in authority aims to intimidate and silence a subject who is in a psychological and existential condition of fragility to transform him into a subjected "other" in order to control or silence him. This happens here, as elsewhere in the text, through one of the procedures of exclusion identified by Michel Foucault in "The Order of Discourse," the prohibition, and by foreclosing access to discourse, the central vehicle in the process whereby people are constituted as individuals and as social subjects. As "the techniques for self-constitution are created by and contained within available discourses,"[24] the exclusion from it leaves the subject constrained in a powerless position, with no agency, as Lev will find out on many occasions, an experience that is profoundly alienating.

The second, more symbolically relevant of these initial boundaries, is a "gate that opened on a square garden" (40), outside which Lev rests during his first working day delivering leaflets for Ahmed's kekab place, watching children play and thinking of his own child. After a few minutes, one of the young mothers, "marching towards him," orders him to go away because it is "a garden for residents only" (41). She also calls him a "foreign nutter" (42) and threatens to call the police, thus invoking the rule of the law against him. In this case, the gate is the marker of a privileged territory that he must not overstep. To the woman, Lev's "face that is so *other* bears the mark of a crossed threshold that irremediably imprints itself as [. . .] anxiety."[25] Ostensibly occupying the place of the difference, Lev is the foreigner to be excluded, perceived as "that which cannot be clearly classified in terms of traditional criteria, or falls between classification boundaries," thus regarded as "polluting" and "dangerous"[26] and to be isolated. He is viewed as a disturbing presence that, with his unacceptable *otherness*, threatens the binary classifications that underpin a society's construction of order as well as the Western discourses, practices, and institutions of bourgeois individualism.

Lev's is an otherness that, both to the policeman's and the woman's eye, is already inscribed in his immigrant's body and is, consequently, subject to forms of exclusion. In fact, in such cases, the physical aspect is "mobilized as marker[. . .] of difference, enabling the security forces whether on the streets, squares, subway stations and other public spaces [. . .] of the host country—to act to impede and/or constrain immigrants."[27]

On a personal level, Lev transgresses the fragile boundaries of the woman's insecure self, thus confirming what Kristeva argues: "The foreigner comes in when the consciousness of my difference arises, and he disappears when we all acknowledge ourselves as foreigners, unamenable to bonds and communities."[28] On a sociocultural level, he compels the woman to interrogate her certainties and this disturbs her vision of herself as belonging to "a benign, welcoming, multi-cultural, liberal society," as Tremain argues in an interview for *The Guardian*[29] and its master narrative that she has never questioned but merely absorbed uncritically. This perception prevents acknowledgment of identities that are deemed to be subaltern within the bourgeois sociocultural framework and its system of interpellations.

Intimidated and helpless to defend himself in a language that he does not master, Lev leaves. As in other circumstances in the novel, being in a limbo, with neither status nor position inside a social system, he is passive and compliant, and accepts in silence the woman's offensive words, a psychological reaction that is a feature of liminal people. Once more, as in the episode previously discussed, Lev's impossibility to have access to the discursive frameworks that circulate in the host country's sociocultural reality, leaves him helpless, in the condition of "separateness of the uprooted person."[30] In both cases, Lev is perceived as an outsider, someone who does not belong, and his "'migrant body' generates estrangement, sets off the alarms of otherness, raises physical and symbolic barriers."[31]

Most of the time, barriers and thresholds are signifiers of exclusion, marginality, and isolation. Yet, paradoxically, at times they mark out a space that can become a shelter, which shows the peculiar ambiguity inherent in the liminal, when in a single representation there can be "the coincidence of opposite [. . .] notions" the coexistence of "that which is neither this nor that, and yet is both."[32] This can be observed also in relation to Lev: the first few nights, the secluded area of a basement flat protected by iron railings, "hidden in the space under the road" (43) and invisible because sheltered from view also by hydrangea bushes, becomes his temporary cardboard house. In these circumstances, borders protect, darkness and invisibility are welcome. The condition of Lev, almost buried "in his hole under the pavement" (50), is strongly reminiscent of the image of some initiation rites observed by Turner, during which the young initiates are taken to a chamber below the surface of the earth, with a hole in its floor.

Reading the names Kowalski and Shepard above the bell next to the door of the basement flat, Lev tries to imagine the comfortable life of the two unknown, absent people behind the framed space of the window, where a cat is curling taking no notice of him. Both thresholds—doors and windows—have a mesmeric quality; at the same time, they resist and invite hermeneutic decodification, with their "combination of porosity and resistance that creates pressures between which the imagination thrives."[33] They signify the captivating invisible presence of other ways of being, other stories to imagine, and other life patterns that entice Lev but out of his reach and which he is barred from penetrating.

Once more, as on the coach and at other moments in the course of the novel, the window becomes "the focal point of feeling"[34] for Lev. It is a physical threshold that protects someone else's intimate domestic world, separating it from both the world outside and Lev's, a boundary that, by activating the thought and the imagination, can open out or close in and that here connotes exclusion. So, thresholds have a Janus-faced nature, being both protective spatial concepts and powerful symbols of isolation and exclusion.

A NEW WORLD, A NEW SELF

A more decisive threshold to step across and move forward and upward, with its accompanying actions and ritual practices to undergo, comes when Lev is engaged to work in G. K. Ashe's high-end restaurant. It is a really transformative moment in Lev's "rite of passage," as it opens a true fracture with his past self and triggers a series of significant changes that structure a different social being via the internalization of new schemes and values. The restaurant is actually a sort of arena in which the acquisition and mastery of some highly specific gestures and skills contribute to "exercise a particularly persuasive effect on the participants' sense of identity."[35]

The trials to access this new professional world entail a two-phase process: first, and profoundly distressing for him, he is to be stripped of his name, the signifier of his identity, and be re-named "Nurse" (75), thus reduced to a mere function. Turner mentions the act of renaming as part of the symbolism attached to liminal personae, when "their very names are taken from them and each is called solely by the generic term."[36] It is a *designation* (76) that Lev silently objects to, though he accepts it without complaint; he affects indifference and appears to be beyond the reach of attacks and rejections but is actually profoundly vulnerable. Yet, indifference is a necessary protective shield for him both against nostalgia of the past and potential wounds in the present. Second, he is to be reeducated in order to conform to very rigid rules and practices, which he dutifully learns by observation and training and has to master a new linguistic code, a proper "glossary" (77). All these sets of practices—"both structured and structuring"are the medium for the simultaneous constitution of both the self and the world of social relations that Lev is entering. They "construct 'social beings' via the internalization of basic schemes and values"[37] that generate new practices, empower the person, and give him the sensation of belonging to the new social organization.

It is as though he is being ground down to be fashioned anew and be enabled to cope with his new station in life. Humble and submissive, ready to obey his instructors implicitly, as all liminal personae in diachronic transitions between states, Lev bends to these new rules submissively, grateful to those who have welcomed him, rating them above himself, ready to be "constantly other, according to others' wishes and to circumstances."[38] So, Lev must repress, and estrange himself from, his most authentic self, because it might jeopardize the integrity of his ego, and "must become an other, a stranger, in order to become a subject."[39] This estrangement transforms him into a foreigner, in exile from his psychological and emotional territory, with the paradoxical outcome that the construction of a new identity expected of him signifies, at the same time, the erasure of his core identity and the emergence of a split self.

Lev's relationship with Ashe, the restaurant's owner, a sort of dialectic of master and slave, with its echoes of Crusoe/Friday, has prompted the criticism of a number of scholars. Reading the novel from a postcolonial perspective, they have raised a number of objections: first that, beneath her undeniable empathy toward her protagonist, Tremain has imposed an "epistemological violence"[40] on Lev's past. Second, that she has read his narrative in the light of dominant Western patterns of representation, at the same time portraying Eastern Europe in primitivist, exoticist terms, as an Arcadian "pastoral world."[41] Lastly, that Lev is "another incarnation of the oriental qualities represented by Caliban [and] Friday."[42]

Indeed, these critical remarks certainly capture a problematic aspect of Tremain's novel. Yet, it should also be observed that, if actually Lev absorbs and is transformed both by his meeting with the British and their cultural models, as well as by his encounter with a number of migrant characters, *he* also discloses his *otherness* to them: human values and beliefs that have shaped him and are his sociocultural constituents. It is a dialogue of differences against the porous and heterogeneous background of multicultural London that is enriching for both and invites a critical reappraisal of their respective certainties and points of view. This is particularly evidenced by the positive influence his warm and hard-working personality has on Christy, for instance, who, thanks to his supportive presence, gives up drinking, resumes working regularly, and finds an affectionate new partner, Jasmina. Against London's multiethnic background, people interact preserving their individuality and identity, but widening the spectrum of their experiences and being affected by each other's stories and personal voices. It is a porous place of crosscultural exchanges, where different routes intersect and "translations" between cultures are long established.

With the successful completion of the trials at G. K. Ashe's restaurant, Lev transitions into his new status. This process is an instance of what Van Gennep maintains, and that has been mentioned in a previous section, that the tripartite structure of the rite of passage is sometimes reduplicated in the transition period itself as will happen again later on in the novel.

Submissiveness, according to Kristeva, is a psychological mask of the foreigner, "a second, impassive personality, an anesthetized skin he wraps himself in, providing a hiding place" for him. Yet, she adds, "beneath his armor as [. . .] tireless 'immigrant worker,' he bleeds body and soul,"[43] humiliated in a position where he has to efface and deny his self.

At Ashe's restaurant, Lev experiences emotional "inner bleeding" in his short-lived but intensely erotic relationship with sexy Sophie, his co-worker, whose "otherness [and] *newness of form* fascinated him" (106), being so unlike his dead wife Marina. The psychological dynamics that pull him so powerfully toward Sophie can be understood in light of Kristeva's observations in *Strangers to Ourselves*. She maintains that "the shattering of repression is what leads one to cross a border and find oneself in a foreign country." Then, she goes on to add that "tearing oneself away from family, language, and country in order to settle down elsewhere is a daring action accompanied by sexual frenzy: no more prohibition, everything is possible." And, whatever form the sense of liberation takes, this rupture with the former self "always involves the shattering of the former body,"[44] a transformation that is often followed by the discovery of a sense of jouissance in one's own body.

Their relationship has longlasting consequences for Lev; the upside is that it has a therapeutic effect, as it helps him to heal the traumatic memory of his wife's death and to make him feel rooted again. Yet, it also hurts Lev profoundly and sets off a chain of events that will have momentous implications and consequences for him, both on his personal and professional life, marking the lowest point of his English period and redirecting his life trajectory in a significant way.

Sophie takes him to the Royal Court Theatre for an avant-garde performance, an episode that occasions Tremain's biting criticism both of Western lifestyle and of contemporary British artistic world, with its pretentiousness and stilted jargon. Lev is both morally outraged by the play's theme of incest and frustrated by Sophie's total neglect of him when she meets her London friends. Once more his feeling of not belonging returns in similar, though magnified, terms as Sophie, at ease in that world and anxious to belong to it, devotes most of her attention to her art friends. They ridicule and scorn him, and their snobbish "intellectual universes" make him feel "helpless and ignorant" (119) not up to their "superior" Western standards. At no point he can really relate to the group of Sophie's friends. He does not fit in and is clearly an "other" to that form of social practice, an extraneousness even visible in his appearance and clothes; his body, "simply by its presence and by the feeling that it produces of being out of place or being in the wrong place [. . .] is capable of producing [. . .] exclusion."[45]

He is once more marginal to her world, "shut out" and abandoned to his own darkness. His brain is "as black, as dark as darkness could be anywhere" (211), actually "striving to become invisible" (200), predominant motifs in this section of the novel, that tend to be quite frequent in relation to Sophie and that recur anytime "he experiences a sense of 'thrownness' into a boundless space, in a world whose linguistic codes and social rules he does not master."[46] Juxtaposing the twofold disappointment and unable to control the tension that has been welling up inside him, Lev falls prey to an explosion of fury, reacts violently and aggressively both with Sophie and her friends, and then gets drunk.

His psychological features in this section are those of a Kristevan *abject*, the subject who discovers that he is radically excluded from the object of his desire, mourning for its loss, and drawn "toward the place where meaning collapses."[47] This condition is formally signalled by the stylistic intensity of Tremain's prose, its halting, staccato rhythm, broken syntax, and cluster of images. It is a narrative that yields to the crying out theme of suffering- horror, "the ultimate evidence of such states of abjection."[48] Giving vent to his choked up rage, his body aching, Lev begins to vomit and spill out foul smelling garbage onto the pavement. He feels that he is "creep[ing] downward [. . .] like an animal that nobody would see or hear" (213), at last falling into "a slippery void" (213). When he is woken up by a policeman, it gradually dawns on him that he has "made [his] life obscene" (215), that he "was lost once more [and] cast out" (215).

He is arrested and rescued by kind Lydia but abandoned by Sophie who has just started a new relationship, and also dismissed by Ashe. This phase of abjection culminates in his final act of raping Sophie during their last meeting. His sexual drive no longer encounters the check of prohibitions, so his "botched up pleasure turns into disease" and he plunges into an abyss of shame, an action that signals to the reader the destruction of psychic identity. And "the disease is all the more serious as sexual liberation was easy but has been suddenly interrupted"[49] by betrayal and abandonment. It is a disturbing action that casts weighty doubts on his character and reveals that there is another Lev: a darker, more instinctive, even occasionally violent, side that he actually cannot control.

The new wound provoked by the loss of both Sophie and his job ends a cycle and pushes him to leave London and set off on a new journey. He goes to work on a farm in Suffolk, picking asparagus with other immigrants like him and sleeping in a leaky old caravan, "back with the dispossessed" (245), feeling that "there was nowhere to go, except further into the darkness"

(250). It is a journey of social regression, an "ordeal" he submits to partly as a tempering of his essence to prepare him for future responsibilities; partly as a form of self-punishment, "for the way he'd wrecked the life he'd had in London" (244); and partly out of disgust at the shallow, "unreal world" (210) of the English and their "small England" (210).

This phase comes to an abrupt end, and his decision to return to London accelerated, when his friend Rudi calls to inform him that his village Auror is about to be flooded and erased by the construction of a dam, and its inhabitants to be relocated to newly built apartments in Baryn, which entails the erasure of his past.

The shock of this news, and the misery of his mother and friends, brings to life yet another Lev, awakening in him a strong sense of responsibility and determination to pursue his dream while his friend Rudy, once self-assured, cocky, resourceful, now is on the border of a psychological breakdown, prey to depression. Lev understands that he needs to make practical plans to help both his family and Rudy himself and seize the opportunity of the momentous transformations the dam will bring about in his town, putting to use the experience and skills he has accumulated in England. He goes back to London, now with a "Great Idea" in mind, which he can vividly picture, in contrast with his first arrival there, when he had no clear plan. He takes a job as a chef both at a retirement home, where he had accompanied Sophie in the past, and at the restaurant of Panno, a Greek friend of Christy, thus facing new trials. He works almost to exhaustion to save money enough and set up his own restaurant in the new Baryn, which he manages to do, also thanks to an unexpected gift of 3.000 pounds from Mrs. Ruby Constad, an old dying woman he had been kind to at the Hospice.

Lev's return to his home country and his reincorporation in his community brings to completion the whole rite of passage cycle. Yet, as he has undergone a many-layered identity, gender, and economic crisis, it is a return with crucial differences, a return to his "roots" but having been transformed by the "routes" he has explored on his journey. First, he reenters his world with a strong sense of self-esteem supportive of others, a transformation socially validated by his ascendancy to a new status inside his community. He has been transformed by the formative experiences and the new work ethos acquired during the transition period, which has not been "a mere acquisition of knowledge, but a change in being."[50] Second, his transformation also reframes the perception of his country, now inevitably assessed through the lens of Western viewpoints and models. No longer transfigured by distance and nostalgia, it is a place of dereliction and ugly suburbs, "abandoned farms and silent factories" (337), isolated from the civilized world, "slipping and sliding on a precipice" (337). On his return home, having completed his journey of self-improvement, Lev's alienation from his country is obvious;

walking alone through his village, "like a ghost" (338), he feels "a stranger in a world newly strange to him" (337). He even wishes to have Christy by his side, a stranger like he himself continues to feel, though now he lives in his native country. He is aware that a cycle has ended and that he is facing the challenge "of another complex and arduous road" (357) ahead of him, a melancholic mood that puzzles Rudy but is caught and understood with emotional empathy by Christy who visits him after a few months.

The novel's closing section, with Lev's final critical view and rejection of his country's past culture and traditions, is certainly another problematic aspect of the novel and has been widely criticized. Tremain's "asymmetrical conceptualization of Britain and 'Eastern Europe'" and the lack of specificity in portraying Lev's country of origin actually erase the Other and its past. This leaves behind "a blank space on which the terms of a new order are inscribed, and this new order is an unmitigated version of Western capitalism,"[51] a view that this chapter upholds, even though such cultural "program" is implemented by an Eastern "son," Lev, and adapted to the specificity of his community.

CONCLUSION

Rose Tremain's *The Road Home* is a quest narrative modeled on the tripartite structure of a rite of passage and its symbolic motifs, as it has been argued in the previous sections of this chapter. Borrowing partly from the *Buildungsroman* model, she reframes the sites of tension between the individual desire and the demands of socialization while revising, and deviating from, the normative formal conventions of the genre in its intersection with trauma narrative and immigrant stories.

On the surface, the novel follows Lev's "rites of passage,", a journey of discovery and psychological transformation charted along the traditional trajectory of the *Buildungsroman*. He moves from an initial condition of loss, marginality, and dependence to his final self-assertion, independence, and agency. His new self is a celebration of the ethics of struggle and perseverance, an ethics that sustains him in the face of despair and loss of community. In the course of the novel, Lev readjusts expectations and convictions both about himself and the foreign culture, which he reconsiders in a new light.

However, the *unconscious* of the text reveals the inscription of a textual *otherness*, a subtext that, read against the grain, problematizes the smooth completion of the transition passage and shows that the final order the text professes "is merely an imagined order, [. . .] the fictive resolution of [. . .] conflicts."[52] Actually, Lev's final return home, unlike the traditional *Buildungsroman* narrative paradigm, does not signal the transparent

celebration of the transformative power of the outward journey on the protagonist's self. As hinted at the beginning of the chapter, the conclusion has
an unresolved ambivalence both in its bitter-sweet atmosphere and in the final
psychological profile of Lev.

In fact, the end of the novel sees him return not to the place he left, which
actually no longer exists as he knew it, but once more to an *other* place he
must adjust to and compromise with; or to the people he left behind, who
also have been transformed by the process of uprootedness they have had
to undergo with the flooding and erasure of Auror. Consequently, his return
journey home has not come full-circle; he continues to feel still a "stranger"
to himself as well as to the people who are closer to him, and he (re)discovers
his own otherness, a phase that he believed he had left behind.

It is an alienating predicament because the emergence of self-conscious-
ness is always linked to self-loss, a process that sees him face a never-ending
journey into a self that is split and decentered, never fixed and finished, still
hollow at heart. In this sense, he exemplifies a Kristevan *subject-in-process*
whose meaning is constituted in relationships, with others as well as with his
own desires, and he traces the postmodern trajectory of a subjectivity characterized by fragmentation.

Lev's psychological portrait at the end of the novel appears to answer in
the affirmative Kristeva's question on the condition of the foreigner: "Should
one recognize that one becomes a foreign in another country because one is
already a foreigner from within?"[53] This is true of Lev; till the very end he is
often out of place or in the wrong place, a painful condition of displacement,
hybridity, and ambiguity that has become a common feature of our alienated
global capitalist world, an alienation that "is etched in sharpest relief in the
migrant's futile search for home."[54]

In conclusion, Tremain's *The Road Home* does not fully interrogate the
common stereotypes about Eastern Europeanness, and certainly the adaptation to sociocultural models is unidirectional as it is mostly Lev who conforms to, and accepts, Western lifestyle. The novel *does* show that the process
of crossing cultural and intellectual borders may be a much more arduous task
than crossing geographical frontiers and that it can be extremely demanding
and often achieved at great costs because for each gain there is a painful
loss. Leaving behind one's roots and affections is a wrenching journey away
from the self into alienation and displacement, as evidenced by the everyday
narratives of immigrant people brought to our attention by the media. This
is especially true at historical moments like ours, when the question of the
absorption of otherness into the social fabric of a nation has a global dimension with serious ethical implications. It is a problem that confronts all countries on an unprecedented scale, an issue made more problematic because the

sociopolitical integration of migrants is unpalatable to societies often dominated by heightened individualism and nationalist discourses.

NOTES

1. Michael Seidel, *Exile and the Narrative Imagination* (New Haven and London: Yale University Press, 1986), 13.

2. Subha Mukherij, ed., *Thinking on Thresholds: The Poetics of Transitive Spaces* (London: Anthem Press, 2013), xviii.

3. Julia Kristeva, *Strangers to Ourselves*, trans. Leon Roudiez (New York: University of Columbia Press, 1991), 36.

4. Eva Luksaite, "Constructing the Diasporic Body: Ritual Practices among South Asians in Britain," *Asia Europe Journal* 8 (June 2010): 22.

5. Rose Tremain, *The Road Home* (London: Vintage, 2008), 69. Further references are to this edition and given after quotation between parenthesis.

6. Victor Turner, *The Forest of Symbols: Aspects of Ndembu Ritual* (Ithaca and London: Cornell University Press, 1967), 100.

7. Turner, *The Forest of Symbols,* 100.

8. Turner, *The Forest of Symbols,* 94.

9. Arnold Van Gennep, *The Rites of Passage*, trans. M. B. Vizedom and G. L. Caffee (London: Routledge & Kegan Paul, 1960), 11.

10. Turner, *The Forest of Symbols*, 94, 97.

11. Van Gennep, *The Rites of Passage*, 18.

12. Homi Bhabha, *The Location of Culture* (London & New York: Routledge, 1994), 1.

13. Turner, *The Forest of Symbols,* 96.

14. Luis Torres, "Exile and Identity," in *Relocating Identities in Latin American Cultures*, ed. Elizabeth Montes Garcés (Calgary: University of Calgary Press, 2007), 65.

15. Gillian Beer, "Windows: Looking in, Looking out, Breaking through," in *Thinking on Thresholds: The Poetics of Transitive Spaces*, ed. Subha Mukherij (London: Anthem Press, 2013), 3.

16. Bhabha, *The Location of Culture*, 7.

17. Turner, *The Forest of Symbols*, 97.

18. Turner, *The Forest of Symbols*, 95.

19. Luksaite, "Constructing the Diasporic Body," 12.

20. André Aciman, ed., *Letters of Transit: Reflections on Exile, Identity, Language, and Loss* (New York: New Press, 1999), 13.

21. Kristeva, *Strangers to Ourselves,* 10.

22. Victor Turner, *The Ritual Process: Structure and Anti-Structure* (London: Routledge & Kegan Paul, 1969), 95.

23. Kristeva, *Strangers to Ourselves,* 6.

24. Luksaite, "Constructing the Diasporic Body," 15.

25. Kristeva, *Strangers to Ourselves,* 4.

26. Turner, *The Ritual Process*, 95.

27. Marcelo Alario Ennes, "Bourdieu and the 'Migrant Body': Embodiment in the Migratory Context," *Revista Brasileira de Sociologia* 8, no. 19 (2020): 37.

28. Kristeva, *Strangers to Ourselves,* 1.

29. Decca Aitkenhead, "Trading Places," *The Guardian,* September 19, 2008.

30. Kristeva, *Strangers to Ourselves,* 29.

31. Annes, "Bordieu and the 'Migrant Body," 28.

32. Turner, *The Forest of Symbols,* 99.

33. Mukherij, ed., *Thinking on Thresholds*, xxi.

34. Beer, "Windows," 14.

35. Catherine Bell, "The Ritual Body and the Dynamics of Ritual Power," *Journal of Ritual Studies* 4, no. 2 (1990): 299.

36. Turner, *The Forest of Symbols*, 96.

37. Bell, "The Ritual Body," 301.

38. Kristeva, *Strangers to Ourselves*, 8.

39. Sylvie Gambaudo, "Europeans: Foreigners in Their Own Land," in *The Idea of Europe in Literature,* ed. Susanne Fendler and Ruth Wittlinger (London: Palgrave Macmillan, 1999), 226.

40. Jozef Jaskulsky, "Friday Reeducated: Orientalizing the East-Central European Other in Rose Tremain's *The Road Home,*" in *Looking at Ourselves: Multiculturalism, Conflict & Belonging,* ed. Katherine Wilson (Oxford: Inter-Disciplinary Press, 2010), 36.

41. Agnes Harastzos, "The Image of the East-Central European in Rose Tremain's *The Road Home,*" *Acta Universitatis Sapientiae, Philologica* 7, no. 1 (2015): 91.

42. Jaskulski, "Friday Reeducated," 34.

43. Kristeva, *Strangers to Ourselves*, 6.

44. Kristeva, *Strangers to Ourselves*, 30.

45. Alario Ennes, "Bourdieu and the 'Migrant Body,'" 37.

46. Corina Crisu, "British Geographies in the Eastern European Mind: Rose Tremain's *The Road Home,*" in *Facing the East in the West: Images of Eastern Europe in British Literature, Film and Culture*, ed. Barbara Korte, Eva Ulrike Pirker and Sissy Helff (Amsterdam and New York: Rodopi, 2010), 370.

47. Julia Kristeva, *Powers of Horror: An Essay in Abjection*, trans. Leon S. Roudiez (New York: Columbia University Press, 1982), 2.

48. Kristeva, *Powers of Horror*, 141.

49. Kristeva, *Strangers to Ourselves,* 31.

50. Turner, *The Forest of Symbols,* 202.

51. Eveline Kilian, "Frames of Recognition under Global Capitalism: Eastern European Migrants in British Fiction," in *Narrating Poverty and Precarity in Britain*, ed. Barbara Korte and Frédérick Regard (Berlin: De Gruyter, 2014), 139.

52. Pierre Macherey, *A Theory of Literary Production* (London: Routledge & Kegan Paul, 1978), 155.

53. Kristeva, *Strangers to Ourselves*, 14.

54. Michael O'Loughlin, "Strangers to Ourselves: On the Displacement, Loss and 'Homelessness of Migrant Experiences," *International Critical Childhood Policy Studies* 3, no. 1 (2010): 146.

BIBLIOGRAPHY

Aciman, André, ed. *Letters of Transit: Reflections on Exile, Identity, Language, and Loss*. New York: New Press, 1999.

Aitkenhead, Decca. "Trading Places." *The Guardian*, September 19, 2008.

Alario Ennes, Marcelo. "Bourdieu and the 'Migrant-Body': Embodiment in the Migratory Context." *Revista Brasileira de Sociologia* 8, no. 19 (2020): 26–58.

Beer, Gillian. "Windows: Looking in, Looking Out, Breaking Through." In *Thinking on Thresholds: The Poetics of Transitive Spaces*, edited by Subha Mukherij, 3–16. London: Anthem Press, 2013.

Bell, Catherine. "The Ritual Body and the Dynamics of Ritual Power." *Journal of Ritual Studies* 4, no. 2 (1990): 299–213.

Bell, Catherine. *Ritual: Perspectives and Dimensions*. Oxford: Oxford University Press, 1997.

Bhabha, Homi. *The Location of Culture*. London & New York: Routledge, 1997.

Crisu, Corina. "British Geographies in the Eastern European Mind: Rose Tremain's *The Road Home*." In *Facing the East in the West: Images of Eastern Europe in British Literature, Film and Culture,* edited by Barbara Korte, Eva Ulrike Pirker, and Sissy Helff, 365–379. Amsterdam and New York: Rodopi, 2010.

Fendler, Susanne and Ruth Wittlinger, eds. *The Idea of Europe in Literature*. London: Palgrave Macmillan, 1999.

Foucault, Michel. "The Order of Discourse." In *Untying the Text: A Post-Structuralist Reader*, edited by Robert Young, 51–78. London: Routledge & Keagan Paul, 1981.

Gambaudo, Sylvie. "Europeans: Foreigners in Their Own Land." In *The Idea of Europe in Literature,* edited by Susanne Fendler and Ruth Wittlinger, 225–239. London: Palgrave Macmillan, 1999.

Harastzos, Agnes. "The Image of the East-Central European in Rose Tremain's *The Road Home*." *Acta Universitatis Sapientiae, Philologica* 7, no. 1 (2015): 83–94.

Jaskulski, Jozef. "Friday Reeducated: Orientalizing the East-Central European Other in Rose Tremain's The Road Home." In *Looking at Ourselves: Multiculturalism, Conflict & Belonging*, edited by Katherine Wilson, 33–42. Oxford: Inter-Disciplinary Press, 2010.

Kilian, Eveline. "Frames of Recognition under Global Capitalism: Eastern European Migrants in British Fiction." In *Narrating Poverty and Precarity in Britain*, edited by Barbara Korte and Frédérick Regard, 131–150. Berlin: De Gruyter, 2014.

Korte, Barbara, Eva Ulrike Pirker, and Sissy Helff, eds. *Facing the East in the West: Images of Eastern Europe in British Literature, Film and Culture*. Amsterdam and New York: Rodopi, 2010.

Korte, Barbara and Frédérick Regard, eds. *Narrating Poverty and Precarity in Britain*. Berlin: De Gruyter, 2014.

Kristeva, Julia. *Powers of Horror: An Essay in Abjection*. Translated by Leon S. Roudiez. New York: Columbia University Press, 1982.

Kristeva, Julia. *Strangers to Ourselves*. Translated by Leon S. Roudiez. New York: University of Columbia Press, 1991.

Luksaite, Eva. "Constructing the Diasporic Body: Ritual Practices among South Asians in Britain." *Asia Europe Journal* 8 (2010): 11–24.

Macherey, Pierre. *A Theory of Literary Production.* London: Routledge & Keagan Paul, 1978.

Montes Garcés, Elizabeth, ed. *Relocating Identities in Latin American Cultures.* Alberta: University of Calgary Press, 2007.

Mukherij, Subha, ed. *Thinking on Thresholds: The Poetics of Transitive Spaces.* London: Anthem Press, 2013.

O'Loughlin, Michael. "Strangers to Ourselves: On the Displacement, Loss and "Homelessness" of Migrant Experiences." *International Critical Childhood Policy Studies* 3 no. 1 (2010): 137–159.

Seidel, Michael. *Exile and the Narrative Imagination.* New Haven, CT and London: Yale University Press, 1986.

Torres, Luis. "Exile and Identity." In *Relocating Identities in Latin American Cultures*, edited by Elizabeth Montes Garcés, 55–84. Calgary: University of Calgary Press, 2007.

Tremain, Rose. *The Road Home.* London: Vintage, 2008.

Turner, Victor. *The Ritual Process: Structure and Anti-Structure.* London: Routledge & Kegan Paul, 1969.

Turner, Victor. *The Forest of Symbols: Aspects of Ndembu Ritual.* Ithaca, NY and London: Cornell University Press, 1967.

van Gennep, Arnold. *The Rites of Passage.* Translated by M. B. Vizedom and G. L. Caffee. London: Routledge & Kegan Paul, 1960.

Wilson, Katherine, ed. *Looking at Ourselves: Multiculturalism, Conflict & Belonging.* Oxford: Inter-Disciplinary Press, 2010.

Section II

LIMINALITY WITHIN

GROUP INTERACTION WITHIN THE LIMINAL SPACE

Chapter 4

Liminal Space and Liminal Place

The Medieval Church Porch

Jamie Ingram

The archetype medieval English parish church is one of nave and chancel, with a simple tower and a south-facing porch situated in a picturesque churchyard. This bucolic modern idyll sits at odds with the historic significance of the parish church to the medieval community. The mother church of the parish was a place of power, divine inspiration, and societal control. The portal to the place of power was its village-facing door, often from the twelfth- and thirteenth centuries sheltered by a porch. These portals became places of contested status, places where the significant but not ultimately powerful sought to be buried, where merchants left their marks and where social ritual took place just within the sight of God. Marriage, christening, churching, and all manner of other ritual encounters with the divine process of recognition and markers of life course events took place in these spaces, safe in the sight of God but outside of God's direct presence on earth.

In this chapter I will explore the unique character of the medieval church porch and its place as a liminal boundary between the secular world and the divine interior illuminated by the deposited medieval graffiti inscriptions found on the walls, doors, and related structures of the church porch and entranceway. This notion of the liminal porch has been explored and discarded in the past[1] described as to chaotic, noisy, and messy. I contest however that it is exactly within this chaos that we will find the liminal nature of the church entrance and particularly the porch. Not only in the ability to transfer supplicants from the secular exterior to the divine interior but also in the capacity of the porch to become a specific space provide a place where transformative liminal ritual behavior can be conducted and self-guided.[2] This liminal function is not isolated to the porch of the parish church but also functions on the porches of the great cathedrals and in the gate houses and entranceways to closed and semi-closed religious establishments.

PORCHES AS PLACES

The typical Anglo-Norman style parish church is a nave and chancel with a small, sometimes later tower. These simple structures can be embellished with aisled naves to widen them, transepts to enlarge them and provides a crossing and a mixture of side chapels and altars. Each of these embellishments and enlargements can be seen in isolation or collected onto a single church to generate the desired form and scale of parish church that the community or local lord desires. Within this structure we normally see a number of doors, usually a pair, north and south, in the nave and on larger churches a grand west ceremonial entrance. The porched entrance, normally positioned on the side of the church that faces toward the majority of the parish community, generally in England this is the south-facing side but is not always the case. In some examples the porch will be found on the north side and on occasions a parish church at the center of its community will be found to have a porch on both the north and south entrances.

The church porch is often a simple structure, two solid walls and a roof attached to the side of the church and the third wall created by the wall of the church and the door, and a large opening in the fourth to the secular world beyond, sometimes arched and sometimes held by columns and a lintel. Other porches have become more elaborate with additional floors to house parish offices or other functional space above the entrance or the addition of great concentric arches and stepped entrances on particularly large structures.[3] In some cases, particularly at cathedrals, the porch can become integrated into the structure of the cloister with the area between the door and the cloister being delineated by the addition of arches and columns to mark it as a different space. In each case this enclosed space enhances and shelters the door to the church in a physical sense but also provides a level of spiritual shelter projecting from the religiosity of the church.

The porch is that space that provides shelter at the entrance, the enlarged doorway that provides unofficial space where religious and semi-religious activity could take place without the mediation of the priest. In the middle ages this was a place that was both secular and divine at the same time. Through the life of the parish, the porch became an important place in its own right not just an adjunct to the church but a space of significance to the community. It is a place where people met to conduct business and transact exchanges either between neighbors or between itinerant merchant and resident. It was also the meeting place for the significant life course events of the parish. For example, until the sacralization and formalization of marriage c. 1200,[4] the rituals around marriage took place in any large structure that could host the couple and the community as witness. Following this process of the church taking control, however, the initial phases of the marriage moved into the porch and then once the secular agreements had been completed witnessed couple were taken into the church for the union to be formally blessed in the sight of God, already joined as a couple not as two individuals. With this, many other life course rituals also moved into the porch; the practice of Churching of women, the christening of infants at the font just inside the door, then ultimately the blessing of the corpse prior to burial.[5] Each are activities that could introduce spiritual pollutants into the sanctified interior of the church but by conducting them in the porch allow the protection of the consecrated to remain.

There is evidence that not only did these life course rituals take place in the church porch but also a number of other related activities. Postles highlights a number of incidents where activity that took place within the church porch was considered "outside" of the church but also identifies activities that are clearly religious in nature such as the permitting of penitent worshipers to observe services from the porch so as not to completely isolate them from the community or the word of God.[6] There are also records of disagreements and fights breaking out in the porches and spilling over into the churchyard,[7] these clearly nonreligious acts taking place in an area that holds a direct connection to the consecrated church demonstrate that the space of the church porch is both spiritually malleable and spatially contested.

It is worth noting however that doctrinally the church porch holds no formal transformative or ritual role, it being within the consecrated bounds of the churchyard[8] and the protective audible area of the sound of the church bells.[9] The nature of usage of this space for ritualized practices of a religious, prereligious, and pseudoreligious nature demonstrates that the true function of the church porch lies not within the formal doctrinal structures of the medieval catholic church but within the operability of the space; driven by the community at large and in many ways the formal and informal practices of the church. The very fact that the church sees fit to perform specific life course rituals within these spaces suggests a level of empowerment that goes beyond that of a simple door and implies a religious function that is not formally encoded.

RITUAL SIGNS OR IDLE HANDS

It is within these unassuming spaces that we find the physical evidence of activity and human presence. The ledger stones of the burials within them, the occasional monuments placed within or on the walls and, of specific interest to this paper, the graffiti. The informal signs of human activity are left by the myriad hands of the parish congregation and occasional visitor to the church.

There is a long history of graffiti creation and study, this wall writing, usually viewed in the modern mind as wholly negative sits in a deeply embedded set of human behaviors that can be seen stretching back to the cave art of prehistory, through the ancient civilizations of the Egyptians, Greeks, and Romans and then on through the development of medieval and early modern Europe and into the modern day. It is within this practice of graffiti making that we find the marks that can be identified within the church porch and that we are now examining, these marks are depositions from the users of the space. While it is tempting to assume that they follow the premise brought forward by the broken windows paper[10] that implies that damaging acts permit damaging acts; in this case graffiti permits graffiti. It would be more accurate to consider the process in terms of people create graffiti, specifically where people spend prolonged periods of time or significant numbers of people spend time there is likely to be an increase in the deposition of graffiti. This can be seen in the studies conducted at Chichester Cathedral and Rochester Cathedral where evidence shows the graffiti is visible in clustered deposits that can be seen in specific religious contexts.[11] The graffiti appears to be deposited in locations that bear a specific purpose based on liturgical, devotional, or local practice-based locations within the space. Large volumes being distributed around locations associated with shrines, reliquaries, chapels, side altars, and with specific relevance to the paper, porches.

When we start to look at the distribution of the graffiti within the church, it becomes apparent that a significant proportion can be found within the church porch, even when a porch has undergone remodeling in the nineteenth century much of the graffiti remains visible (table 4.1) with a significant proportion of the total graffiti present within each church being found within the porch, and as was evidence within Chichester and Rochester Cathedrals, it is common to identify specific clustering of graffiti within the parish churches, this clustering falls broadly into a common pattern (figure 4.1).

GRAFFITI AND PRAYER—MAKING
THE LIMINAL RITUAL

I have mentioned earlier in this work that prayer is a ritual practice and that the graffiti is a component of that ritual. Prayer is performative liminal ritual, intended to generate change either personally or within the world, and is processed through a ritual guide who utilizes the prayer as ritual to establish and maintain social status and movement. The graffiti as a ritual doing fulfills the crucial core of the performative nature of the ritual. The process of creation

Table 4.1 Distribution of graffiti marks within porches at nine churches within Hampshire, UK. Source Hampshire Graffiti Survey and Jamie Ingram

Church	Total graffiti marks	Graffiti marks in Porch	% in porch	Notes
St. James, Bramley	42	28	66.67	
St. Michaels and All Angels, Cheriton	155	65	41.94	
St. Andrew, Chilcomb	51	29	56.86	
All Saints, Dummer	195	162	83.08	Flint church with limestone porch and chancel arch
St. Johns, Farley Chamberlayne	19	11	57.89	
St. Swithun, Headbourne Worthy	106	25	23.58	Porch rebuilt in nineteenth century
St. Peters and St Pauls, Kings Somborne	67	21	31.34	
St. Lawrence, Stratford Sub Castle	465	159	34.19	
St. Mary's, Selborne	287	111	38.68	

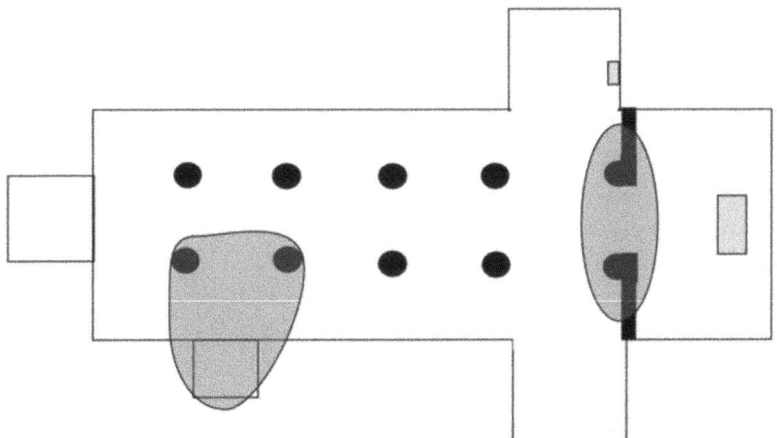

Figure 4.1 Common Distribution Pattern for Religious Graffiti within Parish Churches. A High Distribution Is Present at the Entrance and the Chancel Arch. Implying Higher Levels of Activity in These Areas. *Source*: Jamie Ingram.

being as important, or potentially more important, that the symbolism of the mark itself. There is some suggestion that the resultant dust generated, being a holy matter, may have been collected and used in tinctures and potions.[12]

I now move on to the use of that prayer as learned ritual behavior and the ability of the individual lay worshiper to utilize these rituals in personal improvized practice. This personal prayer-making also remains operable as a ritual, containing all the components that are required for ritual practice; the only significant change is that the ritual guide is also the ritual supplicant. This ritual engagement therefore becomes personal. It is within this prayer-making that the physical performance takes on a material element. Rather than the grand gestures of the ritual guide, the individual worshiper must internalize the practice. This can be contained within genuflexion or the manipulation of prayer beads or some form of iconic object, but in many cases during the middle ages, it is apparent that the making of a mark becomes the preferred method of ensuring that this private performative element gains wider context and form.

The graffiti mark that is created is formed in the manner of symbols that can be seen in the everyday life of the lay worshiper. These are symbols that are utilized in secular and religious environments and can be found in the decoration of homes and churches, used in the marginalia of books, for those who have access to such things, and in the decoration of works of art that may be seen in the great buildings and religious establishments of the medieval world.[13] These designs become performative elements that are in operation for the prayer as a ritual doing.

It is here that we can now identify the graffiti marks as a ritual doing, a material component of the ritual activity that can be both ritualized and non-ritualized in its nature. The graffiti marks are patterns that can be found in myriad locations, from domestic dwellings to agricultural buildings and inscribed onto personal objects, included in the marginalia of texts and in artistic imagery. These are not uncommon designs in society, but their usage makes them empowered components as a part of the ritual in much the same way as Fowles identifies the bowls, which function as water bowls in everyday life and gain significance when used in ritual practice.[14] In function, though, they are much more similar to the peck-marked and painted representations of the masks of the Katsina doings of the Taos and Tiwas Pueblo.[15] The graffiti is about engaging with the spirit world, in this case the divine, while also keeping it at a spiritually safe distance. By creating the graffiti mark during the process of prayer-making, the mark becomes symbolic of the ritual activity involved in that prayer.

In identifying the graffiti marks as ritual doings, they become entangled in the ritual activity of the prayer. The mark becomes the ritual engagement and contains the embodiment of that ritual it empowers, protects, and engages all in the same moment. The power to mark out the ritual becomes an integral component of the ritual performance itself: the graffiti mark becomes entangled with the prayer, the prayer-maker and the entity toward which it is directed, normally the saint, forming a bond through the ritual doings that stabilizes the connection and formalizes the agreement between the prayer-maker and the divinely present being of the saint.

THE RITUAL CONSTRUCTION AND MAINTENANCE OF THE LIMINAL ENTRANCE

By accepting that the graffiti inscriptions within the religious entrance are components of prayer, we can place them into the process of the liminal ritual; they become empowered doings of the ritual activity, each mark connected with a different liminal activity. Each mark would be understood to stand for something specific and significant within the community understanding its own internal language of ritual activity and social development. With this knowledge of marks as ritual doings and their empowered nature of them as such, we must look at them as potential nonhuman agents.[16] The ability of the agent to act on its own and enact some activity or performance is essential to the ability of the graffiti to retain power and to be recognized as the ritual or prayer component that it is. The graffiti marks retain both the essence of the ritual as a part of which it was created and also a component of the person who created it. Acting both as a primary and secondary agent and would have been understood by the medieval populace through the concepts of materiality within the compass of the ability of material to retain the power of the divine, the clergy, and even of the layperson.[17] This operates in much the same way as the power of holy water to remain holy following a blessing or an offering at a shrine to retain the essence of the supplicant in the presence of the saint. It is also this ability of the pilgrim token to retain the essence of the transferred power from the shrine and the blessing in the presence of the saint to enact the power of the saint and the concluded prayer and deeds, such as the protection of a pregnant woman or the blessing of a field, upon returning home. This element of material empowerment was held within the doctrine of the medieval church[18] and formed the very core of the ability of relics and shrines to possess the power to enact miracles and transmit the essence of the saint; it was also believed to be at the heart of the ability of witches and malevolent spirits to act on other individuals.[19] It also enabled the church to teach the value of offerings at shrines, ranging from wax effigies of injured body parts to valuable objects and possessions, all intended to ease the process with the saint and enable them to act upon the supplicants' petition.

Taking this cultural loading of the marks and the resultant nature of them as agents allows us to investigate the nature of the space further and look more deeply into the performance of the space in the medieval world. It places the graffiti into a realm of empowerment that allows them to act as

though the liminal ritual is still in operation. Each mark retains a small proportion of the liminal process that they symbolize and retransmits that back
into the space. The weddings, blessings, churchings, and other rituals each
empowered the space to a small degree and each mark connected through
those rituals to the presence of God, fully present and always aware within
the main body of the church and distant without. This repeated ritual activity
creates a space within the religious entrance that is neither within or without;
a space that can be bound by the rule of God directly but nonetheless lies on
the periphery. This process creates a space where certain activities can be
enacted and where operable change in the sight of God can be undertaken in
an informal setting and without the direct oversight of God. This provides a
space where business agreements can be undertaken, trade can take place and
deals struck; "the money lenders" cast out of the temple (Matthew 21:12) can
operate within sight of it but remain without taking advantage of the liminal
nature, the half and half of the secular and the divine that is created by the
permanent transformative space of the religious entrance. This also provides
a space where civil disagreements can be settled, pacts sworn, and oaths taken
within the sight of God but without the priest being involved and without the
full weight of the church becoming present in the agreement. This can be
seen in the process of wills being read and estates being divided in religious
entrances, the settling of debts and the agreements between parishioners
being made within these spaces.[20] This is not just a convenient spot to conduct
business but a place that allows that business to be witnessed by the ultimate
witness and the agreement enforced by that divine power without breaking
the law of the church and taking business inside the church proper.

The transformative nature of the religious entrance moves beyond the
ability of the space to be used for activities that sit on the periphery of those
permitted within the consecrated church. The empowered semi-divine nature
of the religious entrance enables the separation of the interior and the exterior
to be enforced spiritually as well as physically. When we take the sensorial
nature of the space into account, as well as the ritual doings of the graffiti, we
can see that the space becomes further empowered as a place of transformation, a liminal space between the secular and the divine. Without is the soft
ground, the muddy path, the dirt and pollution of the secular world, with
disease, malodor, and filth present in all aspects of life. Spiritually without is
the presence of demons, devils, and malevolent spirits each vying to corrupt
and pollute the soul. Within the church is a space of brightly lit and decorated
walls, strong colors mixed with gold and silver, and a hard, clean stone floor.
The smell is of incense and clean oils and of wax candles rather than tallow.
On days of worship and activity, the church is filled with liturgy and litany,
the sounds of prayer and thanks, while without is the sound of hard work,
toil, and animals. The religious entrance, the porch, is where this sensorial

evidence mixes and mingles, and as an individual passed through it, they leave behind the secular world without and enter the divine world within. Two ontologically distinct worlds separated and conjoined by the empowered entrance through a gateway, porch, or door from soft ground to hard, from malodor to redolence, and from physical toil to spiritual sanctuary. All this change was/is aided and enabled through the acts of ritual; the prayers are made physical within the graffiti forms that are created alongside the life course rituals that are enacted in this space on the periphery of the church.

This would suggest that the religious entrance is entirely within the purview of the divine, when it is clearly not. The religious entrance also functions without. When agreements fail, fights break out then spill over into the churchyard, and the place of agreement can become the place of dispute with the secular holding sway over the divine. Acts that would be viewed as inappropriate within the church itself are viewed as safe to engage in within the religious entrance, such as the acts that require a notice demanding "no fornication" to be placed near to the porch at St. Mary's Breamore (P. Copeland 2018 personal communication). The entrance is thus notionally still a part of the church but functions within this liminal role as something without on this occasion. This dualistic function, a multifaceted and confused space, is where Mary Douglas's noisy messy space lies.[21] It is here that the liminal is permitted to function. The breakdown of the normal social rules both of the secular and of the holy permit the space to be used for a multiplicity of functions. The religious entrance becomes a place where rites and deals are enacted and a place where the role of the religious becomes confused. It is a space where the religious can be enacted but so can the prereligious and the pseudoreligious. The range of activities becomes numerous and anything that the community wishes to present as holy, blessed, or divinely inspired can be undertaken within the religious entrance. These range from the clearly religious rituals of the church, mandated and controlled life course practices, to personal prayers and the use of holy water upon entrance and to the sometimes dubious claims of merchants to be operating within the sight of god.

As has been discussed, the religious entrance is empowered by the ritualized nature of the activity that is undertaken within it. The special nature of the space as a bridge between the two ontologies, empowered by the liminal agents of the graffiti, as well as the nature of the two worlds it joins and the sensorial interplay between them, allows it to operate in this unique fashion. The permanence of the liminal opens the space to a multitude of interactions and the performance of activities that would not normally be permitted within a consecrated space. The religious entrance becomes a place where acts are undertaken, all within the guise of the empowered religiosity of the space as an extension of both the divine and the secular realms. It is a space where merchants and money lenders can operate, where the faithful can make personal prayer and where the community can gather for ceremony and celebration.

The creation of liminal agents requires the performance of liminal rituals, but once they are created the agent can provide the empowerment for further liminal activity. Marks transmit and transfer the encapsulated power of the change back into the space, allowing it to remain operable for a significant period of time beyond the ritual. This creates a space that is understood to be linked and empowered but not fully understood as to the nature of that empowerment. Such a place is signified as open to the sight and benefice of God but not under direct oversight and governance. This is not a place that people are assessing as active or inactive based on the level of religious and ritual activity present but a place that is understood to be actively connected to the divine in a less formal manner that the rest of the church. It is a space that can be and is used freely and can be the scene to religious and sacrilegious acts.

With this in mind, it becomes evident that the scratched markings within the church porches mean far more than the simple passage of people and in fact stand for the hundreds of prayers and ritual activities that have taken place in each one such as those visible at Selborne in Hampshire (figures 4.2 and 4.3). These prayers also spill over into the threshold space of the church itself, a bubble of ritualized space that envelopes the porch and its immediate surroundings, empowered in a way that stands aside from the rest of the church and the churchyard often encompassing the approximate original location of the font.

The church porch with its religious and ritual context can be seen to stand apart from the body of other significant entrances: town and city gates, castle gates and the doors to great houses and buildings of state, the agricultural barn, and even lesser domestic structures. All these structures show graffiti activity, but the levels of distribution are usually lower. Where areas of concentrated activity are identified, the classes of mark found within display an identifiably different form from those of the religious entrance. A number of the marks can be seen to cross-populate all of these areas but there they show a distinct change in volume and frequency. Within a domestic setting it is frequent that daisy wheel, VV or M marks, and crosses appear over doors, fire places, window surrounds, and on roof timber and floor joists.[22] The density of these marks though is restricted to a low level, usually one or two marks on each opening compared to the many tens or sometimes hundreds that are found in the vicinity of a church porch, in large fortified entrances, it is common to find depictions of people, sometimes being executed, and a large number of merchant marks and heraldic symbols, these are significantly less frequent in church porches, though not completely absent.

Figure 4.2 Porch of St. Mary's Selborne. *Source*: Jamie Ingram.

This asks the question of what is happening with these marks: they are recognized as apotropaic when used in small numbers within domestic dwellings[23] but, within the entrances to churches, already ritually protected spaces, the application of these would appear excessive. With the application of these marks to other parts of a church being linked to ritual prayer making it becomes probable that these marks, when located within the church porch, will follow similar patterns of becoming the physical components of ritual behavior: the "doings" of ritual activities.[24] This is not to say however that all of these marks are ritualized in their formation, there being a separate class of mark relating specifically to the activities of merchants, either as individuals or companies which show only secular value in themselves.

BECOMING A LIMINAL SPACE AND A LIMINAL PLACE

With the plethora of ritualized activities being undertaken within the porch, many of them life course events, it is clear that under normal ritual operability, the space becomes a receptacle for liminal activity, this ritual empowerment

Jamie Ingram

Figure 4.3   Trace of Graffiti in Porch, St. Mary's Selborne. *Source*: Jamie Ingram.

of practice through life course practices as well as ritual of arrival and departure follow the normal markers of a liminal ritual as discussed by van Gennep and Turner:[25] the ritual guide normally being the priest, the porch providing the marker for the location and the outer and inner portals of the porch providing the entry and exit points for the initiates. However, there is something else happening within these porches and this is a residual liminal empowerment.

Under a classical interpretation of the liminal the ritual is the key. The ritual guide enacting the process of change, the break from the normal conventions of society and the movement into the ritual, the process of change and then ultimately the movement back from the ritual space into society, changed in some way by that ritual. This process conforms to the structures laid out by van Gennep and Turner[26] and can be seen in the various rituals undertaken within the porch. Taking the marriage ceremony as an example, the two individuals, the initiates, are brought together in front of the priest, the ritual guide, the priest opens the ritual with a series of blessings and then progresses into the main ritual: the ritual process of transference of the bride from the father to the husband, the exchanging of vows, and the closing of the ritual with the introduction of the new couple. They exit the ritual as a new single social entity within the community where as they entered it as two individuals. The transformation within society is complete, they are released from the liminal and back into the normality of life. This process can be seen to take place within each of the rituals that are undertaken within the church porch, the christening of a new child and the cleansing to make them free of sin, the blessing of women post partem to cleanse them of the stain of original sin following the birth of a child, the burial of a deceased member of the community. Each is an act that requires the performance of a specific liminal ritual, and each of these takes place at least in part within the entrance to the church, normally the porch.

The porch though retains the ability to transform and thus to act as a cleansing portal for entry and exit to the church. It also retains as a result a residual connection to the divine: being of both the secular and the divine the porch offers a place that holds a unique power. It becomes a place where deals, agreements and arguments can be settled both within the gaze of God but also outside of Gods direct imposition. This leaves us with the question of how this retained liminal empowerment can be present as the classic model requires the liminal to fade rapidly once the ritual is no longer in operation.

By accepting that the graffiti inscriptions within the church porch are components of prayer, we can place them into the process of the liminal ritual, they become empowered doings of the ritual activity. Each mark is connected with a different liminal activity, and each is understood to stand for something specific and significant, a community understanding its own internal language of ritual activity and social development. With this understanding of them as ritual doings and the empowered nature of them as such we must look at them as potential nonhuman agents.[27] The ability of the agent to act on its own and enact some activity or performance is essential to the ability of the graffiti to retain power and to be recognized as the ritual or prayer component that it is. The graffiti mark retains both the essence of the ritual that it was created as a part of and also a component of the person who created it. Both act as a primary and secondary agent, and understood by the medieval populace through the concepts of materiality within the compass of the ability of material to retain the power of the divine, the clergy, and even of the lay person:[28] the power of holy water to remain holy following a blessing, of an offering at a shrine to retain the essence of the supplicant in the presence of the saint and the ability of the pilgrim token to retain the essence of the transferred power from the shrine and the blessing in the presence of the saint to enact the power of the saint and the concluded prayer and deeds, such as the protection of a pregnant woman or the blessing of a field, upon returning home. This element of material empowerment was held within the doctrine of the medieval church and formed the very core of the ability of relics and shrines to possess the power to enact miracles and transmit the essence of the saint, it was also believed to be at the heart of the ability of witches and malevolent spirits to be able to act on other individuals. It also enabled the church to teach the value of offerings at shrines, ranging from wax effigies of injured body parts to valuable objects and possessions, all intended to ease the process with the saint and enable them to act upon the supplicants' petition.

By taking this cultural loading of the marks and the resultant nature of them as agents it allows us to investigate the nature of the space further and look more deeply into the performance of the space in the medieval world. It places the graffiti into a realm of empowerment that allows them to act as though the liminal ritual is still in operation, each retaining a small proportion of the liminal process that they symbolize and retransmitting that back into the space, the wedding's, blessing's, churching's, and other rituals each empowering the space to a small degree and each connecting through those rituals to the presence of God, fully present and always aware within the main body of the church and distant without. It creates a space within the porch that is neither within nor without. A space that can be bound by the rule of God directly but on the periphery. This creates a space where certain activities can be enacted, a space where operable change in the sight of God can be undertaken in an informal setting and without the direct oversight of God. This provides a space where business agreements can be undertaken, trade can take place and deals struck, "the money lenders" cast out of the temple can operate within sight of it but remain without, taking advantage of the liminal nature, the half and half of the secular and the divine that is created by the permanent transformative space of the porch. This also provides a space where civil disagreements can be settled, pacts sworn and oaths taken within the sight of God but without the priest being involved and without the full weight of the church becoming present in the agreement. This can be seen in the process of wills being read and estates being divided in porches, the settling of debts and the agreements between parishioners being made within these spaces. This is not just a convenient spot to conduct business but a place that allows that business to be witnessed by the ultimate witness and the agreement enforced by that divine power without breaking the law of the church and taking business inside the church proper.

The transformative nature of the porch moves beyond the ability of the space to be used for activities that sit on the periphery of those permitted within the consecrated church. The empowered semi-divine nature of the porch enables the separation of the interior and the exterior to be enforced spiritually as well as physically. When we take the sensorial nature of the space into account as well as the ritual doings of the graffiti we can see that the space becomes further empowered as a place of transformation, a liminal space between the secular and the divine. Without is the soft ground, the muddy path, the dirt and pollution of the secular world with disease, malodor, and filth present in all aspects of life. Spiritually without is the presence of demons, devils and malevolent spirits each vying to corrupt and pollute the soul. Within the church is a space of brightly lit and decorated walls, strong colours mixed with golds and silvers and the hard, clean stone floor. The smell is of incense and clean oils, and of wax rather than tallow candles. On days of worship and activity the church is filled with liturgy and litany, the sounds of prayer and thanks. While without is the sound of hard work, toil and animals. The religious entrance, the porch, is where this sensorial evidence mixes and mingles as you pass through it you leave behind the secular world without and enter the divine world within. Two ontologically distinct worlds, separated and conjoined by the empowered entrance through gateway or porch from soft ground to hard, from malodor to redolence from physical toil to spiritual sanctuary. All this change aided and enabled through the acts of ritual, the prayers made physical within the graffiti forms that are created alongside the life course rituals that are enacted in this space on the periphery of the church.

This would suggest that the porch is entirely within the prevue of the divine when it is clearly not. The porch also functions without. When agreements fail fights break out then spill over into the churchyard, the place of agreement can become the place of dispute with the secular holding sway over the divine. A dispute that takes place, something that would be viewed as inappropriate within the church its self is viewed as safe to engage in within the porch, such as the acts that require a notice demanding "no fornication" to be place near to the porch at St. Mary's Breamore. Notionally still a part of the church but functioning within this liminal role as something without on this occasion. This dualistic function, a multifaceted and confused space is where the noisy messy space lies. It is here that the liminal is function and permitted to function. The breakdown of the normal social rules both of the secular and of the holy permit the space to be sued for a multiplicity of functions. The porch becomes a place where rites and deals are enacted and a place where the role of the religious becomes confused. It is a space where the religious can be enacted but so can the prereligious and the pseudoreligious. The range of activities becomes endless and anything that the community wishes to present as holy, blessed, or divinely inspired can be undertaken within the porch: from the clearly religious rituals of the church-mandated and -controlled life course practices to the personal prayers and the use of holy water upon entrance to the sometimes dubious claims of merchants to be operating within the sight of god.

It is evident that these empowered liminal boundaries to religious spaces move beyond the church porch, it can encompass much larger spaces at the periphery of religious sites and can encompass activities that are beyond the scope of the parish church. This is most notable at locations such as cathedrals and semi-closed religious houses. One example of such is the significant deposition at the inner gate to the charitable hospital at St. Cross, Winchester, a hospital founded for the care of the noble poor in the twelfth century and enlarged in the fifteenth century. At this location, the four columns that support the gatehouse show large depositions of graffiti, moving from the outer, north side, to the inner, south side, where the inner is considered the area closest to the church and accommodation for the lay brothers (figures 4.4, 4.5, 4.6, and 4.7). This is also the location where a dole of beer and bread was issued to travelers and those in need. The gates were open for much of the day to permit the lay brothers and their relatives to enter and leave providing a key portal into the consecrated space of the hospital. By comparison, the outer gate that encloses the courtyard of the fifteenth-century almshouse has only a handful of marks and the porches on the then chapel, and now parish church, of St. Cross show equally low levels of graffiti. The implication is that the inner gate is the ritualized entry, the place that is empowered by the liminal and operates as the portal between the sacred and the secular worlds, the liminal bridge between the two ontologies.

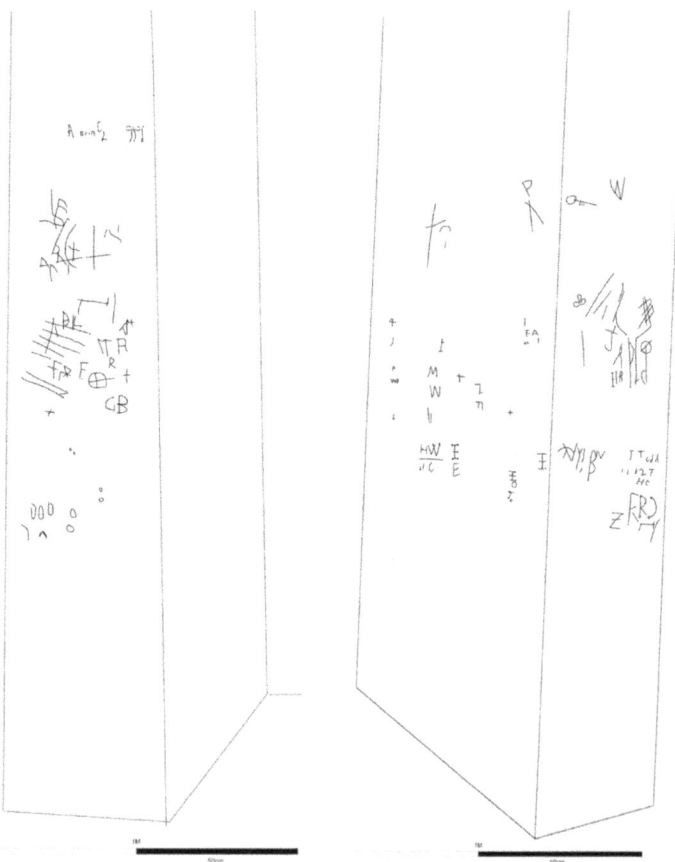

Figure 4.4 St. Cross Inner Gate, NW Column. *Source*: Jamie Ingram.

Figure 4.5 St. Cross Inner Gate, NE Column. *Source*: Jamie Ingram.

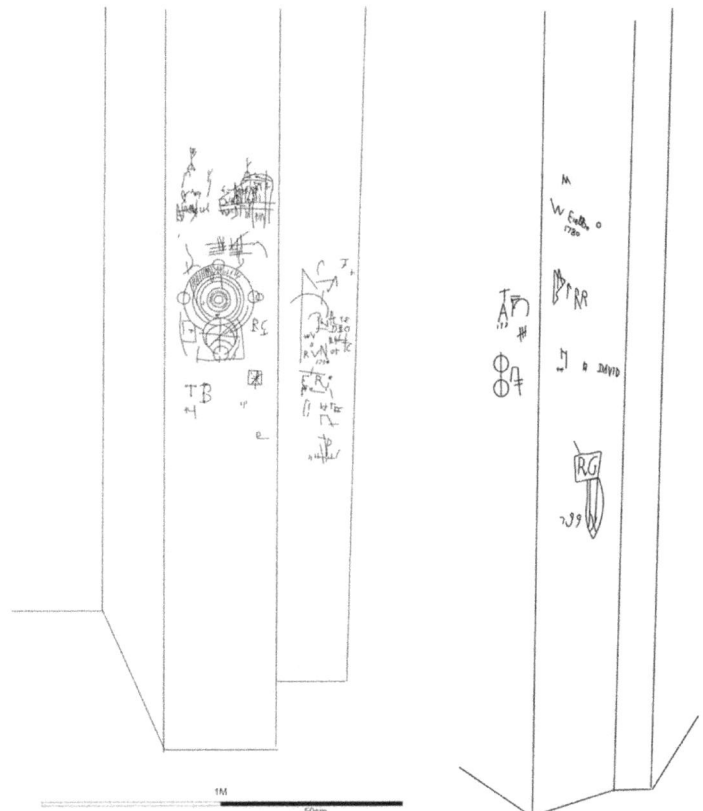

Figure 4.6 St. Cross Inner Gate, SW Column. *Source*: Jamie Ingram.

Figure 4.7 St. Cross Inner Gate, SE Column. *Source*: Jamie Ingram.

CONCLUSION

As has been discussed, the porch or other entranceway into the religious space is empowered by the ritualized nature of the activity that is undertaken within it. The special nature of the space as a bridge between the two ontologies, empowered by the liminal agents of the graffiti, as well as the nature of the two worlds it joins and the sensorial interplay between the two allows it to operate in this unique fashion. The permanence of the liminal opens the space to a multitude of interactions and the performance of activities that would not normally be permitted within a consecrated space. The porch becomes a place where not only religious but prereligious and pseudoreligious activities are undertaken all within the guise of the empowered religiosity of the space as an extension of both the divine reals and the secular. A space where merchants and money lenders can operate, where the faithful can make personal prayer and where the community can gather for ceremony and celebration.

The creation of these liminal agents requires the performance of liminal rituals, but once they are created, the agent can provide the empowerment for further liminal activity. Transmitting and transferring the encapsulated power of the change back into the space and allowing it to remain operable for a significant period of time beyond the ritual. This creates a space that is understood to be linked and empowered but not fully understood as to the nature of that empowerment. A place that is signified as open to the sight and benefice of God but not under direct oversight and governance. This is not a place that people look to and assess the level of activity but a place that is understood to be actively connected to the divine in a less formal manner that the rest of the church. It is a space that can be used freely and is a space that can be the scene of religious and sacrilegious acts.

NOTES

1. Dave Postles, "Micro-Spaces: Church Porches in Pre-Modern England," *Journal of Historical Geography* 33, no. 4 (2007): 749–69, https://doi.org/10.1016/j.jhg.2006.08.003.

2. Jamie Ingram, "Landscapes of Destination: An Archaeology or the Experiential and Ritual Behaviours of Medieval (12th to 16th Century) Worshipers at Religious Centres" (University of Southampton, 2022).

3. Mickey Abel, "Within, around, between: Micro Pilgrimage and the Archivolted Portal," *Hispanic Research Journal* 10, no. 5 (2009): 385–416, https://doi.org/10.1179/146827309X12541437923748.

4. Roberta Gilchrist, *Medieval Life: Archaeology and the Life Course* (Woodbridge: The Boydell Press, 2012).

5. Matthew Champion, *Medieval Graffiti: The Lost Voices of England's Churches* (London: Penguin, 2015), 65–69.

6. Postles, "Micro-Spaces," 757.

7. David Dymond, "God's Disputed Acre," *Journal of Ecclesiastical History* 50, no. 3 (1999): 464–97.

8. Dymond, "God's Disputed Acre."

9. John H. Arnold and Caroline Goodson, "Resounding Community: The History and Meaning of Medieval Church Bells," *Viator* 43, no. 1 (2012): 124–26.

10. James Q. Wilson and George L. Kelling, "Broken Windows," *Atlantic (02769077)* 249, no. 3 (1982): 29, https://doi.org/10.4135/9781412959193.n281.

11. Jamie Ingram, "An Initial Survey to Identify and Understand the Meaning of Medieval Graffiti within Chichester Cathedral : Distinguishing Pilgrim Marks from Other Graffiti and Unofficial Inscriptions," 2015, 1–88; Jacob H. Scott, "Pictorial and Symbolic Graffiti At Rochester Cathedral," *Archaeologia Cantiana* (2018): 47–74.

12. James Wright, "Mediaeval Mythbusting Blog #10: Arrow Stones," Triskele Heritage, 2021, https://triskeleheritage.triskelepublishing.com/mediaeval-mythbusting-blog-10-arrow-stones/?fbclid=IwAR2GPd58zSpZXkEDul2laZtdDVYyKHaZsWsYjWL0mGsWikrJDzovfGT0uEQ.

13. Malcolm Jones, *The Secret Middle Ages: Discovering the Real Medieval World* (Stroud: Sutton Publishing Limited, 2002).

14. (2013: 101–7).

15. (2013: 202–16).

16. Alfred Gell, *Art and Agency* (Oxford: Oxford University Press, 1998).

17. Caroline Walker Bynum, *Christian Materiality* (New York: Zone Books, 2011).

18. Bynum, *Christian Materiality*; Ittai Weinryb, "Votive Materials: Bodies and Beyond," in *Agents of Faith: Votive Objects in Time and Place*, ed. Weinryb Ittai (London: Yale University Press, 2018), 33–59.

19. Alexander Cummins, "Textual Evidence for the Material History of Amulets in Seventeenth-Century England," in *Physical Evidence for Ritual Acts, Sorcery and Witchcraft in Christian Britain*, ed. Ronald Hutton (London: Palgrave Macmillan, 2016), 164–87.

20. Edward Peacock, "Correspondence. The Church Porch," *Archaeological Review* 2, no. 4 (1888); Postles, "Micro-Spaces"; Helen Elizabeth Lunnon, "Making an Entrance : Studies of Medieval Church Porches in Norfolk," (2012): 42–70.

21. 1966.

22. Bob Meeson, "Ritual Marks and Graffiti: Curiosities or Meaningful Symbols?," *Vernacular Architecture* 36, no. 1 (February 1, 2005): 41–48, https://doi.org/10.1179/030554705778553646.

23. Brian Hoggard, *Magical House Protection: The Archaeology of Counter-Witchcraft* (New York: Berghahn Books, 2019), 74–105.

24. Severin M. Fowles, *An Archaeology of Doings: Secularism and the Study of Pueblo Religion* (Santa Fe: School for Advanced Research Press, 2013).

25. Arnold van Gennep, *The Rites of Passage*, 1960; Victor Turner, *The Ritual Process: Structure and Anti-Structure*, 2nd ed. (New Brunswick and London: Aldine Transactions, 2008).

26. Van Gennep, *The Rites of Passage*; Turner, *The Ritual Process: Structure and Anti-Structure*.

27. Gell, *Art and Agency*.

28. Bynum, *Christian Materiality*.

BIBLIOGRAPHY

Abel, Mickey. "Within, around, between: Micro Pilgrimage and the Archivolted Portal." *Hispanic Research Journal* 10, no. 5 (2009): 385–416. https://doi.org/10.1179/146827309X12541437923748.

Arnold, John H. and Caroline Goodson. "Resounding Community: The History and Meaning of Medieval Church Bells." *Viator* 43, no. 1 (2012): 99–130.

Bynum, Caroline Walker. *Christian Materiality*. New York: Zone Books, 2011.

Champion, Matthew. *Medieval Graffiti: The Lost Voices of England's Churches*. London: Penguin, 2015.

Cummins, Alexander. "Textual Evidence for the Material History of Amulets in Seventeenth-Century England." In *Physical Evidence for Ritual Acts, Sorcery and Witchcraft in Christian Britain*, edited by Ronald Hutton, 164–187. London: Palgrave Macmillan, 2016.

Douglas, Mary. *Purity and Danger*. London: Routledge, 1966.

Dymond, David. "God's Disputed Acre." *Journal of Eccleseastical Hoistory* 50, no. 3 (1999): 464–497.

Fowles, Severin M. *An Archaeology of Doings: Secularism and the Study of Pueblo Religion*. Santa Fe, NM: School for Advanced Research Press, 2013.

Gell, Alfred. *Art and Agency*. Oxford: Oxford University Press, 1998.

van Gennep, Arnold. *The Rites of Passage*. London: Routledge & Paul 1960.

Gilchrist, Roberta. *Medieval Life: Archaeology and the Life Course*. Woodbridge: The Boydell Press, 2012.

Hoggard, Brian. *Magical House Protection: The Archaeology of Counter-Witchcraft*. New York: Berghahn Books, 2019.

Ingram, Jamie. "An Initial Survey to Identify and Understand the Meaning of Medieval Graffiti within Chichester Cathedral: Distinguishing Pilgrim Marks from Other Graffiti and Unofficial Inscriptions." University of Southampton (2015): 1–88.

———. "Landscapes of Destination: An Arcaeology or the Experiential and Ritual Behaviours of Medieval (12th to 16th Century) Worshipers at Religious Centres." University of Southampton, 2022.

Jones, Malcolm. *The Secret Middle Ages: Discovering the Real Medieval World*. Stroud: Sutton Publishing Limited, 2002.

Lunnon, Helen Elizabeth. "Making an Entrance: Studies of Medieval Church Porches in Norfolk." University of East Anglia 2012.

Meeson, Bob. "Ritual Marks and Graffiti: Curiosities or Meaningful Symbols?" *Vernacular Architecture* 36, no. 1 (2005): 41–48. https://doi.org/10.1179/030554705778553646.

Peacock, Edward. "Correspondence. The Church Porch." *Arcaeological Review* 2, no. 4 (1888): 283–284.

Postles, Dave. "Micro-Spaces: Church Porches in Pre-Modern England." *Journal of Historical Geography* 33, no. 4 (2007): 749–769. https://doi.org/10.1016/j.jhg.2006.08.003.

Scott, J. H. "Pictorial and symbolic graffti at Rochester Cathedral." *Archaeologia Cantiana* 139 (2018): 47–74.

Turner, Victor. *The Ritual Process: Structure and Anti-Structure,* 2nd edition. New Brunswick, NJ and London: Aldine Transactions, 2008.

Weinryb, Ittai. "Votive Materials: Bodies and Beyond." In *Agents of Faith: Votive Objects in Time and Place*, edited by Ittai Weinryb, 33–59. London: Yale University Press, 2018.

Wilson, James Q. and George L. Kelling. "Broken Windows." *Atlantic (02769077)* 249, no. 3 (1982): 29. https://doi.org/10.4135/9781412959193.n281.

Wright, James. "Mediaeval Mythbusting Blog #10: Arrow Stones." *Triskele Heritage*, 2021. https://triskeleheritage.triskelepublishing.com/mediaeval-myth-busting-blog-10-arrow-stones/?fbclid=IwAR2GPd58zSpZXkEDul2laZtdDVYyK HaZsWsYjWL0mGsWikrJDzovfGT0uEQ.

Chapter 5

Hammering In-between

Liminality and Contingency in Artisanal Practice, Santa Clara del Cobre, Michoacán, Mexico

Michele Avis Feder-Nadoff

INTRODUCING AN ANTHROPOLOGY OF LIMINALITY: A POETICS OF THE HERE AND NOW

This chapter expands upon the concept of liminality through its application to artisanal practice and creative agency.[1] To do so, this chapter weaves the liminal, in-between, the middle and the marginal back into the warp and wefts of practical and ordinary experience. In so doing, it acknowledges the creativity of perception and knowing-in-doing. The analysis provided reflects upon long-term mentor-apprenticeship with the mestizo coppersmiths of Santa Clara del Cobre, Mexico.[2] This project is developed in conversation with the theories of rites of passage and the liminal zone as originally schematized by the Belgian folklorist, Arnold van Gennep in 1907,[3] and subsequently re-discovered in the 1960s, to become widely known, especially through the work of anthropologist, Victor Turner.[4]

Liminal Phases as Performative Schemas

Although originally developed to understand ritual, van Gennep's triadic model of pre-liminal (separation), liminal (margin), and post-liminal (aggregation) has over time become a processual and performative model for socio-cultural experiences of adaptation and transformation. This margin between separation and aggregation makes space for the "gap between signifier and meaning" where theories of culture can become performed and produced.[5]

Van Gennep saw rituals of/and magic as techniques that enacted religious theory. This view, constructed in a world still divided into sacred and profane, presciently proposed praxis as the processual-performative base for theory. In this way, van Gennep also suggested that bodily techniques served as inculcating dispositions of sociocultural fields, ideas developed further by Marcel Mauss and Pierre Bourdieu.[6]

Turner expanded upon van Gennep's interest in the liminal zone, focusing on its performative and reflexive capacities. Applying these concepts to a postmodern world, Turner departed from van Gennep. His performative schema, a quartet of phases, divided the liminal, middle phase, into two—crisis and regressive action. Turner also recognized social conflict in the final phase by acknowledging that reaggregation can fail, resulting in permanent schism. Turner also proposed a contemporary secular liminal state, the liminoid, that functioned as a collective experience of reflexivity inflected by change. Both van Gennep and Turner were concerned with how humans experience and construct meaning around the uncertainties, arbitrariness, inequalities, and indifferent cruelties of human existence (see table 5.1). They both admitted to social and natural precariousness and imbalance.

The world of the coppersmiths of Santa Clara encompasses both these terrains. For this reason, this chapter's exegesis on liminality draws from the perspectives and hierarchies established in lifeworlds divided by the sacred and profane and a secular political world in which margins also include marginalized identities, territories, ethnicities, and class. These factors frame how the liminal zone of the "rites of passage" is cultivated in creative practice and experience in Santa Clara.

Liminality in the Margins: Between Structure and Agency

Liminality has reemerged as a central concept since the 1980s post-postmodern era where nomadism, uncertainty, and change have become modus operandi.[7] As anthropologist and social scientist Bjørn Thomasson explains, liminality imparts a dialectical relationship between agency and structure. As we will see, this is part of a related shift of focus to the margins between tradition, creativity, and innovation. Thomasson states that

> the concept of liminality has the potential to push social and political theory in new directions . . . in line with our notions of "structure" and "practice" . . . Thinking with liminality serves to conceptualize moments where the relationship between structure and agency is not easily resolved or understood . . . In liminality, the very distinction between structure and agency cease to make sense . . . liminality . . . is about how human beings experience and react to change . . . it is likewise about how larger groups or entire societies undergo . . .

transition, how they live through the uncertainties of the in-between, and how they come out on the other side of it—if at all.[8]

In this essay the liminal is a passage whose dialectical meaning as structure and structuring is known through experience: by passing through its undergoing. As described by Johan Fornäs, passage is

either a movement through, across or past some kind of structure (like a walk through a corridor) or that very structure which such a movement goes through (the corridor itself). The structure may be static and fixed, or it may be itself in flux, though then moving differently than the passing subject—like a swimmer passing through a stream of water. Passages are movements in both time and space with some intensified contrast between the moving subject and the surrounding contextual structures.[9]

Table 5.1   Liminal Spaces of the In-Between found in Coppersmithing Apprenticeship in Santa Clara del Cobre, Michoacán

Theory	<--------------Liminal Space------------->	Praxis
Intention	<--------------Liminal Space------------->	Realization
Maestro	<--------------Liminal Space------------->	Apprentice
Ethnographer	<--------------Liminal Space------------->	Subject: Community, or Concepts
Artisan	<--------------Liminal Space------------->	*Obras, ollas,* works, vessls
Materia prima: copper	<--------------Liminal Space------------->	*Obras, ollas,* works, vessls
Obras, ollas, works, vessls	<--------------Liminal Space------------->	Perceivers, spec-actors (Boal, 1985), patients (Gell, 1998)
Everyday Actions	<--------------Liminal Space------------->	Ritual and artisanal performance
Ordinary Life	<--------------Liminal Space------------->	Spiritual Afterlife

This chart illustrates the liminal space charged and active between these aspects and elements encountered and experienced in coppersmithing in santa clara del cobre

LIMINAL RHYTHMS

Liminal experience cannot be detached from the rhythms, streams, ebbs, flows, cadences, ruptures, breeches, and failures of worldly ongoings. Because, doesn't the liminal emerge in this moving thicket? Isn't the liminal felt, experienced, generated and created in everyday life? Certainly, some experiences bound out at us from this grove, their dense intensity outnumbering all the rest, at least for the moment. These then recede, change form and resonance. Their pitch may come back to call us years later, perked by various contingent prompts. Like Marcel Proust's[10] (in)animate things or the transience of Walter Benjamin's aura and trace they call us back involuntarily.[11] These things and events come forward and then recede back into the horizon of our attention.

All experiences can become liminal,[12] extracted and heightened by personal and social reflection and examination, collective or individual subjectivities, rites and rituals, and skilled practice. Attention is prompted by many factors of instability and change, from economic, political, climatic or even pandemic turbulence. Or, by the passage from birth to death, also a great expanse of in-between. For my primary mentor, the master artisan, maestro Jesús Pérez Ornelas a devout Catholic, life was a threshold leading to the after-life (see table 5.2).

This chapter looks at how the Santa Clara coppersmiths cultivate liminality in their life and craft practice, in addition to their faith. How do threshold experiences join artisans with *materia prima,* with techniques of making, with the things they make, with their children, communities, ancestors, and histories? And in turn, how are these things joined with markets which are themselves liminal?[13]Finally, I also reflect upon how the master joins with apprentice, as an ethnographer with subject. But, the objective here is also more than this. As John Dewey[14] stresses, by locating creative practice in experience, we also rebind hierarchical binaries, such as mind and body, labor and thought, whose politics and their outcomes certainly impact Mexican artisans and their marginality. And to add even more, this study means to make room for faith, not only traditional religious observance but faith in doing, in carrying things out across the threshold between the "as-is" and the "as-if" in Turner's[15] terminology.

Maestro Jesús carried out his work as an *artesano*, an *artisan* not solely for tangible gain. "If I counted how many blows it took to make this piece I would go crazy, and besides, no client would be able to afford it!" he would say. His work could not merely be translated into Marx's capital production. Work is a *tributo!* declared Lorena Paredes Rosales, another artisan who studied with my teacher. This means work is a homage and a tribute to those who came before, to the work itself, and to what comes after. Certainly, the threshold finds a spiritual home in the lives of the coppersmiths of this primarily Roman Catholic community. But the point goes further, this chapter argues, that there is always a quotient of effort and feeling in experience that is felt before and after, that is prescient and pressing, and that has the hope to carry on afterward. This standing on the edges of both sides of the in-between, in the margins, in order to act, requires human faith even when we are lost and have doubts. This is also what creativity-in-action means.

Table 5.2 Contingencies and Liminalities

Falla—errors
Perturbance
Failures
Illness
Injury
Place of birth
Birth
Parents
Maturation
Aging
Death
Market factors
Political situations
Natural disasters
Class structures
Ethnicity
Race
Sexual orientation

This chart illustrates the contingent factors of a persons's life as their liminal qualities
Source: Chart designed by author, M. Feder-Nadoff.

Liminal Frames: Temporary Thresholds

Liminal experiences are potentially everywhere. Created by shifting frames—orderly or disorderly—the meaning of these experiences changes over the multiple perspectives provided by time.[16] This is because perspectives, like frames, are also liminal, transitory, and temporal. Their truth and doubts shift when life goes on. Rightly, the term liminal takes its etymological root from the Latin word "limen," or threshold. It is here where changing shadows and illumination take place from the outside and inside.[17] Obscurity moves from the clarity of the present daylight, back to the darkness; like when a door opens or closes or when night settles in. Following this metaphor of the door: the frame consists of two upright jambs that support the protective lintel beam above. This lintel, in turn, supports the opening space that creates the threshold, mirrored underfoot. The flanking doorposts are also signposts, invisibly erected, marked by ritual and rites of passage. They act as watchdogs and can signal storms. In fact, turbulence and rupture can erect them. Together these components provide an opening, a passage by which people can transition from one experience of undergoing to the next.

Thresholds: Limits, Pitch, and Swells

To be effective, transitional phases must surpass their threshold pitch. This means the magnitude or intensity of these phases must be exceeded for a certain reaction phenomena, result or condition to occur or be manifested. This is evident in the artisanal practice of the coppersmiths, whose bodily geographies must stretch their peripheries and also exceed threshold limits.[18] Likewise the *materia prima* must go beyond its molecular threshold as a solid to become annealed in order to be forged. Heated to even higher threshold temperatures, copper is made liquid and smelted to be reformed.[19] In this respect, the threshold then is less a gate or hinge[20] but rather it is more like a membrane—a porous boundary.

Benjamin, aware of van Gennep's theories of rites of passage—"the designation in folklore for the ceremonies that attach to death and birth, to marriage, puberty, and so forth"—complained that in "modern life, these transitions are becoming evermore unrecognizable and impossible to experience [and that we] have grown very poor in threshold experiences." Benjamin explains that the experience of falling asleep "is perhaps the only such experience that remains to us" suggesting that the state in-between, the margin between sleep and wakefulness is like a middle liminal zone full of imagination, altered consciousness and potential.[21] But, Benjamin warns that this threshold "must be carefully distinguished from the boundary" because it is a "zone." He explains that the "*Schwelle* is a zone" and that "Transformation, passage, wave action is in the word *schwellen*, swell, and etymology ought to not to overlook these senses." Benjamin ends this poetic paragraph description enigmatically with the two words: "Dreamhouse."[22]

Liminal Efficacy: Rites of Passage and the Forge

With these words, dreaming and home become linked not only through the creative imagination exercised in the dream-state or liminal zone when life is transformed. But the image of the house in the architectural referral of the door brings up other considerations of the threshold phases. This metaphor also harkens to the home, as the place where we learn to be inculcated in the logics of practice, the realities, meanings, and imaginaries that prepare us for the undertaking of these rites and ceremonies. The structure that generates these techniques of behaviors and where we are inculcated is the family home. In this place of intimacy, through training, the child becomes an adult. Benjamin's text is also a careful reminder of how the somatic sensorial qualities of the dream state echo in threshold experiences. Rites of passage and ritual ceremonies are successful through these abilities to move us through enchantment. These find resonance and relationship to Pierre Bourdieu's description of the relationship between home and habitus because it is certainly there, where the young person is prepared for initiation. It is within this larger structure that the threshold states are prepared, and initiates are then guided through by mentors, leaders, priests, or parents. This cradling structuring structure is ultimately what allows rites to generate agency:

> The house, an opus operatum, lends itself as such to a deciphering, but only to a deciphering which does not forget that the "book" from which the children learn their vision of the world is read with the body, in and through movements and displacements which make the space within which they are enacted as much as they are made by it.[23]

In Santa Clara, the forge is an extension of the home. Like the house, it is the locus of apprenticeship. It is there where fathers teach their sons[24] how to behave socially and it is this dialectical relationship between body and space which forges the artisans. There, they learn not only the techniques of making but also the corporal codes of conduct corresponding to the community's and the family's moral values. It is within this extended context that the efficacy of the threshold must be understood as going beyond "the point at which physiological or psychological effect begins to be produced." Because, the threshold is also a "level point, or value above which something [becomes] true," indicating if something will take place or not.[25]

The Liminal as Transitional Resting Point

This echoes what Winnecot calls the individual's "inner-reality" experiences, which should not be ignored as they function importantly in balancing both inner and outer states of being-in-the-world. Winnecot defines this "intermediate zone" as a "transitional phenomena." In his application to infant development, it is the "intermediate state between a baby's inability and his growing ability to accept reality."[26]

> [This] third part of the life of a human being, [is] a part that we cannot ignore, [. . .] an intermediate area of experiencing, to which inner reality and external life both contribute. It is an area that is not challenged, because no claim is made on its behalf except that it should exist as a resting-place for the individual engaged in the perpetual human task of keeping inner and outer reality separate yet interrelated.[27]

For Winnecot, this is the state in adult life in which art and religion become possible, and if uncontrolled, madness as well. This is also a zone where collectives can form and pulled together by shared imaginaries. As we will see shortly, this conforms to Turner's concept of the liminoid, the collective liminal space of pilgrimage, sports, or play. Winnicot (as Turner, conceives of the intermediate area as a zone of play, artistic creativity and appreciation of religious feeling and dreaming. Winnicot explains that it is in this zone where the child and the individual also become able to accept cultural difference and similarity.[28]

Liminality, Apprenticeship, and Reflexivity

This intermediate zone of in-betweenness is heuristic. It is here, in the middle phase where ritual initiates and apprentices resolve, absorb, and integrate their training directed by community elders, priests, or other guides, such as master artisans. Initiates enter a "suspended state of awareness."[29] This threshold is also an opportunity for "thrashing" things out. The liminal zone is also a messy zone: as van Gennep's original French term "margen" implies it is ambiguous territorially as well as temporally:

> [N]eophytes are withdrawn from their structural positions and consequently from the values, norms, sentiments and techniques associated with those positions. During the liminal period neophytes are alternately forced and encouraged to think about their society, their cosmos, and the powers that generate and sustain them. Liminality may be partly described as a state of reflection. In it those ideas, sentiments, and facts that had been hitherto for the neophytes bound up in configurations and accepted unthinkingly are . . . resolved into their constituents.[30]

People who live in the margins, because of poverty, class, ethnicity, or all three of these, sojourners who arrive from elsewhere, including immigrants and ethnographers, are all initiates, depending on where you stand, your position on the inside and outside shifts and so does your threshold of in-between. In my mentor-apprenticeship with maestro Pérez, I experienced intense reflexive displacement. Although I am also an artist, my autonomy, artistic training, and personal aesthetics had to be put aside, employed only as preliminary kinesthetic preparation, then subsequently in comparative analysis.

Public Reflexivity and Collective Performance

Turner's theory of liminality strove to incorporate these political aspects. He applied liminality to traditional rites of passage as well as to "historical periods of upheaval and reorientation." Importantly, his later work applied liminality to the secular everyday, designating these liminal zones of experience in industrialized society as "liminoid" in which contemporary society formed "communitas." He insisted that the liminal was a performative state of self-reflexivity, not only for the singular neophytes but for communities, audiences, and by implication society as a whole. Like Turner, Erika Fischer-Lichte attaches the liminal to performative modalities, stressing that this creative state not only transforms the actors but also converts participants into active recipients. Creative liminal efficacy then is also based in performances' potential to "collapse dichotomies" such as the "differences between art and life."[31]

Turner described public reflexivity and performance as taking shape in multiple expressions:

> Essentially, public reflexivity takes the form of a performance. The languages through which a group communicates itself to itself are not, of course, confined to talking codes: they include gestures, music, dancing, graphic representation, painting, sculpture, and the fashioning of symbolic objects. They are dramatic, that is literally "doing" codes.[32]

Turner's concepts of liminality—"conflict," "crisis," "social drama," and the "betwixt and between," usually applied to the analysis of theatrical-like or ritual-like performances take on new meaning as enacted in Santa Clara.

THE LIMINALITY OF COLLECTIVE HISTORY AND PERFORMANCE

Santa Clara is a town, that not so long ago, was a village where everybody knew each other not necessarily by their formal names but by "apodos," nicknames. Santa Clara is a village of makers located in a region of many other artisan villages. As much as it is "traditional," it is also very contemporary. Inside community life is connected to the outside through global tourist markets but also through decades-old migratory temporary-work patterns to the United States, Canada, and elsewhere. For the coppersmiths and the community as a whole, the copper craft affirms and responds to profound and complex cultural memories, personal ancestry, and political history passed on corporally, more than orally, through their smithing techniques and skilled use.[33]

Coppersmithing is exceptionally performative, seductive, dramatic, and alchemical. The copper artisan's power of enchantment, their ability to transform gestures of labor into artfulness is evident in the constellating activities of forge, village festivals, religious observance, national fairs, and craft competitions. Santa Clara artisans perform publicly and privately in copper-smithing demonstrations to clients, tourists, and government officials, and for themselves, to their own community members These coppersmithing demonstrations are "social and aesthetic performances of making." Through these theatrical simulacric spectacles Santa Clara artisans conform, assert, resist, and transform their marginalized rural and working-class status.

The Santa Clara artisans are often *campesinos*, farmers and also mestizos, ethnically considered in-between Spanish and indigenous origins. Mexican colonization by the Spanish in the sixteenth century involved the conversion of indigenous villages to Christianity and the transformation of small communities into colonial settlement and congregations by the Franciscans and the Augustinians. Today, these cultural and ethnic mixtures can be seen in the calendar of religious celebrations observed and the style of the objects produced and sold in the town's forges and shops.

In this way liminal rites of passage become traced into the craft production, in addition to the community's many religious events and celebrations marking changes in life status. However, these traditions exhibit more than faith. Community members, including artisans, give careful aesthetic attention to details of material ornamentation. These embellishments contribute to orchestrating the performative drama that makes a rite efficacious, believable, cogent—moving. One such rite is the Fiesta de Sagrario held on the 15th of August and it exhibits the three phases proposed by van Gennep. It is also associated with the timing of the National Copper Fair, another liminal simulacra that celebrates Santa Clara's history and craft-trade and includes a copper *concurso*, competition, in which most of the 250 or so artisans compete for cash prizes.

Fiesta de la virgen de Sagrario

In Santa Clara the 15th of August is a sacred day in which the community holds a procession honoring this Virgen del Sagrario. The beautifully elaborated Virgen wears a crown of copper. From the entrance of the main cathedral outward into the church plaza, a mantel is extended from this patroness to forming a channel or canal beneath. The community procession moves through the town's streets to finally enter beneath this mantle touching the cloth over head with their hands and fingers. It is a powerfully moving sight. Like a great sea, that has parted way, the people pass, a sort of giving birth and redemption simultaneously. The proceeding procession shapes the pre-liminal phase and when passing beneath the mantel the congregants proceed into the liminal phase. Then one by one, each person is delivered, entering the post-liminal, to make their exit after having been graced, by touching the "magical" blue cloth, whose color adds to this sense of watery and celestial passage.

The creativity of the enacted symbolism and orchestration of gestures cannot be separated from the artisans work in the forge and their more public reenactments during the national copper fair, which I will turn to in more detail next. Communal performance of faith and devotion is exercised in not only the events associated with the Catholic Church mixing indigenous adaptations of rites and ceremonies but also in the fair, which was initiated in 1946 when electricity first came to the town. And then, the lights came on only in the plaza outside the church where the first noncommercial exhibition of copper artifacts was held for insiders and outsiders of the community showcasing copper pieces loaned by Santa Clara townspeople.

Crafting Social and Aesthetic Performance

Copper craft and trade in Santa Clara can be seen as a form of ritual or series of rites consisting of epistemological and ontological processes in which the artisan and the objects they produce, as well as their communities, continually come into being and are transformed. In the lifeworld of the artisans of Santa Clara, it is useful to distinguish between social performance and aesthetic performance, or (re)representative and (re)reproductive performances. This echoes the two types of ritual as organized by van Gennep: the first is more individual, marking the person's transformation from one state to another, as it occurs in the funeral. The second type of ritual is more collective and applies to group experiences, such, for example, as the marking of changing seasons or collectively suffered disasters that are expressed by public rituals.

We might conceive of these two types of rituals in relation to the social and aesthetic performances of the artisan in Santa Clara(as first introduced above). The first type is the more intimate private aesthetic work performed in the (family) studio. Aesthetic performance entails reproducing styles and personality and character and identity on a more intimate scale. This can include more accurately a re-reproducing, as the mimetic nature of style is also always evolving. The second social performance is public and a re-representation of self to insiders and outsiders of the community. These performances are also auto-affirming, empowering and as Turner stressed: in their self representation in the theater of acting out oneself in front of others one also comes to be a person or community member. These social performances include, for example, smithing demonstrations during the August fair, in which solitary creation is converted into public social drama, a cultural performance."[34] As Nancy Postero explains, cultural performances are important dramatizations, framed events that enable participants to understand, criticize and change the world in which they live [. . .] This is because such performances are profoundly discursive: they are dialogical and polyphonic fields of action where competing claims can be challenged and negotiated, producing new meanings in the process.[35]

Turner called this reflexive aspect of cultural performance, a "public metasocial ritual" and explained that these utilized liminal time in a distinct manner from that of more secret rituals that are hidden because of their sacred power. Turner thus insisted on the liminal potential of everyday social space.

The events of the August National Copper Fair in Santa Clara mix both in a powerful manner. Turner explained that public metasocial rite involved public liminality, such as the rites of coppersmithing performed in the plaza of the village of Santa Clara in front of everybody, insiders and outsiders, tourist and government officials as well as community members. These are not hidden secret events. Their power is precisely in their public nature. All performances require specifically demarcated space and time, apart from the ordinary currents. However, the metasocial rites employ the every day as its scenario and script of action, sanctified by the liminal time in which it is carried out.[36]

During the fair, this is carried out elaborately in many ways to multiple to present in this short chapter. Suffice it to say that they include demonstrations in the museum courtyard, as well as artisan processions and medieval-guild-related processions, in which elaborately adorned and designed carts drawn by horses and mules pass by with scenes from life in Santa Clara. It is indeed a floating world where the young children dress in indigenous clothing and the accoutrements of the forge, bellows and all its related tools, are carried forth, displayed for all to admire, literally elevated.[37]

The two types of social and aesthetic performances are of course inter-related and even interconstitutive; however, these distinguishing terms are useful for analytical purposes and emphasize central aspects of artisans' life and success. Both of these aesthetic and social performances are composed of "tacit" and "ludic" actions and gestures which embody and transmit "explicit" and "implicit" communal and subjective messages. These are the communal dispositions that insure sociocultural efficacy.[38]

Thresholds of Creativity

Turner relates the liminal zone and its activities with creative experience, insisting on it is a healthy functioning of the life course:

Liminality is full of potency and potentiality. It may also be full of experiment and play . . . Liminality is not confined in its expression to ritual and the performative arts. . . . One might say, without too much exaggeration, that liminal phenomena are at the level of culture what variability is at the level of nature.[39]

Paul Stoller, inspired by Turner, likens the liminal state of "betweenness" to "a space of deep creativity and boundless imagination." Stoller reminds us that although this space can be dialogical, dialectical, and relational, it is also potentially dangerous, as Bourdieu earlier also warned. Stoller illustrates the dangers of the "in-between" by drawing upon the Sufi parable of the "bar-zakh," the footbridge as a threshold state that connects rather than divides the known and the un-known.[40]

Tim Ingold and Elizabeth Hallam stress that improvization is even more important than creativity by linking the past to the future.[41] Edward Bruner, in *Creativity/Anthropology* dedicated to Turner, insisted that ordinary people have the capacity to generate change.[42] The editors of this volume, Rosaldo, Lavie, and Narayan, equally insist upon the democracy of creativity:

> Mundane everyday activities become as much the locus of cultural creativity as the arduous ruminations of the lone artist or scientist. In modern societies the succession of generations requires a similar mix of tradition and change.[43]

Thomasson, a scholar critical of liminality explains that this in-between phase "refers to moments or periods of transition during which the normal limits to thought, self-understanding and behavior are relaxed, opening the way to novelty and imagination, construction and destruction."[44] Thomasson, as Arpad Szakolczai,[45] both take strong views of the liminal, viewing creativity as associated with it, suspiciously, as a lack of borders, limits and boundaries that can ultimately become anarchic, valueless. Thomasson asserts that the liminal state is one of "potentially unlimited freedom from any kind of structure" and blames it for imparting a nihilistic chaos to contemporary life.[46] However, I argue on the contrary that the creativity of the liminal phase functions precisely in processual relationship between structure and agency. In addition, disorder and order are part of the natural spectrum of human existence which is ultimately indeterminate.

The Determinacy of Indeterminacy

The potential of the creativity of threshold experiences then depends upon the determinacy of indeterminacy. This can be understood as the viability and vulnerability of the subjunctive tense. This is what Turner designates as the "as is" and "as if." Each shed the other, like countless snake skins in never-ending reincarnations. But artisans do not return to the same state over and over like the snake; rather, the artisan incarnates new possibilities through creative responses to what cannot be controlled. This fluidity of endings and beginnings can be seen in the products the coppersmiths make, in the primary material—the copper—and how the artisans carry out this work, the subjects we turn to next.

LIMINALITY IN ARTISAN PRACTICE

Technologies of Enchantment

Artisans and made things cross thresholds between themselves and other people. The meaning of these objects is also liminal. Artisanal trade is not only an economic production; its activities are also performances of cultural production that reaffirm the values, tastes, and imagination of artisans and clients who support them in distinct ways in accordance with the historical moment.[47] This means that style is also liminal, simulacra-like. Moving between peoples, places, and things, it adopts and transforms. An object's power to enchant, entangle, and entrap lies in its technical prowess. As Gell stresses, this "technology of enchantment" engenders (social) relationships, senses of attachment, belonging, obligations, reciprocity, the feelings of a place, and its atmospheres of dwelling.[48]

Today the artisans of Santa Clara are known for creating a range of copper objects, from jewelry, sinks, to museum collected sculptural vessels. However, the production of one functional vessel, the copper cauldron or *cazo* introduced by the Spanish during the colonial period persists today. These copper cauldrons range from small pots to cook *atoles*, the sweet liquid corn-gruels or *dulce de membrillo*, sweet fruit jams as well as the enormous drum-like cauldrons for cooking the famous Michoacán style *"carnitas,"* fried pork, and other typical foods. These copper vessels and their accompanying recipes travel over the border with immigrants to Chicago and other cities in *el norte*, the United States or Canada, carrying with them familiar flavors, smells, memories, and deep attachments.[49]

Objects, like old-battered pots, can (magically and liminally) make material absence come alive through immaterial presence—their associated memories, feelings, histories, and attachments. Objects function through the limen in an effort to bind the past and future by maintaining the "tensions between physical presence and the threat of disintegration and absence" in the present.[50]

materia prima

Liminality is expressed in material stories. In West Mexico, copper's story includes mining territories, the Spanish conquest, and ancient metallurgical knowledge. Like the story of clay and the potter that follows, it is imbedded in earthen archaeological records. As Ingold and Hallam describe:

The story of clay does not begin with the potter, since the material he throws on the wheel has already to be dug out from the ground and kneaded so that it is sufficiently pure and the right consistency. Before that is was sedimented through the deposition of water-borne particles, over eons of geological time.[51]

Liminality is also expressed within the material transformation of the metal-smithing (techniques) themselves, conveyed, and carried out through deeply sensorial experiences. Like rites of passage, the materia prima, copper metal, can be seen to pass through three phases of becoming. The first phase of separation is the copper smelting in which the copper ore is transformed from solid to liquid state. The second stage is when the copper is left inbetween in this liminal threshold state, in which its chemical stability is unleashed. It is now plastic and vulnerable, neither liquid nor solid. Then in the third stage it is hammered into form, and the copper becomes work-hardened. In this stage of coalescence the copper, becomes resolved, its metal chemistry stabilized and reintegrated- fixed and formed.

Rites of passage can also be seen in other phases in the life of materials. As Ingold and Hallam describe through the story of clay and the pot:

"Finishing" . . . is but a moment in the life of the pot: a rite of passage, perhaps, where it crosses the threshold from preparation to employment. . . . Clay passes from earth-life to life as a pot. . . . As in rites of passage, one can discern in making the three phases of separation, in which the material is removed from its former life, of transition, in which it is treated in the seclusion of the workshop, and of reincorporation into the settings of its subsequent career.[52]

For the artisans in Santa Clara, finishing things is to begin again. Making things then is an ongoing rite of passage and so is the life of the things they make. To approach material culture and craft-producers via "making" is to conceive of made things as liminal performances, rather than as closed- circuited things, events that exclude, rather than engage.[53] Material culture never finishes; it unfolds and corresponds. It is always unfinished.

In his study of the alchemy of painting, Elkins explains that for the alchemist and artist (like the artisan-maker], *materia prima* is "the way-station between chaos and perfection." Elkins writes that

in alchemy, the Latin word *labor* is used to describe procedures, methods, and techniques—the daily struggle with materials. Also, in Latin, *ora* means prayer, and the alchemists never tired of pointing out that *labor* and *ora* spell laboratory. As in the artists studio, so in the alchemist's laboratory: both of them mingle *labor* and *ora*.[54]

For maestro Jesús, as for most artisans in Santa Clara, his work indeed was "endless labor."[55] It was also a type of "*ofrenda*," an offering. Lorena Paredes

Rosales explained that Maestro Jesús began his classes with a prayer: "En el nombre de la virgen . . ." (in the name of the Virgin). But for this master, it was also a pursuit of perfection which from the outset was impossible. I was reprimanded for attempting to delay moving on to the next piece, by belaboring one. The errors are what carry the artisan to the next piece. Paradoxically, imperfection leads in the pursuit of perfection.

The Mastery of Un-mastery

This is what I identify as the artisan's "mastery of un-mastery." Perfection of execution is aimed for but impossible to obtain. This means the work of the artisan is always indeterminate, processual—in the liminal phase, located in-between intention and realization, perfection and imperfection, and completion and incompletion. Moral imperatives are implicitly part of the aesthetic standard asserted by maestro Perez in his studio. These qualities are also echoed in the work and attitudes toward work expressed by numerous village artisans.

Artisan practice is also kind of endless thinking things out: I will never stop learning how to be an artisans until the day I die!" he would say.

Like the alchemist, the maestro's craft was a kind of "theoalchemy" where he engaged with "questions of eternal life, spirit, resurrection, and incarnation [. . .] The act of making, *labor,* was prayer, *ora.* What counted in the laboratory [of the forge] was endless work [and in] the moment of making, the act is everything."[56]

Artisans's work in the middle of things, *media res.* The processes the artisan engages in expand their sensorial peripheries and in this sense, the artisan also enters into a physiological liminality.

Craft-making requires an ongoing state of attunement of somatic attention. As apprentice this requires a type of nonverbal call and response with one's mentor based on gestures and actions. The adoption of skills is not an acquisition, rather skills are practiced. This continual rehearsal of actions, gestures, and movement occurs in a liminal threshold phase. Rather than a fixed state, skilled practice is always in a state of constant flux. The perturbations and errors that occur in the liminal threshold make things become clear. In apprenticeship, ruptures provide instructions, warnings, descriptions, and clarifications. Separation is prompted by these errors which forces new footing with your mentor-guides to rebalance, recalibrate, and relearn.

For the artisans who learn in their family studios, this all begins almost at birth. Infants, not yet walking, can be seen wrapped in their mothers rebozos, reaching out to join her hands as she moves the handles of the bellows, helping out in the forge. This ongoingness of practice is not extraordinary and forms the culture, like the culture of a petri dish in which the coppersmith develops, day by day and step by step.

When asked what made a good piece, however, my teacher insisted it was not one that you made everyday. A good piece was outside of the routine, but yet this "good piece" could not have been made if the artisan did not labor day in and day out. Ongoing training prepared them for the extraordinary piece. This means that the relationship between ordinary and extraordinary is as structure to agency; it is reciprocal and intertwined, communal and inseparable. At the very least, the training and practice of routine makes the break in routine possible. Just like the ongoingness of experience makes the liminal possible.

Failure, Sin, Freedom, and Choice

Turner's approach to what incites the liminal and the rupture or breakdowns that precede and proceed it through his insertion of a possible permanent schism highlights two types of failures. There are failures that generate creative (re)solutions and those that cannot be redressed. Failure is measured within various contexts as mistakes. This is why there is intentional and unintentional mistakes and errors, especially for initiates.

To follow this further, additionally, it may be possible that as a Catholic Turner was taking up a religiously motivated query as follows: philosophically Turner needed to articulate two types of failures in order to resolve the question of human choice and freedom, after the biblical fall. To eat from the tree of knowledge was ironically when humans began to assert choice and the freedom to fail. The rule against eating from the tree was about having no choice to sin or fail. When humans were expelled from the garden of eden, this meant that not only were they now capable of choices between "good" and "evil," it meant also that they were now responsible to bear the consequences of their errors—or sins. From this perspective, the predicate "as is" and the imaginative subjunctive "as if" tense become linked to human agency in a more fraught or edgy manner.

As metaphysical as this discussion is, it is relevant to the artisans of Santa Clara, who are for the most part very religious Catholics, because their agency is related to concepts of failure and (as I speculate here) original sin. For Maestro Jesús Pérez Ornelas, my mentor teacher, failure was fundamental to the creation of high-quality work. At the same time that he stressed that all his work had flaws, he was also adamant about the pursuit of surface and symmetry perfection. He told me that it was precisely the mistakes of each work that motivated and inspired his following piece.

In a deeply felt sensorial manner, as already described, the works forged in copper passed through van Gennep's triad of ritual phases: separation, transition, and incorporation. The copper, as the artisan, in its raw material state is transgressive; however, in its paring down, cleaning up, comes to be in its refinement: (almost) holy. The raw materials can be seen to embody the maker's original sin and in its intense refining enters a conditional state of grace.

When my pieces turned out *chueca*, crooked, the harshness in which my teacher responded indeed was as if I had sinned by making such an awkward imperfect piece. Vessels in Santa Clara are given an anthropomorphic nomenclature as well. The *olla*, the vessel has a neck, head, feet, a body. My teacher's idiosyncratic work drawing on many styles from West Mexican ceramics to popular art of the region included what he called *caritas*, little heads whose mask-like qualities evoked the myriad of senses of presence and personality elaborated upon by Erving Goffman. The relationship between person and mask made a synthetic evocative unit whose qualities emerged and transformed over the course of Maestro Jesus's lifetime, going from finely groomed and mustached, more Spanish-like gentlemen to more raw, mask-like, even deathlike faces with indigenous features. The objects seemed to mirror the life phases its maker also passed through.

Elkins description of the word "hypostasis" seem to explain an attitude toward materials—the copper—that resonates with my experiences with maestro Jesús and at times, his indignant rage and impatience with my clumsiness and ignorance in the forge. But, his exasperation also expresses his deep respect even reverence, toward making: the techniques and the materials. This included not only the copper, but even the wood first selected for each chore at hand, then chopped with the ax to feed the fire which annealed the copper, among other tasks. As Elkins explains:

> [The] word, *hypostasis* . . . describes what happens when fluids and stones seem to have inner meaning, and when numbers come alive . . . [It] is a religious concept: Jesus was the hypostatic incarnation of the Word of God into the ordinary substance of a human body, meaning that he was spirit that became flesh. A hypostasis is a descent from an incorporeal state into ordinary matter, or . . . an infusion of spirit into something inert. . . . Hypostasis is the feeling that something as dead as paint might also be deeply alive, full of thought and expressive meaning.[57]

For an artist, paint is never inert and for a coppersmith neither is copper. Additionally metalsmithing, as many have acknowledged, is an incredibly volatile and fluid process wherein demarcations from one state to another are margins whose endings and beginnings merge. It has many properties too numerous to discuss at length here, suffice it to say that it too is liminal, superficially a humble modest metal, unlike silver or gold, yet it is resourceful, with chemical properties that make it conductive and even antibacterial.[58]

NEARING CONCLUSIONS: LIMINAL CLARITY

Likewise, thinking with liminality alters the fixed vision of history, time, and the meaning of the ethnographic experience. As researchers our exits and entrances into the lives of others are temporary imaginary points in time. This marginality effects subsequent reflection and retelling. Liminal frames force us to "[i]imagine history [as ethnography] not as an accomplished fact or a formless tendency but as an occupied space of contingency and desire in which people roam."[59] Kathleen Stewart describes history as both determinate and indeterminate: fleeting. Historical experiences move into focus and depart from view. Like the liminal zone, history and ethnography are framed by temporary demarcations and topographies:

> History . . . arises in the present. Grand causes and ultimate consequences gather themselves around the everyday in the trembling space/time . . . . where the question of "meaning" finds itself caught in a signification that is at once contingent and receptive, overwhelming and inconclusive, tactile and uncertain. The past, like the future, comes and goes, drifting in and out of vision, but it haunts things until there's no telling what might happen and what people might do.[60]

Our ethnographies equally enter lives that went on before we entered the scene, walking across thresholds, and will continue afterward once we have walked through. These exits and entrances mean that we hear and listen to our teachers in the field, the "[l]ocal voices . . . within a space of contingency, [and that] the 'truth' of things" we experience are "lodged in the concrete yet shifting life of signs."[61] As ethnographers, this also means that we become part of this "network of tellings and retellings, displacements and re-rememberings" which we then try to share in our writing, as I do here.[62] Maestro Jesús would tell me stories and instruct me: "Now just listen and take notes; later you can write it the way you want to." In this sense, through these triadic phases of remembering and storytelling, (listening, taking notes, re-telling) the ethnographer, as an apprentice, enters the pre-liminal phase, to encounter another cultural order in the liminality of the telling, to then reemerge, post-liminal.

Contingencies and Liminality

Life and its liminal experiences are played out in rhythms in determined and undetermined patterns sensed and perceived in murky, even dangerous, margins. In the introduction to *The Rites of Passage,* Kimball writes that "Van Gennep, with others, accepted the dichotomy of the sacred and the profane; in fact this is a central concept for understanding the transitional stage in which a group finds itself from time to time."[63] Importantly however, Kimball explains that "the sacred is not an absolute value but one relative to the situation."[64] In other words, the frames of the liminal can shift along with the multitude of life's changing axis and contexts. Kimball explains the transitional period, when initiates reintegrate back into society, can be disruptive. Rites of passage can soften these periods of potential social disequilibrium. Yet, these rites can be helpful in many occasions, as "all life is transition, with rhythmic periods of quiescence and heightened activity."[65]

Artisans regularly and routinely enact liminal transitions, joining creatively and generatively with their materials, ecological environment, craft-work, the market, community, and ordinary with extraordinary artisan performance. This going in-between of liminal activity also joins master with apprentice and ethnographer with subject. But the phases of the limen are not like a full moon; although our experiences might wax and wane, we can never return to the same beginning.

The limen, or threshold, is an entry place and exit, a broad thoroughfare. Liminality has neither ending point nor precise location. As objects and persons, it is not fixed. Liminality is neither destination nor demarcation. The liminal is infinite. As the horizon point it is never consumed by our approach; nor does it end.

NOTES

1. This discussion of liminality could enter through an analysis and approach via theories of "play," "ritual," or/and "frame." I have chosen to discuss the concept of liminality in relationship to artisanal practice in Santa Clara del Cobre as the liminal is manifested in a myriad of forms in the lifeworld of the artisans. This chapter is constructed as a multi-faceted prism, bringing together many aspects of liminality revealed through my study of coppersmithing in Santa Clara del Cobre. Each of these facets could easily form an entire chapter. Rather than to delve into only one of these facets, or aspects of liminality, I have chosen to present these facets together. Although this approach is somewhat perfuncturary, it best outlines, albeit non-linearly, "liminality" as a theoretical lens that emerges and assists in an anthropological study of "making" of both craft and human life, more generally.

2. This chapter draws from and expands upon aspects of my doctoral thesis (Michele Feder-Nadoff, "Cuerpo de conocimiento—entre praxis y teoría—la agencia del artesano y su artesanía, Santa Clara del Cobre, Michoacán, México [doctoral dissertation, El Colegio de Michoacán, 2017]); concepts presented here are articulated more granularly in my forthcoming monograph, *Presence of Absence: An Anthropology of Making in Santa Clara del Cobre, Michoácan, Mexico.*

3. Per Zhang, who explains that van Gennep was not the first to develop the idea of transitional rites, their stages and patterns. Henri Hubert and Marcel Mauss had attempted to do this in their treatise on the nature of sacrifice. Juwen Zhang, "Recovering Meanings Lost in Interpretations of Les Rites de Passage," *Western Folklore* 71, no. 2 (2012): 119–147 (122–123). Arnold van Gennep, *Rites of Passage,* trans. M. B. Vizedom y G. L. Caffee (Chicago: The University of Chicago Press, 1960 [1907]). Henri Hubert and Marcel Mauss, *Sacrifice: Its Nature and Functions*, trans. W. D. Halls (Midway Press, 1964 [1898]). See also Adina Hulabaş and Ioana Repciuc, editors, "Introduction," in *The Rites of Passage Time after Time*, 7–23 (Editua Universităţi "Alexandru Ioan Cuza" Iaşi, 2016).

4. Victor Turner, "Betwixt and Between: The Liminal Period in Rites de Passage," *The Proceedings of the American Ethnological Society, Symposium on New Approaches*

to the Study of Religion (1964): 4–20. Victor Turner, *The Forest of Symbols: Aspects of Ndembu Ritual* (Ithaca: Cornell University Press, 1967). Victor Turner, *The Ritual Process* (Chicago: Aldine, 1969). Victor Turner, "Frame, Flow and Reflection. Ritual and Drama as Public Liminality," *Japanese Journal of Religious Studies* 6, no. 4 (1979): 465–499. Victor Turner, *From Ritual to Theatre* (New York: Performing Arts Journal, 1982). Victor Turner, "Liminality and the Performative Genres," in *Rite, Drama, Festival, Spectacle: Rehearsals Towards a Theory of Cultural Performance*, ed. J. J. MacAloon, 19–41 (Philadelphia: Institute for Study of Human Issues, 1984). Victor Turner, *On the Edge of the Bush* (Tucson: University of Arizona Press, 1985). Victor Turner and Edward M. Bruner, ed., *The Anthropology of Experience* (Urbana and Chicago: University of Illinois Press, 1986). See Zhang on this history as well as the introduction to the 1960 translation in English. Zhang, "Recovering Meanings" and Juwen Zhang, "Rites de Passage," in *Theory in Social and Cultural Anthropology: An Encyclopedia*, 2 vols. ed. R. Jon McGee and Richard L. Warms, 2: 702–705 (Sage Publications, 2013). It is also important to contextualize why the study could not gain more recognition at the time of its publication, as there existed a disagreement between Durkheim and van Gennep—see Bjørn Thomassen, "The Hidden Battle that Shaped the History of Sociology: Arnold van Gennep contra Emile Durkheim," *Journal of Classical Sociology* 16, no. 2 (2016): 173–195; Hulabaş and Repciuc, "Introduction."

5. See Kathleen Stewart, *A Space by the Side of the Road* (New Jersey: Princeton University Press, 1996), 5.

6. Marcel Mauss, "Techniques and Technology" [1941–1948]; "Techniques of the Body" [1935–1947]; "Technology," in *Techniques, Technology, and Civilization*, ed. N. Schlanger (Oxford: Bergham Books, 2006). Pierre Bourdieu, *Outline of a Theory of Practice* (Cambridge: Cambridge University Press, 2012 [1972]).

7. Although Delueze and Guattari never utilize the term "liminal" nor mention van Gennep nor Turner, they emphasize the importance of the "middle"—the in-between—in their concept of the rhizome and creative agency. The nomadic, deterritorialized and deterritorializing nature of the rhizome parallels the concept of liminality as a moveable field, area of intensity and transformation. As such, similarly, in this chapter I posit the limen as moveable frames, that is, demarcating moveable fields of consciousness, transformation, reflexivity, and agency. As Delueze and Guattari explain: "The beginning always begins in-between, intermezzo." Similarly they describe how "a line of becoming has only a middle. The middle is not an average; it has fast motion, it is the absolute speed of movement. A becoming is always in raw middle; one can only get it by the middle." Gilles Delueze and Felix Guattari, *One Thousand Plateaus*, trans. and foreword Brian Massumi (Minneapolis and London: University of Minnesota Press, 1987), 293, 380.

This relationship between the concept of the rhizome and the liminal is worthy of a chapter in itself. See, for example, Peixoto Barbara and Valério Curado on a discussion of the performances of the "between" looking at van Gennep, Turner, Schechner, and Delueze and Guattari. Rodrigo Peixoto Barbara and Renata Velério Curado, "Rizo-Liminaridade: Performances do "Entre"/ Rhizo-Liminarity: Performance of the 'Between'," *Revista Arte de Cena* 4, no. 1 (2018): 197–228. DOI: 10.5216/ac.v4i1.51579. Disponível em: https://revistas.ufg.br/artce/article/view/51579. Acesso em: 18 jan. 2023. Interestingly, in terms related to how I look at the liminal (as a moving zone of experience), according to Brian Massumi, Deleuze and Guattari use the word "milieu" to mean "surroundings," "medium" as in chemistry, and "middle." Brian Massumi, "Foreword," in Gilles Deleuze and Felix Guattari, *One Thousand Plateaus*, trans. and foreword by Brian Massumi, xvii (Minneapolis and London: University of Minnesota Press, 1987). Beyond the context of this chapter, although ample discussion is further required, these three allude to the idea that the liminal experience as opposed in this chapter is formed from the everyday, constituted, generated, and produced within. Beyond the scope of this chapter, the liminal implies a proposition of time and space and temporality and territoriality.

8. Bjørn Thomassen, *Liminality and the Modern: Living Through the In-Between* (London and New York: Routledge, 2016), 1.

9. Johan Fornäs, "Passages across Thresholds: Into the Borderlands of Mediation," *Convergence: The Journal of Research into New Media Technologies* 8, no. 4 (2002): 89–106. http://convergence.beds.ac.uk/issues/volumeeight/numberfour.

10. See Marcel Proust, *Swann's Way: In Search of Lost Time, Volume 1,* general ed. Christopher Pendergast, trans. Lydia Clark (New York: Penguin Books, 2002 [1922]), 44.

11. As Benjamin writes in *The Arcades Project:* "Trace and aura. The trace is appearance of a nearness however far removed the thing left behind may be. The aura is appearance of a distance, however close the thing that calls it forth. In the trace, we gain possession of the thing; in the aura, it takes possession of us." The German title of the Arcades Project is Passage-Werk, the passage works. Walter Benjamin, *The Arcades Project*, trans. Howard Ailand and Kevin McLaughlin (Cambridge, MA: Belknap Press of Harvard University Press, 1999), 447.

12. Kimball in his introduction to the first English translation of *Rites of Passage* states that "In one sense all life is transition, with rhythmic periods of quiescence and heightened activity." Solon T. Kimball, "Introduction," in Arnold van Gennep, *Rites of* Passage, trans. M. B. Vizedom and G. L. Caffee (Chicago: The University of Chicago Press, 1960 [1907]), vii.

13. See Patricia Scalco, "Weaving Value: Selling Carpets in the Liminal Space of Istanbul's Grand Bazaar," *Anthropology Toda* 35, no. 5 (2019): 7–10.

14. See John Dewey, *Art as Experience* (New York: Capricorn Books, 1958 [1934]), 3, 6, 7, 8, 13, 14, 15.

15. See, for example, Turner, *The Ritual Process*, VII, 201; "Liminality and the Performative Genres," 21.

16. There is much that could be discussed here relating the limen to frames. Limitations of one chapter and my specific focus limit my attention to its exposition here. Frames are of course a central theoretical element in performance studies, developed from Goffman and also theorized by Bateson in relationship to ritual. See Houseman for a careful analytical distinction between frame in "play" versus in "ritual" critiquing and extending Bateson's approach to frame. Houseman's more non-linear interpretation explains how the "frame" is managed differently in play versus ritual in Bateson's work. Houseman also discusses the topological model of the "moebius" frame and "braided" frames as conceived by Handelman. Erwin Goffman, *Frame Analysis: An Essay on the Organization of Experience* (Boston: Northeastern University, 1986). Gregory Bateson, *Steps to an Ecology of Mind*, foreword Mary Catherine Bateson (Chicago: University of Chicago Press, 2000 [1972]).

M. Houseman, "Pushing Ritual Frames Past Bateson," *Journal of Ritual Studies* 26, no. 2 (2012): 1–5. http://www.jstor.org/stable/44368852.

17. The Spanish word for threshold "umbral" encompasses this shadowy position between two posts, on the verge or the limits of something. The Latin word "umbra" refers to the shadows cast by the eclipsing moon or sun and aptly apply to the poetics of the door, as the threshold too is cast in shadows by the changing angles of cast light caused by the moving positions of sun and moon. In this manner, the threshold becomes like a sun dial, reflecting times of day: its passages of arbitrariness and enchantment. The changing light and shadow of a cloudy day can also effect the illusive appearance of day- or night-time.

18. This is expanded in Feder-Nadoff 2021, where I focus on the instabilities of the peripheral as expressed in the artisan's affective, sensorial, and social geographies. This chapter thus examines un-knowing as an edgy methodological approach to access "peripheral wisdom." Peripheral wisdom is seen here as a form of edgewalking, since to be on the peripheries of knowing means to be on an edge, as observed by art historian Linda Schele (1999). As I write in the chapter: "As an anthropologist who is foremost an artist, my work begins by making things, rather than merely text. I am more comfortable on the margins of the verbal, in the in-between and unsaid, at home when using the language of making and of gestures." Michele Feder-Nadoff, "Hammering on the Edges," in *Peripheral Wisdom: Unlearning, Not Knowing and Ethnographic Limits*, ed. Francisco Martinez, Lili di Puppo and Martin Demant Frederiksen, 2021.

19. This brings to mind the pragmatism of tradition as presented by Mauss, who defined traditional techniques as those which continued to be passed on because they were effective. Marcel Mauss, "Les Techniques du corps," *Journal de Psychologie* 32 ([1936] 2009): 3–4, reissued in M. Mauss, *Sociologie et anthropologie* (París: PDF).

20. The idea of the door as a hinge goes back to Georg Simmel, "Bridge and Door," *Theory, Culture and Society* 11, no. 1 (1994 [1909]): 5–10.

21. Perhaps no doubt, inspired and borrowing from Proust whom Benjamin translated.

22. This swell also harkens to Bergson's swelling analogy related to the waves and the different qualities of memories as they are prompted in experience. Benjamin, *The Arcades Project*, 02a,1.

23. Bourdieu, *Outline of a Theory of Practice*, 90.

24. The forge is predominanlty a patriarchal male space, however women are included. This may involve actual apprenticehsip if the studio requires assistance and has no means to hire male apprentices. Yet, as times it is merely a family business and women are also trained. In most cases woemn are "invisible" assistants. However, the artisan run community school Casa de los Artesanos, is completey egalitarian..

25. See Gadamer's discussion of the experience of art in relationship to the concept of play. He explains that "seriousness" is essential to allowing the "truth" of the art to emerge from the performance and experience of (the) "play." In this sense it must reach a certain "threshold" to have agency as a structure and medium of (a) "truth." This is also achieved by the power of the aesthetics, which require a decision to be taken serious, through the attentiveness of the spectator as well as the creator, as player. Gadamer, 2008.

26. Donald W. Winnecot, *Playing and Reality* (London: Tavistock, 1971), 2–3.

27. Winnecot, *Playing and Reality*, 3.

28. Winnecot, *Playing and Reality*, 4, 8, 40. There can be much more said about the role of play in liminal experience and its structures. See, for example, J. Huizinga, *Homo Ludens: A Study of the Play-Element in Culture* (Eastford, CT: Martino Publishing, 2014 ([1950]); Roberte Hamayon, *Why We Play: An Anthropological* Study, trans. Damien Simon foreword Michael Puett (Chicago: HAU Books, 2016 [2012]); Mijaíl Bajtin, *Teoría y Estética de la Novela*, trans. Helena S. Kriukova (Madrid: Taurus, 1989 [1975]).

29. Turner, *The Forest of Symbols*, 106; as cited by S. Lavie, K. Narayan, and R. Rosaldo, eds., *Creativity/Anthropology* (Ithaca: Cornell University Press, 1993), 2–3.

30. Turner, *The Forest of Symbols*, 105–106.

31. Fischer-Lichte in particular looks at "the collapse of the opposition between art and reality and of all binaries resulting from this opposition transfers the participants into a liminal state." Erika Fischer-Lichte, *The Transformative Power of Performance: A New Aesthetics*, trans. Saskya Iris Jain (New York and London: Routledge, 2008), 176. As we will see later in this text, in the public demonstrations and theatrical reanactments of the community fair, the coppersmith's labor is transformed and does at least temporarily often transform its observers who join in in attempting to mimic the smiths. This would never happen on a construction site or road work crew on the side of a road.

32. Turner, "Frame, Flow and Reflection," 465.

33. Renown for its copper craft production, Santa Clara is located near to the Lake Patzcuaro basin of the northwestern Mexican state of Michoacán, near to many other artisanal communities. Coppersmithing in Santa Clara originates with the indigenous Purhépecha of this region as early as 400 AD. For more information see Michele Feder-Nadoff, "Santa Clara del Cobre: Materia y proceso, destilación e intercambio," in *Ritmo del fuego: El arte y los Artesanos de Santa Clara del Cobre, Michoacán, México*, 32–63 (Chicago: Fundación Cuentos, 2004).

34. The term "cultural performance" originates with Milton Singer cited by Guss, who writes that cultural performance "may be used to articulate a number of different ideas and over time can easily oscillate between religious devotion, ethnic solidarity, political resistance, national identity, and even commercial spectacle." David M. Guss, *The Festive State: Race, Ethnicity, and Nationalism as Cultural Performance* (Oakland: University of California Press, 2000).

35. Nancy Postero, *The Indigenous State: Race, Politics and Performance in Plurinational Bolivia* (Oakland: University of California, 2017), 74; citing Guss, 9.

36. Turner, "Frame, Flow and Reflection," 467.

37. Feder-Nadoff, "Cuerpo de conocimiento," 275.

38. Bourdieu, *Outline of a Theory of Practice*; Mauss, "Les Techniques du corps"; André Leroi Gourhan, *Gesture and Speech*, trans. A. Bostock Berger (Boston: MIT Press, 1993 [1964]);

Pierre Lemonnier, "Mythiques chaînes opératoires," *Techniques et cultures* (2004): 43–44;

David M. Guss, *El Estado festivo: Raza, etnicidad y nacionalismo como representación cultural* (Caracas: Consejo Nacional para la Cultura, 2005).

39. Turner, "Frame, Flow and Reflection," 466.

40. Paul Stoller, "The Parable of the Footbridge. Creativity and Change in the between," *Anthropology Today* 35, no. 5 (2019): 3. Crapanzano (cited by Stoller) explains that "barzakh" is something that separates a known from an unknown, an existent from a nonexistent, a negated from an affirmed, and an intelligible from a

non-intelligible. Vincent Crapanzano, *Imaginative Horizons: An Essay in Literary-Philosophical Anthropology* (University of Chicago Press, 2003), 57–58. See also William C. Chittick, *The Sufi Path of Knowledge: Ibn al-Arabi's Metaphysics of Imagination* (SUNY Press, 1989).

41. Tim Ingold and Elizabeth Hallam, eds., *Making and Growing: Anthropological Studies of Organisms and Artefacts* (Farnham: Ashgate Publishing, 2014).

42. Edward M. Bruner, "Epilogue: Creative Persona and the Problem of Authenticity," in *Creativity/Anthropology*, ed. S. Lavie, K. Narayan, and R. Rosaldo (Ithaca: Cornell University Press, 1993), 321–322.

43. Lavie, Rosaldo, and Narayan, *Creativity/Anthropology*, 5.

44. Thomassen, "The Hidden Battle," 1.

45. For a thorough history of liminality and its roots pre-van Gennep, see Arpad Szakolczai, "Liminality and Experience: Structuring Transitory Situations and Transformative Events," *International Political Anthropology* 2, no. 1 (2009): 141–172.

46. See Thomassen: "In the terminology we propose here—one that Durkhiem certainly would *not* have liked—infinity appears in the horizons of the liminal. Infinity may be a great place to start; it is possibly also the worst place to end. It is therefore also this fascination with boundless liminality and constant flux that we need to scrutinize. The incitation of constant and instant liminal experience that so characterizes cultural life in our contemporary period easily turns into stultifying boredom, senselessness and normative nihilism. . . . The implosion of liminal conditions is becoming still more evident in contemporary culture." Thomassen, *Liminality and the Modern*, 2.

47. See, for example, Frances E. Mascia-Lees, "Aesthetics: Aesthetic Embodiment and Commodity Capitalism," in *A Companion to the Anthropology of the Body and Embodiment,* ed. F. Mascia-Lees, 3–23 (Hoboken: Wiley-Blackwell, 2011).

48. Alfred Gell, "The Technology of Enchantment and the Enchantment of Technology," in *Anthropology, Art and Aesthetics,* ed. J. Coote and A. Shelton, 40–67 (Oxford: Clarendon Press, 1992).

49. See, for example, Judy Boruchoff, "Equipaje cultural: Objetos, identidad y transnacionalismo en Guerrero y Chicago," in *Fronteras fragmentadas: Género, familia e dentidades en la migración mexicana al norte,* ed. G. Mummert (Zamora: El Colegio de Michoacán-CIDEM, 1999), 499–517; and Víctor M. y Álvaro Ochoa Espinosa, "Caminos de Michoacán y lagos que voy pasando . . .," in *Ritmo del fuego: El arte y los artesanos de Santa Clara del Cobre, Michoacán, México,* ed. M. Feder-Nadoff (Chicago: Fundación Cuentos, 2004), 404–409.

50. Elizabeth Hallam and Jenny Hockey, *Death, Memory and Material Culture* (London: Routledge, 2001), 63.

51. Ingold and Hallam, *Making and Growing*, 1–2.

52. Ingold and Hallam, *Making and Growing*, 1–2.

53. Today, resulting from the sensorial, affective and material turns over the last three decades, material culture, as originally modeled by Franz Boas, and his students, is increasingly approached via making. See Coole and Frost, 2010 on the *New Materialisms*.

54. James Elkins, *What Painting Is* (London and New York: Routledge, 2000), 37, 78.

55. Elkins, *What Painting Is*, 72.

56. Ibid.

57. Elkins, *What Painting Is*, 44–45.
58. See Jim Morrison, "Copper's Virus-Killing Powers Were Known Even to the Ancients," *Smithsonian magazine.com*, 2020.
59. Stewar, *A Space by the Side of the Road*, 90.
60. Stewar, *A Space by the Side of the Road*, 116.
61. Stewart, *A Space by the Side of the Road*, 4.
62. Stewart, *A Space by the Side of the Road*, 4.
63. Kimball, "Introduction," viii.
64. Kimball, "Introduction," viii.
65. Kimball, "Introduction," x.

BIBLIOGRAPHY

Bajtin, Mijaíl. *Teoría y Estética de la Novela.* Translated by Helena S. Kriukova. Madrid: Taurus, 1989 [1975].

Barrett, Elinore M. *The Mexican Colonial Copper Industry.* Albuquerque, NM: University of New Mexico Press, 1987.

Bateson, Gregory. *Steps to an Ecology of Mind.* Foreword by Mary Catherine Bateson. Chicago, IL: University of Chicago Press, 2000 [1972].

Benjamin, Walter. *Illuminations: Essays and Reflections.* Translated by H. Zohn. Edited by H. Arendt. New York: Schocken Books, 2007 [1969].

Benjamin, Walter. *Reflections: Essays, Aphorisms, Autobiographical Writings.* Translated by Edmund Jephcott. Edited by Peter Demetz. New York: Schocken Books, 2007 [1955].

Benjamin, Walter. *The Arcades Project.* Translated by Howard Ailand and Kevin McLaughlin. Cambridge, MA: Belknap Press of Harvard University Press, 1999.

Berger, Bennett. "Foreword." In Erwin Goffman, Frame Analysis; An Essay on the Organization of Experience. Boston, MA: Northeastern University, 1986.

Boruchoff, Judy. "Equipaje cultural: Objetos, identidad y transnacionalismo en Guerrero y Chicago." In *Fronteras fragmentadas: Género, familia e dentidades en la migración mexicana al norte,* edited by G. Mummert, 499–517. Zamora: El Colegio de Michoacán-CIDEM, 1999.

Bourdieu, Pierre. *Outline of a Theory of Practice.* Cambridge: Cambridge University Press, 2012 [1972].

Bruner, Edward M. "Epilogue: Creative Persona and the Problem of Authenticity." In *Creativity/Anthropology,* edited by S. Lavie, K. Narayan, and R. Rosaldo, 321–334. Ithaca, NY: Cornell University Press, 1993.

Chittick, William C. *The Sufi Path of Knowledge: Ibn al-Arabi's Metaphysics of Imagination.* New York: SUNY Press, 1989.

Crapanzano, Vincent. *Imaginative Horizons: An Essay in Literary-Philosophical Anthropology.* Chicago and London: University of Chicago Press, 2003.

Delueze, Gilles and Felix Guattari. *One Thousand Plateaus.* Translated and foreword by Brian Massumi. Minneapolis, MN and London: University of Minnesota Press, 1987.

Dewey, John. *Art as Experience.* New York: Capricorn Books, 1958 [1934].

Elkins, James. *What Painting Is.* London and New York: Routledge, 2000.

Espinosa, Víctor M. y Álvaro Ochoa. "Caminos de Michoacán y lagos que voy pasando." In *Ritmo del fuego: El arte y los artesanos de Santa Clara del Cobre, Michoacán, México,* edited by M. Feder-Nadoff, 404–409. Chicago, IL: Fundación Cuentos, 2004.

Feder-Nadoff, M. "Cuerpo de conocimiento—entre praxis y teoría—la agencia del artesano y su artesanía, Santa Clara del Cobre, Michoacán, México." Doctoral dissertation, El Colegio de Michoacán, 2017.

Feder-Nadoff, Michele, ed. *Ritmo del fuego: El arte y los artesanos de Santa Clara del Cobre, Michoacán, México.* Fotografías de M. Feder-Nadoff, Chicago, IL: Fundación Cuentos, 2004.

Feder-Nadoff, Michele. "Hammering on the Edges." In *Peripheral Methodologies: Unlearning, Not Knowing and Ethnographic Limits,* edited by Francisco Martinez, Lili di Puppo, and Martin Demant Frederiksen, 94–112. London: Routledge, 2021.

Feder-Nadoff, Michele. "Santa Clara del Cobre: Materia y proceso, destilación e intercambio." In Ritmo del fuego: *El arte y los Artesanos de Santa Clara del Cobre, Michoacán, México,* edited by Michele Feder-Nadoff, 32–63. Chicago, IL: Fundación Cuentos, 2004.

Fischer-Lichte, Erika. *The Transformative Power of Performance: A New Aesthetics.* Translated by Saskya Iris Jain. New York and London: Routledge, 2008.

Fornäs, Johan. "Passages across Thresholds: Into the Borderlands of Mediation." *Convergence: The Journal of Research into New Media Technologies* 8, no. 4 (2002): 89–106. http://convergence.beds.ac.uk/issues/volumeeight/numberfour.

Gell, Alfred. "The Technology of Enchantment and the Enchantment of Technology." In *Anthropology, Art and Aesthetics,* edited by J. Coote and A. Shelton, 40–67. Oxford: Clarendon Press, 1992.

Gell, Alfred. *Art and Agency: An Anthropological Theory.* Oxford: Clarendon Press, 1998.

Goffman, Erwin. *Frame Analysis: An Essay on the Organization of Experience.* Foreword by Bennett Berger. Boston, MA: Northeastern University, 1986.

Guss, David M. *El Estado festivo: Raza, etnicidad y nacionalismo como representación cultural,* Caracas: Consejo Nacional para la Cultura, 2005.

Guss, David M. *The Festive State: Race, Ethnicity, and Nationalism as Cultural Performance.* Oakland, CA: University of California Press, 2000.

Hallam, Elizabeth and Jenny Hockey. *Death, Memory and Material* Culture. London: Routledge, 2001.

Hamayon, Roberte. *Why We Play: An Anthropological Study.* Translated by Damien Simon. Foreword by Michael Puett. Chicago, IL: HAU Books, 2016 [2012].

Horcasitas de Barros, María Luisa. *Cobre martillado: Vocabulario tradicional, utillaje y técnicas de manufactura.* Cuadernos de trabajo, Técnicas 1. Mexico: INAH, 1974.

Horcasitas de Barros, María Luisa. *La artesanía con raíces prehispánicas de Santa Clara del Cobre.* México: Secretaría de Educación Pública, 1968 [2001].

Hosler, Dorothy. "Mesoamerican Metallurgy: The Perspective from the West." In *Archaeometallurgy in Global Perspective: Methods and Syntheses,* edited by B. W. Roberts and C. P. Thornton, 227–245. New York: Springer, 2014.

Hosler, Dorothy. *The Sounds and Colors of Power: The Sacred Metallurgical Technology of Ancient West Mexico.* Cambridge, MA: MIT Press, 1994.

Houseman, M. "Pushing Ritual Frames Past Bateson." *Journal of Ritual Studies* 26, no. 2 (2012): 1–5. http://www.jstor.org/stable/44368852.

Hubert, Henri and Marcel Mauss. *Sacrifice: Its Nature and Functions*. Translated by W. D. Halls. Chicago and London: University of Chicago Press and Cohen and West LTD, 1964.

Huizinga, J. *Homo Ludens: A Study of the Play-Element in Culture*. Eastford, CT: Martino Publishing, 2014 [1950].

Hulabaş, Adina and Loana Repciuc. "Introduction." In *The Rites of Passage Time after Time*, edited by Adina Hulabaş and Loana Repciuc, 7–23. Editua Universităţi "Alexandru Ioan Cuza" Iaşi, 2016.

Ingold, Tim and Elizabeth Hallam, eds. *Making and Growing: Anthropological Studies of Organisms and Artefacts*. Farnham: Ashgate Publishing, 2014.

Kapferer, Bruce. "Victor Turner and The Ritual Process." Guest Editorial by Bruce Kapferer. *Anthropology Today* 35, no. 3 (2019), 1–2.

Kimball, Solon T. "Introduction." In *Rites of Passage*. Translated by M. B. Vizedom and G. L. Caffee, Edited by Arnold van Gennep, v–xvii. Chicago, IL: The University of Chicago Press, 1907 [1960].

Krippner-Martinez, James. *Rereading the Conquest: Power, Politics, and the History of Early Colonial Michoacán, México, 1521–1565*. University Park, PA: The Pennsylvania University State Press, 2001.

Lemonnier, Pierre, ed. *Technological Choices: Transformation in Material Cultures Since the Neolithic*. London and New York: Routledge, 1993 [2002].

Lemonnier, Pierre. "Mythiques chaînes opératoires." *Techniques et cultures* (2004): 43–44. https://doi.org/10.4000/tc.1054.

Leroi-Gourhan, André. *Gesture and Speech*. Translated by A. Bostock Berger. Boston, MA: MIT Press, 1993 [1964].

Lipstadt, H. "'To See, to Record, to Photograph': Discovering Pierre Bourdieu's Rediscovered Photographs of the Berber House, Uncovering Architecture as an Intellectualist Art." *Thresholds* 27 (2003): 12–17. Accessed March 30, 2020. www.jstor.org/stable/43876174.

Malafouris, Lambros and Chris Gosden. "Mind, Time and Material Engagement." In *The Oxford Handbook of History and Material Culture*, edited by Ivan Gaskell and Sarah Anne Carter, 105–120. Oxford: Oxford University Press, 2020.

Maldonado, Blanca. "Preindustrial Copper Production at the Archaeological Zone of Itzparátzico, a Tarascan Location in Michoacán, Mexico." Doctoral dissertation, University of Pennsylvania, 2006.

Mascia-Lees, Frances E. "Aesthetics: Aesthetic Embodiment and Commodity Capitalism." In *A Companion to the Anthropology of the Body and Embodiment*, edited by F. Mascia-Lees, 3–23. Hoboken, NJ: Wiley-Blackwell, 2011.

Mauss, Marcel. "Les Techniques du corps." *Journal de Psychologie* 32 (1936 [2009]): 3–4. Reissued in M. Mauss. *Sociologie et anthropologie*. París: PDF.

Mauss, Marcel. "Techniques and Technology" [1941–1948]; "Techniques of the Body" [1935–1947]; "Technology." In *Techniques, Technology, and Civilization*, edited by N. Schlanger, 147–154, 77–96, 97–140. Oxford: Bergham Books, 2006.

Mauss, Marcel. *Manual of Ethnography*, edited by N. J. Allen. New York and Oxford: Durkheim Press/Berghahn Books, 2009 [1967].

Morrison, Jim. "Copper's Virus-Killing Powers Were Known Even to the Ancients." *Smithsonian magazine.com*, 2020.

Peixoto, Barbara Rodrigo and Renata Valério Curado. "Rhizo-Liminarity: Performance of the 'Between'." *Revista Arte da Cena* 4, no. 1 (2018): 197–228.

Pérez Pamatz, Felipe. "Fiestas Religiosas en Santa Clara del Cobre." In *Ritmo del Fuego: El Arte y los Artesanos de Santa Clara del Cobre, Michoacán, México,* edited by M. Feder-Nadoff, 410–441. Chicago, IL: Fundación Cuentos, 2004.

Pérez Pamatz, Felipe. "Glosario del cobre martillado." In *Ritmo del Fuego: El Arte y los Artesanos de Santa Clara del Cobre, Michoacán, México,* edited by M. Feder-Nadoff, 392–399. Chicago, IL: Fundación Cuentos, 2004.

Pérez Pamatz, Felipe. "El proceso del cobre martillado." In *Ritmo del Fuego: El Arte y los Artesanos de Santa Clara del Cobre, Michoacán, México,* edited by M. Feder-Nadoff, 376–391. Chicago: Fundación Cuentos, 2004.

Postero, Nancy. *The Indigenous State: Race, Politics and Performance in Plurinational Bolivia.* Oakland, CA: University of California, 2017.

Proust, Marcel. *Remembrance of Things Past.* Translated by C. K. Moncrieff y T. Kilmartin. New York: Random House, 1989 [1928].

Proust, Marcel. *Swann's Way: In Search of Lost Time, Volume 1.* General Editor Christopher Pendergast. Translated by Lydia Clark. New York: Penguin Books, 2002.

Punzo Díaz, José Luis, Juan Morales, and Avto Goguitchaichvili. "Evidencia de escorias de cobre prehispánicas en el área de Santa Clara del Cobre, Michoacán, Occidente de México/Evidence of Prehispanic Copper Slags from the Santa Clara del Cobre area, Michoacan, Western Mexico." *Arqueología Iberoamericana* 28 (2015): 46–51. ISSN 1989–4104. http://purl.orgaia.

Punzo Díaz, José Luis. "Las Fundiciones de Santa Clara del Cobre." In *Santa Clara del Cobre: Zona de Monumentos Históricos*, edited by Susana Casarín, 39–48. México: Instituto Nacional de Antropología e Historia, 2014.

Rosaldo, Renato, et al. *Creativity/Anthropology.* Cornell University Press, 2018. Project MUSE. https://doi.org/10.1353/book.58040.

Roskamp, Hans. "Las caciques indígenas de Xiuhquilan y la defensa de las minas en el siglo XVI: el Lienzo de Jicalán." In *Ritmo del Fuego: El Arte y los Artesanos de Santa Clara del Cobre, Michoacán, México,* edited by M. Feder-Nadoff, 186–197. Chicago, IL: Fundación Cuentos, 2004.

Scalco, Patricia. "Weaving Value: Selling Carpets in the Liminal Space of Istanbul's Grand Bazaar." *Anthropology Toda* 35, no. 5 (2019): 7–10.

Simmel, Georg. "Bridge and Door." *Theory, Culture and Society* 11, no. 1 (1994 [1909]): 5–10.

Simon Martin, and Lori Conley. 1999. *Edgewalker: A Conversation with Linda Schele.* Directed by Andrew Weeks, Home Life Productions. VHS [https://www.youtube.com/watch?v=IOjSnQAszmg]

Stewart, Kathleen. *A Space by the Side of the Road.* Princeton, NJ: Princeton University Press, 1996.

Stoller, Paul. "The Parable of the Footbridge: Creativity and Change in the Between." *Anthropology Today* 35, no. 5 (2019): 3–6.

Szakolczai, Arpad. "Liminality and Experience: Structuring Transitory Situations and Transformative Events." *International Political Anthropology* 2, no. 1 (2009): 141–172.

Thomassen, B. "Thinking with Liminality: To the Boundaries of an Anthropological Concept." In *Breaking Boundaries: Varieties of Liminality*, edited by Á. Horváth, B. Thomassen, and H. Wydra, 39–58. Oxford: Berghahn, 2015.

Thomassen, Bjørn. "Anthropology and Its Many Modernities: When Concepts Matter." *The Journal of the Royal Anthropological Institute* 18, no. 1 (2012): 160–178. Accessed March 29, 2020. www.jstor.org/stable/41350812.

Thomassen, Bjørn. "The Hidden Battle that Shaped the History of Sociology: Arnold van Gennep Contra Emile Durkheim." *Journal of Classical Sociology* 16, no. 2 (2016): 173–195.

Thomassen, Bjørn. *Liminality and the Modern: Living Through the In-Between*. London and New York: Routledge, 2016.

Turner, W. Victor and Edward M. Bruner, eds. *The Anthropology of Experience*. Urbana and Chicago, IL: University of Illinois Press, 1986.

Turner, W. Victor. "Betwixt and Between: The Liminal Period in Rites de Passage." *The Proceedings of the American Ethnological Society, Symposium on New Approaches to the Study of Religion* (1964): 4–20.

Turner, W. Victor. "Body, Brain, and Culture." *Zygon* 18, no. 3 (1983): 221–245.

Turner, W. Victor. "Frame, Flow and Reflection: Ritual and Drama as Public Liminality." *Japanese Journal of Religious Studies* 6, no. 4 (1979): 465–499.

Turner, W. Victor. "Liminality and the Performative Genres." In *Rite, Drama, Festival, Spectacle: Rehearsals Towards a Theory of Cultural Performance*, edited by J. J. MacAloon, 19–41. Philadelphia: Institute for Study of Human Issues, 1984.

Turner, W. Victor. "Social Dramas and Stories about Them." In *Performance: Critical Concepts*, Vol. III, edited by Philip Auslander. London: Routledge, 2003. Originally published in *Critical Inquiry* 7, no. 1 (1980): 141–168.

Turner, W. Victor. *Dramas, Fields, and Metaphors*. Ithaca, NY: Cornell University Press, 1974.

Turner, W. Victor. *From Ritual to Theatre*. New York: Performing Arts Journal, 1982.

Turner, W. Victor. *On the Edge of the Bush*. Tucson, AZ: University of Arizona Press, 1985.

Turner, W. Victor. *The Anthropology of Performance*. New York: Performing Arts Journal Press, 1986.

Turner, W. Victor. *The Forest of Symbols: Aspects of Ndembu Ritual*. Ithaca, NY: Cornell University Press, 1967.

Turner, W. Victor. *The Ritual Process*. Chicago, IL: Aldine, 1969.

Winnecot, Donald W. *Playing and Reality*. London: Tavistock, 1971.

Zhang, Juwen. "Rites de Passage." In *Theory in Social and Cultural Anthropology: An Encyclopedia*, 2 Vols. edited by R. Jon McGee and Richard L. Warms, 702–705. Sage Publications, 2013.

Zhang, Juwen. "Recovering Meanings Lost in Interpretations of Les Rites de Passage." *Western Folklore* 71, no. 2 (2012): 119–147.

Chapter 6

Liminality in Time

The Taipei Dance Circle as a Process

Yu-Chun Chen

Liminality as a concept, established and developed by Arnold van Gennep and Victor Turner, has made interdisciplinary contributions in many areas, including media studies,[1] dance studies,[2] religious studies,[3] and political studies.[4] In June and October 2019, the widely read magazine *Anthropology Today* published by the Royal Anthropological Institute released a two-part special issue entitled "Ritual as Process" (Volume 35). It can be seen that Turner's influence continues in today's academic world. This chapter will focus on Turner's concepts of liminality and social drama to demonstrate a dance troupe's liminal state after losing its leader.

The application of liminality can be time-oriented or space-oriented; sometimes, a liminal state in time can be described through a story or a metaphor in space. For instance, in "The Parable of the Footbridge: Creativity and Change in the Between,"," Paul Stoller uses a Sufi story of crossing a footbridge to describe a sense of uncertainty about a man's future:

> Behind him was his past, a known space from where he had come. Before him was his future, an unknown place to where he was going. In an unsettled state, his mind suddenly cleared. Sparked with an unanticipated jolt of energy and creativity, he envisioned a new world filled with possibilities.[5]

This story perfectly demonstrates how an individual perceives a liminal state between the past, the present and the future in his "lived time"[6] (the subjective feeling of duration), through the metaphor of crossing a footbridge in space. This is a classic usage of liminality, given that the concept was first coined by Arnold van Gennep in *The Rites of Passage* to describe a series of passages from one age to another, such as birth, social puberty, marriage, fatherhood and death, *in time*.[7] In this chapter, I too apply this perspective of using liminality in time by elaborating my ethnographic research findings in the Taipei Dance Circle (the TDC) in Taiwan.

A DANCE TROUPE IN THE GAP

The TDC was founded in 1984 by Shaw-Lu Liu and his wife Wang-Jung Yang. Until Shaw-Lu Liu studied for a master's degree in dance at the Tisch School of the Arts in New York between 1990 and 1992, the troupe was in an initial stage in which it had not discovered its unique aesthetic feature. During his time in the United States, Shaw-Lu Liu came up with the idea of dancing in oil because of how he saw sweat changing the friction between the floor and the dancer's body. On returning to Taiwan, he started experimenting with this oil dance with his dancers. After trying out various types of oil (including olive and cooking) Shaw-Lu Liu and the dancers decided on baby oil because of its particular scent and consistency.

Between 1994 and 2007, a number of famous works (including *Olympics, Ode to a Paramecium, Black Tide, Flow,* and *Of Man and Object*) were released and the TDC toured around the world (including to Tokyo, New York, Germany, Australia, Prague, France, San Francisco, Canada, Singapore, Vietnam, and Korea). This was the golden age of the TDC. Subsequently, from 2007 to 2014, Shaw-Lu Liu experienced a cancer diagnosis and then a struggle with illness and eventually death. His death also brought about an uncertain future for the TDC.

In August 2016, and therefore after Shaw-Lu Liu had passed away, I began my fieldwork in the TDC. To honor Liu's last words about keeping the troupe going, his wife Wang-Jung Yang had taken on the leadership and was work-ing with the remaining dancers. In 2015, she had invited two choreographers, Cheng-Chieh Yu and Wen-Chi Su, along with the sound artist Mark van Tongeren, to create the performance *Lending Ear to Dance, Eye to Sound,* as a tribute to Shaw-Lu Liu in the year after his death. In 2016, the dancers choreographed themselves for the performance *Golden Era.* Nevertheless, because of a lack of government funding, by August 2016 they were facing a financial crisis. My fieldwork lasted for thirteen months, from August 2016 to September 2017, and finished after I had participated in the company's latest work, *Floating Horizons.*

In order to study a troupe that has lost its leader, and during its most dif-ficult time, a series of ontological questions became my research puzzles. What is a dance troupe and what is becoming a dancer in such a situation? Generally, a dance troupe not only is sustained by a group of people but also changes over time. People joined and left this company over its three decades; the TDC is a process in time. In particular, in this special state of losing an important leader I was not able to witness the criteria of kinesthesia with regard to the dancers' bodily training under Shaw-Lu Liu's supervision, even though the members had carried on working under the TDC name. Thus, apart from discussing the basic idea of "changing,"," it is necessary to seek a more analytical concept—liminality—to describe the situation of the TDC after the loss of its leader.

LIMINALITY, SOCIAL DRAMA, AND THE LIMINAL BECOMING

Inspired by Wilhelm Dilthey (1833–1911), Victor Turner took the standpoint of anthropology of experience and developed the processual analysis by using the concepts of liminality, social drama, and the ritual process. As sociologist, anthropologist, and social theorist Arpad Szakolczai suggests in "Liminality and Experience: Structuring Transitory Situations and Transformative Events,"," unlike Immanuel Kant and his followers who treat human experience as a series of chaotic and random things, Dilthey's viewpoint is that experience has a structure of its own. By following Dilthey's perspective, van Gennep and Turner develop the structure of lived experience further by discovering the sequential order of a rite of passage.[8]

According to van Gennep, the rites of passage have three stages: rites of separation (pre-liminal), transition rites (liminal), and rites of incorporation (post-liminal). These three stages might happen in sequence or come about independently.[9] The rites are given by society so that society as a whole will suffer no discomfort or injury when a person moves from one stage to another.[10] The individual must submit to these rites of passage because this is how society is made possible. Following van Gennep, Turner explores the "liminal state" and establishes his theory in *The Ritual Process: Structure and Anti-Structure*. From Turner's viewpoint, during the liminal period the characteristics of the ritual subject (the "passenger") are ambiguous; they pass through a cultural realm that has few or none of the attributes of either the past or the coming state.[11] In this *becoming* state, the passenger is "out of structure" and does not belong anywhere: "They are betwixt and between the positions assigned and arrayed by law, custom, convention, and ceremonial."[12] Turner termed these individuals "threshold people" and linked liminality to death, being in the womb and the eclipse, solar or lunar. This elaboration of liminal features marks Turner's contribution across a number of areas and becomes an important source for interdisciplinary research.

After publishing *The Ritual Process: Structure and Anti-Structure* in 1969, Turner wrote *Dramas, Fields, and Metaphors: Symbolic Action in Human Society* in 1974, proposing the concept of social drama in processual analysis. In comparison with liminality as an in-between period related to living through experiences, social drama is a concept that concerns the structure of lived experience in a broader time span. To elaborate the relationships between liminality, social drama, and the ritual process, Turner's later work manifests a clearer connection. In the chapter "Experience and Performance: Towards a New Processual Anthropology" in his 1985 book *On the Edge of the Bush: Anthropology as Experience*, Turner presented his decision to build life and the experience of life into any disciplined account of human affairs.[13] The reason for this can be seen in his 1986 book *The Anthropology of Performance*. From Turner's viewpoint, sociological and anthropological functionalism aims to set out the conditions of social equilibrium among the components of a social system at a given time and "cannot deal with meaning which always involves retrospection and reflexivity, a past, a history."[14] Thus, following Dilthey, Turner chooses to value the concept of *Erlebnis* ("lived through," an experience). He adopts Rudolf A. Makkreel's translation and interpretation as presented in *Dilthey: Philosopher of the Human Studies*:

> *Erlebnis* is truly temporal and yet it contains a dynamic structural unity which allows the momentary value of the present to become a meaningful presence. [. . .] *Erlebnis*, when interpreted as a "presence," is "able to structure life without fixing it." A tension is set up in any given experience between the determinate character of what is held to be the past—regarded as a source of the reality of the present—and the indeterminacy of the future, which "keeps open the possibilities in relation to which the significance of *Erlebnis* will change and makes it subject to reinterpretation."[15]

To aid comprehension of the meaning of *Erlebnis*, Turner also includes Richard Harvey Brown and Stanford M. Lyman's interpretation from their volume entitled *Structure, Consciousness and History*. Brown and Lyman suggest that *Erlebnis* is not "merely experience . . . but the involvement in, the lived experience of, some whole unit of meaning—as, for example, a work of art, a love affair, a revolution."[16] From this interpretation, Turner links the concept with his idea of social drama; an *Erlebnis* is a social drama. In *Dramas, Fields, and Metaphors: Symbolic Action in Human Society*, Turner defines social drama as "units of aharmonic or disharmonic social process, arising in conflict situations."[17] It comprises four phases: breach, crisis, reflexivity (redressive process), and reintegration. Breach means breaking the rules and crisis is the effects of this first phase. The third phase is the most important because it brings about "the ritual process," which opens up the possibilities for the unknown and uncertain future through a liminal state. Finally, this chaos ends in the fourth phase, which signifies a new beginning.[18] Examples of social drama presented by Turner in *The Anthropology of Performance* are political events such as the American Civil War, the American and French Revolutions, the Jacobite rebellions of 1715 and 1745, and the Mexican Insurgencia of 1810.[19]

By following Turner's concept of social drama, more recent literature continues to explore the liminal character of political revolutions, such as the studies of the 2011 events in Egypt and Tunisia. The anthropologist Mark Allen Peterson points out how the Egyptian revolution started from a carefully orchestrated protest on National Police Day and transformed into a disorganized march against the regime.[20] Also, in Bjørn Thomassen's book chapter "Liminal Politics: Towards an Anthropology of Political Revolutions," van Gennep's idea of "public liminality" is used to describe rituals in public places—how urban squares stimulate crowd formation and let revolutions happen.[21] Both these case studies reflect Turner's theory about social drama and the ritual process by verifying empirical data. Peterson suggests that a basic difference between rituals and social drama is that the latter starts from an unexpected and out-of-control event while the former are rooted in a liminal state under the control of a wider social context.[22] Similarly, Thomassen notes two differences when applying liminality to large-scale situations: (1) the future is inherently unknown and (2) there are no real masters of ceremony because everyone is a layperson.[23] To summarize, both authors point out that the important feature of revolutions is the unexpected beginning (breach) and ending (reintegration).

Coming back to my own research, I agree with these notions because they were detected in my fieldwork experience. Although the present study is not of a political event, the concept of social drama can still be applied to describe the situation being examined. Figure 6.1, which comes from Turner's 1985 book *On the Edge of the Bush: Anthropology as Experience*, shows the relationship between social drama and the ritual process. I created a framework for my PhD thesis by adjusting this model.[24] If we locate the TDC in time and display the events that occur in a particular period, we can understand why this dance troupe is a changing process. As figure 6.2 demonstrates, in the first phase Shaw-Lu Liu's death is the breach that breaks the order. He was the TDC's founder, choreographer, artistic director, and decision-maker; after his death, this important role was missing. Next, this breach produced a financial crisis: the cultural authorities cut the funding and made it more difficult for the TDC to survive. In the third phase, members sought alternative ways to continue their careers and keep the troupe going; they collaborated with other choreographers or choreographed by themselves. During this time, the aesthetic and kinesthetic attentions were gradually changed. As my fieldwork was carried out during the final stage of the TDC, from August 2016 to September 2017, what I experienced was the period of most drastic change for the troupe in the areas of kinesthesia and community. Some members

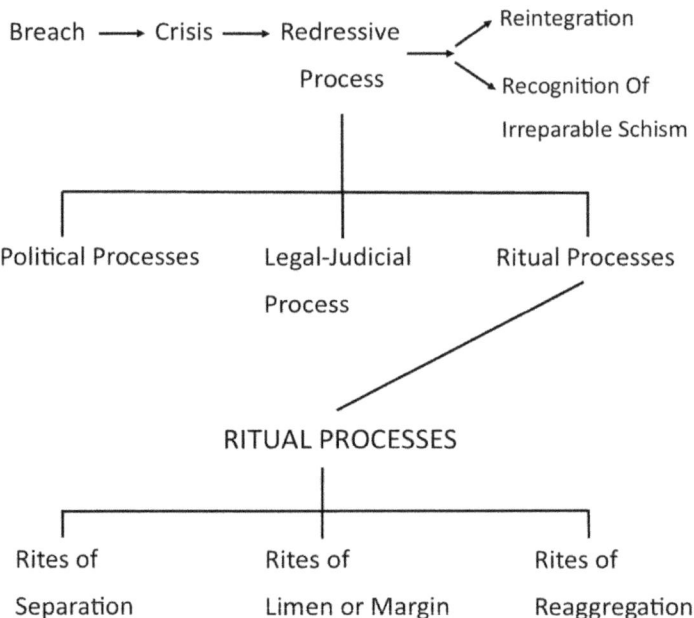

Figure 6.1   The Relationship between Social Drama and the Ritual Process. *Source*: Made by Yu-Chun Chen following Victor Turner (1985).

left or developed new life plans and the kinesthetic attentions were reformed under the leadership of Cheng-Chieh Yu.

In the social drama of the TDC, I replace the ritual process with "liminal becoming" due to the diverse possible applications of the concept of ritual in ritual studies. In "The Ambiguities of Rituals: Introduction," the social anthropologists Jon Henrik Ziegler Remme and Keir Martin point out that rituals contain inherent aspects of uncertainty and indeterminacy even when they offer order, differentiation, and determinacy.[25] These ambiguities mean that the features of rituals are debatable. Thus, I use "liminal becoming" instead to emphasize the liminal features of the ritual process. From this viewpoint, the liminal becoming of the TDC in this redressive process is to struggle and to find alternative ways of solving the problems created by the loss of its leader. The individuals involved lived in the present and waited for miracles, at a time when the future was uncertain. Although the fourth phase—reintegration—comes after the ritual process, there is no particular phase after the state of liminal becoming. From figure 6.2, it can be seen how the TDC passed through the rites of liminality in three dimensions: body, community,

Figure 6.2 *Ode to a Paramecium* **Choreographed by Shaw-Lu Liu in 1998.** *Source*: ©1998 Taipei Dance Circle (Provided by Wang-Jung Yang) / Photo by Ming-Hsun Lee.

and performance. First, the transition of kinesthetic attentions manifests the liminality across dancers' bodies. From the focus on cross and teamwork to the attentions of the head, the spine and individual creativities, the different social formation between individuals and the institution emerged. Second, in the community dimension, the research findings show how a group was gradually changed by an individual's life during this liminal period. Finally, the different performances during these three years reflect different realities after the loss of its leader, echoing the notion that arts are a form through which to express human experiences. More importantly, and different from Turner's framework, I have not included the fourth phase (reintegration) in this figure because the TDC practically stopped working after releasing *Floating Horizons*. If the financial crisis had been resolved, we might have seen a new stage after 2017, but there was no chance of this. In the next two sections, I elaborate the dimension of community in the liminal becoming of the TDC by discussing the ethnographic findings from my fieldwork.

FLOATING SENSE OF BELONGING

After Shaw-Lu Liu's death, the TDC began an alternative collaboration with two choreographers, Cheng-Chieh Yu and Wen-Chi Su, and the sound artist Mark van Tongeren, leading to the performance *Lending Ear to Dance,*

Eye to Sound in 2015. The dancers started learning to work with different performing artists whereas they had previously followed only Shaw-Lu Liu. In 2016, they themselves choreographed the performance *Golden Era*, which was also their first time taking control of everything. As with the idea of the ambiguities of rituals I discussed earlier, these efforts seek to reorder reality but also to bring about new experiences. The dancers might have liked these changes, or they might not. When the crisis—financial interruption because of the government-funding cuts—occurred, a more difficult time emerged and presented a challenge to the continuation of the dance troupe.

The beginning of my fieldwork in the TDC was also the time when Wang-Jung Yang informed all the dancers that they ought to find part-time jobs because she could no longer afford their salaries. In these circumstances, the youngest dancer left to take on a full-time job; only Ben, Kai, and Fon stayed in the troupe. Previously, the TDC's dancers had earned full-time salaries and practically all of them always came to practice from Monday to Friday. They spent a lot of time together and had a strong sense of community. By comparison, their having part-time jobs scattered this shared timetable and produced multiple and uncertain ones, which required more negotiation.

Both Fon, who joined the TDC in 2011, and Kai told me that their identity was that of dancers in a professional troupe rather than that of freelancers or part-time dancers. Fon said, "If you treat a performance as piecework you get away after practising; you cannot build a real relationship with other members or do a great work" (fieldnotes, September 5, 2016). Similarly, Kai shared her feelings with me:

> Being a dancer is not a job between a boss and a member of staff; it is based on his/her aspiration. Now, the thing that is most different from how it was in the past is that I cannot rely on any choreographer because they leave after finishing a performance. Before, Liu was like our father. In the past, we stayed in the troupe for a long time every day; sometimes we had bad tempers or strange behaviour. He could accept everything. (Fieldnotes, October 17, 2016)

For Fon and Kai, this sense of belonging is an important element of being a dancer in the TDC. Through their daily routines and the practice led by Shaw-Lu Liu and Wang-Jung Yang, they had already become "a kind of person" in the group. Thus, their grief at losing their leader not only reveals how they miss those days of the past but also reflects their anxiety in the present. At one of the classes during the choreography camp in 2016, Kai said that she was worried about the TDC's current status: "I think we lose something when practising. During the last choreography camp, we could not get people to stay here. We wanted them to stay, but we did not know how to do that" (transcription, November 24, 2016).

The TDC was a group that formed dancers' identities and made them become "dancers of the TDC" under the leadership of Shaw-Lu Liu. His death as a turning point caused this stable world and the relationships between individuals and the institution to disintegrate. For the dancers who were left behind, so to speak, their adaptation became an existential issue. They faced the question "'Who are we?" when defining themselves as dancers.

BEN'S WITHDRAWAL

The new collaboration after the loss of its leader is related to the dancers' life events. In September 2016, Ben announced that he could not cope with the situation anymore and might leave the troupe in several months' time. We asked him why: "There is no money! How can it continue?" (fieldnotes, September 19, 2016). During the following months, he still came to practice and rehearse. Then, on March 6, 2017, after taking a nap in the afternoon, he suddenly told me that he had decided to leave the TDC and find a full-time job. In contrast to Kai and Fon, since August 2016 Ben had not been able to find a part-time job and had been suffering financial pressures. Furthermore, he had a family, with two children to raise, and his mother had been diagnosed with cancer. Thus, he told everyone that he would be leaving after touring the *Golden Era* performance in April. For this reason, he did not join in the intensive training in March led by Cheng-Chieh Yu, but he did pop into one of the classes. One day in April, I asked him whether he still liked dancing, after staying with the troupe for over three decades. He said that he did, but that he was aging: "I cannot dance like before, when I was young. In particular, carrying people is becoming very difficult" (fieldnotes, April 6, 2017). The troupe held a farewell party for him, but he still sometimes visited Art Space 71 when he was passing by.

KAI'S PREGNANCY

Along with Ben's departure, Kai's pregnancy also facilitated the new collaboration. In December 2016, she announced that she was three months' pregnant and would give birth in July 2017. In order to make the tours of *Golden Era* run smoothly, she asked her good friend and ex-TDC dancer Ying to take over her part. During the choreography of *Floating Horizons* in 2017, she still came to Art Space 71 as often as possible to practice or to help the others. Kai's pregnancy was not an accident but one of her life projects. When I met her, she was almost forty years old. She had tried for a baby before but had had a miscarriage. As a female, "being a dancer" sometimes conflicts with the identity of "being a mother." When Kai's identity of "being a dancer in the TDC" was gradually being challenged by the institution's liminal status, it was possible for the other aspiration in her life to more easily take precedence.

THE NEW COLLABORATION IN *FLOATING HORIZONS*

The TDC's last piece—*Floating Horizons*—was born in the aforementioned situation. The idea of recruiting different dancers for a performance corresponds with Wang-Jung Yang's views about running a dance troupe. Wang-Jung Yang believes that performance is the key element in keeping a troupe alive. Life in the theater is all about continuing to plan for the future. Therefore, after discussing the idea, Cheng-Chieh Yu and Wang-Jung Yang both invited their students from outside the TDC to take part in *Floating Horizons* in 2017. New members Lin, Wen, and Zi who had graduated from the Department of Dance at Taipei National University of the Arts were recruited by Cheng-Chieh Yu while Yi, invited by Wang-Jung Yang, had graduated from the Department of Dance at National Taiwan University of the Arts (table 6.1).

In this project, the outside dancers invited by Cheng-Chieh Yu and Wang-Jung Yang formed the majority, producing a different situation from that which had existed before. As can be seen in the table above, Lin, Wen and Zi all share a common background at Taipei National University of the Arts, with Lin and Wen both gaining their bachelor's degrees from the Department of Dance there. Before joining the project, they had taken Cheng-Chieh Yu's classes and had a greater understanding than others of her thoughts on dance. They were elegant and agile, with highly technical physical abilities. Of these "outsiders," Lin was the only dancer who could do a handstand like Fon, while Wen had a very flexible waist and could bend over backward all the way to the ground. Zi came from the Department of Finance at the National Taiwan University but she had taken courses in the Department of Dance at the University of Oregon as an exchange student and was also in the Legend Lin Dance Theatre for a year.

Yi and Fon were relatively different from these three dancers. Yi was neither Cheng-Chieh Yu's student nor an expert in baby-oil dance while Fon was the only dancer who had been trained by Shaw-Lu Liu. Yi was invited by Wang-Jung Yang, and she was working as a freelancer on four different performances during this time. For Fon, although the production of the performance was under the name of the TDC, she had to work with four dancers who were not familiar to her and this was completely different from her previous experiences in the company. Kai joined the rehearsals at the last minute. When choreography started in June 2017, she was close to her expected delivery date so could practise only limited movements. Also, Cheng-Chieh Yu did not assign her any

Table 6.1   The Background of the Dancers in Floating Horizons Made by Yu-Chun Chen

Lin	Graduated from the Department of Dance, Taipei National University of the Arts, BA. Invited by Cheng-Chieh Yu.
Wen	Studying MA in the Department of Dance, Taipei National University of the Arts. Invited by Cheng-Chieh Yu.
Zi	Studying MA in the Department of Dance, Taipei National University of the Arts. Invited by Cheng-Chieh Yu. Came from a non-formal dance background.
Yi	Graduated from the Department of Dance, National Taiwan University of the Arts, BA. Invited by Wan-Jung Yang.
Fon	Graduated from the Department of Dance, National Taiwan University of the Arts, BA. **Dancer in the TDC**.
Kai	Graduated from the Department of Dance, Folkwang Universität der Künste, Germany, MA. **Dancer in the TDC**.

tasks in the performance. After giving birth on July 26, Kai rested for a month and was then recruited by Cheng-Chieh Yu during the last week of August. She was assigned a character who held a camera to film Lin's solo in the *Walking under the water* section and during the dance on the baby-oil plastic sheet in the second half of the piece. She also simply walked along the edge of the stage in some sections as an observer watching the performance.

Due to the project-oriented nature of *Floating Horizons*, the participants had different timetables and this made it difficult for them all to gather together. Cheng-Chieh Yu once joked about this situation to express her annoyance. She said: 'It is not *Floating Horizons*; it is *Floating Dancers*!."' Almost every dancer had a part-time job outside the project or was participating in other performances at the same time. Under these conditions, Cheng-Chieh Yu's strategy was to let them practise in small groups, in pairs or alone, and then to reorganize these fragments later. In the whole piece, only three sections require five dancers to practise together, with the rest being small collaborations or solos. It can be seen how the choreography was influenced by the dancers' different schedules, which established limitations even before the start. Next, I discuss the dimension of body in the liminal becoming of the TDC, before going on to present my conclusion.

DANCING IN THE LIMINAL TIME

The above two sections paint a new picture of the TDC, as old members left and others joined for the production of *Floating Horizons*. More important than these dancer changes was the fact that the new choreographer

Cheng-Chieh Yu experimented with the plastic sheets and created four surfaces (dry floor, dry plastic, baby-oil floor, baby-oil plastic), thus transforming the relationship that had been created in Shaw-Lu Liu's choreography
between dancers' bodies and the slippery floor. Since dancing on these four
surfaces produces different kinds of friction, dancers had to adapt quickly
while performing. (figure 6.3)

In my interview with the head of the TDC, Wang-Jung Yang offered a
precise observation of and a comparison between Shaw-Lu Liu and Cheng-
Chieh Yu's work:

> The spirit of Shaw-Lu Liu's work was the interaction and collaboration among
> people. Dancers pulled, pushed, grabbed, carried, sat and even stood on each
> other's bodies in his work. Cheng-Chieh Yu's collaboration maintains a distance
> via playing with an object. Shaw-Lu Liu seldom used props; Cheng-Chieh Yu
> used plastic and film to integrate the whole piece. (Fieldnotes, August 30, 2017)

In Shaw-Lu Liu's time, the TDC was in a better financial situation and the
dancers had a monthly income. They rehearsed from Monday to Friday and

Figure 6.3 *Ode to a Paramecium* **Choreographed by Shaw-Lu Liu in 1998.** *Source*: by
Ming-Hsun Lee ©1998 Taipei Dance Circle.

were always able to practice together. Thus, Shaw-Lu Liu could create many sections that involved teamwork. For example, one dancer stands on another dancer's back while he/she is crawling on the baby-oil floor; at the same time, a third dancer uses a different posture to support the dancer who is unbalanced. This collaboration requires tacit knowledge among dancers and demands frequent daily practice, which is impossible to achieve with multiple timetables. By contrast, collaborating in small groups and dancing solos in Cheng-Chieh Yu's choreography allows dancers to practice separately and be responsible individually or collectively for carrying out their duties. In *Floating Horizons*, the sections that require five dancers to practice together are all related to playing with the plastic. The collaboration is based on their interacting with this object as a group. Furthermore, *Floating Horizons* as a performance that combines non-baby-oil and baby-oil dance presents a great number of possibilities. The plastic as the "floating horizon" is an important object with which to experiment and to converse with Shaw-Lu Liu. It is also a key object in linking the dancers' collaborations together (figure 6.4).

Therefore, although *Floating Horizons* was produced under the name of the TDC, the dancers, the choreographer, the aesthetic, and the kinesthetic attention of the movement had changed. Liminality in dance is represented by this new experiment with baby-oil dance. The TDC's baby-oil dance was no longer itself; it became an alternative creation based on different thoughts, elements, and content. However, the state of transformation in baby-oil dance remains when it comes to liminality during a performance. As Victor Turner's colleague Richard Schechner points out, "performer training focuses its techniques not on making one person into another but on permitting the performer to act in between identities; in this sense performing is a paradigm of liminality."[26] In other words, during a performance the performer is in a role different from that of his or her daily self. Schechner calls this "the transformation of being, which means that multiple selves coexist in an unresolved dialectical tension."[27]

Just like the process of swimming, baby-oil dance requires a state of transformation that makes dancers go through a certain procedure every time. They change their clothes and put oil-suits on and then take showers after they finish dancing; finally, they put their normal clothes back on again. This is a cycle of being in contact with baby oil and removing it. During this ritual process, the dancers experience a mind–body alteration that is different from their everyday life, even from their dance on the dry floor. With the movements of pull, push, roll, slide, run, jump, fall, and turn, dancers adapt themselves to the sense of slipperiness and develop a distinct mindset. For instance, Zi made a distinction between her kinesthesia when dancing on baby-oil surfaces and when on dry surfaces: "dancing on baby-oil surfaces needs slower kinetic sensation in movements that require a calm mind and body" (fieldnotes,September 2, 2017).

Figure 6.4 *Floating Horizons* **Choreographed by Cheng-Chieh Yu in 2017.** *Source*: ©2017 Taipei Dance Circle (Provided by Wang-Jung Yang) / Photo by Ming-Hsun Lee.

CONCLUSION

The previous sections show the TDC's process of liminal becoming in the dimension of community and body from August 2016 to September 2017. Individuals' life projects deeply influence the collective in this small dance troupe and make it seek alternative ways to keep itself going. In the making of *Floating Horizons*, new members' participation creates a totally different environment from the one that existed before, even though the work is produced under the name of the TDC. During the previous decades, dancers had come and gone. However, Shaw-Lu Liu was alive then and this was treated as a natural occurrence. After his death, the troupe entered a liminal state and these changes should not be viewed simply as changes. Every move is vital and leads to significant consequences. More importantly, the aforementioned discussion also demonstrates how the new collaboration led to different ways of choreographing and presenting a performance. When dancers had different timetables and could not always gather together to practice, the teamwork sections had to be reduced and replaced with sections involving small groups and solos. The making of this performance brings about new experiences for every participant; they were "threshold people" passing through a liminal stage.

To sum up, by adopting the notion of "liminality as experience,"[28] this chapter explores the structure of lived experience through a presentation of the ethnographic findings of my fieldwork. As Szakolczai suggests, "An 'experience' means that once previous certainties are removed and one enters a delicate, uncertain, malleable state, something might happen to one that alters the very core of one's being."[29] The best example of this is "death," as the ultimate interruption in our social life. This is what created the social drama for the TDC and brought about a series of actions and events both individually and collectively in time.

NOTES

1. Mihai Coman, "Liminality in Media Studies: From Everyday Life to Media Events," in *Victor Turner and Contemporary Cultural Performances*, ed. Graham St John (Berghahn Publication, 2008); Daniel Dayan and Elihu Katz, *Media Events: The Live Broadcasting of History* (Cambridge: Harvard University Press, 1992).

2. Paul Spencer, "Introduction: Interpretations of the Dance in Anthropology," in *Society and the Dance: The Social Anthropology of Process and Performance*, ed. Paul Spencer (Cambridge University Press, 1985); Graham St John, "Trance Tribes and Dance Vibes: Victor Turner and Electronic Dance Music Culture," in *Victor Turner and Contemporary Cultural Performance*, ed. Graham St John (Berghahn Publications, 2008).

3. Edith Turner, "Communitas," in *The Encyclopedia of Religious Rituals*, ed. Frank Salamone (Great Barrington, MA: Berkshire, 2004); Tom Driver, *The Magic of Ritual: Our Need for Liberating Rites that Transform Our Lives and Our Communities* (San Francisco: Harper San Francisco, 1992).

4. Mark Allen Peterson, "In Search of Antistructure: The Meaning of Tahrir Square in Egypt's Ongoing Social Drama," in *Breaking Boundaries: Varieties of Liminality*, eds. Agnes Horvath, Bjørn Thomassen, and Harald Wydra (Berghahn Books, 2015); Bjørn Thomassen, *Liminality and the Modern: Living Through the In-Between* (Routledge Publication, 2016).

5. Paul Stoller, "The Parable of the Footbridge: Creativity and Change in the Between," *Anthropology Today* 35, no. 5 (2019): 3.

6. Alfred Schutz, *The Phenomenology of the Social World* (Northwestern University Press, 1967).

7. Arnold van Gennep, *The Rites of Passage*, trans. Monika B. Vizedom and Gabrielle L. Caffee (London: Routledge, 2010), 2–3.

8. Arpad Szakolczai, "Liminality and Experience: Structuring Transitory Situations and Transformative Events," in *Breaking Boundaries: Varieties of Liminality*, eds. Agnes Horvath, Bjørn Thomassen, and Harald Wydra (Berghahn Books, 2018), 16.

9. van Gennep, *The Rites of Passage*, 11.

10. Ibid., 3.

11. Victor Turner, *The Ritual Process: Structure and Anti-Structure* (New York: Aldine de Gruyter, 1969), 94.

12. Ibid., 95.

13. Victor Turner, *On the Edge of the Bush: Anthropology as Experience* (The University of Arizona Press, 1985), 206–7.

14. Victor Turner, *The Anthropology of Performance* (PAJ Publications, 1986), 97.

15. Rudolf A. Makkreel, *Dilthey: Philosopher of the Human Studies* (New Jersey: Princeton University Press, 1979), 389–90 (my emphasis).

16. Richard Harvey Brown and Stanford M. Lyman, eds., *Structure, Consciousness and History* (Cambridge University Press, 1978), 41.

17. Victor Turner, *Dramas, Fields, and Metaphors: Symbolic Action in Human Society* (Ithaca and London: Cornell University Press, 1974), 37.

18. Turner, *On the Edge of the Bush: Anthropology as Experience*, 215–20.

19. Turner, *The Anthropology of Performance,* 91.

20. Peterson, "In Search of Antistructure: The Meaning of Tahrir Square in Egypt's Ongoing Social Drama," 164.

21. Thomassen, *Liminality and the Modern: Living Through the In-Between*, 206.

22. Peterson, "In Search of Antistructure: The Meaning of Tahrir Square in Egypt's Ongoing Social Drama," 176.

23. Thomassen, *Liminality and the Modern: Living Through the In-Between*, 210.

24. Yu-Chun Chen, "'Become and Becoming a Dancer': An Ethnography of the Taipei Dance Circle" (doctoral dissertation, University of Roehampton, 2019), 35.

25. Jon Henrik Ziegler Remme, and Keir Martin, "The Ambiguities of Rituals: Introduction," *Ethnos* (2019): 7.

26. Richard Schechner, *Between Theater and Anthropology* (University of Pennsylvania Press, 1985), 6.

27. Ibid.

28. Szakolczai, "Liminality and Experience: Structuring Transitory Situations and Transformative Events," 16.

29. Ibid., 18.

BIBLIOGRAPHY

Brown, Richard Harvey and Stanford M. Lyman, eds. *Structure, Consciousness and History*. Cambridge University Press, 1978.

Chen, Yu-Chun, "'Become and Becoming a Dancer': An Ethnography of the Taipei Dance Circle." Doctoral dissertation, University of Roehampton, 2019.

Coman, Mihai. "Liminality in Media Studies: From Everyday Life to Media Events." In *Victor Turner and Contemporary Cultural Performances*, edited by Graham St John, 94–108. Berghahn Publication, 2008.

Dayan, Daniel and Elihu Katz. *Media Events: The Live Broadcasting of History*. Cambridge, MA: Harvard University Press, 1992.

Driver, Tom. *The Magic of Ritual: Our Need for Liberating Rites that Transform Our Lives and Our Communities*. San Francisco, CA: Harper San Francisco, 1992.

Makkreel, Rudolf A. *Dilthey: Philosopher of the Human Studies*. Princeton, NJ: Princeton University Press, 1979.

Peterson, Mark Allen. "In Search of Antistructure: The Meaning of Tahrir Square in Egypt's Ongoing Social Drama." In *Breaking Boundaries: Varieties of Liminality*, edited by Agnes Horvath, Bjørn Thomassen, and Harald Wydra, 164–182. Berghahn Books, 2015.

Remme, Jon Henrik Ziegler, and Keir Martin. "The Ambiguities of Rituals: Introduction." *Ethnos* (2019). https://doi.org/10.1080/00141844.2019.1699142.

Schechner, Richard. *Between Theater and Anthropology*. University of Pennsylvania Press, 1985.

Schutz, Alfred. *The Phenomenology of the Social World*. Northwestern University Press, 1967.

Spencer, Paul. "Introduction: Interpretations of the Dance in Anthropology." In *Society and the Dance: The Social Anthropology of Process and Performance*, edited by Paul Spencer, 1–46. Cambridge University Press, 1985.

St John, Graham. "Trance Tribes and Dance Vibes: Victor Turner and Electronic Dance Music Culture." In *Victor Turner and Contemporary Cultural Performance*, edited by Graham St John, 149–173. Berghahn Publications, 2008.

Stoller, Paul. "The Parable of the Footbridge: Creativity and Change in the Between." *Anthropology Today* 35, no. 5 (2019): 3–6.

Szakolczai, Arpad. "Liminality and Experience: Structuring Transitory Situations and Transformative Events." In *Breaking Boundaries: Varieties of Liminality*, edited by Agnes Horvath, Bjørn Thomassen, and Harald Wydra, 11–38. Berghahn Books, 2018.

Thomassen, Bjørn. *Liminality and the Modern: Living Through the In-Between*. Routledge Publication, 2016.

Turner, Edith. "Communitas." In *The Encyclopedia of Religious Rituals*, edited by Frank Salamone, 97–101. Great Barrington, MA: Berkshire/Routledge Religion and Society Series, 2004.

Turner, Victor. *The Ritual Process: Structure and Anti-Structure*. New York: Aldine de Gruyter, 1969.

Turner, Victor. *Dramas, Fields, and Metaphors: Symbolic Action in Human Society*. Ithaca, NY and London: Cornell University Press, 1974.

Turner, Victor. *On the Edge of the Bush: Anthropology as Experience*. The University of Arizona Press, 1985.

Turner, Victor. *The Anthropology of Performance*. PAJ Publications, 1986.

van Gennep, Arnold. *The Rites of Passage*. Translated by Monika B. Vizedom and Gabrielle L. Caffee. London: Routledge, 2010.

Chapter 7

Mormon Polygamy

Liminal or Normative?

Michael Hubbard MacKay

Victor Turner's anthropological work is valued in numerous disciplines. It even made an impact in Mormon Studies and Latter-Day Saint (LDS) history through the work of Lawrence Foster. Using Turner's theories about ritual and liminality as a framework for his historical case studies about marriage and polygamy, Foster writes, "the Mormon experience may in many respects serve as a paradigmatic illustration of such transition states . . . the 'liminal' phase of rites of passage or larger social transitions is especially applicable to the Mormons."[1] Foster's historical work paraleled Turner's theories in which social transition like maturation or marriage places individuals in a liminal state from which they later return to society changed and reintegrated. Turner's model fits LDS nineteenth-century polygamy like an oversized glove, ultimately helpful, but also easily replaced with new theories that fit slightly better. Theories often take on a life of their own when they are used in new contexts. Outside of the ethnographies that developed the theories in the first place, they are used and applied in other case studies or historically relevant examples, but they rarely maintain a costume fit, even if they were intended to be comprehensive. One way of valuing Turner's theories is by carefully using them, expanding them, and in some cases excluding them.

This chapter will briefly examine the long history of the LDS rite of polygamy to contend that liminality was a relevant description but is better understood as normative discourse, even when that discourse is labeled as "liminal." To make this argument using LDS polygamy as a case study, a few foundational points need to be made. First, the postmodern turn in anthropology evokes questions about whether rites can be examined individually, like a single individual's ritual movement into adulthood. The LDS experience of polygamy is hard to understand without a sociological viewpoint, especially since it affected the community so deeply even though upwards of 75 percent of the LDS population at any given moment in the nineteenth century were *not* practicing polygamy. Catherine Bell argues convincingly for the value of practice theory and the idea of ritualization and its relationship to cultural reproduction, instead of independent/individual ritual action. This chapter will examine polygamy at a community level across five decades to chart the relationship between the LDS community and American society in general. This is in contrast with examining polygamy as an individual act bound to the LDS community, which is the way Foster used Turner's theories. As such, it will focus on the tension between the state and religion evoked by disestablishment and nineteenth-century secularism. The site of this tension is also on liberalism's secular forces that oppose abnormal marriage practices and rites, like polygamy. Finally, it will focus on the rite of marriage not on sex, since it is not part of the ritual but rather a characteristic outcome of the ritual. This is important since the state did not have jurisprudence over sex, just marriage.

These preliminaries expand the context and allow ritual to be examined at a higher sociological level and part of an extended timeline. Focusing on the relationship between sex and polygamy has an abrupt end in the 1890s when LDS leaders banned polygamous sexual unions after decades of legal and social battles with the United States. This narrative does not consider that the rite of marriage continued with the caveat that women could still be married to husbands polygamously in the next life. Polygamy was the site of discursive change and by the end of the nineteenth century, the state ended polygamy but it remained a normative discourse within the LDS population. Polygamy enabled LDS to negotiate kinship on earth and after death. The rite was pliable enough that they only ended *living* polygamous marriage, leaving the rite open to continue to perpetuate polygamy after death. As theological as this rite may have been and as uninterested in the theology as the state may have been, it is still a cognizant reality to LDS families well over 100 years later.

This ritual dilemma helps demonstrate that LDS polygamy reveals some of the critiques of Turner's theories, since female liminars found themselves at deeper odds with normal society after their rites of passage and even after polygamy (in mortality) was ended. In fact, Turner idealizes society in the name of stability. In the case LDS polygamy rites, it appears that the idea of reaggregation back into normal society after a liminal stage is better understood as the tensions between the secular and the religious and their normative discourses. By examining the long history of LDS polygamy from the 1840s to the present, this tension will be demonstrated. First, I will examine the current state of polygamy among the LDS population and briefly discuss the politics of examining the topic academically. Then I will turn to the beginning and the ritualization of the polygamy as a rite in Joseph Smith's ministry. In the process, I will argue for the flexibility and process of ritualization for LDS marriage rites then chart the fall of sexual polygamy across the second half of the nineteenth century. I will end this chapter by describing the twentieth-century practice of ritual polygamy and the issues that arise from using Turner's theory of liminality to examine it.

THE PROBLEM OF POLYGAMY

To twenty-first-century LDS, polygamy is pejorative even though their history and genealogies are filled with polygamists. Plural marriages were outlawed well over a century ago and the practice is viewed as wrong and foreign. The paradox lies with the tension that foments around their modern sensibilities that oppose the practice and their explicit defense of its use in nineteenth-century LDS history. They are reticent to embrace or justify polygamy, yet recognition of the tension between it and the normative monogamous practice of marriage may be the only way to understand the nineteenth-century LDS ritual. If one must always understand polygamy as poor behavior, then how could one examine it at face value? Caught in the same dilemma, Pulitzer-prize-winning scholar Laurel Thatcher-Ulrich recently examined Mormon polygamy to highlight its ability to enfranchise women and even empower them in a society dominated by a hierarchical patriarchy. While this seems to justify polygamy, it also embraces modern liberal ideals, considering that Thatcher-Ulrich's feminist writing produced the bumper-sticker-worthy statement, "Well-Behaved Women Seldom Make History." The domestic recesses of society, as her research reveals, show women shaping the contours of society even within polygamy, perhaps elongating their exclusion from nineteenth-century American society.[2] Historian Sarah Pearsall makes sense of American polygamy by demonstrating its broad social impact, writing "Polygamy controversies place us amid major events in early America because such clashes were about the organization and governance not just of house-holds but of societies, nations, and empires." She argues that polygamy was part of the change and formation of "the infrastructure of monogamy" and the foundations of American society.[3] Though this is critical of polygamy, her research reveals that it is a cog in a much broader social machine, excepting that "bad" marriage helped define "good" marriage in America. Thatcher-Ullrich and Pearsall help demonstrate the difficulty of examining nineteenth-century polygamy.

Polygamy's relationship to normative monogamous marriage vilifies it in a secular world that disregards its significance to religion. Its rouge nature makes it potentially more religious and even marks its practitioners as a liminal utopian community set apart outside normative society because of its abnormal practices (one can see the allure to use Turner's theories here). In this way, nineteenth-century LDS polygamy is a counter-religious practice to secularism and a communal rite practiced across the second half of the century. The return to secular society in the early twentieth century is inevitably disappointing to a religiously driven reader, even though it came by way of the dismissal of LDS polygamy, at least in practice.

The choice seems to be between secularism (as the right choice) and polygamy (the wrong choice). Yet, the end of polygamy, starting in the 1890s, stopped the practice of polygamy—well, at least the practice of illegal polygamy. This was the triumph of liberalism to stop multiple LDS women from cohabitating with and marrying one LDS man. Nonetheless, this also ended the female enfranchisement described by Thatcher-Ullrich garnered through this kind of polygamy and exchanged it with a new kind of polygamy that was potentially more dangerous to women and their roles in society. Though men could no longer marry more than one woman in life, polygamy remained as an option for them.

THE RITUALIZATION OF LDS MARRIAGE RITES

It is tempting to make LDS marriage about sex, especially since marriage provided an appropriate space for sex and tried to avoid the "carnality" of sexual relationships outside of marriage in antebellum America. Kathleen Flake argues, "Records show early Mormonism rejecting, over a remarkably short period of time, Christian marriage's traditional role as a defense against carnality."[4] The ritualization of civic marriage in LDS history certainly includes sex and governs it differently, but the rite itself can be seen more holistically in which sex was one part of a complex social-cultural norm of LDS kinship. Flake developed several key points in the ritualization of marriage demonstrating its movement away from the Protestant celebration of marriage as an earthly institution to govern carnality and to a heavenly institution governing kinship networks on earth and in heaven.

The practice of marriage was normative and embodied in the lives of the earliest LDS in antebellum America, and yet they became radicalized in ritual to eventually embrace polygamous marriages. Pierre Bourdieu's ideas help answer how social agents can construct new objects like religious rites, though they do not always or necessarily produce or create these things consciously. Catherine Bell values Bourdieu's theory in the fact that action is not straightforwardly determined by society, nor is it symbolically representing society. Action is not determined but rather objectively dynamic, where an actor is defined by a system of dispositions that not only organize perceptions and classification but also generate parts of the action—like the polygamous part of marriage for LDS. For Joseph Smith, his religious ministry is constructed and structured by normal actions and structures structuring other structures, as Bourdieu would contend, to shape his actions. He not only was part of the reproduction of marriage rites but also used that institution to enable new religious rites of marriage. Catherine Bell relies upon Bourdieu to move from ritual to ritualization by focusing on what is done to action to make it ritual action or religious behavior.[5] In the first decade of LDS polygamy, marriage became eternal/religious, and then complicated social relationships became deeply associated with relational theologies after death and earthly familial and community relationships that polygamy assuaged—or complicated even further.

The first point of movement toward ritualization is transgressive and happens when Joseph Smith elopes, but it is still a fully normative action.[6] Marriage laws and the juridical and governmental control over marriage were systematic structures constantly making demands upon Smith and his community and family. His adult life began with Isaac Hale refusing to give his blessing for him to marry his daughter Emma Hale. Marriage was expected, yet all the structural demands that came with it limited options for them to be married. Marriage laws and culture were given structures that could not be eliminated but instead caused tension and offered shape to his religious life. Their actions were strategic, shifting the intentionality of marriage, by eloping and reproducing the habitus. Even an act of rebellion was still determinate within the habitus but became retrospectively part of the ritualization of an alternative marriage system. Talal Asad would see this as the binary critique of secularism, in which eloping was bad and parental consent for marriage was good.[7] Eloping was both part of the system and acting against the system. Ritualization emerges at this early point as simply action that demonstrates the dynamics of practice, but it was not religious yet given that marriage and marriage ceremonies had not transformed from generic sociocultural practice into concepts in Mormon theology. The secular world of law and marriage worked against the structure of class and culture, Emma's religion, and Joseph Smith's class and family. If eloping was secularism's earliest critique of Smith's marriage practices, polygamy would be its last critique of Joseph Smith's marriage practices, which opens the possibility of liminal spaces like eloping be counternormative measures of power.

As Mormonism grew, Smith created local economies, formed armies, and constructed a lay priesthood as they migrated from New York to Ohio and Missouri. Within his Zion society, he spoke for God. Though Smith had the power to muster an army and organize thousands of antebellum Americans, he had little to no control over one of the most fundamental social building blocks in his society. Legal restrictions and cultural norms stripped the LDSs of control over marriage, divorce, and basic structures of the American society they lived within. Since he was trying to build Zion in America and a society that would consist of God's chosen people (even modern Israel), his lack of control over marriage eventually surfaced. LDS leaders, like Oliver Cowdery and Martin Harris, exhibited some of the earliest signs of struggle, since Cowdery was betrothed and had an additional relationship and Harris had no power to divorce even though he was estranged from his wife. Interestingly, though they were also particularly worried about marriage and the threat *unrighteous* men posed for married *righteous* women. For example, *The Book of Mormon* highlights the problem of monogamous marriage for women because of "the wickedness and abominations of their husbands."[8] Marriage was important under the Mormon theology that embraced a sote-riology in which they were saved as a people, as a nation of Israel. This was particularly important under the idea that one could be adopted into the house of Israel and that a soul could be lost if those who you were attached to choose not to be adopted into Israel. As he built "Zion," he gathered converts who were Gentiles (outsiders or non-LDS) adopted into the house of Israel. But believers also moved to Missouri to convert the Lost Tribes of Israel, the Native Americans, who had recently moved to reservations on the borders of the United States. Smith was creating a community of new relationships, but like his marriage, limits were placed upon his control of civic marriage. They were denied access to the Native Americans by the US government, their land was taken from them in Missouri, and Mormon priests were denied legal authority to perform marriages or obtain marriage licenses by 1835. Society upheld civic and governmental structures that determined the boundaries that Smith was working within and against, but it also allowed him to change marriage. Normative structures also existed because of the possibility of non-normative possibilities, in which Smith could invest in strategies to change marriage at risk of creating bad marriage or religion. The legal structures of marriage were secular and created a secular community, whereas Smith's movements toward a non-civic religious rite for marriage were part of the secular and religious binary.[9] Marrying without a license from the state was transgressive.

The follies of antebellum marriage were structural actions predetermined and given to the LDSs, yet Joseph Smith used those structures to shape other actions and create them into religious action. Before 1835, marriage was not sacramental, in the sense that baptism was for the LDSs. But in 1835, for the first time, Smith made marriage an eternal rite that could *only* be performed by the elders of his church. This is a clear example of when a secular structure was used to create a religious structure, in Bordieuian terms. Because religion was part of the habitus, one can see the civic structure shaping the actions of individuals as that structure shaped the structure of Mormonism. Ritualization began with Joseph and Emma Smith eloping, already demonstrating the tension between the given structure of marriage and their religious lives but then became even more distinct when they fought against the civic structures by making marriage sacramental and under the control of religious authority, not the state. They did not give up on the structure of marriage. They ritualized it.

In the winter of 1835, Joseph Smith made "marriage a locus of its priesthood restorationism and its marriage rite gave women and men rights to access heavenly powers to accomplish divine purposes here and in the hereafter."[10] With civic authority Joseph married Newel Knight and Lydia Goldwaite Bailey on November 24, 1835. Though marriage was not introduced as an essentially sacrament, yet it became a rite that determined that marriages could be preserved into the next life, since it was then identified as an "institution of heaven." In fact, Joseph went on to council the couple that God instituted marriage on earth "in the garden of Eden" to Adam and Eve making it an ancient rite, not just modern. Joseph stated that "it was necessary that [their marriage] be Solemnized by the authority of the everlasting priesthood."[11]

This marriage separated the rite from civic authority by declaring that it had to be done exclusively by LDS authority, marked its ancient origins with Adam and Eve, and assured that marriages lasted after death. Newel's journal entry included that they "received much Instruction from the Prophet concerning matrimony, & what the ancient order of God was, & what it must be again concerning marriage."[12] Joseph was clearly associating marriage with the most ancient marriage rites of Adam and Eve, calling it an "ancient order of God," as if it was like the priesthood which was also an ancient order of God according to Joseph. Newel indicated that this ancient order of marriage needs to be restored and that his marriage marked the beginning, though not the complete fulfillment, of the restoration of the ancient order or marriage. This statement about kinship was a kinship stretching back to Adam and forward into the eternities. Joseph Smith also wrote in his journal that "the ceremony was original with me . . . I pronounced them husband & Wife in the name of God and also the blessings that the lord conferred upon adam & Eve in the garden of Eden."[13] The marriage rites were inseparable from the priesthood and instituted in the beginning, representing a heavenly and eternal principle.

The fact that the new LDS marriage rite emphasized eternal relationships demanded a new kind of flexibility. Marriage was not just to avoid the carnality of humankind, it governed complicated new kinship networks and even the unknown imagined kinship networks of the next life in heaven. This was certainly an empowering idea, but it also added a complexity that required bold new relationships to "seal" or marry families and generations together, one of which was polygamy.

SEALING AND MARRIAGE RITES

The marriage rite introduced in 1835 has had relative stability throughout LDS history. Glimpses of the marriage ceremony of Newel and Lydia marked three primary points of departure: (1) it was done only by LDS authority; (2) it was an ancient rite from Adam; and (3) it sealed couples together for the next life. The next glimpse of the ceremony came in 1842 when Joseph Smith was married to Sara Ann Whitney polygamously. Her father sealed them together in marriage with similar points of emphasis as the 1835 marriage, this time the prayer was recorded in a letter, making the rite explicit. Finally, by 1853, a formalized prayer was published by LDS Apostle Orson Pratt that distilled the principles of LDS marriage rites given before. Though there have been several adjustments throughout the nineteenth and twentieth century, the marriage rite has stayed remarkably similar, never retracting the earliest principles of the rite.

Nonetheless, the sealing or marriage rite has been extremely flexible in its ability to adapt to the needs and desires of LDS kinship networks on earth and imagined networks in heaven. That flexibility ultimately included polygamy. Some of Joseph's earliest polygamous marriages demonstrate this point very well, such as when he married Louisa Beaman (27) who had been a longtime family friend. She had yet to marry and her marriage to Joseph placed her in a line of patriarchal priesthood she had not belonged to before the marriage. This affected not only her status in heaven but also her kinship in Nauvoo. Sisters Zina Diantha Huntington Jacobs (21) and Presendia Huntington Beull (32) were sealed to Joseph next, but they were already married, whereas Joseph's marriage to them was intended to join them with the eternal priesthood that their husbands could not offer them. Fourth was his brother Carlos's widow, Agnes Coolbrith Smith, who would be sealed into the family. Fifth was forty-seven-year-old midwife Patty Bartlett Sessions who was deeply important to the LDS kinship and unlikely to marry.

Marriage rites were powerful. Not just because of the community they created among living LDS, but because it created strong lines of authority connecting back to the ancient prophets and into the eternities in heaven. In fact, the dynastic lines and mortal demands of marriage rites became a major administrative duty of LDS leaders. Heaven and earth became relational, even salvation became relational. Jonathan Stapley argues, "The relationships formed by sealing are the basis for Joseph Smith's understanding of perseverance" or assurance of salvation in the next life. (17) Sealing between spouses also assured that children were in a line of authority that also guaranteed salvation or perseverance. This marked the basic core of the sealing sacrament. Authority of the prophets going back to Adam and through Joseph Smith linked spouses eternally in marriage. But, kinship networks were complicated as seen in Joseph's polygamous relationships and then the supple ritual also allowed for Joseph brother's deceased spouse to be sealed to him. This created a basic kinship network of biologically unrelated LDS families and created a way to negotiate death and secure relationships across the divide between heaven and earth.

Jonathan Stapley has demonstrated that the demands of kinship under the rules of LDS sealing rites constantly rearranged themselves with real-world problems and heavenly worries. (1) At the broadest level, LDS were sealed into a line of patriarchs in a successive line back to Adam. This was the priesthood of God, like a body of ancient patriarchs bound by their order and including their community, a Holy Order of God. This also created a hierarchy on earth in which the living prophets were the link to the ancient prophets. (2) The LDS marriage rites accommodated this network by allowing for adoptions (sealings as children to non-biological parents) into the dynastic structure. Like Sara Ann Whitney's family being sealed to Joseph's family through marriage, Joseph's doctor's family could be adopted to his family too, without a daughter who could be married polygamously to Joseph. Instead, the doctor could be adopted as a son. Wilford Woodruff (a succeeding prophet) explained that he was eventually sealed to hundreds of LDS families by way of adoption. (3) Decades after Joseph's death Woodruff sealed his own father to Joseph Smith, both of whom were dead. Hiram Smith, Joseph's brother, breached this sealing practice very early on and it continues until today. Women who died unmarried were also sealed polygamously to living men. (4) Multiple women were sealed to one man within the priesthood order. Polygamy was a powerful tool for kinship networks and the value of priesthood leaders. Though this created problems, it also attempted to heal social fissures. (5) LDS marriage rites were also about preservation of spousal relationships not just polygamous relationships. (6) Finally, and perhaps, the most important point is LDS marriage rites' secured salvation and kinship salvation (table 7.1).

Table 7.1   The Supple Nature of LDS Marriage Rites

1. Patriarchal Dynasty: Seals generations of Saints through prophets back to Adam.
2. Adoption and Dynasty: Sealing non-biological families to the living prophets.
3. Death and Sealing: Seals individuals posthumously to living spouses.
4. Polygamy: Kinship networks are created through marriage of multiple women to one priesthood leader.
5. Spousal Stability: LDS marriage secured long lasting spousal relationship, lasting beyond mortality.
6. Perseverance: Secures relationships and salvation for loved ones.

These adjustments to the value and use of LDS marriage rites developed over time. They were additions and adjustments not inborn realities from the beginning. LDS polygamy also never developed a one-size-fits-all set of practices. Instead, it was carefully and sometimes uncarefully negotiated, offering freedoms and follies, but constantly formed the LDS demographics and kinships across the nineteenth century. The marriage rite was supple and relevant but eventually ran out of steam in its fight against American secularism and liberalizing tendencies.

POLYGAMY AND ITS DOWNFALL

Working against the normativity of secularism, Smith inculcated polygamy into the religious rites of Mormonism. Marriage was translated to and redefined within Mormon structures, from which it began to determine relationships differently. Marriage stopped being just a civic bond and became an eternal reality for LDS. The concept of eternality established the LDS social structure by means of its reference and maintenance of stability. Terryl Givens explained, "The sealing [marriage rite] . . . is for Latter-day Saints an eternal bond or connection to other human beings, within the kingdom of God."[14] The rite of marriage, as such, could be described as liminal space caught between life on earth and heaven, the space betwixt and between. They believed that the Second Coming was near and would free them from their bondage soon. "Heavenly sociability" of the eternities encouraged marriage as liminal space in which humans glimpsed the eternities with God, given its claim that the network of divine interrelation was built of social connections ritualized by marriage. Turner explained that social transitions included liminality and *communitas* from which social inversion occurred, even the flattening of hierarchical social relationships.[15] In antebellum America, Mormonism pushed against the grain of the democratic religious sensibilities of Protestant America.[16] Turner's theories may have fit better if the Kingdom of God had been established before polygamy was ended, and the practice of polygamy enabled LDS to be safely reintroduced to a heavenly society. But eventually, a secular age was their landing pad.

Lawrence Foster writes, "Less than a decade later, when the main body of the Saints had settled the Great Basin region, plural marriage had become a generally accepted part of Mormon patriarchal family arrangements in the West."[17] Mormon polygamy was publicly practiced and openly discussed, Mormonism in the Great Basin quickly became the quintessential example of what religion was *not* in America. Spencer J. Fluhman argues that Mormonism was treated as a foil against "true American religion" in the eyes of the rest of the populace. He explains,

Anti-Mormons let Polygamy do the lion's share of the work in the various formulations of Mormon foreignness. . . . Where Mormonism itself had borne that burden for decades, polygamy increasingly became the rhetorical battleground for what could be rightly considered religious in American culture.[18]

Peter Coviello goes even further to argue that what makes "early Mormonism properly heretical is its rupture not of some transhistorical 'Christianity' but of *proper* belief as codified under conditions of secularism."[19] Brigham Young was recorded saying,

If I had forty wives in the United States, they did not know it, and could not substantiate it, neither did I ask any lawyer, judge, or magistrate for them. I live above the law, and so do this people.[20]

During this same time period, historian Paul Reeve argues that "Protestants believed Mormons were physically different" and racially suspect. In fact, he explains that Mormonism was Orientalized due to polygamy, relating LDSs with Muslims, Turks, and the Chinese.[21]

Yet, polygamy was nonetheless still a normative discourse and even cultural capital inside LDS society. Like one side of the same coin, they may have been what religion was not, but religion was also being defined by their countervailing position, as Fluhman argues. Polygamy was a socially produced resource used to secure power and improve social and religious status from within. It certainly enfranchised women, but it also acted like a weapon of "symbolic violence" cementing women in lower stations of the society. Bourdieu argues that this kind of symbolic violence is a "coercion which is set up only through the consent that the dominated cannot fail to give the dominator."[22] Moving from structure to performance, the practice of polygamy became the embodied drama that drove a feeling of normative collectiveness.

Brigham Young was a colonizer, an organizer, and determined to gather LDS from around the world to the Great Basin. He declared that polygamy was an eternal principle and it bound them together while keeping others out. He preached,

Monogamy, or restrictions by law to one wife, is not part of the economy of heaven among men. Such a system was commenced by the founders of the Roman Empire . . . and introduced this order of monogamy wherever her sway acknowledged. Thus, this monogamic order of marriage, so esteemed by modern Christians as a whole sacrament and divine institution, is nothing but a system established by a set of robbers.[23]

He perpetuated the difference, in his mind, between the secular and the religious, demanding that polygamy marked the practice and discourse of religion. Polygamy defined and created the LDS community. Never imagining that there would be an end to the practice of polygamy, the symbolic violence was not cognizant in the minds of the polygamists, as a kind of maintenance practice of a normative discourse.

If Mormons had established a liminal space in the Great Basin, marked by the practice of polygamy, manifest destiny and the imperial expansion of the United States eventually consumed that space. Polygamy eventually brought the LDSs into direct conflict with the courts. By the early 1860s, the US government passed laws to stop polygamy among the Mormons. The laws addressed institutionalized liberalism, by campaigning against practices that could potentially hurt women and erode American society. Decades in the courts, fighting against the new laws against polygamy only resulted in the US Supreme Court upholding the laws in 1879. For a decade after the court case, federal officers prosecuted polygamists, imprisoning them, fining them, and seizing Mormon lands.[24] It was not stability that marked the Mormon ritual, it was chaos. Like what Saba Mahmood does with women in Cairo, the normative "liberal assumptions" should be interrogated for their limiting and distorting effects.

The end of polygamy in 1894 brought the dramatic transition of Utah from American territory to statehood in 1896.[25] "Polygamy had knit Mormon communities tightly, while bloodlines and dynastic connections had defined LDS leadership for at least two generations," Fluhman explains. But, "Across the twentieth century, Mormons would less and less view themselves as a peculiar people." Polygamy became a historical digression, a liminal space, in the middle of transition. The Mormon prophet Wilford Woodruff declared "that plural marriage and the practice of adoption was a way of extending kinship lines and building dynastic associations did not follow naturally or logically from Smith's original vision." Polygamy was ended and Mormonism emerged into American society, embracing traditional Western marriage as an eternal system but still intended to create a "heavenly sociability."[26] In part, the transition failed because they were now Americans and because Christ had not returned. Secularism in the United States would be their kingdom.

POLYGAMY DID NOT GO AWAY

When the liberal triumph over polygamy was realized, the marriage rites that secured polygamous relationships were left untouched. The ceremony and ritual were still as efficacious as ever. The civic authority to control marriage in the United States successfully eliminated the practice of polygamy among the LDS, eventually, but they had no interest in their authority stretching beyond mortality. Secularism is a normative project, but its mission is not to make an enemy of religion. Secularism's enemy is defined under the auspices of "bad religion" defined by liberalism's standards. It has no hostility toward religion, nor does it want to replace or create religion. Instead, as a discipline it directed strategies to combat polygamy as bad religion, but left those interests for LDS to decide, when they became theological. The LDS could support polygamy if the marriages were efficacious in the next life, instead of now. They could use the same marriage rites to marry polygamously, as long it was done for someone who was dead, but not to mark a mortal relationship that included sex or cohabitation. Polygamy in this sense was not bad, but polygamy was only bad when it was associated with sex and actual relationships that the civic government controlled. Religion was left free for LDS to negotiate, but that does not mean that men and women were left free from polygamy and its effects theologically.

Just like the LDS marriage rites had adjusted to strengthen and make sense of LDS kinship on earth and in heaven in the nineteenth century, the second half of the twentieth century used heavenly polygamy to satisfy the demand of sealings when someone was divorced or a spouse died. Instead of seeing polygamy as a reaction to the demands of kinship in the nineteenth century, it continued as an operative form of marriage in heaven and the rite of marriage remained the same. This theological point was not just cognitive, it was important enough that the same LDS marriage rituals were done by living members to mark the reality of polygamy in the heavens. Stapley explained "widowers and male divorcees were able to be sealed to subsequent spouses in the temple, a practice that continues to be permitted under church policy today. While lived monogamy is strictly enforced upon penalty of excommunication"[27] (Stapley, 48). This created additional options and possibilities for LDS men but left women in a difficult position when they began negotiating their eternal relationship with spouses and children.

While the flexible nature of LDS marriage rites is clear, it is less flexible for women due to the increasing number of divorces since the second half of the twentieth century. One of the primary issues is that polyandry is prohibited. This made it difficult for women who were sealed to a man who died because they cannot easily be remarried to another man and sealed for eternity. Men in this scenario are just married polygamously, while women must get special permission to enol the first marriage. Another dilemma is the negotiation to determine who their children will be sealed to. Ultimately this causes serious psychological distress and major contention for marriage rites in contemporary LDS culture. The prophets of this generation are also not free from these dilemmas as their spouses die and they are remarried too.

An LDS poet and writer, Carol Lynn Pearson reached out to thousands of LDS men and women to learn about their experiences in 2015. In her book *The Ghost of Eternal Polygamy,* she tells their stories with passion and resolve to end polygamy, again. She writes,

> In our small Mormon universe, I submit that the first large step toward that better day . . . the first large step has got to be disassembling the paradigm of polygamy. That pattern functions as a unique and sad overlay to ordinary, run-of-the-mill patriarchy, and seeps through as a powerful glue that holds firmly in place the fiction of male centrality.[28]

Her impassioned plea is not completely dissimilar to the secular strategies instigated to end polygamy in the nineteenth century, yet secularism's inability to imagine the impact of theological realities in the real world make the laws, rules, and standards of Western liberalism seem more like fiction. Secularism had the power to control and end the cohabitation of polygamists, yet it did not have the character or sensibilities to notice the devastating realities of theology's potentially devastating effects.

CONCLUSION

The failure of polygamy marked the taming of Mormonism through the normative power of secularism in nineteenth-century America. Turner's anthropological theory is less helpful on this account since society could not be idealized nor could all liminars return satisfied or in alignment with society. The liminal space defined by polygamy was no longer ritually efficacious and the entirety of the dynastic structure of heaven and earth was rearranged to fit a secularly certified monogamous family structure by the end of the nineteenth century. Ritual marriage became a place to seal families together, mimicking secular family structures, instead of extending the prophetic and dynastic lines back to God. LDS priesthood became at least partially marked by the virtues of liberal individualism. Jonathan Stapley described this shift as going from a priesthood community bound on earth and heaven (cosmological priesthood) to an individualized priesthood in which leaders wield the power of God in their own hands and monogamous marriages are normative.[29]

Once LDS ended polygamy, they did not rejoin normal society. Reintegration could have happened in this case as LDS increasingly aligned with religious norms in the United States, but it didn't happen that way. Critics of Turner, like Renato Renaldo, explain that reintegration in society is utopian and ahistorical since it idealizes normal society or in this sense the secular world.[30] This critique makes sense in nineteenth-century Mormon polygamy since a return to the secular world was hardly the goal of the LDS community. Polygamy was a ritual system that fostered the establishment of the Kingdom of God on earth and its failures were the realization of the power of secularism to identify and demand "good" religion. Furthermore, the secular strategies were so uninterested in theology that polygamy continued, this time introducing problems in kinship.

In this account of polygamy, social and cultural reproduction explain what happened, with at least some sense of reality, challenging the sense of radical change. The tension between radical change and social and cultural reproduction in ritual polygamy demonstrates that the tension itself is more realistic than the two positions taken individually or separately from each other. Rituals can represent radical change like the change from civic marriage to polygamous rites in Mormonism, yet the strong arm of normative secular forces still shaped LDS marriage rites in undeniable ways and the LDS apologies for nineteenth-century polygamy carry on into the twenty-first century. The negotiation granted by Bourdieuian theory and Catherine Bell are relevant to social and cultural reproduction to explain LDS polygamy in America. Ritual did not create a liminal space to negotiate change and reintegration. Instead, the ritual was just another normative discourse, even if it was in opposition to the normalizing secular discourse in America. The LDS rite of marriage never changed but the normativity of the rite's impact addressed kinship relationships in heaven and on earth, even though it was disciplined in its ability to govern kinds of sex in marriage by the secular state.

NOTES

1. Lawrence Foster, *Religion and Sexuality: The Shakers, the Mormons, and the Oneida Community* (Urbana, IL: University of Illinois Press, 1984), 166.

2. Lauren Thatcher-Ullrich, *A House Full of Females: Plural Marriage and Women's Rights in Early Mormonism, 1835–1870* (Vintage, 2018).

3. Sarah Pearsall, *Polygamy: An Early American History* (Yale University Press, 2019).

4. Kathleen Flake, "The Development of Early Latter-day Saint Marriage Rites, 1831-53," *The Journal of Mormon History* 41, no. 1 (2015): 78–9.

5. Catherine Bell, *Ritual Theory, Ritual Practice* (New York: Oxford University Press, 1992), 92.

6. Samuel Brown, *In Heaven as it is on Earth: Joseph Smith and the Early Mormon Conquest of Death* (New York: Oxford University Press, 2012). Samuel Brown analyzed Smith's life in terms of how death and his existential fears led to Mormon rituals, temples, scripture, community, and salvation. Death was the motivating factor caught up in the complicated cultural milieu of antebellum America.

7. Talal Asad, *Genealogies of Religion: Discipline and Reasons of Power in Christianity and Islam* (Baltimore: Johns Hopkins University Press, 1993).

8. Book of Mormon, Jacob 2:32.

9. Talal Asad, *Formations of the Secular: Christianity, Islam, Modernity* (Stanford: Stanford University Press, 2003).

10. Flake, "The Development of Early Latter-day Saint Marriage Rites, 183153," 78–9.

11. *Joseph Smith Papers, Journals*, 1:110.

12. Michael Hubbard MacKay and William Hartley, eds., *Rise of the Church of Jesus Christ of Latter-day Saints: The Journals and History of Newel Knight* (Provo: RSC and Deseret Book, 2019).

13. *Joseph Smith Papers, Journals*, 1:110.

14. Terryl Givens, *Feeding the Flock* (Oxford: Oxford University Press, 2017), 181.

15. Victor Turner, *The Ritual Process: Structure and Anti-Structure* (Ithaca, NY: Cornell University Press, 1969), 94–130.

16. Nathan O. Hatch, *The Democratization of American Christianity* (New Haven, CT: Yale University Press, 1989) compared against Amanda Porterfield, *Conceived in Doubt: Religion and Politics in the New American Nation* (Chicago: University of Chicago Press, 2012).

17. Foster, *Religion and Sexuality*, 182.

18. Spencer Fluhman, *"A Peculiar People": Anti-Mormonism and the Making of Religion in Nineteenth-century America* (Chapel Hill: The University of North Carolina Press, 2012), 123.

19. Peter Coviello, *Makes Themselves Gods: Mormons and the Unfinished Business of American Secularism* (Chicago: Chicago University Press, 2019), 138.

20. Brigham Young, in *Journal of Discourses*, 1:361.

21. Paul Reeve, *Religion of a Different Color: Race and the Mormon Struggle for Whiteness* (New York: Oxford University Press, 2015), 3, 52–5.

22. Pierre Bourdieu, *Pascalian Meditations*, trans. Richard Nice (Standford: Stanford University Press, 2000), 170.

23. Brigham Young, in *Deseret News*, 6 August 1862.

24. Sarah Barringer Gordon, *The Mormon Question: Polygamy and Constituional Conflict in Nineteenth-Century America* (Chapel Hill: University of North Carolina Press, 2002).

25. Thomas Alexander, *Things in Heaven and Earth: The Life and Times of Wilford Woodruff, a Mormon Prophet* (Salt Lake City: Signature Books, 1991), 261–87; Armand L. Mauss, *The Angel and the Beehive: The Mormon Struggle with Assimilation* (Urbana: University of Illinois Press, 1994), 21–32.

26. Fluhman, *"A Peculiar People,"* 146.

27. Jonathan Stapley, *The Power of Godliness: Mormon Liturgy and Cosmology* (New York: Oxford University Press, 2018), 48.

28. Carol Lynn Pearson, *The Ghost of Eternal Polygamy: Haunting the Hearts and Heaven of Mormon Women and Men* (Pivot Point Books, 2016), 176.

29. Stapley, *The Power of Godliness*, 17.

30. Renato Rosaldo, *Culture and Truth: The Remaking of Social Analysis* (Boston: Beacon Press, 1993), 96–97.

BIBLIOGRAPHY

Alexander, Thomas. *Things in Heaven and Earth: The Life and Times of Wilford Woodruff, a Mormon Prophet.* Salt Lake City, UT: Signature Books, 1991.

Asad, Talal. *Genealogies of Religion.* Baltimore, MD: Johns Hopkins University Press, 1993.

Blythe, Christopher. "The Council of Fifty Minutes and Latter Day Saint Studies on Succession." *John Whitmer Historical Association* 37, no. 1 (Spring/Summer 2017): 83–94.

Bourdieu, Pierre. *Pascalian Meditations.* Translated by Richard Nice. Stanford, CA: Stanford University Press, 2000.

Bringhurst, Newell and Craig L. Foster, eds. *The Persistence of Polygamy: Joseph Smith and the Origins of Mormon Polygamy.* Independence, MO: John Whitmer Books, 2010.

Bringhurst, Newell G., Craig L. Foster, and Carmon B. Hardy, eds., *The Persistence of Polygamy: From Joseph Smith's Martyrdom to the First Manifesto, 1844–1890.* Independence, MO: John Whitmer Books, 2013.

Compton, Todd. *Sacred Loneliness: The Plural Wives of Joseph Smith.* Salt Lake City, UT: Signature Books, 1997.

Coviello, Peter. *Makes Themselves Gods: Mormons and the Unfinished Business of American Secularism.* Chicago, IL: Chicago University Press, 2019.

Daynes, Kathryn. *More Wives Than One: Transformation of the Mormon Marriage System.* Urbana, IL: University of Illinois Press, 2001.

Flake, Kathleen. "The Development of Early Latter-day Saint Marriage Rites, 1831–53." *The Journal of Mormon History* (2015): 78–79.

Flake, Kathleen. "Ordering Antinomy: An Analysis of Early: Mormonism's Priestly Offices, Councils, and Kinship." *Religion and American Culture: A Journal of Interpretation* 26, no. 2 (2016): 141–142.

Fluhman, Spencer. *"A Peculiar People": Anti-Mormonism and the Making of Religion in Nineteenth-Century America.* Chapel Hill, NC: The University of North Carolina Press, 2012.

Foster, Lawrence. *Religion and Sexuality: The Shakers, the Mormons, and the Oneida Community.* Urbana, IL: University of Illinois Press, 1984, Illini Books edition.

Foster, Lawrence. *Women, Family, and Utopia: Communal Experiments of the Shakers, the Oneida Community, and the Mormons.* Syracuse, NY: Syracuse University Press, 1992.

Givens, Terryl L. *Feeding the Flock: The Foundations of Mormon Thought: Church and Praxis.* New York: Oxford University Press, 2017.

Gordon, Sarah Barringer. *The Mormon Question: Polygamy and Constituional Conflict in Nineteenth-Century America.* Chapel Hill, NC: University of North Carolina Press, 2002.

Hales, Brian C. *Joseph Smith's Polygamy,* 3 vols. Salt Lake City, UT: Greg Kofford Books, 2013.

Hardy, B. Carmon. *Doing the Works of Abraham: Mormon Polygamy, Its Origin, Practice, and Demise.* Norman, OK: Arthur H. Clark, 2007.

Hatch, Nathan O. *The Democratization of American Christianity.* New Haven, CT: Yale University Press, 1989.

Kern, Louis J. *An Ordered Love: Sex Roles and Sexuality in Victorian Utopias—The Shakers, the Mormons, and the Oneida Community.* Chapel Hill, NC: University of North Carolina Press, 1981.

MacKay, Michael Hubbard. *Prophetic Authority: Democratic Hierarchy and the Mormon Priesthood.* Urbana, IL: University of Illinois Press, 2020.

Mauss, Armand L. *The Angel and the Beehive: The Mormon Struggle with Assimilation.* Urbana, IL: University of Illinois Press, 1994.

Pearsall, Sarah M. S. *Polygamy: An Early American History.* New Haven, CT and London: University of Yale Press, 2019.

Porterfield, Amanda. *Conceived in Doubt: Religion and Politics in the New American Nation.* Chicago, IL: University of Chicago Press, 2012.

Reeve, Paul. *Religion of a Different Color: Race and the Mormon Struggle for Whiteness.* New York: Oxford University Press, 2015.

Smith, Merina. *Revelation, Resistance & Mormon Polygamy: The Introduction and Implementation of the Principle: 1830–1853.* Logan, UT: Utah State University Press, 2013.

Stapley, Jonathan. *The Powers of Godliness.* New York: Oxford University Press, 2018.

Turner, Victor. "Betwixt and Between: The Liminal Period in Rites de Passage." In *The Forest of Symbols: Aspects of Ndembu Ritual*, edited by Victor Turner. Ithaca, NY: Cornell University Press, 1967.

Turner, Victor. *The Ritual Process: Structure and Anti-Structure.* Ithaca, NY: Cornell University Press, 1969.

Van Wagoner, Richard. *Mormon Polygamy: A History,* 2nd edition. Salt Lake City, UT: Signature Books, 1992.

Walker, Ronald W. "Six Days in August: Brigham Young and the Succession Crisis of 1844." In *A Firm Foundation: Church Organization and Administration*, edited by Arnold Garr and David Whittaker, 161–196. Provo, UT: Religious Studies Center, BYU, 2011, and Deseret Book, 2011.

WITHIN AND WITHOUT

LIMINALITY AND DIALOGUE

Chapter 8

Liminal Dialogue

Solomon Ibn Verga's Tale of Ephraim Ibn Sanjo and King Pedro I of Aragon

Eric Ziolkowski

The German-born Dutch-French anthropologist and folklorist Arnold van Gennep (1873–1957) and his younger Russian contemporary, the philosopher and literary theorist Mikhail Mikhailovich Bakhtin (1895–1975) did not know each other. Nor is there any indication I am aware of that either one of them knew of, or was influenced by, the other's work. Nonetheless there is a striking commonality—an elective affinity of sorts—between van Gennep's famous ethnographic concept of "liminal" or "threshold" rites,[1] especially as adapted and elaborated into Victor Turner's (1920–1983) even broader notion of ritual "liminality,"[2] and Bakhtin's equally famous narratological notion of the "threshold situation," which emerges as the chief "chronotope" in Bakhtin's study of Feodor Dostoevsky's narrative "poetics."[3] This commonality stems from but extends beyond the linguistic, metaphoric connection betokened by the Latin root of "liminality," *limen*, meaning "threshold."[4]

As van Gennep construes them in his seminal study *The Rites of Passage* (*Les rites de passage*, 1909), liminal or threshold rites (prominent in pregnancy, betrothal, and initiation) occur during the second, transitional stage in the three-stage ceremonial pattern of the rites of passage—that is, following the "pre-liminal" rites that mark the initiate's separation from a previous world or condition of life (prominent in, e.g., funeral ceremonies) and preceding the "post-liminal" rites marking the initiate's "incorporation" into a new world or life condition (prominent in, e.g., marriage ceremonies).[5] The attraction of Turner to van Gennep's work stemmed from his interest in comparative symbology, for which the data, Turner explains, are mainly found in *cultural genres* or *subsystems* of expressive culture, including "both oral and literate genres, and one may reckon among them *activities* combining verbal and nonverbal symbolic actions, such as ritual and drama, as well as narrative *genres*, such as myth, epic, ballad, the novel and ideological systems"[6]—and also, we might add, the kind of parable-like tale that will be the main focus of this present chapter. While van Gennep seemed to intend the term "rite of passage" to apply *both* to rituals accompanying a human individual's or social group's change in social status *and* to rituals associated with a whole society's seasonal changes, Turner notes that van Gennep concentrated on the former type, and "the term has come to be used almost exclusively in connection with these 'life-crisis' rituals."[7] This is the sense of the term that informs most often my evocations of van Gennep's theory in this chapter, though I also draw upon various aspects of the term's employment by Turner, who tries "to revert to van Gennep's earlier usage in regarding almost all types of rites as having the processual form of *'passage.'*"[8]

In what follows, I bring the three-stage ceremonial process, and especially the related concepts of ritual liminality and the threshold experience, to bear upon a particular Renaissance Hebrew account of an imagined medieval Jewish-Christian encounter, with the aim of exposing a certain kinship between ritual pattern and narrative structure.

SOLOMON IBN VERGA AND HIS SHEVEṬ YEHUDAH

Little is known about Solomon ibn Verga, a leading exemplar of what David Nirenberg calls the "lachrymose school"[9] of sixteenth-century exiled Spanish Jewish historiographers,[10] and one whose views are regarded as anticipating both the anti-talmudic movement that began a century later among the conversos,[11] and the nineteenth-century Reform movement.[12] What *is* clear is that he knew well the medieval Jewish experience of persecution, expulsion, and banishment. Born in Castile, avowedly of Davidic lineage (through a thirteenth-century ancestor he claims, one don Samuel ha-nasiy),[13] he may—or so it is speculated—have been a frequent participant in the Jewish-Christian interreligious disputations that were fashionable at that time. After leaving Spain with the Jewish expulsion of 1492, he remained in Portugal, where in 1497 he was compelled to become a Marrano. Almost a decade later, living in or near Lisbon, he witnessed in 1506 the massacre of several thousand Jews in one of that city's public squares. There are different views on what happened next in his life. According to one view, in the following year, when King Manuel I revoked his previous edict that forbade conversos from leaving Portugal, Ibn Verga emigrated to Italy, where he spent the rest of his life, remaining for a while in Rome.[14] Another view holds that "Ibn Verga never came to Italy, but died in Flanders shortly after fleeing from Portugal in 1508."[15]

Our main concern in this chapter is with the tale of the two stones which is found in Ibn Verga's *Shevet Yehudah* (The staff [*or* rod *or* scepter] of Judah),[16] a book modern scholars have pronounced "one of the outstanding achievements of the Hebrew literature of the Renaissance"[17] and "one of the most curious Hebrew literary productions of the age."[18] Apparently based upon the chronicle of Jewish persecution composed by a martyred relation, the historian and kabbalist Rabbi Yehudah ibn Verga of Seville (fifteenth century),[19] this book probably relies heavily on the now-lost *Ma'amar Zikhron ha-Shemadot* (Treatise on the history of the persecutions) by the Spanish Jewish anti-Christian polemicist Profiat Duran (Isaac b. Moses ha-Levi, also known by his pseudonym Ephod; d. c. 1414).[20] Solomon ibn Verga wrote his *Shevet Yehudah* sometime during the 1520s or in the several decades prior to that decade.[21] It was first published with some supplemental materials by his son, the rabbi and דיין/*dayyan* (halakhic scholar and judge) Joseph ibn Verga (d. c. 1559), in or around 1554 in the Ottoman Empire, perhaps at Uscudama or Uscudam (the Turkish name for Adrianople or Hadrianopolis; Arabic: Edirne),[22] and then in Sabbioneta, near Venice, in 1567.[23] A century later, the book was translated from Hebrew to Latin by Georg Gentz (1618–1687; Latin: Gentius). Recounting stories, disputations, and traditions of much earlier dates, interweaving fiction and history (or *Dichtung und Wahrheit*, as Israel Zinberg puts it, applying Goethe's famous terms),[24] and reflecting some of Ibn Verga's own life in exile, the book chronicles the persecutions of the Jews throughout the Diaspora, from the destruction of the Second Temple to Ibn Verga's time. The question of why the Jews were always persecuted and oppressed, although King Alfonso poses it to the Christian scholar Thomas in the first major disputation presented in *Shevet Yehudah*,[25] is not Alfonso's alone. Rather, as Zinberg points out, this question really is "the leitmotif, the life nerve"[26] of the whole book.

PRE-LIMINAL

The overarching liminal theme of גלות/*galut* (exile) and oppression in the *Shevet Yehudah* haunts the putatively fictive anecdote involving "Pedro the Old (Elder, הזקן/*hazaqen*)," presumably King Pedro I of Aragon (c. 1069/74–1104),[27] who ruled Aragon and Navarre from 1094 until his death. Like his father King Sancho Ramírez (1036?–1094, r. Aragon 1063/64–1094, and r. Navarre 1076–1094), Pedro was heavily involved in the *reconquista*, in close alliance with the celebrated Cid Campeador.[28] Aside from the narrative with which we shall be concerned in *Shevet Yehudah*, and another, historically fallacious allusion to him elsewhere in Ibn Verga's text,[29] there are no Jewish reports or records on Pedro, and modern Jewish historiography is all but utterly silent regarding him.[30] The anecdote we shall now consider, which constitutes one of the dialogues and debates in various Spanish Christian courts included in *Shevet Yehudah*,[31] opens with a conversation between Pedro and his (apparently fictitious) minister Nicolao of Valencia,[32] a pair whose representation here Jeremy Cohen construes as "a beneficent king" of "tolerant, enlightened disposition," and "his hateful counselor."[33] Aware that the king desired to launch a military expedition against the infidels, meaning the Muslims, Nicolao asks him why he wants to attack the enemy abroad and spare the infidels in his own land, meaning the Jews. This rhetorical question is hardly new. It accords with the rationale that was reportedly voiced in the periods leading up to the First and Second Crusades to justify the pogroms conducted against Jewish communities in different areas of Europe on both those occasions by Christian troops en route to wage war against the Muslims in the Holy Land: before we travel afar to avenge ourselves on the Ishmaelites (Muslims) abroad, let us first avenge ourselves on the Jews here in our midst, for their having crucified Christ.[34] Nicolao not only plays out the deeply established folkloric role of Jew-hater.[35] In casting the Jews as an enemy within the realm of a non-Jewish potentate, and hence as a people to be persecuted, Nicolao also evokes a stereotype with deep roots in Christian Spain,[36] and as old as the Hebrew Bible—as exemplified in Pharaoh's fear about the enslaved but multiplying Israelites within Egypt (Exod. 1:8–10) or in Ahasuerus's planned pogrom against the Jews in Persia on the contention that their laws differ from those of other people (Esth. 3:8–11).

This entire *pre-liminal* phase of Ibn Verga's narrative unfolds before the initial manifestation of the alienated, *liminal* protagonist, the summoned Jewish sage who will appear in Pedro's court after having already been *othered* a priori and in absentia through Nicolao's disparagement of the entire Jewish people to Pedro. Nicolao repeats rumors he claims to have heard from a Jewish convert or משומד / *meshummad* (apostate from Judaism) about the Jews treating Christians with contempt and calling the Christian faith false. To this claim the king's initial, instinctive response is to express suspicion about the believability of any religious convert, "for whoever changes his religion," says Pedro, "it is easy for him to change his words."[37] However, the king proceeds to submit somewhat discrepantly that religious hatred is simply an offshoot of an incidental hatred (שנאה מקרית/*sin'ah mikrit*), in contradistinction to a directly, naturally caused and occasioned hatred.[38] And notwithstanding any of his expressed skepticism, the king orders that a Jewish sage be summoned for questioning.

At this point the story shifts from its pre-liminal phase into the second, *liminal* phase of the Gennepian/Turnerian ceremonial pattern. The summoned Jewish sage will now enter Pedro's court, through an implicit albeit unmentioned Bakhtinian threshold, effectually ready to play

Mordecai—the quintessentially liminal, exilic Jew—to Nicolao's Haman.[39] Meanwhile Nicolao also finds an analogue in the conspiratorial wisemen of Nebuchadnezzar as depicted in the geonic satiric narrative *Alphabet of Ben Sira*, when the fame of its eponymous sagely protagonist becomes so widespread as to attract the curiosity of that villainous Babylonian king. From whom, the story's narrator asks, did Nebuchadnezzar hear of Ben Sira?

> From his own wise men! When Nebuchadnezzar's wise men heard of Ben Sira's wisdom, they said, "Woe to us! Nebuchadnezzar will now destroy us. Let us defame Ben Sira before the king. He will summon him, and we will ask Ben Sira a difficult question concerning something we know but he does not. If he does not give the correct answer, we will have him killed."[40]

LIMINAL

With no transition following the command by King Pedro that a Jewish sage be summoned before him in order to respond to the question of whether the Christian religion is false, Ibn Verga's narrative shifts to the arrival of one such Jewish sage. Generically speaking, the moment this Jew enters Pedro's court, the narrative will morph into a kind of hybrid of both the widespread folkloric tale-type about the king setting tasks to a Jew,[41] and the related biblical genre, the court narrative, which finds ample exemplification in the Tanakh and certain apocryphal scriptures.[42] The summoning of a Jew for questioning on his religious beliefs by a royal figure also constitutes a common motif in medieval and Renaissance literature, and this particular form of court narrative, I contend, almost always constitutes both a liminal situation in Turner's sense and a threshold dialogue in Bakhtin's sense. The situation is *liminal* because it almost inevitably reduces the summoned Jewish interviewee under duress into a "cultural realm . . . 'out of time,'" "neither here nor there," as Turner famously characterizes the condition of a liminal initiand or neophyte, "betwixt and between the positions assigned and arrayed by law, custom, convention, and ceremonial."[43] Because such a predicament for a Jew can involve literally life-or-death consequences, whatever conversation the Jew is compelled to engage in with the potentate can almost invariably take the form of what Bakhtin would identify as a "threshold dialogue," one reflecting "life poised *on the threshold*."[44]

Consistent with David Nirenberg's disclaimer about the oft-romanticized notion of *convivencia* in medieval Islamic Spain, that "God and his lash hovered over those places where religions met and mingled,"[45] the situation of the Jewish wise man in the presence of the Christian king Pedro is inherently precarious. Like any diasporic Jew when summoned to a foreign potentate's court, he shares the sense of powerlessness and futility the biblical Moses felt at the prospect of confronting Pharaoh in the Egyptian ruler's court: "Who am I, that I should go unto Pharaoh . . . ?" (Exod. 3:11). To be sure, a monarch who summoned a stranger might be implicitly bound to conventional rules of hospitality and also, perhaps, to traditions of extending to the summoned stranger some variant of the right of asylum, with its ritual purpose of "incorporating" the stranger into the host-society.[46] Yet, pertinent to Ephraim's predicament in King Pedro's presence is the generalization offered by the pioneering Dutch phenomenologist of religion Gerardus van der Leeuw (1890–1950) about the element of *tabu* (taboo) or danger that is thought to be inevitably present, whether blatantly or latently, in any encounter between a king and a stranger.

> To the Greek the *king* and the *foreigner* or *stranger* appeared as objects of *aidos*, of awe, to be duly respected by keeping one's distance. Almost everywhere the king is looked upon as powerful, so that he should be approached only with the greatest caution, while the foreigner, bearer of a power unknown and therefore to be doubly feared, stands on an equal footing with an enemy; *hostis* is both stranger or foreigner, and enemy. One may either kill the alien, if one is in a position so to do, or bid him welcome; but in no case are his coming and going to be regarded with indifference.[47]

Accordingly, the Jew entering Pedro's court, although the physical threshold through which he had to pass goes unmentioned, appears there as a stranger separated from his own (Jewish minority and ghettoized [?]) community and placed in an unmistakably liminal, *threshold* situation—what Bakhtin would describe as one of those narrative "*points of crisis, . . . turning points and catastrophes*" constituting "*crisis time*";[48] or what van Gennep and Turner both construe as life crises that necessitate specific processual rites of passage for the individual to get through them—that is, "'life-crisis' rituals,"[49] often "irreversible . . . one-shot-only affairs,"[50] like Ephraim's current ordeal in Pedro's court. Such life-crises or threshold situations epitomize Turner's Gennepian notion of liminality or *communitas*, typified by marginal, "liminal *personae*" or "threshold people,"[51] often "[m]embers of despised or outlawed ethnic and cultural groups [who] play major roles in myths and popular tales as representatives or expressions of universal human values"[52]—for example, the Good Samaritan, the Jewish musician Rothschild in Chekhov's tale "Rothschild's Violin" ("Skripka Rotshil'da," 1894),[53] and the fugitive African American slave Jim in Mark Twain's novel *Adventures of Huckleberry Finn* (1884). Like all those other figures in their own respective contexts, Ephraim the Jew enters King Pedro's court as a physically or bodily, but *not* mentally or spiritually, helpless being. With respect to the distinction between his physical/social self vs. his spiritual/private self, his predicament in Pedro's court resembles that of a person pressured to attend a political ritual in a totalitarian state, as Catherine Bell describes that scenario in discussing the power of ritualization. Such an attendee "might assert that her physical presence is consenting to what is going on, but her mind is resisting. Such a participation creates the relations and the very hold of power within her person in terms of a consenting physical body experienced as distinct from a resisting mind."[54] "When he came" to Pedro's court, writes Ibn Verga of Ephraim the Jew,

> the king said to him, "O Jewish sage, what is your name?" He said to him, "Ephraim ben Sanjo [שאנגו, apparently Sancho]. Said the king, "As is evident, there is conjoint-ness within you [or: you are apparently a hybrid[55]], as from your middle downward, wherein is the sign of the covenant, your name may be called Ephraim, whereas from your middle upward you are a Christian, as your name Sanjo reveals."
>
> Replied the Jew, "My lord the king! Sanjo is my surname, which is [really] Sanji [Sanchi?], save that it has been misformed in the vernacular."
>
> Said the king, "Was I asking [for the hand of] your daughter that you have told me your family?"
>
> The Jew replied, "My lord the king! I said Sanjo in order to make a distinction, for there are several Ephraims in the streets, whereas my lord the king sought to get to know me since he asked my name."

Here, the very real danger for the Jewish stranger upon his arrival before the king would hardly have been obscured by the initial, polite, and seemingly trivial banter about his patronymic, "son of Sancho" (ibn Sanjo). This banter begins to create the ritual decorum of the proceeding interview—decorum, that is, in Ronald Grimes's sense, denoting "the ritual dimensions of face-to-face interaction, usually involving exchange of polite gestures,"[56] including speech acts such as introductions and recognitions.[57] To be sure, Ephraim the Jew would undoubtedly have known that his appellation established an implicit albeit purely coincidental, nominal link between him and King Pedro, who was likewise, as already mentioned, the son of a Sancho (Ramírez). Even more significant, however, is the Jew's given name, a designation for the Northern Kingdom of Israel during the eighth century BCE (reflected in Isa. 7:2, 5; 9:8–9; 17:3; and Hos. 5:3, 5; 6:10; 10:6), taken from that Israelite tribe named for the specially blessed, eponymous second son of Joseph and Asenath: Ephraim, the tribe designated as God's "firstborn" (Jer. 31:9b).

Also noteworthy is that Pedro, surprisingly for a monarch, opened up the conversation in a tone and manner resembling the kind of "low," non-"official," parodic "folk carnival humor" that, as Bakhtin shows, set itself subversively against the "official," "high" culture of late medieval and Renaissance Europe. Pedro did this by, in effect, assuming momentarily the role of a joker or court jester, the antithesis of a king, in a kind of role reversal typical of Renaissance carnival,[58] as well as of ritual liminality. With no reference to Bakhtin, Turner elsewhere analyzes *Carnaval* in present-day Rio de Janeiro as a "dynamic many-leveled, liminal domain of multiframed antistructures and spontaneous communitas."[59] For Turner, "in liminality people 'play' with elements of the familiar and defamiliarize them."[60] Hence the jester or joker is both quintessentially carnivalesque in Bakhtin's sense, and liminal in the sense whereby Turner includes court jesters in the same classification of liminal types as "neophytes in the liminal phase of ritual, subjugated autochthones, . . . holy mendicants, good Samaritans, . . . 'dharma bums,'"[61] and so forth.

King Pedro, qua momentary jester, called attention to Ephraim's liminality and then sought to endow it with a seemingly ludic veneer by jokingly evoking two different rites of passage. One of these was the initiatory rite of circumcision, which van Gennep construes as a rite of separation, and which zeroes in on what Bakhtin calls the "lower bodily stratum"[62] that carnival so raucously liberates. The other rite, the epitomic rite of incorporation for van Gennep, was marriage. This seeming playfulness of Pedro, though perhaps unexpected and a bit unsettling, especially given our awareness of his devious motivation for summoning the Jew in the first place, only confirms the liminal nature of the unfolding tale: "But to my mind," states Turner, "it is the analysis of culture into factors and their free or 'ludic' recombination in any and every possible pattern, however weird, that is the essence of liminality, liminality *par excellence*."[63]

Turner, again, was almost surely unaware of Bakhtin's notion of carnival and its cultural subversiveness. Yet, as if to link his own theory of liminality with that Bakhtinian notion, Turner notes of "tribal societies" that their

> *liminal* phases . . . invert but do not usually subvert the status quo, the structural form, of society; reversal underlines that chaos is the alternative to cosmos, so they had better stick to cosmos, that is, the traditional order of culture—though they can for a brief while have a heck of a good time being chaotic, in some saturnalian or lupercalian revelry, some charivari, or institutionalized orgy.[64]

Bakhtin likewise discusses the "laughter" and "licentiousness" of Roman Saturnalias as an ancient precursor to medieval and Renaissance carnival licentiousness,[65] which finds classic literary expression in François Rabelais's (1494?–c. 1553) sprawling novel of five installments, which began to appear a decade or so after Ibn Verga's *Sheveṭ Yehudah*: *La vie de Gargantua et de Pantagruel* (1532 or 1533–1564, *The Life of Gargantua and of Pantagruel*).[66]

Bakhtin and Turner arrive at remarkably similar conclusions regarding what Bakhtin finds to be the regenerative tendency of medieval parody, typified by Rabelaisian "grotesque realism" and its principle of "degradation," which entails "the lowering of all that is high, spiritual, ideal, abstract; . . . a transfer to the material level, to the sphere of earth and body in their indissoluble unity."[67] "To degrade," writes Bakhtin,

> is to bury, to sow, and to kill simultaneously, in order to bring forth something more and better. To degrade also means to concern oneself with the lower stratum of the body, the life of the belly and the reproductive organs.[68]

There was more than a hint of such degradation in passage from *Shevet Yehudah* quoted above, specifically in Pedro's jocular shifting of focus away from the assumed *wisdom* of the Jewish *sage* or *wise man* to the starkly *physical*, telltale lower-bodily-stratal mark that defines his Jewish otherness: circumcision ("from your middle downward, wherein is the sign of the covenant"). Given the focus here on Ephraim's sexual organ, it may not be too much of a Freudian stretch to note that Pedro's subsequently expressed assumption that Ephraim has a daughter, a suggestion that highlights the thought of Ephraim as a physical agent of human procreation and hence of *birth*, connects the king's revealingly associative thought process further with Bakhtin's theory, which stresses the paradoxical linkage of Rabelaisian degradation with "new birth" and regeneration:

> Degradation digs a bodily grave for a new birth; it has not only a destructive, negative aspect, but also a regenerating one. To degrade an object does not imply merely hurling it into the void of nonexistence, into absolute destruction, but to hurl it down to the reproductive lower stratum, the zone in which conception and a new birth take place.[69]

With a closely related phenomenon in mind, Turner observes that "in liminality people 'play' with the elements of the familiar and defamiliarize them. Novelty emerges from unprecedented combinations of familiar elements."[70] As we shall later see, the "new birth" (Bakhtin) or "novelty" (Turner) to which this liminal and at least lightly carnivalesque encounter between the monarchic "jester" Pedro and the "degraded" Jew Ephraim leads will be nothing less than an apparent overhauling and reformation of the king's attitude toward the Jewish people—a significant development in view of the destructive design that Pedro's sinister minister is seeking to foster in the king's mind against the Jews.

Pedro, in his manner of mildly Rabelaisian jocularity, bifurcates his guest into a man of hybridity or "conjoint-ness," a man who is *half-Jew* ("from [his] middle downward, wherein is the sign of the covenant," that is, his circumcision, signified by his Israelite given name) and *half-Christian* ("from [his] middle upward . . . , as [his Christian] name Sanjo reveals"). Accordingly, the king's next joke about requesting the hand of Ephraim's daughter in marriage could be taken in either one of two ways. The joke could seem, on the one hand, a comfortingly playful evocation of an image of religious intermarriage and interreligious reconciliation, and hence a carnivalesque regenerative inversion of the Christian-dominant Aragonese social order. Or, on the other hand, Pedro could seem to be making a jocularly threatening allusion to something akin to the *jus primae noctis* or *droit du seigneur*, a reminder that he as monarch had the power to lay claim to any possession the Jew had, including the Jew's daughter. The status of the Jews in Aragon was that of aliens with no rights, totally dependent upon the protection of the king. In effect, they were his slaves.[71] In this light, if Pedro's joke about Ephraim's daughter were interpreted as a subtle threat and its veiled logic played out, the daughter would presumably be expected or forced to convert from Judaism to Christianity.

Now let us return to Ibn Verga's narrative. With no transition, King Pedro springs his trap, proposing that he and Ephraim stop the joking—the joking that Pedro himself initiated—about Ephraim's name, his circumcision, and his daughter's hand in marriage, and turn to the real reason for Ephraim's having been summoned:

> The king said, "Let us leave this be, for the reason you have been brought before me is so that you should respond [to the question], which of the two religions [or laws, דתות / *datot*] is better, the religion [or law, דת / *dat*] of Jesus or your religion [דת / *dat*]?"
>
> Replied the Jew, "My religion is better for me as far as concerns me, since I was the basest slave [slave of slaves] in Egypt, whereupon God brought me forth from there with miracles and signs. Your religion is good for you insofar as your dominion is enduring."
>
> Said the king, "I am asking about the religions in and of themselves, and not with respect to those who have received them."
>
> The sage replied, "After contemplating for three days I shall reply to my lord, if that seem good in his eyes."
>
> The king replied, "Let it be so!"

Here we might pause to consider what Ephraim's state of mind might be at this point. If there were any similarity between the socio-economic factors at play in Jewish-Christian relations in and around Aragon in Pedro I's time and those that governed the same relations there a couple of centuries later, in the time of the Aragonese monarch John I (1350–1396, r. 1387–1396),

Ephraim could expect to encounter in Pedro an attitude of tolerance that he would be entitled not to expect among commoners on the street. As T. N. Bisson explains, the massacring of the Jews in Castilian and Aragonese cities during summer 1391

> revealed a deep chasm between the tolerance generally shared by the kings, the higher clergy, and the aristocracy, and the distrust felt by the lower classes, often in debt, and incapable of accepting those who failed to share in their credulous Christianity or even scorned it. John I, *like his ancestors*, drew on the services of Jews and protected them. . . . Denouncing the violence, he ordered that Jews everywhere be protected.[72]

In Ibn Verga's anecdote, when finally asked by King Pedro whose religion or law is better, Ephraim did not respond directly, because doing so would have been to fall into a pitfall. Instead, Ephraim first requested three days to contemplate the king's question, a well-established delaying tactic[73] that finds its scriptural locus classicus in the three-day delay by Esther—and the simultaneous three-day fast she orders for the Jews of Susa to engage in on her behalf—before she goes to her husband, King Ahasuerus, as a first step toward preventing Haman's planned destruction of her people, the Israelites (Esth. 4:15–16). Subsequent Jewish folklore and literature recount other notable instances of this lapse of three days needed prior to taking a critical action of some sort or required in a decision-making process. For example, in the Jewish account of the inquiries with a Jew, a Christian, a Muslim, and a philosopher that led the Khazar kagan to convert to Judaism either in 740 CE or sometime during the Caliphate of Hārūn al-Rashīd (AH 145 or 149– 193/763 or 766–809 CE, r. 170–193/786–809), the kagan required three days to conclude that, from among the four disputants, the Jew was the one with the most convincing case.[74] An analogous three-day lag for decision-making occurs in a medieval Jewish legend about the origin of the first royal dynasty of Poland and the relation of the Jews to Polish society. Set in the ninth century, when Jews are thought by some to have first arrived in that land from mainly the west and southwest, the legend astonishingly suggests that the first king of Poland was, albeit very briefly, a Jew, one Abraham Prohovnik (Polish: Prochownik): after acceding to that position unintentionally and by chance, he immediately rejected the crown, and, after taking three days (in most versions) to consider the matter, convinced the citizens to crown the peasant-farmer Piast, the legendary progenitor of the medieval Polish dynasty that bears his name.[75]

The delaying tactic used by Ibn Verga's Ephraim also finds a much earlier, classical Latin precedent in an exemplum Cicero relates about the Greek poet Simonides (c. 556–468 BCE), although in that case the number of days requested was not limited to three. Rather, anticipating Scheherazade's temporally open-ended delaying tactic in *The One Thousand and One Nights*, the ingenuity of Simonides becomes manifest precisely through his perpetually extending the number of days he says he needs in order to answer a difficult question. Reportedly, when the tyrant Hiero asked him what God is, Simonides requested a day to consider the question. Yet, when asked for his answer the next day, he begged for two more days. And as he continued on each successive day of questioning to double the number of days he had last requested to ponder further the question before providing an answer, Hiero finally asked him what he meant by doing so: "The longer I deliberate," he said, "the more obscure the matter seems to me."[76]

Although their delaying tactics are comparable, Simonides and Ibn Verga's Ephraim use them for opposite reasons. Ephraim, an obedient, believing Jew, presumably *does have* an answer for Pedro (i.e., that the Jewish religion is better than the religion of Jesus) but must refrain from disclosing it because of the precarious liminal situation the king has put him in, whereas Simonides appears genuinely not to know the answer to Hiero's question. As Cicero infers, Simonides, who was said to be not only a charming poet but also an erudite and learned man in other fields of knowledge, had so many acute and subtle arguments come to his mind that he was doubtful which of them was the truest, and so he entirely despaired of the truth.

What happened next in the tale told by Ibn Verga's Ephraim?

Trying the Christian Monarch in a Halakhic Court

Three days later the sage returned, his manner wroth and his face sullen.

The king said, "Wherefore are you sad?"

He said in reply, "I have been cursed today through no wrongdoing on my part, and you, my lord, must take my side in contention. The matter is as follows: about one month ago my neighbor left for distant parts, and in order to appease his sons, he left them two precious stones. The two brothers have just come to me and asked that I inform them of the quality of each stone and the difference between the two. I said to them, 'Who knows this better than your father? For he is a great craftsman in the recognition of stones and their design, who is called a *lapidarius*. Send to him and he will tell you the truth.' For this answer they struck and abused me."

The king replied, "They abused you unjustly and they deserve punishment."

Replied the sage, "May thy ears, O king, hearken unto the issue of thy mouth! For Esau and Jacob were brothers who were each given a stone. My lord asks, 'Which is more precious?' Let my lord send an emissary to our father who is in Heaven, for he is the greatest *lapidarius*, who will tell the difference between the stones."

While the anecdote from *Sheveṭ Yehudah* about King Pedro and the Jew Ephraim is of uncertain provenance, the parable of the two stones told within the anecdote is generally assumed to have originated among the Jews in Muslim Spain at least several centuries before Ibn Verga's time, and to be somehow— perhaps seminally—related to the celebrated parable of the three rings, best known from its versions in day 1, tale 3 of Giovanni Boccaccio's *Decameron* (written 1348–1353) and Gotthold Ephraim Lessing's drama *Nathan the Wise* (*Nathan der Weise*, published 1779, first performed 1783 in Berlin).[77] The ring parable, various versions of which were recorded outside Spain by Christian authors in Latin, Old French, and Italian during the thirteenth and fourteenth centuries, is thought by Karl-Josef Kuschel to find its own underlying idea (*Uridee*) in the Jewish will to survival (*Jüdische Überlebenswille*).[78] However, Yitzhak Baer, apparently dissenting from the supposition of Ernest Renan and others after him that the parable of the stones originated in Andalusia, opines that Ibn Verga rehearses "in a shortened and distorted form the well-known Italian parable of the three jewels—that symbol of religious tolerance which Lessing later made famous."[79] Supportive of the possibility of some sort of direct kinship between Ibn Verga's parable of the two stones and the Italian versions of the three rings parable[80] is the aforementioned surmise that Ibn Verga sojourned in Italy following his departure from Portugal. However, Yerushalmi, in rejecting that theory, also denies the supposition that *Sheveṭ Yehudah* betrays Italian Renaissance influences.[81] Whatever the case may have been, the fact that Ibn Verga knew Latin and adopted many narratives from Latin sources[82] allows for at least the possibility that he came across a Latin version of the parable, such as the one in the *Gesta Romanorum*.

Ibn Verga's Ephraim, when he did finally respond to the king after the passage of three days, resorted to two rhetorical techniques that, it is said, typified ancient Jewish diplomacy: he answered a question by posing another question (a ploy Gaston Paris finds to display "oriental shrewdness [*la finesse orientale*]"[83]), and later employed the parabolic tale (about the father, the two sons, and the stones), to which he then added the little epimythium or *nimshal* (about Jacob and Esau). These two rhetorical techniques find paradigms in Jesus's interrogative riposte to the Pharisees' question about the taxes due to Caesar (Matt. 22:15; cf. Mark 12:13–17; Luke 20:20–26), and in the prophet Nathan's telling of the ewe-lamb parable to King David (2 Sam. 12:1–13a). Nathan's predicament in David's presence was hardly less threatening than was Ephraim's predicament in Pedro's presence.[84] Yet, by telling the parable, the prophet impelled David to judge himself guilty for Uriah's death, just as the tale and accompanying moral told by Ibn Verga's Ephraim led King Pedro to recognize *himself* as guilty of trying to embarrass the Jew with an unfair, dangerous question.

Here, it should be qualified that Ephraim's tale of the stones is not, as some have suggested, most aptly labeled a מָשָׁל/*mashal*.[85] That term, denoting an extended metaphor, simile, comparison, or saying, is usually rendered in the Septuagint as παραβολή/*parabolē* (literally "juxtaposition"), of which "parable" is a transliteration.[86] Identified by David Stern as "the preeminent form of narrative in Rabbinic literature,"[87] the mashal by definition "suggests a set of parallels between an imagined fictional event and an immediate, 'real' situation confronting the parable's author and his audience."[88] Whereas meshalim "do not make even a rhetorical claim to be historically true,"[89] Ibn Verga's Ephraim made no pretense that there is anything imagined or fictional about his tale. On the contrary, in asking for three days to ponder the king's question and, then, with the permission granted, in absenting himself for that length of time, he had created a long enough time frame to enable himself credibly to pass off his tale as something that really could have transpired within it.

For this reason, Ephraim's tale resembles more closely a מַעֲשֶׂה/*ma'aseh*, another oft-used rabbinic rhetorical technique. The ma'aseh is often confused with the *mashal* but has to do more specifically with Jewish law or halakhah. Customarily employed by the pre-mishnaic sages known as the *tannaim* (first and second century CE) and equivalent to the word עוּבְדָה/*uvda* in the Babylonian Talmud and, sometimes, to דִּילְמָא/*dilma* in the Jerusalem Talmud, the term *ma'aseh* denotes literally a "happening" or "occurrence" that serves as a source for determining a halakhic rule or principle regarding both civil law (*dinei mamonot*) and ritual law (*dinei issur ve-hetter*).[90] "Like the *mashal*," Stern points out, "the ma'aseh is a brief narrative form whose function is openly didactic. But where the *mashal*'s narrative is fictional, the *ma'aseh* purports to tell a story that actually took place. To be sure," as in the case of Ephraim's tale of the stones, we may note, "this claim is primarily rhetorical; it has no bearing on the separate question of whether the incident in the *ma'aseh* actually did occur as narrated."[91]

In failing to recognize Ephraim's tale of the stones as a *ma'aseh*, scholars commenting upon it have overlooked its legalistic framework. King Pedro and Nicolao, in their ignorance of talmudic jurisprudence, remained totally unaware of what the Jewish sage was doing as he in effect transformed the Christian royal court into a halakhic hearing room. He did so from the moment he began recounting his tale of woe about his mistreatment by the two brothers, playing the role of complainant against them and, through another Bakhtinian-carnivalesque role-reversal, placing the unwitting Pedro in the role of rabbinic adjudicator—that is, as an unwitting *dayyan* or halakhic scholar, as it were. This was already implied in Ephraim's telling him, "You, my lord, must take my side in contention."[92] Yet the *coup de grâce* was now the declaration Ephraim made after leading Pedro to agree that the two brothers had unjustly abused him and that they therefore deserved to be punished:

"May thy ears, O king, hearken unto the issue of thy mouth!" Here, Ephraim was echoing an expression that the tanakhic patriarch-to-be Abraham himself uttered first to his father, Terah, and then to Nimrod, after similarly tricking them to acknowledge the justice of Abraham's having destroyed Terah's idols in a tale recorded by the Spanish exegete Bahya Ben Asher ibn Halawa (1255–1340):

> When his father came back home he found his idols burned and asked Abraham: My son, why did you burn my gods?
>
> He said: I didn't do it, but the big one got mad and burned his mates.
>
> He said: my son, you are a fool, they can't do this, I myself made them from wood.
>
> He said: *your ears should listen to your mouth*, if they are useless why did you tell me they created the sky and the earth?
>
> Then Terach went to Nimrod and said: my son burned my gods and your gods.
>
> Nimrod called for Abraham and asked: why did you do this?
>
> He said I didn't do this but the big idol burned them.
>
> Nimrod said: they are not alive, they can't do this.
>
> He said: *your ears should hear [the words of] your mouth*, if they have no power why don't you believe in He who created the sky and the earth and you worship a piece of wood?[93]

Back in Ibn Verga's tale, Ephraim, having led King Pedro to acknowledge that the two brothers deserved punishment for having abused him, further led the king to recognize the applicability of this same logic to Ephraim's current predicament of having been asked by the king to identify which religion is the one most precious. Ephraim then recasts Pedro from his role as an unwitting *dayyan* into another juridical role of which Pedro was unaware: the role of the *accused*, an analogue to the two abusive brothers in the *ma'aseh*. Ephraim did this by instructing the king to "send an emissary to our father . . . in Heaven, . . . the greatest *lapidarius*, who will tell the difference between the stones"— that is, just as Ephraim avowedly told the two brothers that their father was "a great craftsman in the recognition of stones and their design, . . . a *lapidarius*" whom they should contact to "tell [them] the truth."

In response, King Pedro does something remarkable. Having just been issued two bold imperatives by his otherwise seemingly docile Jewish subject ("May thy ears, O king, hearken to the issue of thy mouth!" "Let my lord send an emissary to our father who is in Heaven"), Pedro might have been expected to rebuke him or even to have ordered him to be punished for such an impropriety, especially since it was committed in the presence of another person (Nicolao). Instead, without replying directly to the Jew (indeed, he never says another word to him),[94] the king immediately shifted his attention to Nicolao, whom he now blamed for having "spoken falsehood about the community of the Jews." In this way, albeit still unwittingly, Pedro exposed Nicolao as the guilty defendant in Ephraim's halakhic suit, and Ephraim, whether wittingly or not, fulfilled the rabbinic teaching that if someone wants to kill you, slay that person first.[95]

Ephraim's Coded Response to King Pedro's Question

The crucial question remains, however: Did Ephraim really *not*, as scholars have always suggested he did *not*, answer the king's question about which religion is better? Instructive here is a reflection recorded in the early eighteenth century by a French traveler in Ottoman Turkey, based on his observations of the Jews whose ancestors had immigrated there after fleeing persecution in Spain. Contributing significantly to the success of the Jews in international business trade, observed François Aubry de La Mottraye, were "their Humility and Submission in suffering any Affronts or Injuries, even Blows, without shewing any Resentment in their Countenance, or making any Complaints."[96] In the words of two later scholars, the Jews of the Diaspora, having endured centuries of repression and persecution, "had to be always very circumspect and to defend themselves without attacking"[97] and "knew how to bow when the storm blew over them."[98] For these reasons, three things have often been assumed about Ephraim's *ma'aseh*: first, that it reflected the Jews' anxiety of existence (*Existenzangst*)[99] under an intolerant, repressive Christianity, here epitomized by the Jew-hating Nicolao;[100] second, that Ephraim's telling of it amounts to a prudent avoidance of answering the king's question; and third, that by conveying a message of mutual respect and even a perception of equality between the Christian and Jewish "laws," the *ma'aseh* enables Ephraim to affirm the legitimacy of Christianity without denying the legitimacy of his own religion. The metaphor of the stones, it is argued, "allows for more than one 'true religion,' recognized as such in the present. . . . Here, only the relative difference between the (two) religions remains unresolved as God's secret, to be revealed eschatologically,"[101] a conclusion that accords with Ephraim's original response that each religion is best suited to its own adherents.

While concurring with the first point enumerated previously, I disagree with the other two. My own contention is that Ephraim *does* answer the king's question, albeit in a coded manner, and that his response, when interpreted properly, is hardly neutral, but instead favors Judaism strongly and unequivocally. Remarkably, the codedness and hence the true meaning of Ephraim's response have been overlooked in previous scholarship on this tale.[102]

Ephraim's *ma'aseh* no doubt seems to convey a lesson of interfaith respect and tolerance; Baer, as mentioned earlier, links this *ma'aseh* with the parable of the three rings as a "symbol of religious tolerance," and this squares with other stories told by Ibn Verga in *Shevet Yehudah* that "preach quite plainly—and almost frivolously—the doctrine of tolerance toward members of other religions."[103] Considered in isolation, despite Nirenberg's view of Baer as a modern epitome of the pessimistic, lachrymose tendency of Jewish historical interpretation,[104] this point may seem to support the widespread supposition that the three rings parable originated in medieval Islamic Spain as a product and reflection of *convivencia*, referring to the "coexistence" of Jews, Muslims, and Christians in close proximity with each other, especially in Islamic Spain (al-Andalus) from 711 to 1492. Américo Castro asserts that the king could grasp the meaning of Ephraim's tale "thanks to a situation in which different beliefs intermingled harmoniously in the common life of the inhabitants of the Iberian Peninsula. (This was not a situation of mere tolerance)."[105] In accord with Me'ir Wiener's ascription of "the greatest ethical value"[106] to Ephraim's tale, Poul Borchsenius views it as "a gentle smile [that] . . . casts a gleam of light on an important lesson: respect one another, whether you are Christian or Jew, you are both children of the same father."[107]

However, care must be taken not to romanticize the *ma'aseh* of the stones or its supposed message of tolerance, or the cultural situation that seems to have originally produced the tale. Marcus Landau infers from Ephraim's *ma'aseh* that "at the time when it would have first been told, the Jews certainly were acquainted with tolerance, which it taught, ever so slightly."[108] However, he further suggests that such tolerance hardly amounted to unbridled religious freedom. Like the Christians and the Muslims, the Jews had no doubt about the authenticity (*Aechtheit*) of their own "ring" (religion),

> but Christians and Mohammedans had no reason to conceal their judgment, whereas the Jews, everywhere in the minority, dejected and persecuted . . . , had to pretend to be satisfied if they were allowed to express the possibility of the genuineness of their "ring," and not be forced to acknowledge the genuineness of the rings of their "brothers" and the falsehood of their own.[109]

Hence rather than to idealize Ibn Verga's *ma'aseh*, its context, or the notion that its point is to teach tolerance, it is best to share in Nirenberg's cautious effort to steer a middle course between the optimistic "rose-tinted" perception of medieval Spain as a grand bastion of tolerance and the oppositely pessimistic, lachrymose view of it as a "darkening valley of tears."[110]

What has been overlooked in previous scholarship is that Ibn Verga's Ephraim employs his *ma'aseh* to do more than only to express a plea for tolerance or to feign humble contentment at being allowed to consider his religion as being possibly genuine or even as being possibly no less genuine than King Pedro's religion. To accede to the hackneyed interpretation of his *ma'aseh* as not going beyond those two accomplishments would be to miss the deeper, religiously partisan message of the tale.

Taken at face value, Ephraim's tale and moral might seem to convey a sense of religio-philosophical relativism approximating the sort that is ascribed to, and condemned in, rationalist philosophy by another, earlier Andalusian, the scholar, and poet Judah Halevi (before 1075–1141), whose philosophy Ibn Verga parodies.[111] In his classic work composed in Arabic over a period of at least ten years up to 1140, *Kitāb al-Ḥujja wal-Dalīl fī Naṣr al-Dīn al-Dhalīl* (the book of argument and proof in defense of the despised faith),[112] which was translated to Hebrew in 1167[113] by Judah ibn Tibbon under the title *Sefer ha-Hokhaḥah ve-ha-Re'ayah le-Hagganat ha-Dat ha-Bezuyah*, popularly known as *Sefer ha-Kuzari* (book of the Kuzari [Khazars]),[114] Judah Halevi writes:

> In the opinion of the philosophers, however, he becomes a pious man who does not mind in which way he approaches God, whether as a Jew or a Christian, or anything else he chooses. . . . According to this everyone might endeavour to belong to a creed dictated by his own speculating, a thing which would be absurd.[115]

Had Ibn Verga's Ephraim told his *ma'aseh* in a different time and place, or if he were not a made-up character in a fictive tale in *Shevet Yehudah*, the relativism his *ma'aseh* seems to express might have elicited from a Christian audience anything but the approbation it drew from King Pedro in Ibn Verga's account. Ephraim's apparent suggestion that God alone can judge whose religion is more genuine, the Jews' or the Christians', seems in harmony with the talmudic saying that "the pious among the Gentiles [i.e., those of them who fear God] have a share in the world to come [עולם הבא / *olam ha-ba*]."[116] Moses Maimonides affirms this statement in his *Mishneh Torah*[117] and quotes it in one of his *teshuvot* or responsa, although not without pronouncing Judaism the only divinely revealed religion and hence the only wholly true one. He elaborates:

> There is no doubt that every man who ennobles his soul with excellent morals and wisdom based on the faith in God, certainly belongs to the men of the world to come. That is why our sages said, "Even a non-Jew who studies the Torah of our teacher Moses resembles a High Priest" [Baba Qamma 38a]. What is essential is nothing else than that one tries to elevate his soul toward God through the Torah.[118]

By the fifteenth century, in part because of their perceived relativism, the Jews were thought to threaten ecclesiastical and papal authority even more insidiously than the Muslims. The Catholic position that there is no salvation outside the church (*salus extra Ecclesiam non est*) had been first articulated by Cyprian in the third century.[119] This maxim was continuously reaffirmed by popes and councils in the centuries leading up through Ibn Verga's time, as in the confession of faith prescribed in 1208 by Pope Innocent III;[120] in 1215 by the Fourth Lateran Council;[121] and in 1442 by the Council of Florence, which added language to specify the exclusion of Jews, heretics, and schismatics along with pagans.[122] Between those two councils, the bull *Unam sanctam* (one salvation) promulgated in 1302 by Pope Boniface VIII adds the infamous flourish that subjection to the pope is requisite to the salvation of every creature[123]—an addition that the Fifth Lateran Council in 1516, less than a decade after Ibn Verga's death, reaffirmed, and approved (*innovamus et approbamus*) while reiterating that "subjection to the Roman pontiff is necessary for salvation [*de necessitate salutis existat . . . Romano pontifici subesse*]."[124] St. John of Capistrano (1386–1456), a Franciscan who earned the nickname "The Scourge of the Jews" warned Christians in sermons preached in Germany that the Jews tried to spread a "deceitful" idea: "The Jews say that everyone can be saved in his own faith, which is impossible."[125] "If everyone can find salvation through his own religion," John reflected, "then there must be as many religions as human beings."[126] Regarding such passages, Bernard Lewis explains:

> For St. John of Capistrano and others like him, it was easy to understand the triumphalism of Islam, so akin to their own, and to confront it appropriately—that is, on the battlefield. The religious relativism of their unarmed Jewish neighbors posed a different challenge, requiring a different response.[127]

Ibn Verga seems almost to satirize this Christian anxiety when, in a disputation, he records in *Shevet Yehudah* prior to the account of Ephraim's encounter with King Pedro, he has a Spanish Christian king who gives voice to the heretically relativistic notion that all religions, including Judaism, Christianity, and Islam, are the products of imagination.[128]

Let us return to the *ma'aseh* of Ibn Verga's Ephraim, the moral of which, I shall argue, is only *seemingly* relativistic, for it only *ostensibly* represents an avoidance of answering the king's question. As a Jew under duress in a Christian royal court, Ibn Verga's wise man had to be as cautious in his speech as did the actual Jewish representatives at any of the famous Jewish-Christian disputations. Maimonides had taught that the content of what a person says must be the same as the content of his or her heart, and so: "It is forbidden to delude [literally, steal the opinion of] one's fellow creatures, even a Gentile."[129] Accordingly, despite a social environment conditioned by Christian repression and persecution of Jews, the French scholar, tosafist, and preacher Moses ben Jacob of Coucy, a participant at the Paris Disputation of 1240, once stated that the Jews were never to deceive anyone, including Christians or Muslims, because God "scatters Israel among the nations so that proselytes shall be gathered unto them; so long as they behave deceitfully toward them (non-Jews), who will cleave to them? Jews should not lie either to a Jew or to a gentile, nor mislead them in any matter."[130]

However, not to deceive one's persecutor or potential persecutor is one matter; it is quite another matter to take commonsensical, preemptive precaution against being unjustly indicted or persecuted, whether one does so by keeping silent when necessary or by speaking in a coded language laced with double entendre. As the *Kuzari* explains, the rabbis of antiquity employed parables to convey "mysterious teachings" that were meant not for the public but only for "a few select persons."[131] Ibn Verga's Ephraim uses a similar tactic in his interlocution with King Pedro, as we shall see.

As reported in *Shevet Yehudah* itself, the rabbis who participated in the Tortosa Disputation of 1413–1414 realized that their remarks, all of which were being written down by Christian scribes, might be falsified and later used by the presiding pope to convict them: "So we agreed to be guarded in our speech, and to keep silent as much as possible; but this proved impossible, for the Pope ordered us to reply in every matter."[132] Silence proved no more of an option for Ibn Verga's Ephraim in King Pedro's court. Given his endangerment, there, his only recourse was to speak "between the lines" in Leo Strauss's famous sense of the phrase: "Persecution, then, gives rise to a peculiar technique of writing, . . . in which the truth about all crucial things is presented exclusively between the lines. That literature is addressed, not to all readers, but to trustworthy and intelligent readers only."[133] Although Strauss here is referring to written texts,[134] his point would be equally applicable to oral speech, as in Ephraim's case.

Shevet Yehudah, which Strauss does not mention, furnishes a remarkable illustration of his thesis, as Ibn Verga levels criticisms both against his own people, to promote internal Jewish reforms, and, even more daringly, against Christian doctrine. On the one hand, the fabricated scenario in a Christian court, where most of the debaters are Christians, allows Ibn Verga to ascribe to them harshly critical statements about Judaism which he could not convey through the mouth of a Jew.[135] The Christian attitude toward the strife between Christians and Jews, as Ibn Verga undertands it, is unsparingly granted prominence next to the Jewish view. Though Ibn Verga is well aware that the hatred and persecution of the Jews was largely propagated by fanatical Catholic priests who called for them to be persecuted for having allegedly "crucified Christ," numerous other factors are also asserted: most notably, the puffed-up pride of the Jews over their brilliance and wealth, which stirred up the mob's jealousy; the large fortunes that particular portions of the Jewish population accumulated through loans and usury; and the Jews' separateness and their restrictive dietary and drinking customs.[136] But the underlying cause of the Jews' vulnerability in history preceded the Diaspora, as the Christian scholar Thomas explains to King Alfonso in the *Shevet Yehuda*:

> That originally while the Jews found favor in the eyes of God, he would fight their wars, as it is known to all. . . . Therefore they did not learn the ways of war for they did not need them . . . and when they sinned God turned away his face from them and they thus remained losers on all counts—they were ignorant of weapons of war and its invention, and the will of God was not with them; they remained naked and fell like sheep without a shepherd.[137]

While allowing Christian personages to voice criticisms of certain Jewish cultural and social habits, Ibn Verga never questions the Judaic religion itself. On the other hand, he carefully subverts, albeit between the lines, specific articles of Christian faith. In Zinberg's words, Ibn Verga often feigns ignorance and employs the Christian disputants as mouthpieces through which to imply "the fullest denial of the foundations of Christian doctrine."[138]

Ibn Verga's Ephraim seems already to have spoken between the lines in his initial response to the religious question posed to him by King Pedro. In saying that his own Jewish law was better for himself, since he had been divinely delivered out of slavery in Egypt, Ephraim was paraphrasing those crucial thoughts that have been rehearsed for two millennia at the Seder table during the Maggid, the recounting of the Exodus in the Passover Haggadah: "We were Pharaoh's slaves in Egypt, and the Lord our God brought us forth from there with a mighty hand and an outstretched arm" and "In every generation let each man look on himself as if *he* came forth out of Egypt." During the First Crusade, the Jews of the Rhineland invoked the same Mosaic narrative in their effort to view the ferocious Christian attacks against their communities "as a continuum of Biblical history."[139] As a contemporary Hebrew chronicler, Solomon bar Simson, put it,

> They cried out to the Lord with all their hearts, saying: "O Lord, God of Israel, will You completely annihilate the remnant of Israel? Where are all your wonders which our forefathers related to us, saying: 'Did You not bring us up from Egypt and from Babylonia and rescue us on numerous occasions?' How, then, have You now forsaken and abandoned us, O Lord, giving us over into the hands of evil Edom so that they may destroy us?"[140]

The last sentence parallels the present persecution of the Jews by the Christian crusaders ("evil Edom"[141]) with the ancient scriptural account of the assaults on the Israelites by the Midianites, which prompted the heroic Gideon to recall Israel's divine deliverance from Egypt.[142] A no less poignant example of this age-old practice of paralleling a present situation of the Jewish people with some epochal turning point in their history was furnished by the Lisbon-born philosopher and statesman Isaac ben Judah Abravanel (1437–1508), the most influential among the Jews at the royal court of Ferdinand and Isabella of Spain. After failing to persuade the monarchs to revoke the edict of expulsion of Spanish Jewry, signed March 31, 1492, Abravanel did succeed in negotiating the brief postponement of the deadline for the Jews' departure, from the originally set date of July 31 (exactly four months after the edict's signing) to August 2, which in that year coincided with the ninth of Ab in the Hebrew calendar, the traditional anniversary of the destruction of Jerusalem by the Babylonians (587 or 586 BCE) and the Romans (70 CE), both of which catastrophes led the Jews into exile. As the late María Rosa Menocal pointed out, by orchestrating this shift of the date for the expulsion from Spain, Abravanel ensured that posterity would forever remember this later diaspora when commemorating the first: "Abravanel wanted it to remain forever clear that the expulsion from Spain, called Sefarad, marked the cataclysmic end of a long sojourn in a promised land."[143]

Considered in view of these comparable evocations of the Exodus and the Diaspora, Ibn Verga's Ephraim is revealed to have been hardly neutral in claiming that the Christian law was better for King Pedro because it was currently "dominant." Coming right after Ephraim identified himself with the Israelites of Moses's time, that claim, in a coded manner, casts the king as a latter-day analogue to ancient Pharaoh. After all, Pharaoh, although initially "dominant" over the Israelites, wound up thwarted by their God, who had charged Moses with informing Pharaoh about Israel's status as God's "first-born son,"[144] a clear indication of Yahweh's special regard for the Israelites. Because it is with them and with their diasporic descendants that "Jacob" is implicitly identifiable in Ephraim's moral, Ephraim's acknowledgment of the dominance of Christianity hearkens back between the lines to the talmudic contention that the descendants of Esau were to be delivered into the hands of Jacob's descendants.[145] It was said that Jacob himself, upon resigning all earthly treasures to Esau, had declared: "But I do not demur, you may exercise your dominion and wear your crown until the time *when the Messiah springs from my loins, and receives the rule from you.*"[146]

Given his straits in Pedro's court, it was only natural for Ephraim to resort to telling a parable or mashal, a rhetorical device that the rabbis had honed "for a covert political purpose as an oblique means of expressing opinions that were too dangerous to be spoken openly."[147] However, as we have already observed, he further protected himself by guising his mashal as a ma'aseh, that is, by presenting his parable as an account of something that had actually happened to him, with the twist being that he clearly contrived the whole story about the two brothers with the stones and of the abuse Ephraim suffered at their hands to draw a particular response from the king.

The differences between Ephraim's ma'aseh and the Renaissance Italian versions of the ring parable to which scholars have often sought to link it are patent. The Jew tells it to a Christian king rather than the Muslim sultan, Saladin (Ṣalāḥ al-Dīn, 532–589/1138–1193), the Ayyūbid ruler and anti-crusader *jihādist*, who is always the Jew's interrogator in the Italian versions. The *ma'aseh* involves a rivalry between two brothers signifying Christianity and Judaism rather than three, signifying Judaism, Christianity, and Islam. And the concerns of the two sets of brothers are notably different. The two brothers' concern in the *ma'aseh* is over their two precious stones, which are presumably not identical, and whose values in relation to one are knowable only by God, not by human beings, whereas the three brothers' concern in the three rings parable is over a single precious ring, of which two identical duplicates are artificially fabricated.[148] There is no reason to doubt that both stones in Ephraim's *ma'aseh* are genuine; what the brothers are wondering about is their *relative value*.[149] Which stone is worth more than the other?

The moral of Ephraim's tale—that Esau (representing the Christians) and Jacob (representing the Jews) each received a precious stone, and that God alone, as the supreme jeweler, can distinguish between the stones—allows the wise man *ostensibly* to avoid answering the king's question about the relative merits of the Christian and Jewish religions. In deferring to God's judgment, this moral recalls the Qur'ān's pronouncement about the denials by Jews and Christians of one another's religious claims: God alone will adjudicate their differences on Judgment Day.[150] Also comparable is a later proverbial response to the question of which religion is the best, the Turkish or the Christian: "As you love equally your two eyes, so God loves both religions: they are both equally good."[151]

However, we remarked that ibn Verga's wise man *ostensibly* avoided answering the king's question. Only *ostensibly* because, as a liminal Jew under duress in a Christian royal court, Ephraim had reason to speak between the lines in Strauss's sense of that phrase. Regardless of whether his parable is based upon Judah Halevi's (c. 1075–1141) comparison of the Jews to glittering jewels,[152] or whether it derives from the parable about a father, a son, and a pearl told by the thirteenth-century Spanish kabbalist Abraham Abulafia,[153] the scriptural referents of Ephraim's moral *do covertly* favor Jacob's "stone" over Esau's. (This point is always overlooked in the scholarship on this tale.) Were the image of the stone construed as a symbol of birthright, the *ma'aseh* about *two* stones would make no sense, because there was only *one*

birthright to be had between Jacob and his older twin, and Jacob obtained
it from Esau by outwitting him (Gen. 27:1–45). Yet if each brother's stone
symbolizes his own blessing by the father, then, to be scripturally consistent,
Jacob's "stone" or blessing must assume an immeasurably greater value than
Esau's (Gen. 27:27–29, 39–40). Thus Jacob's tricking of his dull brother out
of his birthright, a theme extended by Israel's dominion over his "brother"
Edom (=Esau),[154] bears humorously upon the advantage that Ibn Verga's
Ephraim took of his royal interrogator's presumed ignorance of the Tanakh
and the Talmud. Perhaps Ephraim enjoyed a secret laugh at this "clueless"
Christian monarch who had attempted to embarrass him. For he could count
on the king's having no idea, *first*, that the scriptural Jacob and Esau never
did receive precious stones from their father Isaac or from God; *second*, that,
instead, according to a midrashic legend, Jacob, after obtaining the birthright,
presented the avaricious Esau with pearls and precious stones simply as a
tactic to appease Esau's wrath;[155] and, *third*, that rabbinic and medieval Jews
read Jacob as a symbol of the Jews, and Esau (and also Edom) as a symbol
of Rome and, later, of the Christians. This Jewish construal of the two rival
brothers inverts the medieval Christian typological interpretation, in which
Jacob prefigures the divinely favored Christians and Esau, the accursed Jews.

The Question of Conversion

In Ibn Verga's account of the interrogation of Ephraim ibn Sanjo by Pedro
I, the Jew's submission to the gentile ruler's authority is never questioned.
Ephraim's apparent confidence in the king's judgment and fairness squares
with Ibn Verga's overarching view that the Jews, while hated and resented
by the ignorant Christian populace, were generally favored by the enlightened
Christian rulers. In beseeching the king to side with him in his contention
against his two alleged assaulters, Ephraim conveys, or convincingly feigns,
a respect for the Christian monarch's judicial sense. Also reflected here is
Ibn Verga's desire to cast the king as the sole bearer of proper authority to
ensure that justice will be done in response to Nicolao's spreading of rumors
against the Jews.

Such rumormongering amounted to a verbal assault, of which the alleged
physical assault upon Ephraim by the two brothers is an obvious allegory. At
stake is the slanderous question Nicolao raised about Jewish attitudes toward
Christians and the Christian faith. In this respect, the anecdote accords with
specific aspects of actual earlier Jewish-Christian disputations. The allegations that Nicolao repeats of anti-Christian injunctions in the Jews' "books"
(possibly an allusion to talmudic texts), of Jewish two-facedness toward
Christians on the street (greeting them kindly, then cursing them behind their

backs), and of the Jews' readiness to pronounce the Christian religion false to a Christian's face (a charge that contradicts the preceding one about two-facedness) would have anticipated the principal foci of the Paris Disputation of 1240: above all, the charge that certain contents of the Talmud contradict Christian doctrine, insult Christians, and blaspheme God.[156] Moreover, Nicolao's revelation that the source of his anti-Jewish hearsay was a converso ("one of them who has come over to our religion") squares with the fact that the accuser who argued the Christian case against the Talmud at the Paris Disputation was a Jewish apostate/convert, Nicholas Donin of La Rochelle, as was also the Christian spokesman at the Tortosa Disputation, Gerónimo de Santa Fé (Hieronymus de Sancta, né Joshua Lorki, d. c. 1419), whom the Jews called "the blasphemer" (מגדף / *megaddef*).[157]

Shevet Yehuda elsewhere includes an account of the Tortosa Disputation, written in the form of a report by one of the Jewish participants, Bonastruc Desmaîtres, and augmented by Ibn Verga.[158] This account, though much scantier than one might expect of an event still so recent at that time, and so traumatic in Jewish history,[159] squares with King Pedro's disparagement of the anonymous converso mentioned in the anecdote that contains the parable of the stones. The king's dismissal of the converso's credibility on the grounds that "whoever changes his religion, it is easy for him to change his words" is comparable to the disparaging quips, recorded in *Shevet Yehuda*, that were made about Geronimo by the Aragonese antipope Benedict XIII (Pedro Martínez de Luna, r. 1394–1417), who chaired the Tortosa Disputation. For example, to an objection raised by the chief Jewish spokesman Don Vidal ben Benvenista, over an inimical comment by Geronimo, the pope responds that Don Vidal should not be surprised at this bad behavior, since Geronimo "is one of you."[160] In another instance, the pontiff chides the Jewish delegates: "Why do you not understand Geronimo? He is one of you, and comes at you with cunning."[161] Reminiscent of the qur'ānic condemnation of apostasy from Islam as something unforgivable and punishable by God,[162] *Shevet Yehuda* in these instances seems to issue two implicit warnings to any Jew who might consider converting to the Christian faith. First, such a convert risks merely substantiating, from a Christian perspective, the reductive vulgarism, "once a Jew, always a Jew," which is clearly the pope's insinuation about Geronimo. Second, as King Pedro's remark to Nicolao illustrates, the trustworthiness of any religious convert will always be deemed suspect, because one faith's convert is another faith's apostate. In this respect, the king's thinking recalls Saladin's reported comment that a bad Christian never becomes a good Muslim, and that a bad Muslim never becomes a good Christian, implying that Christians and Muslims should remain faithful to their own creeds and never convert.[163]

POST-LIMINAL

Following the close of the ma'aseh told by Ephraim, his *nimshal* about Esau
and Jacob, and then his halakhic-rhetorical plea for Pedro to dispatch an emissary to God as "the greatest *lapidarius*" to distinguish between the "stones,"
the king's first utterance expresses the widely held, often pejoratively
expressed, folkloric notion of the Jews as an inherently "clever" people.[164]
This notion underlies the representation not only of Ephraim ben Sancho but
also of the analogous Jewish wise man in the frame stories of virtually every
other telling of the three rings parable:

> The king said, "Have you, Nicolao, beheld the cleverness of the Jews? This sage
> is worthy of gifts and honor, while for you punishment should be appropriate for
> you have spoken falsehood about the community of the Jews."
>
> Nicolao said, "However that may be, the statute of the holy kings [ordains]
> the subjugating all religions to his religion. Why then, would he not make these
> submit?"

To be sure, Ibn Verga's tale does *not* end with the sort of explicit Gennepian
ritual incorporation its variant in the *Decameron* ends with. With the Sultan
Saladin and Melchizedek, the Jew figuring as counterparts of Pedro and
Ephraim and with Melchizedek's parable of the three rings having replaced
Ephraim's ma'aseh of the two stones, Boccaccio's tale ends with the disclo-
sure that Saladin made Melchizedek his lifelong friend and kept him at his
court in a position of significance and honor. If the ending of Ibn Verga's tale
stops short of such full-fledged incorporation, it does hint at the possibility of
a new or renewed need for Christian tolerance of the Jews—something akin
to the sort of novelty or "new birth" that Turner and Bakhtin find following
in the wake of liminal, carnivalesque, and degradative ritual stages. Such a
regenerative outcome seems betokened by Pedro's suggestion that Nicolao
should be punished for having slandered Ephraim's community; by the subsequent advice of the king, a seeming paraphrase of Qur'ān 2:256,[165] that
success in matters of religious faith is never achieved through compulsion;
and by his concluding rebuke of Nicolao: "Would that we had sufficient time
to seek the perfection of our own souls, rather than waste our time seeking to
perfect the souls of the Jews."[166] It is no wonder that this episode in *Shevet
Yehudah* is immediately followed by one in which the argument between a
Christian scholar and a Jew exposes the "futility" and "uselessness of the
enterprise of interreligious disputation."[167]

As we know, this lofty promise of tolerance, reached here through a narrative patterned in accord with the logic of the three-phase ritual process, was
later dashed repeatedly by cruel realities of history.

NOTES

1. Arnold van Gennep, *The Rites of Passage*, trans. Monika B. Vizedom and Gabrielle L. Caffee (Chicago: University of Chicago Press, 1960).

2. Victor Turner, *The Ritual Process: Structure and Anti-Structure* [1969] (New Brunswick, NJ/London: Transaction, 1979; repr. 2009), 95–96; and idem, "Liminal to Liminoid in Play, Flow, and Ritual: An Essay in Comparative Symbology," *Rice University Studies* 60, no. 3 (1974): 53–92.

3. Mikhail Bakhtin, *Problems of Dostoevsky's Poetics*, ed. and trans. Caryl Emerson, Theory and History of Literature 8 (Minneapolis: University of Minnesota Press, 1984), 61, 63, 73, etc. Michael Holquist defines "chronotope" (*xronotop*) as follows in M. M. Bakhtin, *The Dialogic Imagination*, ed. M. Holquist, trans. Caryl Emerson and M. Holquist (Austin: University of Texas Press, 1981), 425: "Literally, 'time-space.' A unit of analysis for studying texts according to the ratio and nature of the temporal and special categories represented. . . . The chronotope is an optic for reading texts as x-rays of the forces at work in the culture system from which they spring."

4. Cf. Turner, *The Ritual Process*, 94; and idem, "Liminal to Liminoid," 57, 72.

5. van Gennep, *The Rites of Passage*, 10–11, 21.

6. Turner, "Liminal to Liminoid," 54, italics in text.

7. Ibid., 56.

8. *Ibid.*

9. The term was coined, and the tendency in Jewish historiography that it designates was dismissed, by Salo Wittmayer Baron, *History and Jewish Historians: Essays and Addresses*, compiled by Arthur Hertzberg and Leon A. Feldman (Philadelphia: Jewish Publication Society of America, 1964), 64, 88, 96.

10. David Nirenberg, *Communities of Violence: Persecution of Minorities in the Middle Ages* (Princeton, NJ: Princeton University Press, 1996), 90; and idem, "Religious and Sexual Boundaries in the Medieval Crown of Aragon," in *Christians, Muslims, and Jews in Medieval and Early Modern Spain: Interaction and Cultural Change*, Mark D. Meyerson and Edward D. English, eds., (Notre Dame, IN: University of Notre Dame Press, 2000), 141: "The lachrymose school, which dates back to medieval chronicle traditions, sees the history of Judaism since the fall of Jerusalem in 70 C.E. as a vale of tears, a progression of violent tragedies. It is in part an eschatological vision, with each disaster increasing in magnitude until the last and greatest disaster precipitates the coming of the Messiah and redemption."

11. Azriel Shochat, "Ibn Verga, Solomon," in *Encyclopaedia Judaica*, 22 vols., 2nd edition, ed. Fred Skolnik and Michael Berenbaum (Detroit: Macmillan Reference USA in association with the Keter Publishing House, 2007), 9:695.

12. Joseph Dan, "Fiction, Hebrew," in *Encyclopaedia Judaica*, 2nd edition, ed. Skolnik/Berenbaum, 7:15.

13. Solomon ibn Verga, ספר שבט יהודה/ *Sefer Sheveṭ Yehudah*, ed. Azriel Shochat [Shoḥet], with introduction by Yitzhak Baer (Jerusalem: Mosad Byaliḳ, 1946; hereafter *SY*), 120 [§50]. On this claim by Ibn Verga see Norman Roth, *Jews, Visogoths and Muslims: Cooperation and Conflict*, Medieval Iberian Peninsula Texts and Studies 10 (Leiden/New York/Cologne: E. J. Brill, 1994), 165, 300n. 9.

14. See, e.g., Israel Zinberg, *A History of Jewish Literature*, 12 vols., trans. and ed. Bernard Martin (Cleveland: Press of Case Western Reserve University, 1972–78 [vols. 4–12, Cincinnati: Hebrew Union College Press, 1974–78]), 4 (1974): 66; Yitzhak F. Baer, *Galut*, trans. Robert Warshow (New York: Schocken, 1947), 77; and Shochat, "Ibn Verga, Solomon," 695.

15. Yosef Hayim Yerushalmi, *Zakhor: Jewish History and Jewish Memory* (Seattle: University of Washington Press, 1996), 60.

16. *SY*, 78–86 [§32B]. Except where otherwise indicated, English renderings hereafter are by the late Howard J. Marblestone. Me'ir Wiener's German rendering of this passage occurs in Solomon Ibn Verga (Salomone aben Verga), ספר שבט יהודה [*Sefer Sheveṭ Yehudah*]/*Liber Schevet Jehuda*, 2 vols., trans. [from Hebrew to German] M. Wiener (Hannover: Carl Rümpler, 1856), 2:106–108; repr. in Friedrich Niewöhner, *Veritas sive Varietas: Lessings Toleranzparabel und das Buch Von den drei Betrügern* (Heidelberg: Lambert Schneider, 1988), 48–50. August Wünsche offers a different, condensed German paraphrase of the same anecdote ("Der Ursprung der Parabel von den drei Ringen," *Lessing-Mendelssohn-Gedenkbuch*, publ. Deutsch-Israelitische Gemeindebunde (Leipzig: Baumgärtner, 1879), 329–49; see 338–40). Another German rendering, even more condensed, constitutes tale no. 253 in Micha Josef Bin Gorion [né Berdyczewski], *Der Born Judas: Legenden, Märchen und Erzählungen* (Berlin: Schocken, 1934), 610–12. In French, a translation of the main portion of the tale is offered in Nicholas, "Le Conte des trois anneaux" (1857), 205–6; and a condensed paraphrase by Gaston Paris, "La parabole des trois anneaux. Conférence faite a la Société des Études Juives le 9 Mai 1884" (1885), in idem, *La poésie du Moyen Age. Leçons et lectures*, 2 vols., 2nd ser., 7th ed. (Paris: Hachette, 1922), 2:136–37. A literal Italian translation is given by Giuseppe Levi, ed., *Cristiani ed ebrei nel medio evo. Quadro di costume* (Florence: Successori le Monnier, 1866), 411–13; and condensed English paraphrases by Kaufmann Kohler, *Jewish Theology Systematically and Historically Considered* (New York: Macmillan, 1918), 431, from Wiener's above-cited German translation; and Poul Borchsenius, *The History of the Jews*, 5 vols., trans. F. H. Lyon et al. (New York: Simon and Schuster, 1960–64), vol. 2, *The Three Rings: A History of the Golden Age of Jewish Culture in Spain*, trans. Michael Heron (1965), 16–17. For Cantera Burgos's Spanish rendering, see ibn Verga, *Chébet Jehuda* §32, p. 144.

17. Shochat, "Ibn Verga, Solomon," 696.

18. Cecil Roth, "Historiography," in *Encyclopaedia Judaica*, 2nd edition, ed. Skolnik/Berenbaum, 9:156.

19. Zinberg identifies Yehudah ibn Verga as the grandfather of Solomon (*A History of Jewish Literature*, 4:66); C. Roth, as his father ("Historiography," 156); and Shochat, as his "relative or . . . uncle" ("Ibn Verga, Solomon," 695). Richard Gottheil and M. Seligsohn reiterate the supposition that Yehudah was Solomon's grandfather ("Ibn Verga, Judah," in *The Jewish Encyclopedia: A Descriptive Record of the History, Religion, Literature, and Customs of the Jewish People from the Earliest Times to the Present Day*, 12 vols., ed. Isidore Singer [New York/London: Funk and Wagnalls, 1901–1906], 6 [1904]: 550), and the same two scholars else-where insist that Yehudah could not be Solomon's son ("Ibn Verga, Solomon," in *The Jewish Encyclopedia*, 6 [1904]: 550).

20. See Jacob S. Levinger, Irene Garbell, and Colette Sirat, "Duran, Profiat," in *Encyclopaedia Judaica*, 2nd edition, ed. Skolnik/Berenbaum, 6:56.

21. See Baer, *Galut*, 77–82; and Shochat, who dates the author's lifespan as "second half of 15th century–first quarter of 16th century," and says the *Shevet Yehudah* was written "during the 1520s" ("Ibn Verga, Solomon," 695). Other scholars date its composition in the late fifteenth century.

22. The book's first publication is dated "about 1550" by Simon Marcus, "Ibn Verga, Joseph," in *Encyclopaedia Judaica*, 2nd edition, ed. Skolnik/Berenbaum, 9:694; 1553 by Roth, "Historiography," 156; and 1554 by Jeremy Cohen, *A Historian in Exile: Solomon ibn Verga, "Shevet Yehudah," and the Jewish-Christian Encounter* (Philadelphia: University of Pennsylvania Press, 2017), 2.

23. Cohen, *A Historian*, 2.

24. Zinberg, *A History of Jewish Literature*, 4:66, 69.

25. *SY*, 26–46 [§7].

26. Zinberg, *A History of Jewish Literature*, 4:70.

27. Paris ascribes "1094–1104" ("La parabole des trois anneaux," 136). Kohler ascribes to him the years "1196–1213" (*Jewish Theology*, 431), the lifespan of King Pedro II [*sic*] of Aragon (r. 1196–1213), with whom Marcelino Menéndez y Pelayo likewise identifies the King Pedro of *Shevet Yehudah*'s account in his *Orígenes de la novela*, 4 vols. (Madrid: Bailly-Ballière, 1905–15), 1:xxxiin. 2. Yitzhak Baer assumes that the King Pedro of Ibn Verga's story, like Nicolao, is fictitious: Baer, "Introduction," *SY*, 10; cited by Alan Middleman, "Toleration, Liberty, and Truth: A Parable," *Harvard Theological Review* 95, no. 4 (2002): 353–72, at 360n. 15.

28. An account of the deeds of Pedro I, especially of his military victories over the Moors, is found in *The Chronicle of San Juan de la Peña: A Fourteenth-Century Official History of the Crown of Aragon* [ca. 1370], trans. [from Latin] Lynn H. Nelson (Philadelphia: University of Pennsylvania Press, 1991), 19–21, 24, 25 [chaps. 17–18]. See also Henry John Chaytor, *A History of Aragon and Catalonia* (London: Methuen, 1933), 47–48, 52; and T. N. Bisson, *The Medieval Crown of Aragon: A Short History* (Oxford: Clarendon Press, 1986), 15.

29. See *SY*, 103, line 2, where it is suggested, mistakenly and anachronistically, that the Jewish-Christian Disputation of Barcelona, July 20–31 (or July 20–27), 1263 was conducted "before the pious king Don Pedro the Old" (quoted by Cohen, *A Historian*, 54, 55) rather than King James I of Aragon, whom all other historical records identify as that Disputation's presider. This same passage in *SY* is unique in quoting (anti) Pope Benedict XIII at the later Disputation of Tortosa (Disputation of Tortosa [1413–14]) as quipping that King Pedro "was pious but not clever" (*SY*, 103, line 5, quoted by Cohen, *A Historian*, 54). On the inaccuracy of Ibn Verga's portrayal of this pope see ibid., 42.

30. Cf. Niewöhner, *Veritas sive Varietas*, 51.

31. Although C. Roth dismisses these dialogues as fabrications of Ibn Verga's "perplexed imagination" ("Historiography," 156), various other scholars find them "the most interesting thing in *Shevet Yehudah*," displaying "originality" and "exceptional literary gifts" (Zinberg, *A History of Jewish Literature*, 4:68; Dan, "Fiction, Hebrew," 15; Shochat, "Ibn Verga, Solomon," 696). As Zinberg points out, the disputations "take up almost half the entire book," though "only one, that in Tortosa, has

any historical foundation. But even in the description of this disputation numerous details of significant historical value are interwoven with fantastic legends. All the other disputations, however, are things that never were; they are purely legendary in character" (Zinberg, *A History of Jewish Literature*, 4:68–69).

32. I am aware of no historical record of this personage. Nor does he find a counterpart in any of the narratives that frame other versions of the parable of the three rings.

33. Cohen, *A Historian*, 138–39.

34. See, e.g., the articulation of this argument in the contemporary Chronicle of Solomon bar Simson [fl. 1140] translated in *The Jews and the Crusaders. The Hebrew Chronicles of the First and Second Crusades*, ed. and trans. S. Eidelberg (Madison: University of Wisconsin Press, 1977; repr. Hoboken, NJ: KTAV, 1996), 22, 26, and also Eidelberg's comments, ibid., 5–6. As Eidelberg further notes (143n. 9), Solomon bar Simson's argument, made at the commencement of the First Crusade, parallels the argument reported by Guibert of Nogent, *De vita sua* 2.5, in *Recueil des historiens des Gaules et de la France*, ed. M. Bouquet et al., 24 vols. in fol. (Paris, 1738–1904), vol. 12 (1877): 240B. The striking linguistic parallels with the text of a Geniza letter of the eleventh-century Norman convert Obadyah (Johannes), published in A. Scheiber, "Ein aus arabishcer Gefangenschaft befreiter christlicher Proselyt in Jerusalem," *Hebrew Union College Annual* 39 (1968): 163–75, prompt Eidelberg to wonder: "Did Obadyah see an early prototype of the Jewish chronicle, or perhaps both he and our chronicler drew from a common Gentile pamphlet circulating at the time of the Crusade?" (*The Jews and the Crusaders*, ed. and trans. Eidelberg, 143n. 9). The same argument for attacking the Jews before warring with the "Ishmaelites" is quoted almost verbatim in the Chronicle of Rabbi Eliezer bar Nathan (in *The Jews and the Crusaders*, ed. and trans. Eidelberg, 80), which, as Eidelberg (ibid., 74) points out, "derived from the same parent sources" as Solomon bar Simson's Chronicle. Cf. the argument quoted in *The Narrative of the Old Persecutions, or Mainz Anonymous* (in *The Jews and the Crusaders*, ed. and trans. Eidelberg, 99). Another comparable exhortation, alleged to have been made by the Cistercian priest Raoul or Radulf at the time of the Second Crusade, is quoted by Rabbi Ephraim of Bonn in the latter's *Sefer Zekhirah* (late twelfth century; *The Book of Remembrance*), translated in *The Jews and the Crusaders*, ed. and trans. Eidelberg, 122. Several centuries later, in 1478, the same sort of unsubstantiated allegation against the New Christians—"that this fifth column was rotting the Church from within and mocking Christianity" (Chris Lowney, *A Vanished World: Medieval Spain's Golden Age of Enlightenment* [New York: Free Press, 2005], 232)—alarmed King Ferdinand and Isabella into petitioning the pope to approve a Castilian inquisition.

35. *P715.2–*A hater of Jews* (*Folktales of the Jews*, series ed. Ellen Frankel, vol. 2: *Tales from Eastern Europe*, ed. Dan Ben-Amos, consulting ed. Dov Noy, trans. Leonard J. Schramm [Philadelphia: Jewish Publication Society, 2007], 601); e.g., Israel Folklore Archive (IFA) tales 3892, 6306, and 7812. In this respect, Nicolao finds a strikingly direct counterpart in the villainous, Jew-hating character named Dayenu in the folktale "The Stolen Ring" (documented in *Tales from Eastern Europe*, ed. Ben-Amos, 382), which circulated orally in different forms among several Jewish ethnic groups.

36. On Christian "conspiracy" theories about alleged Jewish "perfidy" and "collaboration" in the Muslim conquest of Spain, see, e.g., Norman Roth, *Jews, Visogoths and Muslims*, 32–34, 129, 205.

37. *SY*, 79, trans. Marblestone.

38. *SY*, 79, line 7. On this point, Cohen elaborates: "It remains unclear whether the king thus refers to the apostate's hatred for the Jews or the Jews' hatred of Christians that the apostate has denounced. Curiously, when Ibn Verga subsequently enumerates the genuine causes of the Jews' exile and suffering, he suggests that religiously grounded hatred does have its roots in the nature of things. . . . Should one conclude that it is specifically the apostate's hatred that is only incidental, rather than natural? Perhaps, despite his zeal and avowed intention to the contrary, the *meshummad* [voluntary convert] cannot assume a different nature but somehow retains his innate Jewishness" (*A Historian*, 142).

39. Cf. Middleman, "Toleration, Liberty, and Truth," 360.

40. אלפא ביתא אחרת לבן סירא / *Alpha betha aharat Ben Sira* [*The Alphabet of Ben Sira*], in *Ozar midrashim: A Library of Two Hundred Minor Midrashim*, 2 vols., ed. Judah David Eisenstein (New York: J. D. Eisenstein, 1915), 1:45 / *The Alphabet of Ben Sira*, trans. Bronznick, 177–78.

41. Antti Aarne, *The Types of the Folktale: A Classification and Bibliography*, trans. and enlarged by Stith Thompson, 2nd rev. (Helsinki: Academia Scientiarum Fennica, 1961 = *Folklore Fellows Communications* 184), 933*C–*King Sets Tasks to Jew* = IFA tale 922*C; Heda Jason, "Types of Jewish-Oriental Oral Tales," *Fabula: Zeitschrift für Erzählforschung* 7, no. 1 (1965): 115–224; see 182–83; and Heda Jason, *Types of Oral Tales in Israel: Part 2*, ed. Dimitri Segal, Israel Ethnographic Society Studies 2 (Jerusalem: Israel Ethnographic Studies, 1975), 51–52.

42. See Lawrence Mitchell Wills, *The Jew in the Court of the Foreign King: Ancient Jewish Court Legends*, Harvard Dissertations in Religion 26 (Minneapolis: Fortress, 1990), which considers examples including the Joseph story in Gen. 37–50; Esth.; Dan. 1–6; Bel and the Dragon; and 1 Esd. 3–4.

43. Turner, *The Ritual Process*, 95.

44. Bakhtin, *Problems of Dostoevsky's Poetics*, 63.

45. Nirenberg, "Religious and Sexual Boundaries," 145. For a romanticized image of Islamic Spain, see María Rosa Menocal, *The Ornament of the World: How Muslims, Jews, and Christians Created a Culture of Tolerance in Medieval Spain* (Boston: Little, Brown and Company, 2002). For an alternative, opposed view, see Dario Fernandez-Morera, *The Myth of the Andalusian Paradise: Muslims, Christians, and Jews Under Islamic Rule in Medieval Spain* (Wilmington, DE: ISI Books, 2016).

46. Much has been written on the right of asylum found even among "uncivilized" peoples. See, e.g., Henry Clay Trumbull, *The Threshold Covenant: The Beginning of Religious Rites*, 2nd edition (New York: Charles Scribner, 1896), 58–59; Gennep, *The Rites of Passage*, trans. Vizedom/Caffee, 32.

47. Leeuw 1986, 44 [pt. 1, sec. 4], italics in text. Leeuw would certainly have read the discussion of "Taboos on Intercourse with Strangers" in James George Frazer, *The Golden Bough: A Study in Magic and Religion* [1890; 2nd ed., rev. and enl., 1900; 3rd ed., rev. and enl., 1911–15], abridged edition (New York: Macmillan,

1922), 225–30 [chap. 19, §1], which includes the observation: "As the object of the royal taboos is to isolate the king from all sources of danger, their general effect is to compel him to live in a state of seclusion" (226) and "It is probably that the . . . dread of strangers, rather than any desire to do them honour, is the motive of certain ceremonies which are sometimes observed at their reception" (227).

48. Bakhtin, *Problems in Dostoevsky's Poetics*, 149, 169, italics in text.

49. See, e.g., Turner, "Liminal to Liminoid," 56.

50. Turner, "Liminal to Liminoid," 57.

51. Turner, *The Ritual Process*, 95.

52. Ibid., 110.

53. Although Turner refers to the eponymous Jewish musician in Chekhov's tale as "the Jewish fiddler," Rothschild is actually a flutist who only takes up playing the violin after he is given the instrument of the main protagonist, the violinist Yakov, at the latter's death near the story's end.

54. Catherine Bell, *Ritual Theory, Ritual Practice* (Oxford/New York: Oxford University Press, 1992; repr. 2009), 208.

55. As translated by Cohen, *A Historian*, 139.

56. Ronald L. Grimes, *The Craft of Ritual Studies* (Oxford/New York: Oxford University Press, 2014), 340.

57. Ibid., 276.

58. A classic example of such role reversal is the ritual and literary theme of the mock-king-for-day, considered in Eric Ziolkowski, "Sancho Panza and Nemi's Priest: Reflections on the Relationship of Literature and Myth," in *Myth and Method*, ed. Laurie L. Patton and Wendy Doniger (Charlottesville/London: University Press of Virginia, 1996), 247–99, see esp. 265–78.

59. Victor Turner, "Carnival, Ritual, and Play in Rio de Janeiro," in *Time Out of Time: Essays on the Festival*, ed. Alessandro Falassi (Albuquerque: University of New Mexico Press, 1987), 74–90, here 89.

60. Turner, "Liminal to Liminoid," 60.

61. Turner, *The Ritual Process*, 125. On jokers and jesters as liminal figures, see also ibid., 109–110.

62. See Mikhail Bakhtin, *Rabelais and His World*, trans. Hélène Iswolsky (Bloomington: Indiana University Press, 1984), 368–436.

63. Turner, "Liminal to Liminoid," 60–61.

64. Ibid., 72, italics in text. Here, Turner is adapting to his own theory certain observations, most notably regarding charivaris and Saturnalia, that he earlier drew explicitly from fellow anthropologist Brian Sutton-Smith; see ibid., 60 and 73.

65. See Bakhtin, *Rabelais*, 6–8, 10, 13n., 14, 70, and intermittently thereafter.

66. The first installment of Rabelais's novel, *Pantagruel*, appeared in 1532 or 1533; the second, *Gargantua*, in 1534; *Tiers livre de Pantagruel* (*Third Book of Pantagruel*) in 1546; *Quart livre* (*Fourth Book*) partially in 1548 and as a whole in 1552; and the mostly or possibly entirely spurious fifth book, partially (i.e., chaps. 1–16) in 1562 under the title *L'isle sonnante*, and as a whole in 1564.

67. Bakhtin, *Rabelais*, 19–20.

68. Ibid., 21.

69. Ibid.

70. Turner, "Liminal to Liminoid," 60.

71. See Fritz Baer, *Studien zur Geschichte der Juden im Königreich Aragonien während des 13. und 14. Jahrhunderts* (Berlin: Emil Ebering, 1913), 11–13; Niewöhner, *Veritas sive Varietas*, 51; Marcel Poorthuis, "The Three Rings: Between Exclusivity and Tolerance," in *The Three Rings: Textual Studies in the Historical Trialogue of Judaism, Christianity, and Islam*, ed. Barbara Roggema, Marcel Poorthuis, and Pim Valkenberg (Leuven: Peeters, 2005), 278n. 50.

72. Bisson, *The Medieval Crown of Aragon*, 124, emphasis mine.

73. Cohen correctly calls this a "good medieval" motif (*A Historian*, 165).

74. "The Answer of Joseph, King of the Togarmi, to Chisdai, the Head of the Captivity, Son of Isaac, Son of Ezra, the Spaniard, Beloved and Honored by Us," in *Miscellany of Hebrew Literature*, 2 vols., ed. Albert Löwy (London: N. Trübner, 1872–77), 1:107.

75. Herman Sternberg gives a full account of this legend in his *Versuch einer Geschichte der Juden in Polen, seit deren Einwanderung in dieses Land (um das IX Jahrh.) bis zum Jahre 1848, 1. Theil: Polen unter der Regierung der Piasten* (Vienna: [n.p.], 1860), 5–8. See also Haya Bar-Itzhak, "The Legend of Abraham the Jew, King of Poland," in idem, *Jewish Poland: Legends of Origin. Ethnopoetics and Legendary Chronicles* (Detroit: Wayne State University Press, 2001), 89–112.

76. Cicero, *De natura deorum* 1.22.60, in idem, *De natura deorum. Academica*, parallel Latin text and English translation, trans. H. Rackham, Loeb Classical Library 268 (Cambridge, MA/London: Harvard University Press, 1933; rev. and repr. 1951), 59.

77. Writing in the mid-nineteenth century, Ernest Renan speculated that the parable of the three rings had derived from medieval Islamic Spain (al-Andalus, Andalusia), where "the mingling [*le mélange*] of religions was bound to inspire similar thoughts" (*Averroès et l'averoïsme* [1852], 8th ed. [Paris: Calmann-Lévy, 1925], 294). Renan is followed in this speculation by, e.g., Michel Nicolas, "Le Conte des trois anneaux [I]," *La Correspondance Littéraire*, 1st year, no. 9 (5 July 1857): 205–206; idem, "Le Conte des trois anneaux [II]," in idem, *Essais de philosophie et d'histoire religieuse* [Paris: Michel Lévy frères, 1863], 241; and Ernest Fontanés, *Le Christianisme modern: étude sur Lessing* [Paris/London/New York: Germer Baillière, 1867], 9). M. Wiener, pronouncing the parable of the two stones the "Hebrew source" of the parable of the three rings, opined that the version of that parable recorded by ibn Verga "not only is the oldest, but also has the most historical authenticity" ("Das Märchen von den drei Ringen, auf seinen Ursprung zurückgeführt und in seinen verschiedenen Relationen gewürdigt," in *Jahrbuch für Israeliten 5617 (1856–1857)*, n.s., 3rd year, ed. Josef Wertheimer [Vienna: Leopold Sommer, 1856], 179, my translation; see also 177). Subsequent scholars sharing this view include Nicolas, "Le conte des trois anneaux [I]" (1857); Nicolas, "Le conte des trois anneaux [II]" (1863), 241–45; Levi, *Cristiani ed ebrei nel medio evo*, 411n. 1; Menéndez y Pelayo, *Orígenes de la novela*, 1:xxxin.2–xxxii. Cf. Hermann Reuter, *Geschichte der religiösen Aufklärung im Mittelalter, vom Ende des achten Jahrhunderts bis zum Anfange des vierzehnten*, 2 vols. (Berlin: Wilhelm Hertz,

1875–77), 2:303; Wünsche, "Der Ursprung der Parabel von den drei Ringen," 338, 349; Marcus Landau, *Die Quellen des Dekameron*, 2nd ed. (Stuttgart: J. Scheible, 1884), 185; Alessandro D'Ancona, "Del Novellino e delle sue fonti," in idem, *Studj di critica e storia letteraria* (Bologna: Nicola Zanichelli), 332. D. M. (Douglas Morton) Dunlop, while supposing the *Shevet Yehudah* to have been composed sometime prior to 1453, submits that "the stories related in it had long been current among the Jewish Rabbins" (*The History of the Jewish Khazars* [1954], "new ed." [New York: Schocken, 1967], 2:65). Edward Storer likewise believes that the variant of the three rings parable in the *Libro di novelle e di bel parlar gentile* (Book of novellas and of elegant noble speech)—also known as the *Novellino* or *Cento novelle antike* (*The Hundred Old Tales*), a collection of apologues anonymously compiled sometime between the 1280s and the 1320s—derived "from Jewish sources" and "appeared for . . . probably the first time in" the *Shevet Yehudah* (*Il Novellino: The Hundred Old Tales*, trans. E. Storer [London: George Routledge, 1925], 169n. 1). Gaston Paris, in a lecture to the Society of Jewish Studies in 1884, does not doubt that ibn Verga's narrative—"the ingenious Spanish Jewish apologue" ("La parabole des trois anneaux," 143)—"presents to us the most ancient and most authentic form [*la forme la plus ancienne et la plus authentique*] of the parable [of the three rings]" (ibid., 138). This parable cannot be proven to have been "invented by a contemporary of Pedro of Aragon, . . . but it is more than likely that it is of Jewish invention, and also that it was born in Spain, where the relations between Jews and Christians were very close and often came to give rise to difficulties of this sort" (ibid., 139). To be sure, "it is probable that it is not entirely original; yet, at its heart, [Ibn Verga's] story has conserved for us the first contrivance [*la première invention*]" of the tale that evolved into the parable of the three rings (ibid.). Cf. Friedrich Niewöhner, "Are the Founders of Religions Impostors?," in *Maimonides and Philosophy. Papers Presented at the Sixth Jerusalem Philosophical Encounter, May 1985*, ed. Shlomo Pines and Yirmiyahu Yovel (Dordrecht: Nihoff, 1986), 244; idem, *Veritas sive Varietas*, 46; Karl-Josef Kuschel, *Vom Streit zum Wettstreit der Religionen: Lessing und die Herausforderung des Islam* (Düsseldorf: Patmos, 1998), 281–85. In the opinion of Isaac Garti, "Boccaccio, Giovanni," in *Encyclopaedia Judaica*, 2nd edition, ed. Skolnik/Berenbaum, 4:25, "[Ibn Verga] was undoubtedly quoting a story that was well known long before he wrote his book." In Cohen's view, Ephraim's speech in Ibn Verga's text places *Shevet Yehudah* within "the history of the famed parable of the three rings, which evidently originated in an eastern, Islamic cultural setting before 'moving' westward, appearing in Boccaccio's *Decameron* and ultimately making its way into Lessing's *Nathan the Wise*" (*A Historian*, 166; see also 25, 185n.16). Iris Shagrir likewise considers it likely that *Shevet Yehudah*'s parable of the stones is "based on a long-standing popular version originating from Spain" (*The Parable of the Three Rings and the Idea of Religious Toleration in European Culture*, trans. Ilana Goldberg (New York: Macmillan Palgrave, 2019), 41. Borchsenius dates the parable of the two stones "back to about 1100" (Borchsenius, *The Three Rings*, 2:16) whereas Paris deems it "nullement assuré" that the parable was "inventée" during that time ("La parabole des trois anneaux," 139).

78. Kuschel, *Vom Streit zum Wettstreit der Religionen*, 285.

79. Baer, *Galut*, 81; see also idem, introduction to Ibn Verga, *Shevet Yehudah*, ed. Shochat, 14. Cf. Middleman, "Toleration, Liberty, and Truth," 360.

80. For example, with respect to the *Shevet Yehudah*'s parable, Shagrir deems it "quite likely that its author was familiar with the Catholic versions—especially the Italian ones," and that *Shevet Yehudah*'s version "merges" Abulafia's parable of the pearl (see below) with "the Christian *Parable of Three Rings*—especially in the latter's Italian version" (Shagrir, *The Parable of the Three Rings*, 41). Cf. Cohen, *A Historian*, 166.

81. Yerushalmi (*Zakhor*, 136n.16) finds the origin of this view in Y. Baer's introduction to *SY*, 11, 13–14. Cf. Baer, *Galut*, 77.

82. See Gottheil/Seligsohn, "Ibn Verga, Solomon," 551.

83. Paris, "La parabole des trois anneaux," 131–63.

84. See also Paris, "La parabole des trois anneaux," 138–39; Borchsenius, *The Three Rings*, 15.

85. E.g., Helen Adolf, "Wesen und Art des Rings: Lessings Parabel, nach mittelalterlichen Quellen gedeutet," *The German Quarterly* 34, no. 3 (1961): 228–34; see 229, 232.

86. L. Mowry, "Parable," in *The Interpreter's Dictionary of the Bible: An Illustrated Encyclopedia*, 5 vols., gen ed. George Arthur Buttrick (Nashville: Abingdon Press, 1962), 3:649; B. Y. Robert Scott, "Parable," in *Encyclopaedia Judaica*, 2nd edition, ed. Skolnik/Berenbaum, 15:620; Charles W. Hedrick, "Parable," in *The New Interpreter's Dictionary of the Bible*, 5 vols., ed. Katharine Doob Sakenfeld et al. (Nashville: Abingdon, 2006–2009), 4 (2009): 368. As noted by Dov Noy, ed., with assistance of Dan Ben-Amos, *Folktales of Israel*, trans. Gene Baharav (Chicago: University of Chicago Press, 1963), 194, the term in the Bible also denotes proverbs; see 1 Sam. 24:13; Prov. 1:1.

87. David Stern, *Parables in Midrash: Narratives and Exegesis in Rabbinic Literature* (Cambridge, MA: Harvard University Press, 1991), 2.

88. Ibid., 5.

89. Ibid., 20.

90. Menachem Elon, "Ma'aseh," in *Encyclopaedia Judaica*, 2nd edition, ed. Skolnik/Berenbaum, 13:308.

91. Stern, *Parables in Midrash*, 13.

92. The translation Poorthuis offers of this same passage puts its litigious aspect in even sharper relief: "I ask you, my lord, to hear my case" ("The Three Rings: Between Exclusivity and Tolerance," 276).

93. Quoted by Vered Tohar, "The Exegesis of Bahya Ben Asher for Gen. 15:7," *European Journal of Jewish Studies* 9, no. 2 (2015): 134–53, here 147–48, emphasis mine.

94. As noted also by Middleman, "Toleration, Liberty, and Truth," 361.

95. *Alpha betha aharat Ben Sira*, ed. Eisenstein, 1:47; *The Alphabet of Ben Sira*, trans. Bronznick, 183. Cf. b.Sanhedrin 72a.

96. François Aubry de La Mottraye, *A. de La Motraye's Travels Through Europe, Asia, and Into Part of Africa; with Proper Cutts and Maps*, 2 vols. (London: Printed for the Author, 1723), 1:84.

97. Paris, "La parabole des trois anneaux," 136.

98. Borchsenius, *The Three Rings*, 14.

99. Kuschel, *Vom Streit zum Wettstreit der Religionen*, 283.

100. Poorthuis, "The Three Rings: Between Exclusivity and Tolerance," 278.

101. Ibid.

102. Regarding this tale, Poorthuis considers it "highly improbable that the Jew really viewed Christianity as being on an equal footing with Judaism" (ibid., 277). However, Poorthuis does not pursue this point; rather, he reiterates the standard interpretation: "His [i.e., Ephraim's] cleverness consists in his maintaining his loyalty towards his own religion without insulting that of the other" (ibid.).

103. Baer, *Galut*, 81.

104. Nirenberg, *Communities of Violence*, 8–9. See Yitzhak F. Baer, *A History of the Jews in Christian Spain*, 2 vols. (Philadelphia: Jewish Publication Society of America, 1961–66).

105. Américo Castro, "The Presence of the Sultan Saladin in the Romance Literatures," trans. Edmund L. King (1954), in *The Idea of History: Selected Essays of Americo Castro*, ed. and trans. Stephen Gilman and E. L. King (Columbus: Ohio State University Press, 1977), 250.

106. Wiener, "Das Märchen von den drei Ringen," 179. Cf. Paris, "La parabole des trois anneaux," intermittently throughout.

107. Borchsenius, *The Three Rings*, 17.

108. Landau, *Die Quellen des Dekameron*, 185.

109. Ibid., 186.

110. Nirenberg, *Communities of Violence*, 9.

111. As noted by Shochat, "Ibn Verga, Solomon," 695. Cf. Cohen, *A Historian*, 166.

112. Slonimsky places the composition of this work "between 1130–1140" ("Introduction" to Judah Halevi, *The Kuzari (Kitab al Khazari): An Argument for the Faith of Israel*, trans. Hartwig Hirschfeld, ed. Henry Slonimsky [New York: Schocken, 1964], 23). According to Eliezer Schweid, "Judah Halevi. His Philosophy," in *Encyclopaedia Judaica*, 16 vols., 1st edition (New York: Macmillan, 1971–72), 10: col. 363: "Halevi worked on the *Kuzari* for 20 years, completing its final draft shortly before his departure for Erez Israel [i.e., in 1140]." Peter B. Golden says simply that it was "written in Arabic in 1140" ("The Conversion of the Khazars to Judaism," in idem, *Turks and Khazars: Origins, Institutions, and Interactions in Pre-Mongol Eurasia* (Farnham: Ashgate, 2010), 28 (article "XI").

113. As dated by Golden, "The Conversion of the Khazars," 28. Schweid dates the Hebrew translation "in the middle of the 12th century" ("Judah Halevi," col. 362).

114. Schweid, "Judah Halevi," cols. 362–63; Leo Strauss, *Persecution and the Art of Writing* [1952] (Chicago: The University of Chicago Press, 1988), 98n. 9.

115. Judah Halevi, *Kuzari* 2.49, trans. Hirschfeld, 112.

116. This claim is made by Rabbi Yehoshua (b.Sanhedrin 105a), contradicting Eliezer ben Hyrcanus's contention that gentiles have no share in the life to come (Tosefta Sanhedrin 13:2).

117. MishT, div. *Hamada* (Knowledge): *Hilchot teshuvah* (Laws of Repentance) 3:5, trans. Touger, 4 (2010): 640–41: "the 'pious of the nations of the world' have a portion

in the world to come." Cf. MishT, div. *Shoftim* (Judges): *Hilchot Melachim* (Laws of the Kings) 8:11, trans. Touger, 23 (2001): 582–83: "Anyone who accepts upon himself the fulfillment of these seven mitzvot and is precise in their observance is considered 'one of the pious among the gentiles' and will merit a share in the world to come."

118. Moses Maimonides, *Letter to Hasdai ha-Levi*, in Maimonides, *A Maimonides Reader*, ed. Isadore Twersky, Library of Jewish Studies (New York: Behrman House, 1972), 478.

119. Cyprian, *Epistola ad Jubaianum, de haereticis baptizandis* (256 CE) [Oxford ed.: letter 73], par. 21, in Patrologiae cursus completes, series Latina, 222 vols., publ. J.-P. Migne (Paris, 1844–55; 1862–64; hereafter PL), 3 (1844): col. 1123B.

120. Pope Innocent III, *Epistola* 196, *Archiepiscopo et suffraganeis Terraconensis ecclesiae. De negotio Durandi de Osca et sociorum ejus*, in PL 215 (1855): col. 1511A.

121. Lateran IV (1215), constitution 1 (*De fide catholica* [On the catholic faith]), in *Decrees of the Ecumenical Councils*, 2 vols., parallel Latin text and English translation, ed. Norman P. Tanner (London: Sheed and Ward, 1990), 1:230, lines 33–34.

122. Basel–Ferrera–Florence–Rome (1431–1445), session 11 (4 February 1442, Florence), in *Decrees*, ed. Tanner, 1:578, lines 8–14.

123. Boniface VIII, *Unam sanctam*, in *Corpus Iuris Canonici*, 2 vols., ed. Emil Friedberg (Leipzig: Bernhard Tauchnitz, 1879–81), 2: cols. 1245–46.

124. Lateran V (1512–17), session 11 (19 December 1516), in *Decrees*, ed. Tanner, 1:643, lines 38–39 and 644, line 5.

125. Munich Cod. lat. 161911 f. 225r; quoted by Johannes Hofer, *Johannes Kapistran: ein Leben im Kampf um die Reform der Kirche*, 2 vols., new, rev. edn. (Heidelberg: F. H. Kerle, 1964), 2:155n. 30; translated by Bernard Lewis, *Cultures in Conflict: Christians, Muslims, and Jews in the Age of Discovery* (New York: Oxford University Press, 1995), 34–35. Cf. Abraham Malamat et al., *A History of the Jewish People*, ed. Haim Hillel Ben-Sasson (Cambridge, MA: Harvard University Press, 1976), 580.

126. See Munich Cod. lat. 161911 f. 225r; quoted by Hofer, *Johannes Kapistran*, 2:155.

127. Lewis, *Cultures in Conflict*, 35.

128. See *SY*, 16, cited by Zinberg, *A History of Jewish Literature*, 4:69–70.

129. Moses Maimonides, *Laws Concerning Character Traits* 2.6, in *Ethical Writings of Maimonides*, ed. Raymond L. Weiss with Charles Butterworth (New York: New York University Press, 1975), 33.

130. Moses of Coucy, *Semag Asayim* no. 82; quoted by Theodore Friedman, "Gentile: In the Middle Ages," in *Encyclopaedia Judaica*, 2nd edition, ed. Skolnik/Berenbaum, 7:487. Known also as Moses ha-Darshan, Moses of Coucy is not to be confused with the eleventh-century scholar and aggadist Moses ha-Darshan of Narbonne.

131. *The Kuzari* 3.73, trans. Hirschfeld, 195.

132. *SY*, 102 [§40]; in *Judaism on Trial: Jewish-Christian Disputations in the Middle Ages*, ed. and trans. Hyam Maccoby (East Brunswick, NJ: Associated University Presses, 1982; repr. 1996), 178.

133. Strauss, *Persecution and the Art of Writing*, 25.

134. Most notably Maimonides's *Guide for the Perplexed*, Judah Halevi's *Kuzari*, and Spinoza's *Theologico-Political Treatise*.

135. As observed by Shochat, "Ibn Verga, Solomon," 696.

136. Zinberg ascribes these allegations to Ibn Verga himself (*A History of Jewish Literature*, 4:71).

137. *SY*, 44 [§7]; as rendered in English by Haim Hillel Ben-Sasson, "History. The Middle Ages," in *Encyclopedia Judaica*, 2nd edition, ed. Skolnik/Berenbaum, 9:225.

138. Zinberg, *A History of Jewish Literature*, 4:69. See ibid. for illustrative examples from Ibn Verga's text.

139. *The Jews and the Crusaders*, ed. and trans. Eidelberg, 5; see also 10.

140. From the Chronicle of Solomon bar Simson, in *The Jews and the Crusaders*, ed. and trans. Eidelberg, 24. See also the analogous passage in the so-called Narrative of the Old Persecutions, or the Mainz Anonymous, in *The Jews and the Crusaders*, 105.

141. This same phrase is again used later in the Chronicle of Solomon bar Simson: "Our people's strength flagged when they saw that the hand of evil Edom was prevailing against them" (in *The Jews and the Crusaders*, ed. and trans. Eidelberg, 30).

142. Exod. 6:13: "And where are all [the Lord's] wonderful deeds which our fathers recounted to us, saying, 'Did not the Lord bring us up from Egypt?' But now the Lord has cast us off, and given us into the hand of Midian."

143. Menocal, *The Ornament of the World*, 249.

144. Exod. 4:22b.

145. Baba Batra 123b.

146. Quoted by Louis Ginzberg, *The Legends of the Jews*, 7 vols., trans. Henrietta Szold et al. (Philadelphia: Jewish Publication Society, 1909–38), 1:393; language modernized by me; emphasis mine.

147. Stern, *Parables in Midrash*, 46.

148. Nothing is said in the tale about the appearances of the stones in Ibn Verga's tale, nor is it even hinted that they resemble each other. Niewöhner says of this tale that "all rings [*sic*!] are genuine" (*Veritas sive Varietas*, 244), an inadvertency which Poorthuis is quick to correct ("The Three Rings: Between Exclusivity and Tolerance," 275n. 45). See also Cohen, *A Historian*, 166.

149. Poorthuis, "The Three Rings: Between Exclusivity and Tolerance," 277.

150. Qur'ān 2:113.

151. Walter Anderson, *Kaiser und Abt: Die Geschichte eines Schwanks* (Helsinki: Academia Scientiarum Fennica, 1923), 237, Z65, my translation. Cf. Mario Penna, *La Parabola dei tre anelli e la tolleranza nel Medio Evo* (Turin: Gheroni, 1952), 86n.1.

152. See Adolf, "Wesen und Art des Rings," 230. See Halevi, *The Kuzari*, 220 (4.15).

153. In Abraham ben Samuel Abulafia, *Ohr Ha-Sechel: Light of the Intellect* [composed in Messina, ca. 1285] ("Integral edition in English and Hebrew"), trans. Avi Solomon, Adam Shohom, and Sharron Shatil (United States: Providence University Press, 2008), 48–49.

154. Contrast Deut. 23:7–8 with Jer. 49:8; Obad. 6–8, 19–21; Rom. 9:10–13.

155. *Midrash Tanhuma*, 2 vols., ed. Salomon Buber (Wilna [Vilnius], 1885), 1:162, 169; cited by Ginzberg, *The Legends of the Jews*, 1:381, 391.

156. See *Judaism on Trial*, ed. and trans. Maccoby, 26–36. As Y. Baer notes, the attention of the Scholastics was drawn to the Talmud in the thirteenth century by their struggle against the neo-Manicheans and the Averroists (*Galut*, 43).

157. Ibn Verga, *Shevet Yehuda*, 94 [§40]/*Judaism on Trial*, ed. and trans. Maccoby, 168.

158. *Shevet Yehuda*, 94–107 [§40]/*Judaism on Trial*, ed. and trans. Maccoby, 168–86.

159. Regarding this account of the disputation, Cecil Roth points out that Ibn Verga "knew details of only five sessions out of the total of 69, the antipope Benedict XIII appearing in these pages as a kindly sponsor rather than the venomous oppressor that he was . . . . In fact, there is barely any record of the disputation after the first few days in any medieval Jewish source, such was the historiographical myopia of even the most erudite Jewish writers of the period" ("Historiography," 156–57).

160. Ibn Verga, *Shevet Yehuda*, 96/*Judaism on Trial*, ed. and trans. Maccoby, 171.

161. Ibn Verga, *Shevet Yehuda*, 100/*Judaism on Trial*, ed. and trans. Maccoby, 176.

162. Qur'ān 3:86–88; 4:137; 5:54; 16:106

163. Jean sire de Joinville, *Histoire de Saint Louis*, 12th ed. [original text], ed. Natalis de Wailly (Paris: Hachette, [n.d.]), 137 [chap. 65, §331]. Joinville reports that this statement was quoted to him and ascribed to Saladin, by the grand admiral of Egypt, where Joinville was taken captive in 1250.

164. AT 1528*B–*Jewish Cleverness*; see Jason, *Types of Oral Tales in Israel: Part 2*, 76. *Folktales of Israel*, ed. Noy/Ben-Amos, trans. Baharav, 91–110 (pt. 5, "Clever Jews"), includes ten examples: tales 36–45 (IFA tales 327, 252, 505, 250, 332, 249, 142, 423, 342, 13).

165. Cf. the Muslim king who, in another account near the opening of Ibn Verga's book, affirmed his conviction that "there is never any advantage to a forced religion" (*SY*, 21; quoted by Cohen, *A Historian*, 139).

166. SY, 83, lines 1–2; quoted by Cohen, *A Historian*, 166.

167. Cohen, *A Historian*, 166–67, commenting on *SY*, 8–90 [§32C].

BIBLIOGRAPHY

Aarne, Antti. *The Types of the Folktale: A Classification and Bibliography*. Translated by and enlarged by Stith Thompson. 2nd rev. Helsinki: Academia Scientiarum Fennica, 1961 = *Folklore Fellows Communications* 184.

Abulafia, Abraham ben Samuel. *Ohr Ha-Sechel: Light of the Intellect* [composed in Messina, ca. 1285]. "Integral edition in English and Hebrew." Translated by Avi Solomon, Adam Shohom, and Sharron Shatil. [United States]: Providence University Press, 2008.

Adolf, Helen. "Wesen und Art des Rings: Lessings Parabel, nach mittelalterlichen Quellen gedeutet." *The German Quarterly* 34, no. 3 (1961): 228–234.

Alphabet of Ben Sira, The. Trans. Norman Bronznick et al. In *Rabbinic Fantasies: Imaginative Narratives from Classical Hebrew Literature* [1990]. Edited by David Stern and Mark Jay Mirsky. Yale Judaica Series 29, 167–202. New Haven, CT and London: Yale University Press, 1998.

Anderson, Walter. *Kaiser und Abt: Die Geschichte eines Schwanks.* Helsinki: Academia Scientiarum Fennica, 1923.

"The Answer of Joseph, King of the Togarmi, to Chisdai, the Head of the Captivity, Son of Isaac, Son of Ezra, the Spaniard, Beloved and Honored by Us." In *Miscellany of Hebrew Literature.* 2 vols. Edited by Albert Löwy. London: N. Trübner, 1872–77, 1:104–112.

Baer, Fritz. *Studien zur Geschichte der Juden im Königreich Aragonien während des 13. und 14. Jahrhunderts.* Berlin: Emil Ebering, 1913.

Baer, Yitzhak F. *Galut.* Translated by Robert Warshow. New York: Schocken, 1947.

Baer, Yitzhak F. *A History of the Jews in Christian Spain*, 2 vols. Philadelphia, PA: Jewish Publication Society of America, 1961–66.

Bakhtin, Mikhail M. *The Dialogic Imagination.* Edited by M. Holquist. Translated by Caryl Emerson and M. Holquist. Austin, TX: University of Texas Press, 1981.

Bakhtin, Mikhail M. *Problems of Dostoevsky's Poetics.* Edited by and translated by Caryl Emerson, Theory and History of Literature 8. Minneapolis, MN: University of Minnesota Press, 1984.

Bakhtin, Mikhail. *Rabelais and His World.* Translated by Hélène Iswolsky. Bloomington, IN: Indiana University Press, 1984.

Bar-Itzhak, Haya. "The Legend of Abraham the Jew, King of Poland." In idem. *Jewish Poland: Legends of Origin. Ethnopoetics and Legendary Chronicles*, 89–112. Detroit: Wayne State University Press, 2001.

Baron, Salo Wittmayer. *History and Jewish Historians: Essays and Addresses.* Compiled by Arthur Hertzberg and Leon A. Feldman. Philadelphia, PA: Jewish Publication Society of America, 1964.

Bell, Catherine. *Ritual Theory, Ritual Practice.* Oxford and New York: Oxford University Press, 1992; repr. 2009.

Ben-Sasson, Haim Hillel. "History. The Middle Ages." In *Encyclopaedia Judaica.* 22 vols. 2nd edition. Edited by Fred Skolnik and Michael Berenbaum. Detroit: Macmillan Reference USA in association with the Keter Publishing House, 2007, 9: 208–228.

Bin Gorion [né Berdyczewski], Micha Josef, comp. *Der Born Judas: Legenden, Märchen und Erzählungen.* Berlin: Schocken, 1934.

Bisson, T. N. *The Medieval Crown of Aragon: A Short History.* Oxford: Clarendon Press, 1986.

Boniface VIII, Pope (Benedetto Caetani). *Unam sanctam* [issued 18 November, 1302]. In *Corpus Iuris Canonici.* 2 vols. Edited by Emil Friedberg. Leipzig: Bernhard Tauchnitz, 1879–81, 2: cols. 1245–1246.

Borchsenius, Poul. *The History of the Jews.* 5 vols. [1960–64]; Trans. F. H. Lyon et al. New York: Simon and Schuster, 1965. Including vol. 3: *The Three Rings: A History of the Golden Age of Jewish Culture in Spain*, trans. Michael Heron [1963].

Castro, Américo. "The Presence of the Sultan Saladin in the Romance Literatures." Trans. E. L. King. *Diogenes* (London) (1954): 1–23. Repr. in: *The Idea of History: Selected Essays of Americo Castro,* edited by and translated by Stephen Gilman and Edmund L. King, 241–269. Columbus, OH: Ohio State University Press..

Chaytor, Henry John. *A History of Aragon and Catalonia.* London: Methuen, 1933.

The Chronicle of San Juan de la Peña: A Fourteenth-Century Official History of the Crown of Aragon [ca. 1370]. Translated. [from Latin] by Lynn H. Nelson Philadelphia, PA: University of Pennsylvania Press, 1991.

Cicero. *De natura deorum. Academica.* Parallel Latin text and English translation. Translated. H. Rackham. Loeb Classical Library 268. Cambridge, MA and London: Harvard University Press, 1933. Rev. 1951.

Cohen, Jeremy Cohen. *A Historian in Exile: Solomon ibn Verga, "Shevet Yehudah," and the Jewish-Christian Encounter.* Philadelphia, PA: University of Pennsylvania Press, 2017.

Cyprian, *Epistola ad Jubaianum, de haereticis baptizandis* [256 CE] [Oxford ed.: letter 73]. In Patrologiae cursus completes, series Latina. 222 vols. Publ. J.-P. Migne. Paris, 1844–55; 1862–64, 3 (1944): cols. 1109A–1127A.

Dan, Joseph. "Fiction, Hebrew." In *Encyclopaedia Judaica.* 22 vols. 2nd edition. Edited by Fred Skolnik and Michael Berenbaum. Detroit: Macmillan Reference USA in association with the Keter Publishing House, 2007, 7:10–16.

D'Ancona, Alessandro. "Del Novellino e delle sue fonti." In idem. *Studj di critica e storia letteraria,* 219–359. Bologna: Nicola Zanichelli, 1880.

Decrees of the Ecumenical Councils. 2 vols. Parallel Latin text and English translation. Edited by Norman P. Tanner. London: Sheed and Ward, 1990.

Dunlop, D. M. [Douglas Morton]. *The History of the Jewish Khazars* [1954]. "New ed." New York: Schocken, 1967.

Elon, Menachem. "Ma'aseh." In *Encyclopaedia Judaica.* 22 vols. 2nd edition. Edited by Fred Skolnik and Michael Berenbaum. Detroit: Macmillan Reference USA in association with the Keter Publishing House, 2007, 13:308–312.

Fernandez-Morera, Dario. *The Myth of the Andalusian Paradise: Muslims, Christians, and Jews Under Islamic Rule in Medieval Spain,* Wilmington, DE: ISI Books, 2016.

Fontanés, Ernest. *Le Christianisme modern: étude sur Lessing.* Paris, London and New York: Germer Baillière, 1867.

Frazer, James George. *The Golden Bough: A Study in Magic and Religion* [1890; 2nd ed., rev. and enl., 1900; 3rd ed., rev. and enl., 1911–15]. Abridged edition. New York: Macmillan, 1922.

Friedman, Theodore. "Gentile: In the Middle Ages." In *Encyclopaedia Judaica.* 22 vols. 2nd edition. Edited by Fred Skolnik and Michael Berenbaum. Detroit: Macmillan Reference USA in association with the Keter Publishing House, 2007, 7:486–487.

Garti, Isaac. "Boccaccio, Giovanni." In *Encyclopaedia Judaica.* 22 vols. 2nd edition. Edited by Fred Skolnik and Michael Berenbaum. Detroit: Macmillan Reference USA in association with the Keter Publishing House, 2007, 4:25.

Ginzberg, Louis. *The Legends of the Jews.* 7 vols. Translated by Henrietta Szold et al. Philadelphia, PA: Jewish Publication Society, 1909–38.

Golden, Peter B. "The Conversion of the Khazars to Judaism." In *The World of the Khazars,* edited by P. B. Golden, H. Ben-Shammai, and A. Róna-Tas, 123–162. Leiden: Brill, 2007. Repr. in: P. B. Golden. *Turks and Khazars: Origins, Insitutions, and Interactions in Pre-Mongol Eurasia.* Farnham, England: Ashgate, 2010. Article "XI," 1–40.

Gottheil, Richard, and M. Seligsohn. "Ibn Verga, Judah." In *The Jewish Encyclopedia: A Descriptive Record of the History, Religion, Literature, and Customs of the Jewish People from the Earliest Times to the Present Day.* 12 vols. Edited by Isidore Singer. New York and London: Funk and Wagnalls, 1901–1906, 6 (1904): 550.

Gottheil, Richard, and M. Seligsohn. "Ibn Verga, Solomon." In *The Jewish Encyclopedia: A Descriptive Record of the History, Religion, Literature, and Customs of the Jewish People from the Earliest Times to the Present Day.* 12 vols. Edited by Isidore Singer. New York and London: Funk and Wagnalls, 1901–1906, 6 (1904): 550–551.

Grimes, Ronald L. *The Craft of Ritual Studies.* Oxford and New York: Oxford University Press, 2014.

Guibert of Nogent. *De vita sua.* In *Recueil des historiens des Gaules et de la France.* Edited by . M. Bouquet et al. 24 vols. in fol. Paris, 1738–1904, 12 (1877): 235A–266C.

Halevi, Judah. *The Kuzari (Kitab al Khazari): An Argument for the Faith of Israel.* Translated by Hartwig Hirschfeld. Edited by Henry Slonimsky. New York: Schocken, 1964.

Hedrick, Charles W. "Parable." In *The New Interpreter's Dictionary of the Bible.* 5 vols. Edited by Katharine Doob Sakenfeld et al. Nashville, TN: Abingdon, 2006–2009, 4 (2009): 368.

Hofer, Johannes. *Johannes Kapistran: ein Leben im Kampf um die Reform der Kirche.* 2 vols. New, rev. edn. Heidelberg: F. H. Kerle, 1964.

Ibn Verga, Solomon [Salomone aben Verga]. ספר שבט יהודה [*Sefer Sheveṭ Yehudah*] / *Liber Schevet Jehuda.* 2 vols. Translated [from Hebrew to German] by M. Wiener. Hannover: Carl Rümpler, 1856.

Ibn Verga, Solomon. ספר שבט יהודה / *Sefer Sheveṭ Yehudah.* Ed. Azriel Shochat [Shoḥet]. With introduction by Yitzhak Baer. Jerusalem: Mosad Byaliḳ, 1946. [*SY*]

Il Novellino: The Hundred Old Tales. Translated by E. Storer. London: George Routledge, 1925.

Innocent III, Pope. *Epistola* 196. *Archiepiscopo et suffraganeis Terraconensis ecclesiae. De negotio Durandi de Osca et sociorum ejus.* In Patrologiae cursus completes, series Latina, 222 vols., publ. J.-P. Migne. Paris, 1844–55; 1862–64, 215 (1855): cols. 1510A–1513D.

Jason, Heda. "Types of Jewish-Oriental Oral Tales." *Fabula: Zeitschrift für Erzählforschung* 7, no. 1 (1965): 115–224.

Jason, Heda. *Types of Oral Tales in Israel: Part 2.* Edited by Dimitri Segal. Israel Ethnographic Society Studies 2. Jerusalem: Israel Ethnographic Studies, 1975.

The Jews and the Crusaders. The Hebrew Chronicles of the First and Second Crusades. Edited by and translated by S. Eidelberg. Madison, WI: University of Wisconsin Press, 1977. Repr. Hoboken, NJ: KTAV, 1996.

Joinville, Jean sire de. *Histoire de Saint Louis.* 12th ed. [original text]. Edited by Natalis de Wailly. Paris: Hachette, [n.d.].

Judaism on Trial: Jewish-Christian Disputations in the Middle Ages. Edited and translated by Hyam Maccoby. East Brunswick, NJ: Associated University Presses, 1982; repr. 1996.

Kohler, Kaufmann. *Jewish Theology Systematically and Historically Considered.* New York: Macmillan 1918.

Kuschel, Karl-Josef. *Vom Streit zum Wettstreit der Religionen: Lessing und die Herausforderung des Islam.* Düsseldorf: Patmos, 1998.

La Mottraye, François Aubry de. *A. de La Motraye's Travels Through Europe, Asia, and Into Part of Africa; with Proper Cutts and Maps.* 2 vols. London: Printed for the Author, 1723.

Landau, Marcus. *Die Quellen des Dekameron,* 2nd edition. Stuttgart: J. Scheible, 1884.

Levi, Giuseppe, ed. *Cristiani ed ebrei nel medio evo. Quadro di costume.* Florence: Successori le Monnier, 1866.

Levinger, Jacob S., Irene Garbell, and Colette Sirat. "Duran, Profiat." In *Encyclopaedia Judaica.* 22 vols. 2nd edition. Edited by Fred Skolnik and Michael Berenbaum. Detroit: Macmillan Reference USA in association with the Keter Publishing House, 2007, 6:56–58.

Lewis, Bernard. *Cultures in Conflict: Christians, Muslims, and Jews in the Age of Discovery.* New York: Oxford University Press, 1995.

Lowney, Chris. *A Vanished World: Medieval Spain's Golden Age of Enlightenment.* New York: Free Press, 2005.

Maimonides, Moses [Moses ben Maimon]. *Letter to Hasdai ha-Levi.* In *A Maimonides Reader,* edited by Isadore Twersky, 47–78. Library of Jewish Studies. New York: Behrman House, 1972.

Maimonides, Moses. *Ethical Writings of Maimonides.* Edited by Raymond L. Weiss with Charles Butterworth. New York: New York University Press, 1975.

Maimonides, Moses. *Mishneh Torah.* 25 vols. Translated by Eliyahu Touger. New York and Jerusalem: Moznaim, 1988–2001.

Malamat, Abraham, H. Tadmor, M. Stern, S. Safrai, H. H. Ben-Sasson, and S. Ettinger. *A History of the Jewish People.* Edited by Haim Hillel Ben-Sasson. Cambridge, MA: Harvard University Press, 1976.

Marcus, Simon. "Ibn Verga, Joseph." In *Encyclopaedia Judaica.* 22 vols. 2nd edition. Edited by Fred Skolnik and Michael Berenbaum. Detroit: Macmillan Reference USA in association with the Keter Publishing House, 2007, 9: 694–695.

Menéndez y Pelayo, Marcelino. *Orígenes de la novela.* 4 vols. Madrid: Bailly-Ballière, 1905–15.

Menocal, María Rosa. *The Ornament of the World: How Muslims, Jews, and Christians Created a Culture of Tolerance in Medieval Spain.* Boston, MA: Little, Brown and Company, 2002.

Middleman, Alan. "Toleration, Liberty, and Truth: A Parable." *Harvard Theological Review* 95, no. 4 (2002): 353–372.

Midrash Tanhuma. 2 vols. Edited by Salomon Buber. Wilna [Vilnius], 1885.

Mowry, L. 1962. "Parable." In *The Interpreter's Dictionary of the Bible: An Illustrated Encyclopedia.* 5 vols. Gen ed. George Arthur Buttrick. Nashville, TN: Abingdon Press, 1962, 3:649–654.

Nicolas, Michel. "Le Conte des trois anneaux." *La Correspondance Littéraire.* 1st year, no. 9 (July 5 1857): 205–206.

Nicolas, Michel. "Le Conte des trois anneaux." In idem. *Essais de philosophie et d'histoire religieuse*, 225–245. Paris: Michel Lévy frères, 1863.

Niewöhner, Friedrich. "Are the Founders of Religions Impostors?" In *Maimonides and Philosophy. Papers Presented at the Sixth Jerusalem Philosophical Encounter, May 1985.* Edited by Shlomo Pines and Yirmiyahu Yovel. Dordrecht: Nihoff, 1986.

Niewöhner, Friedrich. *Veritas sive Varietas: Lessings Toleranzparabel und das Buch Von den drei Betrügern.* Heidelberg: Lambert Schneider, 1988.

Nirenberg, David. *Communities of Violence: Persecution of Minorities in the Middle Ages.* Princeton, NJ: Princeton University Press, 1996.

Nirenberg, David. "Religious and Sexual Boundaries in the Medieval Crown of Aragon." In *Christians, Muslims, and Jews in Medieval and Early Modern Spain: Interaction and Cultural Change.* Edited by Mark D. Meyerson and Edward D. English, 141–160. Notre Dame, IN: University of Notre Dame Press, 2000.

Noy, Dov, ed., with assistance of Dan Ben-Amos. *Folktales of Israel.* Translated by Gene Baharav. Chicago, IL: University of Chicago Press, 1963.

Ozar midrashim: A Library of Two Hundred Minor Midrashim. 2 vols. Edited by Judah David Eisenstein. New York: J. D. Eisenstein, 1915.

Paris, Gaston Paris. "La parabole des trois anneaux. Conférence faite a la Société des Études Juives le 9 Mai 1884" [1885]. In idem. *La poésie du Moyen Age. Leçons et lectures.* 2 vols. 2nd ser. 7th edition. Paris: Hachette, 1922, 2:131–163.

Penna, Mario. *La Parabola dei tre anelli e la tolleranza nel Medio Evo.* Turin: Gheroni, 1952.

Poorthuis, Marcel. "The Three Rings: Between Exclusivity and Tolerance." In *The Three Rings: Textual Studies in the Historical Trialogue of Judaism, Christianity, and Islam*, edited by Barbara Roggema, Marcel Poorthuis, and Pim Valkenberg, 257–285. Leuven: Peeters, 2005.

Renan, Ernest. *Averroès et l'averroïsme* [1852]. 8th edition. Paris: Calmann-Lévy, 1925.

Reuter, Hermann. *Geschichte der religiösen Aufklärung im Mittelalter, vom Ende des achten Jahrhunderts bis zum Anfange des vierzehnten.* 2 vols. Berlin: Wilhelm Hertz, 1875–77.

Roth, Cecil. "Historiography." In *Encyclopaedia Judaica.* 22 vols. 2nd edition. Edited by Fred Skolnik and Michael Berenbaum. Detroit: Macmillan Reference USA in association with the Keter Publishing House, 2007, 9:153–161 [pp. 153–154 updated by S. David Sperling].

Roth, Norman. *Jews, Visogoths and Muslims: Cooperation and Conflict.* Medieval Iberian Peninsula Texts and Studies 10. Leiden, New York and Cologne: E. J. Brill, 1994.

Schweid, Eliezer. "Judah Halevi. His Philosophy." In *Encyclopaedia Judaica.* 16 vols. 1st edition. New York: Macmillan, 1971–72, 10: cols. 362–65.

Scott, B. Y. Robert. "Parable." In *Encyclopaedia Judaica.* 22 vols. 2nd edition. Ed. Fred Skolnik and Michael Berenbaum. Detroit: Macmillan Reference USA in association with the Keter Publishing House, 2007, 15:620–621.

Shagrir, Iris. *The Parable of the Three Rings and the Idea of Religious Toleration in European Culture.* Translated by Ilana Goldberg. New York: Macmillan Palgrave, 2019.

Shochat, Azriel. "Ibn Verga, Solomon." In *Encyclopaedia Judaica.* 22 vols. 2nd edition. Ed. Fred Skolnik and Michael Berenbaum. Detroit: Macmillan Reference USA in association with the Keter Publishing House, 2007, 9:695–696.

Stern, David. *Parables in Midrash: Narratives and Exegesis in Rabbinic Literature.* Cambridge, MA: Harvard University Press, 1991.

Sternberg, Herman. *Versuch einer Geschichte der Juden in Polen, seit deren Einwanderung in dieses Land (um das IX Jahrh.) bis zum Jahre 1848, 1. Theil: Polen unter der regierung der Piasten.* Vienna: [n.p.], 1860.

Strauss, Leo. *Persecution and the Art of Writing* [1952]. Chicago, IL: The University of Chicago Press, 1988.

Tales from Eastern Europe. Edited by Dan Ben-Amos. Consulting ed. Dov Noy. Translated by Leonard J. Schramm. Vol. 2 of *Folktales of the Jews.* Series ed. Ellen Frankel. Philadelphia, PAJewish Publication Society, 2007.

Tohar, Vered. "The Exegesis of Bahya Ben Asher for Gen. 15:7." *European Journal of Jewish Studies* 9, no. 2 (2015): 134–153.

Trumbull, Henry Clay. *The Threshold Covenant: The Beginning of Religious Rites.* 2nd edition. New York: Charles Scribner, 1896.

Turner, Victor. "Liminal to Liminoid in Play, Flow, and Ritual: An Essay in Comparative Symbology." *Rice University Studies* 60, no. 3 (1974): 53–92.

Turner, Victor. *The Ritual Process: Structure and Anti-Structure* [1969]. New Brunswick, NJ and London: Transaction, 1979. Repr. 2009.

Turner, Victor. "Carnival, Ritual, and Play in Rio de Janeiro." In *Time Out of Time: Essays on the Festival,* edited by Alessandro Falassi, 74–90. Albuquerque: University of New Mexico Press, 1987.

van Gennep, Arnold. *The Rites of Passage.* Translated by Monika B. Vizedom and Gabrielle L. Caffee. Chicago, IL: University of Chicago Press, 1960.

Wiener, M. "Das Märchen von den drei Ringen, auf seinen Ursprung zurückgeführt und in seinen verschiedenen Relationen gewürdigt." In *Jahrbuch für Israeliten 5617 (1856–1857),* n.s., 3rd year, edited by Josef Wertheimer, 171–179. Vienna: Leopold Sommer, 1856.

Wills, Lawrence Mitchell. *The Jew in the Court of the Foreign King: Ancient Jewish Court Legends.* Harvard Dissertations in Religion 26, Minneapolis, MN: Fortress, 1990.

Wünsche, August. "Der Ursprung der Parabel von den drei Ringen." In *Lessing-Mendelssohn-Gedenkbuch*. Publ. Deutsch-Israelitische Gemeindebunde, 329–349. Leipzig: Baumgärtner, 1879.

Yerushalmi, Yosef Hayim Yerushalmi. *Zakhor: Jewish History and Jewish Memory*. Seattle, WA: University of Washington Press, 1996.

Zinberg, Israel. *A History of Jewish Literature*. 12 vols. Translated and edited by Bernard Martin. Cleveland, OH: Press of Case Western Reserve University, 1972–78.

Ziolkowski, Eric. "Sancho Panza and Nemi's Priest: Reflections on the Relationship of Literature and Myth." In *Myth and Method*. Edited by Laurie L. Patton and Wendy Doniger, 247–299. Charlottesville, VT and London: University Press of Virginia, 1996.

Chapter 9

Intermediality

Performing the Liminal in the Dance Work Falling

Pauline Brooks

The explosion of modern technologies into the world of performance has meant a challenge for some, while for others, such as Bigger, Broadhurst, Fenton, and Friedman,[1] it has provided a new, exciting territory in which to experiment and to be playfully creative. The evolution of technology and its infiltration into the performing art disciplines has enabled an environment for liminal performance and thus has "given performance practice powerful new dimensions."[2] These developments have included intermedial theater-based work—where live performance interacts with digital or virtual technology; the design of wearable technology that can be part of costume worn by performers and interactive technology, such as *Isadora*, as used most notably by the dance company *Troika Ranch* to explore greater interactivity between performer and device. In addition, telematic—or networked—performances have enabled geographically distanced artists to create and perform together with both live and virtual audiences. The focus of this chapter will be on intermedial dance performance, specifically the intermedial dance work *Falling* (2019)[3] involving live dancers who interact and connect with digital video projections of themselves. The lens through which I write and through which I will provide a reading of the dance is that of both codirector/choreographer and lecturer/teacher. The dancers were twelve final year undergraduate dance students from a university in northwest England. They had never performed in an intermedial dance work before but chose to be part of the project (a final year course) as cocreators and performers. *Falling* is a work where visceral and virtual performers play with being separate and together. It explores how interactions between the live and the digital dancers create connections between them. These connections can transport the performers

213

(and the audience) into a "brave new world," a place of possibilities, one perceived as a threshold to something new, that of liminal performance through intermediality.

I will examine the concept (and practice) of intermediality and consider how our specialist intermedial performance environment, our digital dance laboratory/theater formed our "in-between state."[4] By mingling the real and the virtual, through the interplay between them, we were able to enter that liminal-like state of creative performance in the work. I will discuss the three-stage intermedial creative process of preparation, playful creativity, and performance. I will explain how the first stage includes separation, part of which meant the live dancers creating movement that was filmed and edited to generate the digital dancers. Then choreographic exploration took place to make phrases of movement for the live dancers. In stage two, creative play supported the live dancers to combine their movement with the digital dancers. In the third and final stage, that of an intermedial performance, the live dancers refined their movement to interact and coexist with the digital performers. I will also consider how ludic strategies are a key part of the creative and devising process. Firstly, the use of play and creative tasks helped us to explore and to create movement as well as to aid the dancers in becoming more familiar with the intermedial environment. Secondly, the introduction of rules into the creative tasks supported the live performers to integrate with the digital performers. Finally, I will offer my close reading, an analysis and explanation of *Falling*, and how the development of connections between the live and digital dancers establishes liminal performance.

INTERMEDIALITY

What differentiates liminality from intermediality in terms of performance? While there are overlapping and shared features, for me, what it boils down to as an intermedial dance artist is that I work with live performers and a range of media all of which serve as tools to intermingle and to create dance performance that is interdisciplinary and intermedial. It is the intermingling, the layering of different media (live and digital in this instance), that allows for exploration where the two overlap and coexist and permits that crossing of borders into a new performance space. These liminal settings within which I work mean that I can play creatively, experimenting in what at times is a chaotic "order and disorderliness,"[5] as we discover new creative spaces and interactions and seek to unravel the disorder and find new connections for the performers (and the audience), which allows me to explore new physical, technical, and conceptual possibilities for dance performance.

In the 1960s, Hans Breder was an early adopter of video into the visual arts in a genre he called *intermedia*. What was key for him was the term "inter" as opposed to "multi"-media. He likened the concept to that of a "quest for new kinds of conjunctions."[6] Such a pursuit to challenge performance practice through the fusing of varied media, especially that of digital technology, drives those artists today who continue to explore the liminal, blending the real and the virtual. Through that interplay with the live and the virtual artist, the performer reveals to the audience new thoughts and processes. In attempting to explain the term "intermedia" to others, he explained it as artists working with a hybrid of different media and approaches to create their art. There is still debate today surrounding the use of the term "hybrid" or "hybridity" as a feature of intermediality or as a concept for the bringing together of two (or more) different art forms or media. Commonly the word "hybrid" refers to the progeny of crossing two different animals, or by agriculturists to the result of cross-pollinating plants from two varieties, and, more frequently today, for instance, in relation to hybrid cars of two different power sources. There are certain negative connotations held by some theater/performance traditionalists who may see intermedial theater productions as not belonging to *pure* or traditional theater practice. I would strongly suggest that is the point; it is something different, but akin to. something different, but akin to. A new branch, a new genre. Nelson, in his chapter in *Mapping Intermediality in Performance,*[7] reminds us how Jenson (2007) argues in favor of the use of the term "hybridity" because of the unique potential she believes results from the competition and collaboration between different media and for the potential offerings that it has for the spectator, too. In the same chapter, Nelson balances Jenson's view by drawing on the remarks made by Müller on how fashionable a term it has become, suggesting that there is not yet clarity or conformity in either the use of the term hybridity or intermediality. So, as Rajewsky[8] suggests, it is best if each user makes clear their own definition, because of the range and variety of definitions of intermediality and of where a person stands in relation to a definition of it and their position in relation to hybridity as an *inter*-media form (either merely as a "mongrel" or with the capacity to reveal new potentials).

In the hybridity debate, I position myself in a way I can best explain in relation to my understanding of the hybrid car. It has the potential for two power sources but only as either one or the other never both together. Intermediality involves the separation of the live and the digitized media, which is reaggregated and remediated into a new form. They come together in a liminoid artifact. One without the other would not convey the artistic intent. Working in an intermedial setting in the project *Falling,* with film projection of digital performers alongside live performers (in addition to audio and theater lighting), the idea was very much about how the two can be both separate *and* how they can come together to be something new and something where the performers intersect and cross borders. It is comparable to an ambiguous state, that threshold stage which Turner describes where people are "neither here nor there; they are betwixt and between."[9] It is this threshold, a boundary between past and future, between old and new that is a central part of my intermedial liminal performance work. The blurring of traditional (live) theater performance with different disciplines, different media intermixed, allows for the conception of something new, an emergent form, intermedial.

Combining art forms in the theater is not a new phenomenon. Greek theater brought together different amalgamations of words, movement, sound, and visuals in amphitheaters, specialized places for performance. In the past half century "dance artists have played a pivotal role in using *new media* and their displays, software and interfaces on stage," writes Boenisch.[10] The motivation by dance artists for exploring with new media may come from our position of working in a visual art form, speaking through a language that is movement-based rather than text-based. Or, as Greek theater and the history of dance and theater has demonstrated, because we have always been open to interdisciplinary approaches.

Chapple and Kattenbelt, in their chapter on "The Issues in Intermediality in Theatre and Performance,"[11] refer to the fact that a "significant trend" in twentieth-century theater is how traditional theater practice has adopted the use of digital technology, both in and with the traditional. They also acknowledge the liminal in intermediality because it "operates in the spaces where the strict formal boundaries become blurred."[12] Similarly, I have found that our intermedial space, our digital dance lab, becomes a revolving door of possibilities that offers us new creative spaces in which to devise and perform, as well as for explorations in the new layering of aesthetics for the audience perception.[13] Working with a blend of art forms (more commonly mediatised technology) and live performance, intermediality allows me to soften or "blur boundaries" between what is the virtual and the visceral. I can play "in-between" the thresholds of the live and the digital, experiment with "shape-shifting"[14] time and space with and for the performers and the audience, or as one of the performers in *Falling* wrote in their reflective evaluation:

> We aimed to push the boundaries as far as possible with our live bodies with regards to falling, learning to trust ourselves and each other, but we also wanted to create a more impossible universe using our virtual bodies [. . .] the virtual bodies start with the laws of our universe, for example falling off the ledge at the expected rate, but consequently seem to move away from our universe's reality by reversing the falls. This juxtaposition of the live bodies' reality and the virtual bodies' seemingly impossible reality helped to bring the piece to a climax.

As a choreographer I have frequently worked with music (live and recorded), with voice (sung and spoken), with sets, lighting, costume, with projections of slides onto the cyclorama and through the performers (before we had computers and mediatized technology) and now with film, and even networked performance using videoconferencing and projection that truly allows for the live and the virtual in the performance. In the intermingling of the media, I find the potential for new revelations and the potential to create the "magic" of performance. Without exploring options as they arise and without allowing for experimenting with hybrid or inter-media or multimedia forms, we would not move forward and would never find the otherwise, unimagined possibilities for performance, or as Chapple and Kattenbelt conclude:

> [. . .] the art forms of theatre, opera and dance meet, interact and integrate the media of cinema, television, video and the new technologies; creating profusions of texts, inter-texts, inter-media and spaces in-between. It is in the intersections and the spaces in-between the intersections that we locate intermediality.[15]

Broadhurst[16] writes that corporeality (as well as technology) is important in liminal performance and, of course, that presents us with opportunities to experiment and to discover new aesthetic features where we layer and blend the two. In that scenario, there is a sense of hybridization, certainly a passage through a portal to a new borderland for liminal performance. Various theorists who write on intermediality such as Chapple and Kattenbelt and Nelson,[17] as well as those who write on liminal performance (for instance, Broadhurst, Broadhurst and Machon, Fenton, and Rogers)[18] consider a central aesthetic of the form to be postmodernism. One of the key features of postmodernism in theater is the loss of the hierarchy of the center of the stage, which is replaced by an acknowledgment of the importance of every point on the stage space, while another trait is that of rejecting absolute meaning. Similarly, intermedial practice is concerned with changing perceptions of performance. Like postmodernism, intermedial performance can seek to surprise, to challenge, to excite, and even to disturb and play with perceptions as to what is real and what is virtual. Certainly, one of my concerns as an intermedial artist is to influence the perception of the viewer, for them to be actively involved in deciding where to look and on what to focus as my work presents the audience with multiple perspectives. Ideally, through such an active engagement, they become a part of the performance because of their involvement in the making of the meaning, their interpretation of what *they* see and experience.

THREE STAGES OF THE INTERMEDIAL CREATIVE PROCESS

For me there are three stages of the creative process I use for devising an intermedial liminal dance performance, one that I have especially made use of when working with university dance students (see table 9.1). There are several acts of "separation"—to borrow from Van Gennep's "Rites of

Table 9.1   Stages of Intermedial Creative Process

Stage 1 Preparation:	Stage 2 Playful Creativity:	Stage 3 Performance:
Audition.	Deconstruction of live and digital/virtual.	Convergence of live and digital/virtual.
Rehearsal activity— separation of live action & digital/virtual action.	*(Playing)*	Embodied experience.
	Reflection/Evaluation.	*(Being)*
(Doing)		
	Recombination and refinement of old traditions (live performance) and new explorations (intermedial)	Presentation of multiple perspectives (by performers)
Specialist place (studio/ theater/scenography)		Perception of varied interpretations (by audience)

Passage"[19] at the *preparation stage* of a creative performance process, be it intermedial or traditional performance. These include auditioning for performers, selecting those to take part (and thus separating them from those not chosen). In university performance departments, the audition process may not formally take place, instead student choice immediately separates those who select the module option from those who choose not to take that module (as it was in our case). Other separations may then occur during the creative process as the directors decide who performs which parts or in what sections. The rehearsals and workshops for the physical preparation of the body for physical activity (dance) and the creativity activity occur in a specialist place—a studio or theater, somewhere separated from the everyday. In our case, this was a digital dance lab, a studio theater with large projection screens on three sides: upstage cyclorama and stage left and right (see figure 9.1). For the preparation of *Falling,* all film work took place in the first three weeks of the project in the black box studio theater, with dancers performing, for instance, falling actions from masked raised stage sections onto (unseen) crash mats, as well as walking along the platform and balancing on it (rather as if on a tight rope or looking over a precipice). The edited film material provided us with a part of that transitional "other world" within which we could make playful explorations with the live dancers.

The second phase, or what Kűpers describes as the "limen of liminality,"[20] is where we can be playfully creative, it is a place for experimentation in intermedial performance practice. Turner considers how it is from Sutton-Smith's "order-disorder of play in games"[21] and in the settings of the "liminoid state" that we are able to explore the potential for new artistic realms.

Figure 9.1 View of Theater Performance of *Falling* with Live Dancers on Stage Surrounded by Digital Dancers on Three Screens. *Source*: Pauline Brooks.

Certainly, it is in the playful experimentation or in the order-disorder of the "fructile chaos" where we find that *storehouse of possibilities*[22] that leads us to discovering new performance insights.

In Stage 2, we spent time with the live dancers encouraging improvization that involved playing with falling, catching, leaning and molding in a variety of groupings—solos, duets, and small groups, as well as in learning to be more sensitive to the live dancers around them and, what was more difficult for them, to draw more deeply on their senses to the projected digital dancers they could not hear nor smell, but only see (I shall write more on this point later in the essay). We spent time at the end of sessions discussing what had happened, what they felt had worked and why, and what should happen next. The dancers kept reflective journals to help them to deepen their understanding of the process. While some of the student dancers were able to become more sensitive to *all* the performers in the company, others admitted in their reflections *I believe I could have explored my connections and contact [much more] with the other live bodies as well as the virtual bodies*. It was evident that a number of the student performers did not recognzse themselves in the digital dancers—but saw them as another being, one they found difficult to connect to in the same manner as they could with the live dancers. There was a sense of "them and us" and, however, at points also, a sense of "we," where the "us" became all thirty-six digital dancers and twelve live dancers into a connected company of forty-eight. It was in those moments that, through the recombination and refinement of old traditions (live performance) and new explorations (intermedial performance), we were able to find the "blurring of boundaries" to create an emergent form within a new genre and to work toward becoming an intermedial company in a liminal performance.

The third stage in my intermedial creative process is that of performance. This involves refining the material and clarifying the connections between between the live and digital/virtual in order to enable the live performers to pass from merely "doing" to "being." As another of the dancers wrote in their reflective evaluation *making that connection between the visuals displayed on the screen whilst performing in the live space was sometimes more difficult that I originally thought it would be.* Seeking to collaborate with our dancers to help them to discover an embodied state, which Turner refers to as *communitas*, is the common experience that helps humans to bond and for performers to connect. Turner subdivides *communitas* into three forms: *spontaneous, ideological,* and *normative,* and it is the first two forms that relate to our process and our intended final realization for the performers. He likens *spontaneous communitas* to that "magical" moment, for instance, that friends experience a "flash of lucid mutual understanding."[23] His *ideological communitas* involves a set of theoretical concepts. In his 1974 essay, Turner begins to consider the connection of *communitas* with the flow theory of Mihaly Csikszentmihalyi[24] (more colloquially referred to it as "being in the zone"). Turner emphasizes that *ideological communitas* is not so much a community as a shared feeling of *being.*[25] Certainly, this transformation of a performer from the mere superficial repetition of action (however, technically proficient), from the just "doing" to the deeper, more informed "lived" experience (embodied) of "being" is what we seek to attain through our process. The facility of "being" allows for the manifestation of the artistic intent, the creative expression articulated by and through the movement. It resonates with what Lowell terms an "intercorporeality,"[26] a communication shared between performers (live and/or digital), while also connecting with the audience. Another of the performers wrote of the challenges they had faced engaging with the digital dancers during their fall and recovery grounded solo at the end of Section 1 (see video from 2.28 to 3.30), but in "letting go" or by "being in the zone," they found that connection of "being" (*communitas*) with the digital dancers as they walked off the stage seemingly leading the walking digital dancers off too:

> On the night of the performance. [. . .] Although I was nervous before starting my solo, I realised that as it was an improvisation and I had rehearsed it over and over again, meticulously improving the dynamics and range of movement that I didn't need to be nervous and [. . .] just had to let go of any apprehension I had and trust myself and my movement memory. Using the cues I had been [using] throughout the rehearsal process, I walked as though I was leading the screen dancers off stage; something which I had struggled to do during every rehearsal.

Broadhurst[27] notes that the introduction of technology provides artists with the potential for new avenues of creative enquiry, while the combination of the physical and the virtual blurs, or softens, boundaries and makes the spaces used liminal. Blazek, in his discussion of textual liminality, writes of the "fluid passageway"[28] that, for instance, enables readers to pass back and forth geographically and historically with regard to time and space. My consideration is of a fluidity that allows us to play with time and space within intermedial constructions. We can slow down, speed up and even freeze the movement of the digital dancers in ways impossible for live dancers, and we can also suggest ways in which the digital and live dancers share space (and time). Blazek, along with Bay-Cheng et al., speak of the "portals"[29] or gateways that open in these thresholds and transformational moments. Intermediality presents us with those insightful moments of playful creativity and experimentation when we as creators see through those portals into the new realms for performance. Those moments provide performers (and creators) with opportunities for both *experiencing* the liminal and to experiment with the form liminality, culminating in a liminal performance.[30]

PLAY AND LUDIC STRATEGIES
FOR PLAYFUL CREATIVITY

Richard Schechner writes how "Playing, like ritual, is at the heart of performance" and goes on to say "performance may be defined as ritualized behaviour conditioned/permeated by play."[31] Play Theory acknowledges the central role of play in human culture as noted by authors such as Caillois, Huizinga, and Sutton-Smith,[32] and it has regained importance in performance studies— partly from postmodernist interests in playful, spontaneous improvization and partly from its appropriation by those in games design and theory.[33] Alexander F. Chamberlain made a significant connection between play and adult activities and, more significantly for my work as a choreographer/dance artist, when he noted that "the orator, the poet, the artist, the seeker after knowledge 'play' as surely and as *naively* as the child."[34] I appreciate how the essence of working creatively *must* involve us in playful experimentation. While Abraham Maslow is acknowledged for saying "almost all creativity involves *purposeful* play" (my italics), there are times in my devising phases when the purpose of playful creativity is to have the *freedom* to explore. In his study of Huizinga's *Homo Ludens,* Rodriguez notes how Huizinga describes play as a "free and meaningful activity, carried out for its own sake, spatially and temporally segregated from the requirements of practical life, and bound by a self-contained system of rules."[35] This feature of playful creativity, or *playing*, is situated in the central phase of my three stages of intermedial creative process.

In a situation where student dancers have not worked in intermedial settings before, playful improvization in creative workshops is a fruitful way to "break the ice" and to introduce them to the performance skills strived for by the genre. Creative experimentation allowed each of the performers (players) the freedom to "see what happens." This idea of allowing them to play is to enable them to experiment, to explore, and to build trust without fearing they might "get it wrong." As the "outside eye," I was seeking how together we would discover moments of movement that I considered were innovative and unexpected that could be used in the dance work and in movements they acknowledged "felt right." To allow for improvization, creative play is a means by which we can nurture creativity in students of performance. It allows for the discovery of new movement patterns away from formulaic reproduction of taught or set phrases and actions that can be the result of overthinking, talking, and rigid planning that involves, for example, performers in plotting "if I reach here, then you turn there, and then we can step together and create a shape." Rather, we aim for a more organic devising process, what Gill writes of as the "skilled *play* of musicians and dancers"[36] (my italics). In the same online article, Gill reminds us that Schiller wrote in 1793 "man plays only when he is in the full sense of the word a human being, and he is only fully a human being when he plays."[37] That sense of "skilled play" and fully developed humans (and artists) is certainly one that we (as dance educators) seek to encourage and support. Schechner agrees, noting how in the twentieth century we have returned to play as a category of creative thought and action; acknowledging Turner, he writes that "playing, like ritual, is at the heart of performance."[38] Schechner writes the element of play, that of make-believe, is a key part of performance because it draws upon and embodies the "as if." And while we did use that element in our playful suggestions, for instance, "how might you cross the stage *as if* you were on a tight rope?" Or "how would you balance *as if* you were on the edge of a high building?" However, to generate movement that uses space and time to create phrases of dance, I use a playful activity I call the what if game: "what if you and your (live) partner now respond to the digital dancer on the screen by you?" And "*what if* you seem to catch, or initiate a push and become a trio?" Or "*what if* you explore contrasting the levels to your digital partner?" (see figure 9.2). And "*what if* you match and mirror your digital partners actions?" (See figure 9.3)

The goal of the play-like experimentation, or these ludic strategies, is to illicit responses to and interaction with both live and digital performers. Providing a place for performers to play and to discover more about each other, about the technology, and about the intermedial space in which they will perform means they were able to develop skills which they could share

Figure 9.2   Rehearsal Footage of Live Dancers (Upstage by the Screen) Forming a Trio with Their Digital Dancer by Contrasting Levels. *Source*: Pauline Brooks.

between them, so enhancing their potential for creativity. By starting with play, we can help to transform the performers and to build connections—connections between the live performers, between the live performers and the digital performers, and with the liminal intermedial spaces in which they will finally enter to perform.

Caillois[39] added to Huizinga's theories of play by introducing four classifications of games and play: *Agon* (games that involve competition), *Alea* (games that involve luck or chance), *Mimicry* (games that utilize the imagination, create a fictitious universe, such as in make-believe games and the theater), and *Ilinx* (or vertigo, games that involve spinning building dizziness/falling, or more ritualized aspects that bring the player to a transcendental state). Note how the *what if* game falls into the *Mimicry* classification along with the *as if* that Schechner writes of. But of more use is the spectrum or continuum of play suggested by Caillois that ranges from the extremes of two poles. At one end is *Paidia*—free improvization, free expression, and carefree gaiety, and at the other extreme of the continuum *Ludus,* where Caillois states, "there is a growing tendency to bind it with [. . .] purposely tedious conventions."[40]

For us, the participants in *Falling,* free improvization (*Paidia*) was encouraged, and the improvizational tasks suggested to encourage creative

Figure 9.3   Rehearsal Footage Showing Two Live Dancers Preparing to Match Their Digital Partners on the Screen with an Upside-Down Lift. *Source*: Pauline Brooks.

collaboration between live dance partners and, more importantly, with the virtual (or digital) dance partners projected on the screen. Because as tutors working within set timetable parameters with student performers, there were time restrictions placed upon us and we were not always successful in achieving the level of connection between the dancers in the thirty-three hours allotted to create the movement for the film, to edit the film, and to create the whole work for performance. As one of the dancers noted in their reflections on exploration and play:

> I believe I could have explored [further] my connections and contact with other live bodies as well as the virtual bodies [. . .] a deeper connection between live and media could have been enhanced by a heightened state of awareness during improvised sections.

Playfulness through improvization was a means by which to bring the dancers into the performance arena with each other and with the digital performers/technology, although as the creative performance process progressed, we did introduce rules. Thus, at the other extreme of the continuum, *Ludus* became how we, as the directors and cocreators, introduced more technical skills and refinement of the movement to transition from playful process to a final performance product. We brought in rules so that the performers had to remember certain phrases and connections that were set, rehearsed, refined, and were repeatable. These set moments provided key structures or islands, in the dance work around and between which we allowed the dancers to continue to improvize. *Falling* still incorporated aspects of playfulness, with moments of improvization to entice and intrigue the viewing audience and to aid the dancers to continue to be present to "be in the moment." Our more refined acts of play (or *Ludus*) fell into three groups:

1. Playfulness through interaction (action-reaction)
2. Playfulness through Mirroring (copying)
3. Playfulness through Framing (of other)

For example, two dancers had to slowly walk diagonally across the stage while everyone else, without touching, had to run as fast as possible creating speed and chaos on stage (as we see in figure 9.4 where the photographer, Noel Jones, has managed to capture the running dancers as blurred images contrasting the clarity and focus of the two slow walkers).

Live dancers had to find a moment to mirror (copy) the action of their digital partner(s), bringing them into a moment of unison and matching actions (see figure 9.3). Small groups of dancers had to use their bodies to frame their digital partner(s) or have the digital partner frame them by varying their levels (see figure 9.2). The games allowed them to play, The games allowed them to play, to explore, to create, to interact with each other, and to be open to dancing with both virtual and live partners. The introduction of rules into aspects of the play allowed for reflection, for evaluation, The introduction of rules into aspects of the play allowed for reflection, for evaluation, and then for the refinement of the material, thus ensuring that those found, liminal moments always occurred, those moments when portals of new perspectives opened. What followed was a transformation of the performers from being separate live and digital dancers to becoming one cohesive company of forty-eight rather than twelve dancers—a *communitas*. Through play, performance, and participation with each other and with the technology, live and digital performers became increasingly interwoven. Or as one of the performers noted (see figure 9.2 and video from 4.58 to 5.30):

> Within Section 2 I connected with [a live] dancer, creating a duet which turned into a trio with a virtual dancer [. . .] Timing was key to ensure the duet happened at the same time the virtual dancer appeared, this took practice, but in the later stages of the process, it became habitual [. . .] It was effective to connect to the projections [. . .] it gave the piece another dimension.

Figure 9.4   The Slow Walkers Focus on Each Other Despite the "Chaos" Around Them—Illustrated by the Blurred Images of the Runners. *Source*: Pauline Brooks.

FALLING: AN INSIDER'S READING

Three Artistic directors from the Dance Department at Liverpool John Moores University (LJMU) created and directed *Falling* (2019). Noel Jones was the director-in-charge of filming and the digital media production. Bernard Pierre-Louis was the director of sound, while I led the shaping of the live and digital choreography along with my colleagues. We worked with twelve final year undergraduate dance students, who were cocreators in the creative and performance process with us as well as performers.[41] The performers contributed to the discussion relating to the connotations of falling, by creating spider diagrams in small groups, based on the word falling as a starting point for ideas. They participated in devising the movement for the choreography, creating and editing the sound for all three sections, and for filming and editing of Sections 1 and 2 of the film with the digital dancers. (Noel Jones edited and completed Section 3. He also created the adapted screen version that is available to you in the URL to the work through this essay). *Falling* is approximately twelve minutes in length and is comprised of three sections—Section 1: Balancing Introductions (00–3.45); Section 2: Catching and Falling (3.45–9.12); Section 3: Falling (9.15–12.20). The premiere of the live version of the work was in Sudley Theatre at Liverpool John Moores University on April 8, 2019, and then subsequently at the *Liverpool*

Light Night Festival on May 17, 2019. Noel Jones created the screen dance version presented at the Third Interdisciplinary Falls Studies Workshop, *Liminal Spaces, Images and Texts: Mind the Gap,* June 12–13, 2019, at Trinity College, Dublin. Discussion will refer to both live and screen dance versions.

When introducing an audience to a dance work where familiar boundaries are blurred, it is helpful to not overload them with too many visual perspectives. However, presenting the familiar in unfamiliar ways is, of course, another way to lead them into elements of surprise, to the unexpected liminal performance that will unfold before them. We chose to separate the live and the digital performers at the beginning, gradually introducing each as, for instance, at the beginning of Section 1. The dance opens with a sparseness. The lights go up and the live dancers are on a bare stage, surrounded by blank screens, they exit, and from the darkness the first digital dancer appears on the back cyclorama—the first suggestion of the "threshold" to a new world (see video at 0.21 seconds). For the young boy sitting in the middle of the seating in the dark auditorium, his audible gasp of amazement as the digital dancer unexpectedly appears on the back screen was that spine tingling moment of when a gateway, or portal, opening into another world occurs. We enabled the creation of such an interplay of "in-between the different realities"[42] by carefully scaling the size of the digital dancers to match those of the live dancers. Consequently, throughout the work it was possible to present multiple perspectives of the performers. The projections and lighting of the digital dancers would "pop" on the screens in contrast to the more muted lighting on the live dancers. These devices meant we could, as Turner wrote "play with the elements of the familiar,"[43] and by presenting multiple perspectives and possibilities for the performer and the spectator so "defamiliarize them." Although the digital dancers could only appear on the screens, we were able to establish a sense of one company, a *communitas,* through the interplay between the live and digital dancers, the carefully constructed spacing of the live dancers in relation to the digital, our "reterritorialization" of the space,[44] and the sharing of the performer hierarchy or focus of attention.

As has been mentioned, a central feature of intermedial and liminal performance is the postmodernist idea of encouraging an active viewing by challenging and disturbing the audience through the perceptions of both embodied presence and digital presentation.[45] However, we need to consider not just how to challenge and disorientate audience perspectives but also how to "contribute and optimise an experience of intermediality."[46] It is key to find a balance in the multiple perspectives for viewing, so that the audience does not become overwhelmed and disengaged. I agree with Broadhurst[47] that it is important to be creative in order not just to construct a tension or a rivalry between the corporeal and the digital—a sense of their separateness from each other—but also to build a relationship of cooperation, a "communion of equal individuals" expressed in and through liminal performance.[48] Total domination by one media (usually digital over live) is detrimental to the total effect. Finding a balance, in the blending of the media, between projection and live action is important.[49]

The gradual interplay of live and digital dancers in Section 1 enables the audience to become accustomed to the different perspectives presented as we see each dancer (live and digital) enter and disappear and stay and interact—if only by looking at each other. By placing the live dancers in proximity to the digital dancers on the screen at the beginning of the work, we gradually develop the relationship between the live and digital dancers. Being close to the screens, the live dancers inhabit the outer margins of the stage *with* the digital dancers. For the live audience sitting as they are in the raked seating of the dark theater, separated from the performers and the stage space by that invisible but keenly felt boundary of the "fourth wall", there was the additional experience of hearing at times the footsteps of the dancers on the stage or their breathing—an embodied presence that perhaps was more real that can be encapsulated in the screen dance version available for you in this essay, where the live performers have also been transformed into a digital presence. Gradually, we play with time and space, so that by the end of Section 1 (in the live theater version) we present a live solo dancer, fluidly moving low on the ground of the central space of the stage watched over by the digital dancers looking down at her from all three screens. (In the screen dance version some elements of this can be seen in the video between 2.28 and 3.30). They turn away and exit into the blackness, only to reappear downstage right on the screen and proceed to walk to the upstage screen. The solo live dancer stands and walks as if in front of them, leading the line of screen dancers, live and digital dancers in one line, one size. While she exits through the gap between the screens upstage left, the digital dancers continue to walk around the perimeter of the stage onto the screen stage left. As the digital dancers exit that screen, the live dancers reappear, taking the place of the digital dancers as it were, from down stage left, forming a horizontal line across the stage (along the boundary of the fourth wall), with their backs to the audience. The start of Section 2 (see video at 3.45) is signaled by the exit of the digital dancers and the entrance of the live dancers as well as by the changes in the lighting and in the sound score. The live dancers travel back upstage and exit, leaving one pair of live dancers to traverse the stage, struggling to balance as if on a tight rope, while the digital dancers appear only on the side screens and walk back and forth, challenging the live couple to fall.

In Section 2, small groups of live and digital dancers appear and disappear. They are balancing and counterbalancing, running and catching, gradually increasing speed and numbers of groupings on all three screens and in the live space. We increase the multiples of viewing perspectives, leaving it to the viewer to make their choices as to where to look. We aim to maintain the strong connection between the live performers (drawing on traditional theatre form) and to build a bond between the live and digital performers. However, we challenge that connection for the viewers (and performers) by bringing the live dancers into the central stage space, thus increasing the physical distance between them and the digital dancers. In figure 9.4, we see the two (live) performers and how their intense eye contact emphasizes their connection as they walk slowly toward each other across the diagonal of the stage, to meet center stage, pass by and exit (see video from 5.30). We present them as a focal point, a contrast to the "fructile chaos" around them created by increasing intensity of the running, falling live dancers, and the appearing and disappearing digital dancers.

In the final section, we present the digital dancers seemingly raised on a dais or wall of light (see figure 9.1) surrounding the live dancers, who fall and catch themselves and then, for the first (and only) time, dance in unison as an ensemble of live dancers, beneath the digital dancers, who sit with their backs to both the live performers and the audience. The live dancers reclaim the space. A moment of challenge and competition occurs between the two, until all the live dancers fall (see at video at 10.20), the digital dancers fall from sitting on the wall of light, and then that too falls. There comes a moment of tension, as the digital dancers take ownership of the space, appearing to repeatedly jump on the live dancers and to disappear through the floor, until all the dancers recover, reappear, and interact once more in small groups to wobble, balance, support, frame, and mirror each other. All dancers exit, leaving a pair of dancers (one live and one digital—we see they are the *same* dancer by means of the costume), to fall off the stage/screen in unison (see video at 11.25). Mischievous editing by speeding up and reversing the video footage allows for a "trickster" moment[50] when after falling and disappearing into the floor (see video from 11.28 to 11.47), the digital dancers reappear back onto the screens, but reversing their jumps, as only the digital dancers can (see video at 11.47). The whole company reenters stage and screen (see video at 12.00), there is a pause, a breath, and then all but one performer falls. A lone individual remains standing before the snap blackout, leaving the audience to reflect on their own making of meaning from their viewing of the dance work.

CONCLUSION

To create the intermedial work *Falling,* we had to remain open to the portals of inspiration and glimpses into the liminal realms of possibilities that playful exploration and creative experimentation with and by the technology and the scenography of the space provided for us. As directors, we were limited only by the boundaries of our imagination, by the capabilities of our performers/cocreators, by the technological facilities in and with which we worked, and the time we had from the preparatory start of the process to the presentation of the performance (eleven weeks at three hours a week with the performance in week twelve). Directors and performers worked in active partnership throughout the process. For the dancers who were new to inter-mediality, they experienced challenges and frustrations as they experimented with new concepts and with what at times felt like the "disorderliness" of the creative exploration.[51] However, through playing, they also discovered "magical moments", flashes of shared insights and exhilaration (*spontaneous communitas*) when they experienced "order" among the chaos, enabling them to link with "other" as well as "self." In *Falling*, we have experimented with the "storehouse of possibilities"[52] that the technology, the space, and playful creativeness with both have enabled us to find. Dancers criss-cross thresholds. We present the audience with multiple perspectives "betwixt and between" live and virtual dance worlds, leaving opportunities for new insights, which may seem challenging at times, at others, provoking and even unexpectedly exciting. We have sought to create that "detached, still almost sacred liminal [performance] space"[53] that has allowed us to search for and find new possibilities of expression between the intermedial world of the live theater and digital technology, so that *Falling* becomes, and is, an example of performing the liminal.

NOTES

1. Stephen Bigger, "Thresholds and Fruitful Chaos: Revolutionary Change in Education?" 2010. https://eprints.worc.ac.uk/id/eprint/834; Susan Broadhurst, *Liminal Acts: A Critical Overview of Contemporary Performance and Theory* (London: Cassell, 1999); David Fenton, "Unstable Acts: A Practitioner's Case Study of the Poetics of Postdramatic Theatre and Intermediality," PhD diss. (Queensland University of Technology, 2007); Dan Friedman, "Performance as Revolutionary Activity: Liminality and Social Change," *Body, Space and Technology* 1, no. 1 (2000), doi:10.16995/bst.281.

2. Susan Broadhurst, "Theorising Performance and Technology: Aesthetic and Neuroaesthetic Approaches," *Australasian Drama Studies* 65 (October 2014): 213.

3. *Falling* (screen dance adaptation), created and directed by Pauline Brooks, Noel Jones, and Bernard Pierre-Louis, presented at the Interdisciplinary Falls Studies Workshop, *Liminal Spaces, Images and Texts: Mind the Gap*, Trinity College, Dublin, June 13, 2019, https://www.paulinebrooks-dance.com/choreography-inter-medial/falling-2019.

4. Bigger, "Thresholds and Fruitful Chaos," 3.

5. Brian Sutton-Smith, "Games of Order and Disorder," Paper presented to Symposium on *Forms of Symbolic Inversion,* American Anthropological Association, Toronto, December 1, 1972, quoted in Victor Turner, "Liminal to Liminoid, in Play, Flow, and Ritual," *Rice University Studies* 60, no. 3 (1974): 60, https://hdl.handle.net /1911/63159.

6. Hans Breder, "Intermedia: Enacting the Liminal," *Performing Arts Journal* 17, nos. 2–3: 115, www.jstor.org/stable/3245784.

7. Robin Nelson, "Introduction: Prospective Mapping and Network of Terms," in *Mapping Intermediality in Performance,* ed. Sarah Bay-Cheng, et al. (Amsterdam: Amsterdam University Press, 2010), 18.

8. Irina O Rajewsky, "Intermediality, Intertextuality, and Remediation: A Literary Perspective on Intermediality," *Intermédialités* 6 (2005): 43–64, doi:10.7202/1005505ar.

9. Victor Turner, *The Ritual Process: Structure and Anti-Structure* (Ithaca, New York: Cornell University Press, 1969), 95.

10. Peter M. Boenisch, "Mediation Unfinished: Choreographing Intermediality in Contemporary Dance Performance," in *Intermediality in Theatre and Performance,* 3rd ed., ed. Freda Chapple and Chiel Kattenbelt (Amsterdam: Rofopi, 2007), 151–166.

11. Freda Chapple and Chiel Kattenbelt, "Key Issues in Intermediality in Theatre and Performance," in *Intermediality in Theatre and Performance,* 3rd ed., ed. Freda Chapple and Chiel Kattenbelt (Amsterdam: Rofopi, 2007), 11–15.

12. Chapple and Kattenbelt, "Key Issues," 24.

13. Pauline Brooks, "Creating New Spaces: Dancing in a Telematic World," *International Journal of Performance Arts and Digital Media* 6, no. 1 (2010): 49–60, doi: 10.1386/padm.6.1.49_1.

14. Broadhurst, *Liminal Acts,* 13.

15. Chapple and Kattenbelt, "Key Issues," 24.

16. Broadhurst, *Liminal Acts,* 9.

17. Chapple and Kattenbelt, "Key Issues," 2007; Nelson, "Prospective Mapping," 2010.

18. Susan Broadhurst and Josephine Machon, "Introduction: Body, Space and Technology," in *Performance and Technology Practices of Virtual Embodiment and Interactivity,* ed. Susan Broadhurst and Josephine Machon (Hampshire and New York: Palgrave Macmillan, 2006), XV–XX; Fenton, "Unstable Acts," 2007; and Holly Rogers, "Betwixt and Between Worlds: Spatial and Temporal Liminality in Video Art-Music," in *The Oxford Handbook of New Audiovisual Aesthetics,* ed. Claudia Gorbman, John Richardson, and Carol Verallis (New York: Oxford University Press, 2013), 525–542.

19. Arnold van Gennep, *The Rites of Passage,* trans. Monika B. Vizedom and Gabrielle L. Caffee (London: Routledge and Kegan Paul, 1960), 21.

20. Wendelin Kűpers, "Dancing on the Limen-Embodied and Creative Inter-Places as Thresholds of Be(com)ing: Phenomenological Perspectives on Liminality and Transitional Spaces in Organisation and Leadership," *Tamara Journal for Critical Organisation Inquiry* 9, no. 3–4 (2011): 46. https://tamarajournal.com/index .php/tamara/article/view/139/114.

21. Sutton-Smith, "Order and Disorder," quoted in Turner, "Liminal to Liminoid," 60.

22. Victor Turner, "Are there Universals of Performance in Myth, Ritual, and Drama?," in *By Means of Performance*, ed. Richard Schechner and Willa Appel (Cambridge: Cambridge University Press, 1990), 12. (Schechner explains that the book is published in honor of Turner. The chapter is from Turner's 1982 paper prepared for participants in Symposium 89, Wenner-Gren Foundation for Anthropological Research).

23. Turner, "Liminal to Liminoid," 79.

24. Mihaly Csikszentmihalyi, "Flowing: A General Model of Intrinsically Rewarding Experiences," *Journal of Humanistic Psychology* 15, no. 3 (1975): 41–63, doi:10.1177/002216787501500306.

25. Turner, "Liminal to Liminoid," 79.

26. Lewis J. Lowell, "Toward a Unified Theory of Cultural Performance: A Reconstructive Introduction to Victor Turner," in *Victor Turner and Contemporary Cultural Performance,* ed. Graham St. John (New York, Oxford: Berghahn Books, 2008), 53.

27. Susan Broadhurst, "Intelligence, Interaction, Reaction, and Performance," in *Performance and Technology Practices of Virtual Embodiment and Interactivity,* ed. Susan Broadhurst and Josephine Machon (Hampshire and New York: Palgrave Macmillan, 2006), 141.

28. William Blazek, "A Moving World: The Port of Liverpool in American Fiction," in *Mapping Liminalities: Thresholds in Cultural and Literary Texts*, ed. Lucy Kay, et al. (Bern: Peter Lang, 2008), 37.

29. Blazek, "A Moving World"; Sarah Bay-Cheng, et al., ed. "How to Approach this Book," in *Mapping Intermediality in Performance (*Amsterdam: Amsterdam University Press, 2010), 9–11.

30. Fenton, "Unstable Acts*,"* 36.

31. Richard Schechner, *Performance studies: An Introduction,* 3rd ed. (London and New York: Routledge, 2013), 89.

32. Roger Caillois, *Man, Play and Games* (New York: Schocken Books, 1979); Johan Huizinga, *Homo Ludens: A Study of the Play-Element in Culture (*Abingdon, Oxon and New York: Routledge, 1949); Brian Sutton-Smith, "A Structural Grammar of Games and Sport," *International Review of Sport Sociology* 11, no. 2 (1976): 117–137, doi:10.1177/101269027601100207.

33. Alice Bayliss et al., "Emergent Objects: Designing through Performance," *International Journal of Performance Arts and Digital Media* 3, no. 2–3 (2007): 269–279.

34. Alexander F. Chamberlain, *The Child: A Study in the Evolution of Man* (London: Walter Scott Ltd., 1900), 27. https://wellcomecollection.org/works/tarzp3za.

35. Hector Rodriguez, "The Playful and the Serious: An Approximation to Huizinga's *Homo Ludens,"* *The International Journal of Computer Game Research* 6, no. 1 (2006): para 1, http://gamestudies.org/0601/articles/rodriges.

36. Sam Gill, "The Powerful Play Goes On: Friedrich Schiller to Jacques Derrida on Play" (2009), accessed May 24, 2019, http://sam-gill.com/conversations-controversies/.

37. Gill, "The Powerful Play Goes On."
38. Schechner, *Performance Studies,* 89.
39. Caillois, *Man, Play and Games*, 1979.
40. Caillois, *Man, Play and Games*, 13.
41. Pauline Brooks, "Performers, Creators and Audience: Co-participants in an Interconnected Model of Performance and Creative Process," *Research in Dance Education* 15, no. 2 (2014): 120–137, doi: 10.1080/14647893.2014.891846.
42. Chapple and Kattenbelt, "Key Issues," 11.
43. Turner, "Liminal to Liminoid," 60.
44. Giles Deleuze and Felix Guattari, *A Thousand Plateaus: Capitalism and Schizophrenia,* trans. Brian Massumi (Minneapolis: University of Minnesota Press, 1987).
45. Liesbeth Groot Nibbelink and Sigrid Merx, "Presence and Perception: Analysing Intermediality in Performance," in *Mapping Intermediality in Performance,* ed. Sarah Bay-Cheng, et al. (Amsterdam: Amsterdam University Press, 2010), 219.
46. Nibbelink and Sigrid, "Presence and Perception," 220.
47. Broadhurst, *Liminal Acts,* 1999.
48. Turner, *The Ritual Process,* 96.
49. Brooks, "Co-Participants," 2014; Steve Dixon, "Uncanny Interactions," *Performance Research: A Journal of the Performing Arts* 11, no. 4 (2011): 67–75, doi:10.1080/13528160701363473; Nik Haffner, "Embrace Your Television," in *Dance and Technology: Moving Towards Media Productions,* ed. Söke Dinkla and Martina Leeker (Berlin: Alexander Verlag, 2002), 104–117.
50. Barbara Babcock-Abrahams, "A Tolerated Margin of Mess: The Trickster and His Tales Reconsidered," *Journal of the Folklore Institute* 11, no. 3 (March 1975): 147–186, http://www.jstor.com/stable/3813932.
51. Sutton-Smith, "Order and Disorder," 1972, as in Turner, 1974.
52. Turner, "Liminal to Liminoid," 1974.
53. Turner, "Universals of Performance," 12.

BIBLIOGRAPHY

Babcock-Abrahams, Barbara. "A Tolerated Margin of Mess: The Trickster and His Tales Reconsidered." *Journal of the Folklore Institute* 11, no. 3 (March 1975): 147–186. doi:10.2307/3813932.
Bayliss, Alice, Joslin McKinney, Sita Popat, and Mick Wallis. "Emergent Objects: Designing through Performance." *International Journal of Performance Arts and Digital Media* 3, no. 2–3 (2007): 269–279. doi:10.1386/padm.3.2-3.269_1.
Bigger, Stephen. "Thresholds and Fruitful Chaos: Revolutionary Change in Education?" https://eprints.worc.ac.uk/id/eprint/834.
Bay-Cheng, Sarah, Chiel Kattenbelt, Andy Lavender, and Robin Nelson. "How to Approach this Book." In *Mapping Intermediality in Performance,* edited by Sarah Bay-Cheng, Chiel Kattenbelt, Andy Lavender, and Robin Nelson, 9–11. Amsterdam: Amsterdam University Press, 2010.

Bay-Cheng, Sarah, Chiel Kattenbelt, Andy Lavender, and Robin Nelson, eds. *Mapping Intermediality in Performance.* Amsterdam: Amsterdam University Press, 2010.

Blazek, William. "A Moving World: The Port of Liverpool in American Fiction." In *Mapping Liminalities: Thresholds in Cultural and Literary Texts*, edited by Lucy Kay, Zoë Kinsley, Terry Phillips, and Alan Roughley, 17–40. Bern: Peter Lang, 2008.

Boenisch, Peter M. "Mediation Unfinished: Choreographing Intermediality in Contemporary Dance Performance." In *Intermediality in Theatre and Performance,* edited by Freda Chapple and Chiel Kattenbelt, 151–166. Amsterdam: Rofopi, 2007.

Breder, Hans. "Intermedia: Enacting the Liminal." *Performing Arts Journal* 17, no. 2–3 (1995): 112–130. www.jstor.org/stable/3245784.

Broadhurst, Susan. *Liminal Acts: A Critical Overview of Contemporary Performance and Theory.* London: Cassell, 1999.

Broadhurst, Susan. "Intelligence, Interaction, Reaction, and Performance." In *Performance and Technology Practices of Virtual Embodiment and Interactivity,* edited by Susan Broadhurst and Josephine Machon, 141–152. Hampshire and New York: Palgrave Macmillan, 2006.

Broadhurst, Susan. "Theorising Performance and Technology: Aesthetic and Neuroaesthetic Approaches." *Australasian Drama Studies* 65 (October 2014): 213–236.

Broadhurst, Susan and Josephine Machon. "Introduction: Body, Space and Technology." In *Performance and Technology Practices of Virtual Embodiment and Interactivity,* edited by Susan Broadhurst and Josephine Machon, XV–XX. Hampshire and New York: Palgrave Macmillan, 2006.

Brooks, Pauline. "Creating New Spaces: Dancing in a Telematic World." *International Journal of Performance Arts and Digital Media* 6, no. 1 (2010): 49–60. doi:10.1386/padm.6.1.49_1.

Brooks, Pauline. "Performers, Creators and Audience: Co-participants in an Interconnected Model of Performance and Creative Process." *Research in Dance Education* 15, no. 2 (2014): 120–137: doi:10.1080/14647893.2014.891846.

Caillois, Roger. *Man, Play and Games.* New York: Schocken Books, 1979.

Chamberlain, Alexander F. *The Child: A Study in the Evolution of Man.* London: Walter Scott Ltd., 1900. https://wellcomecollection.org/works/tarzp3za.

Chapple, Freda and Chiel Kattenbelt. "Key Issues in Intermediality in Theatre and Performance." In *Intermediality in Theatre and Performance,* edited by Freda Chapple and Chiel Kattenbelt, 11–15. Amsterdam: Rofopi, 2007.

Csikszentmihalyi, Mihaly. "Flowing: A General Model of Intrinsically Rewarding Experiences." *Journal of Humanistic Psychology* 15, no. 3 (July 1975): 41–63. doi:10.1177/002216787501500306.

Deleuze, Giles and Felix Guattari. *A Thousand Plateaus: Capitalism and Schizophrenia.* Translated by Brian Massumi. Minneapolis, MN: University of Minnesota Press, 1987.

Dixon, Steve. "Uncanny Interactions." *Performance Research: A Journal of the Performing Arts* 11, no. 4 (2011): 67–75. doi:10.1080/13528160701363473.

Falling, (screen dance adaptation*),* created and directed by Pauline Brooks, Noel Jones and Bernard Pierre-Louis, presented at the Interdisciplinary Falls Studies Workshop, *Liminal Spaces, Images and Texts: Mind the Gap,* Trinity College, Dublin, June 13, 2019. https://www.paulinebrooks-dance.com/choreography-intermedial/falling-2019.

Fenton, David. "Unstable Acts: A Practitioner's Case Study of the Poetics of Postdramatic Theatre and Intermediality." PhD diss., Queensland University of Technology, 2007.

Friedman, Dan. "Performance as Revolutionary Activity: Liminality and Social Change." *Body, Space and Technology* 1, no. 1 (2000). doi:10.16995/bst.281.

Gill, Sam. "The Powerful Play Goes On: Friedrich Schiller to Jacques Derrida on Play." (2009). Accessed May 24, 2019. http://sam-gill.com/conversations -controversies/.

Haffner, Nik. "Embrace Your Television." In *Dance and Technology: Moving Towards Media Productions,* edited by Söke Dinkla and Martina Leeker, 104–117. Berlin: Alexander Verlag, 2002.

Huizinga, Johan. *Homo Ludens: A Study of the Play-Element in Culture.* Abingdon, Oxon and New York: Routledge, 1949.

Kűpers, Wendelin. "Dancing on the Limen-Embodied and Creative Inter-places as Thresholds of Be(com)ing: Phenomenological Perspectives on Liminality and Transitional Spaces in Organisation and Leadership." *Tamara Journal for Critical Organisation Inquiry* 9, no. 3–4 (2011): 45–59. https://tamarajournal.com/index .php/tamara/article/view/139/114.

Lowell, Lewis J. "Toward a Unified Theory of Cultural Performance: A Reconstructive Introduction to Victor Turner." In *Victor Turner and Contemporary Cultural Performance,* edited by Graham St. John, 41–58. New York. Oxford: Berghahn Books, 2008.

Nelson, Robin. "Introduction: Prospective Mapping and Network of Terms." In *Mapping Intermediality in Performance,* edited by Sarah Bay-Cheng, Chiel Kattenbelt, Andy Lavender, and Robin Nelson, 13–23. Amsterdam: Amsterdam University Press, 2010.

Nibbelink, Liesbeth Groot and Sigrid Merx. "Presence and Perception: Analysing Intermediality in Performance." In *Mapping Intermediality in Performance,* edited by Sarah Bay-Cheng, Chiel Kattenbelt, Andy Lavender, and Robin Nelson, 218– 229. Amsterdam: Amsterdam University Press, 2010.

Rajewsky, Irina O. "Intermediality, Intertextuality, and Remediation: A Literary Perspective on Intermediality." *Intermédialités* 6 (2005): 43–64. doi:10.7202/1005505ar.

Rodriguez, Hector. "The Playful and the Serious: An Approximation to Huizinga's *Homo Ludens.*" *Game Studies: The International Journal of Computer Game Research* 6, no. 1 (2006). http://gamestudies.org/0601/articles/rodriges.

Rogers, Holly. "Betwixt and Between Worlds: Spatial and Temporal Liminality in Video Art-Music.'" In *The Oxford Handbook of New Audiovisual Aesthetics,* edited by Claudia Gorbman, John Richardson, and Carol Verallis, 525–542. New York: Oxford University Press, 2013.

Schechner, Richard. *Performance Studies: An Introduction.* 3rd edition. London and New York: Routledge, 2013.

Sutton-Smith, Brian. "Games of Order and Disorder." Paper presented to Symposium on *Forms of Symbolic Inversion,* American Anthropological Association, Toronto, December 1, 1972. Quoted in Victor Turner, "Liminal to Liminoid, in Play, Flow, and Ritual: An Essay in Comparative Symbology," *Rice University Studies* 60, no. 3 (1974): 52–92. https://hdl.handle.net/1911/63159.

Sutton-Smith, Brian. "A Structural Grammar of Games and Sport." *International Review of Sport Sociology* 11, no. 2 (1976): 117–137. doi: 10.1177/101269027601100207.

Turner, Victor. *The Ritual Process: Structure and Anti-Structure.* Ithaca, NY: Cornell University Press, 1969.

Turner, Victor. "Liminal to liminoid, in Play, Flow, and Ritual: An Essay in Comparative Symbology." *Rice University Studies* 60, no. 3 (1974): 52–92. https://hdl.handle.net/1911/63159.

Turner, Victor. "Are there Universals of Performance in Myth, Ritual, and Drama?" In *By Means of Performance: Intercultural Studies of Theatre and Ritual,* edited by Richard Schechner and Willa Appel, 8–18. Cambridge: Cambridge University Press, 1990.

van Gennep, Arnold. *The Rites of Passage,* Translated by Monika B. Vizedom and Gabrielle L. Caffee. London: Routledge and Kegan Paul, 1960.

Section IV

LIMINALITY AS AN AGENT OF CHANGE

Chapter 10

The Pedagogics of Liminality

Ivan Illich and the Critique of Institutional Ritualization

José R. Irizarry

The title for this chapter can build expectations, in the most literary-minded readers, for some form of critical engagement with Leo Tolstoy's novella *The Death of Ivan Illich*. While that expectation will send the reader off course, it may in fact be proper to this chapter's topic since the name conjured in the title of the Russian master's story is indeed a *liminal* subject, a representation of an agonistic memory recreated in the *threshold* between death and life. With the opening sentences announcing that "Ivan Illich is dead," Tolstoy has introduced us to an absent-presence whose literary function will be to evoke in the living characters—those who breathe, reason, speak, and move with purpose—their innermost longings and intentions. In Tolstoy's narrative, those who name themselves "friends" of Ivan Illich evoke his name to ponder who will take his place in the bureaucratic judicial system where he served for long and who will get what position once the chairs of the systemic game of power are reorganized following his death. Illich's wife evokes his name to assert her right, as a grieving widow, to manipulate the system in order to get a more substantial government's pension. The fictional Illich appears as a symbolic corpse, an enunciation that signals the demise of authentic relationships and community faced by the necrotic tendencies of unexamined institutional systems. In *The Death of Ivan Illich* Tolstoy, experiencing the fast-paced progressivism that characterized social transitions into the twentieth century, advances once again his doctrinal "rejection of the state and all the institutions associated with it, because they inherently operated through violence and oppression."[1]

It is a this point where, for the purpose of this chapter, I recall a nonfictional Ivan Illich, the Austrian priest who in the 1960s and 1970s prophesized the impending death of institutional systems and the revisionist historian who radically promoted the reinstitution of "the commons," that unclaimable shared public space political theorist Hanna Arendt termed our *common world.*[2] Much like Tolstoy' social commentary at the turn of the twentieth century, Illich sought to interpret what can be considered a transitional period in history when the radical movements of the late sixties initiate their process of commodification into the legal and programmatic systems of mainstream institutions during the seventies. Living in this threshold of institutional change posits "liminality," according to American journalist Eric Davis, as a key characteristic of this decade[3] In accepting this judgment, one needs to be reminded that this is the same sociocultural context that compelled anthropologist Victor Turner to recover the concept of "the liminal" in his anthropological analysis of rites of passage.

In attempting to interpret the transformational character of the postindustrial age, Illich's critical project was ambitious. His goal was to endeavor a historical analysis of every single modern institution that was engendered to support the ideology of progress and development and to identify the systemic flaws that made those institutions counterproductive to their intended purposes. Even when he ventured into a historical examination of unrelated ideas at different stages of his scholarly career such as the written text, the body, social meanings of water, work, human needs, and gender, there were three main systems he aimed at with consistent eagerness: compulsory schooling, the medical establishment, and the ecology of transportation.[4] These three systems, according to Illich's periodization, consolidated their social dependencies in the early twentieth century, when industrial nations stirred toward the normalization and export of managerial efficiency to promote social growth and the personal wellness of its citizens.

While the historical analysis Illich conducts in each of these systems is robust and nuanced, at times self-corrective with each iteration, the counterproductive argument he advanced was simple and consistent; modern schools make people less educated, medical professionalization promotes iatrogenic results thus making people unhealthier, and mass transportation decreases kinesthetic displacement, hence hindering free movement. As counterintuitive arguments go, these conclusions seem to be deconstructive axioms in need of very sensible elaboration. After all, critics of well-established institutional systems that achieve social permanency and become accepted as conventions are likely to be rebuffed. Illich tries to be an effective critic by identifying the historical contingencies of each system and the transiency of the ideas that produced them whether those ideas are education, health, or energy.

In *De-schooling Society*, Illich articulates his first and more complete manifesto against educational systems turned functional arms of a society self-trapped in the normativity discourse of scarcity and needs that sees the ability to produce and consume market goods as the only path toward human progress.[5] Once we have accepted the idea that the optimum realization of the person is not to live life but to commodify life as an expression of socially acceptable personhood, we have arrived at an ontological axiom, "We are what we have," a statement of modern identity that more than often refuses interrogation. In the words of James Conroy, we have arrived at a *discursive closure* that is exposed to measured re/form but rarely gives itself to critical displacement.[6]

Against such a discursive closure that seeks to reform schooling to make its processes better without discerning the values and theoretical axioms that conform the system itself, Illich suggests a qualitative break with the institution of schooling to reinstitute what he considers to be a historical focus of education on learning and the formation of mind and soul for *convivial* existence.[7] What modern schools produce is technical knowledge that preserves the ritual propagation of systems but not the habits of mind needed to instill awareness of the way those systems inhibit human freedom. Educating for these habits of mind is important since, according to Illich, when individuals learn free from institutional ritualization (what schooling seems to provide), they break away from ideologies that foster inequality as well as from their traditional sources for wellness and happiness. Borrowing Max Gluckman's idea of the purposes of ritual, Illich makes this argument more poignant by saying:

> Rituals can hide from their participants even discrepancies and conflicts between social principle and social organization. As long as an individual is not explicitly conscious of the ritual character of the process through which he was initiated to the forces which shapes his cosmos, he cannot break the spell and shape a new cosmos. As long as we are not aware of the ritual through which school shapes the progressive consumer—the economy's major source—we cannot break the spell of this economy and shape a new one.[8]

One of Illich's most contentious works, apart from his brief but controversial incursion into the topic of gender, was his incisive take on the health system on his *Medical Nemesis*. If medical expertise has achieved the social status of a modern idol granting it a soteriological role that which we cannot live without and on which the salvation of our bodies depend, Illich attempted to be an iconoclast from the opening sentence of this work by stating that "[the] medical establishment has become a major threat to health."[9] In his searing critique of what he calls the rituals conducted by the medical profession to appropriate the knowledge of another person's body and to create a dependency in a pathogenic system, he concludes that such an establishment can only survive with the production of more sickness.[10] This critique may have been perceived as an outlandish claim at the moment he wrote the text as many professed a blind faith in the possibilities of medical science but will sound as a reasonable argument to contemporary readers who witness the pervasive mediatic commercialization of drugs always accompanied by a long advisory list of side-effects demanding additional treatment and medication and the widening scope of diagnostics for which these are required.[11]

In making this critique of the medical establishment, Illich foreshadowed the over-professionalization of medicine in order to build a system that, like the public school, will serve the needs and subsistence market of a consumer society—more present today in the mechanization of treatments, insurance coverage costs, and increased pharmaceutical manufacturing. In lieu of this trend, Illich suggests the autonomy of individuals to know and cope with the state of their bodies as they enjoy various experiences of health (without the inscription of and a professional diagnosis) and to practice the historically acceptable art of suffering. In a very insightful way, Illich summarizes this point:

> Professionally organized medicine has come to function as a domineering moral enterprise that advertises industrial expansion as a war against suffering. It has thereby undermined the ability of individuals to face their reality, to express their own values, and to accept the inevitable and often irremediable pain and impairment, decline, and death.[12]

At this point, it is important to note that out of his resistance to the expropriation of the body by medical professionals and their advocates within the system (hospitals and government), Illich positioned himself as a staunch supporter, even as a Catholic priest challenging the orthodoxy of the moment, of a woman's right to choose over her body and the right of patients to determine the terms of their existential demise.

Conversely, another capacity of the free body is limited by industrial society according to Illich—that of unrestricted mobility within the spaces that used the constitute the commons (i.e., the promenade or the plaza at the center of town where unprompted encounters were possible, an open field with leafy trees providing shade to weary sojourners, the traditional market where domestically produced goods could be exchanged). Restituting the commons is an imperative critical move in challenging the fetishization of private spaces as sites for individual consumption.[13] In *Energy and Equity*, he argues that the ideology of continuous growth on both socialist and capitalist economic systems imposes insufferable social inequalities when overconsumption of energy becomes detrimental not only to the shared natural environment but to the integration of the community itself. In fact, in Illich's humanistic view, destruction of the environment is the lesser injurious effect of energy overconsumption as the "far more bitter results are the multiplication of psychic frustration . . . (for) the passenger who agrees to live in a world monopolized by transport becomes harassed, overburdened consumer of distances whose shape and length he can no longer control."[14]

As the argument goes, energy used in traffic over a determined period of time translates into high levels of acceleration.[15] Energy allows growth to happen at a pace seeking to reach the expected stage of social development in the shortest period of time. In this context of energy consumption to improve levels of speed, people are dependent on technology that can provide rapid transitions from one spatial position to the next, whether these spaces are the interactive online environments of today or the ecology of mass transportation in Illich's days. To facilitate the efficiency of that movement via transportation systems, vehicles, roads, bridges, and directional signs are needed. Movement becomes then a private and mechanized endeavor controlled by these spatial and visual artifacts within an ecology where the "other" and the natural environment disappear.[16] Illich suggests that in such context, the person has lost the power to imagine herself outside of the role of the passenger who is carried along in time and space. In analyzing the high industrialization of movement as "traffic" in relation to the individual subject he says:

> The occasional chance to spend a few hours strapped into a high-powered seat makes him an accomplice in the distortion of human space, and prompts him to consent to the design of hiscountry's geography around vehicles rather than around people. . . . His self-image requires as itscomplement a life-space and a life-time integrated by the pace at which he moves. If that relationship is determined by the velocity of vehicles rather than by the movement of people, man the architect is reduced to the status of a mere commuter.[17]

Therefore, according to Illich, the individual loses control over the physical and psychological power that resides in the capacity to use her metabolic energy to move freely unobstructed by regulatory signage, the strict directionality of roads, and the isolationism of an encapsulated car.[18] While those who still use the metabolic energy of their legs to walk or to ride bicycles experience some of the freedom that allows for more human connection and contemplative enjoyment of the environment, their lack of participation in the consumption of transport energy will ultimately render them deficient participants in the consumer-oriented society.[19]

Whereas education, curative practices, and modes of movement have existed in every society across time, Illich strives to demonstrate how the shape these necessary human practices have taken in late modernity find no antecedent in history and that they have emerged as natural byproducts of an idea of social progress and development that provides the foundation for the global culture of consumption. Unquestionably, Illich is not a singular and unique voice in the scholarly critique of postindustrial systems promoted by the unquestioned ideology of progress and the technocratically guided development that depends on professional tutelage. Well known is Karl Popper's assessment of progress as an inadequate scientific explanation of actual social phenomena.[20] Oswald Spengler, in proposing the decline of the West after the two great wars, pointed to the failure of technological improvements to guarantee democracy and moral advancement.[21] More recently, postmodern scholars of every strand have convincingly shown how progress, as the meta-narrative of human flourishing, is not more than an instrument of power and control over both the psyche and the political agency of individuals.[22]

What gives Illich's work particularity among the many critics of institutional systems is the epistemology that guides his methods of analysis. As Giorgio Agamben suggests in his foreword to a collection of Illich's early writings, "The concepts of Illich as a critic of modernity and archeologist of conviviality originates as a radical and coherent development of theological categories already present in the thought of the priest."[23] This theological *substratum* underpinning his epistemological approach to cultural critique makes his sociological analysis a proper interlocutor with studies of religion and ritual. His call for a restituted space of social relationships (God's Kingdom) and the invitation to consider the limits of social institutions (the boundaries of divine transcendence) frame the overall methodology for tearing down the idols of modern consumerist culture. Today, Illich's iconoclastic approach to systems may not seem as subversive as they seemed following the socially eager sixties and seventies and the *stiz im leben's* appetitive for utopian ideas. In fact, Illich's works fell into scholarly oblivion as the eighties eclipsed. Why then recover his work to position him as a privileged conversation partner in the twenty-first-century cybernetic, post-Taylorism society? Why should the reader endure a dialogical engagement with an author whose scholarly originality has been superseded? Why do we need to witness the *Resurrection of Ivan Illich*?

I cannot deny that my interest in Illich's revisionist historiographical method, the hermeneutical creativity of his argumentation, and the biographical coincidences that have found me sharing Illich's places of living and study make his work intellectually attractive. But personal considerations aside, it is my contention that Illich's work should be provided with a new context for the interpretation of his ostensible deconstructionist approach to institutions and the recovery of the scope and intentions of his critical project. Was Illich suggesting a society deprived of schools and teachers? Was he devaluing the role of health professionals and seeking the eradication of places dedicated to the treatment of unhealthy bodies? Was he envisioning a society where cars and means of transportation become outmoded? If that was the fundamental expectation of his critical project, the current permanence and growth of these systems will render his extensive discursive treatment of these institutions a washout. Yet, as a historian with a Braudelian taste for *longue durée's,* conceptions of continually evolving structures, such a proposal for institutional obsolescence will be acknowledged an impossibility by Illich himself.

What can still happen if his method and critique of systems is applied to current institutions is that we may treat these systems as open discursive arenas. In doing so we may recover a consciousness of the impermanence of the idea of the system itself so that we are able to have choices in the ways we participate in and reintegrate ourselves into social systems without being coopted by their imposed social necessity.[24] By engaging a historical analysis of each system, we realize that the current institutional arrangements of schools, hospitals, and transportation systems are important stages of an evolving society tooling itself for full participation in a commodifying, market-oriented culture though a process of ritualization. In this ritualization of systems, institutions are accepted as an imperative social need and professionals conceived as a new "priesthood caste" mediating effective responses to immediate social demands. After all, as Catherine Bells reminds us, "ritualization is generally a way of engaging some wide consensus that those acting are doing so as a type of natural response to a world conceived and interpreted as affected by forces that transcend it- transcend it in time, influence, and meaning, if not in ontological status. Ritualization tends to posit the existence of a type of authoritative reality that is seen to dictate to the immediate situation."[25] However, these institutional systems are not to be taken for granted as eternal realities with a status of permanence, even if they are solidified in the consensus of ritualization. When it comes to examining them there should be no discursive closure as all institutions are open to contestation when they cease to affirm their purported aims.

What can break our almost ritualistic trance with modern institutions to allow us to consider their demise as something within the realm of the possible? My thesis, in rereading Illich's work, is that there is a substantive lack of consciousness that we have enveloped ourselves, epistemologically and ontologically, into the ritualist structure of modern systems without considering that point of transition in which the institutions established to promote human (and ecological I may add) well-being become counterproductive.[26] Illich called this point of transition into counterproductivity, using language familiar to Turner's study of ritual transitions, a *threshold.* Modern institutions provide tools that can partially remedy the ills of the human condition but only *to a certain point.* Beyond that critical threshold remain lack of individual choice, communal erosion, and ultimately self-inflicted cultural captivity.

In response to calls for a pragmatic ethics that seeks to develop strategies for institutional reform or for a postmodern surrendering to cultural inevitability that suspends ethical engagement with the world when dealing with repressive social systems, Illich responded with a call for an *askesis* of knowledge that can only happen in the impermanent realm of that threshold. Pretty much as ritual practices in the liminal space promote complete surrender of status—achieved in the past and expected in the future—Illich's counter-systemic threshold surrenders knowledge based on the social determinations of institutional certainties and opens the person to alternative forms of human flourishing. This will require an acute exploration of history as those certainties solidify themselves in the temporal continuum of past and future. This threshold appears, in Illich's words, as a space for purging those corrupting concepts that give "fictitious substances" the semblance of sensible existence.[27]

Read without that *threshold* as a hermeneutical key, Illich's work can be perceived as either recovering a past to promote a traditionalist, premodern view of society without institutions, where *communitas* was still valued or, alternatively, as a postinstitutional visioning process with no particular project to make that vision a concrete reality. Nevertheless, Illich was a historian not yearning for a tradition that has been neglected or abandoned even if much have been lost to our impoverishment. In turn, as he does not celebrate the Hegelian notion of progress, he does not anticipate what should happen as a result of his critical analysis. Past and future do not determine the way of recovery from the trance that makes us automatons of modern systems, only what we learn in the instance of a convivial experience within the threshold can show us the way out.

I suggest that Illich's unresolved conflict with the idea of education as a coopted system for the production of institutional experts could be then addressed by describing his analysis as a search for what Turner called in the *Ritual Process,* a *pedagogics of liminality*.[28] While Turner did not define methodically what he meant by "pedagogics," one would have to assume the emerging faith in the interpretative capacities of the social sciences at the time he conducts his study of rituals,[29] informed his interest in "the relationship between those social, technological, and material means through which cultural practices are transmitted, the varied experiences of those involved in this learning, and the embodied outcomes of these processes," what for Chris Shilling defines the nature of pedagogics.[30] The pedagogical function of the liminal experience can be understood here then as the promotion of (trans) formative processes that foster the realization of the self as no other than "the other," which can only happen in the context of a community that finds itself outside the social system or in and out of the formal structure of systems where social status is implied and expected. The pedagogics of liminality makes evident that in an (institutional) oriented existence "the person desires to possess for oneself what ought to be shared for the common good" and that *communitas* will be threatened if the institutional expert acts only "in terms of the rights conferred by the incumbency of (his) office in the social structure" and if he "follows (his) . . . urges at the expense of his fellows."[31] Illich called this formative process of liminal pedagogics, preferring the Spanish language as heuristic tool, *convivencia* (conviviality)—an active and conscious form of living together in order to sustain *communitas*.

Unlike Victor Turner who understood this pedagogics to be a functional process toward the appropriate reintegration of the individual to the social structure, a necessary developmental instance such to speak, Illich, who was not fond of developmental claims, wanted to give the liminal experience a status of recurrent permanence. More in tune with what we can call liturgical imagination than with ritual practice, Illich saw the liminal pedagogics as convivial experiences of awareness that could be performed and rehearsed more than once offering the necessary interruptions in an institutionally structured life to instill a critical and even contesting disposition toward the world.[32] This will require an epistemological act of suspension that goes together with an existential act of renunciation. Liminal pedagogics will not require us to abandon or deny our role in the social structure (as experts or consumers, agents or recipients, priests or neophytes), but it will require sporadic instances of suspension or interruption where we reconsider the ways we know and describe ourselves and our relationship with the world within a range of metaphors that break open the linguistic determinations of the *en-massed* individual (the student, the patient, the conductor, the expert, the consumer). This pedagogics of the liminal requires the creation of hermeneutically innovative and heuristically inspiring perspectives. In tandem, it requires a determination to experience life as given, without the excesses we add to it within a discourse of needs and scarcity, practicing self-limitation in the context of subsistence.

Illich can be described within this framework as a liminal being for he sought both the epistemological basis for a critique of systems and an existential expression of convivial life. He pursued the epistemological goal by recovering in his work a myriad of metaphors hidden in common-use language thus making any discourse with totalizing pretensions an illusion of reality. The existential expression of conviviality was fostered by his creation of small communities of friends who as equals, lay and expert, will influence each other and commit to a life of basic subsistence where the vernacular, the peoples' own tools, were the main resources of work, health, learning, and movement. Illich experimented with the creation of these intentional communities among Puerto Rican immigrants as a priest in New York City and with a group of international friends and locals in his Center for Intercultural Documentation (CIDOC) in Cuernavaca Mexico.

Borrowing from Brazilian dramatist Augusto Boal's theory of the theater, I suggest this liminal pedagogics allows the formation of an *aesthetic space*, where actors see themselves in the act of acting, speaking languages that reframe the structure of their own experience and acting with the limited resources at their disposition to create a possible world for the audience—if just for the interstitial moment of performance and nothing more.[33] As Turner will say referring to social drama, such performative ritual "probes the community weaknesses, calls the community leaders to account, desacralize its most cherished beliefs, portraits its conflicts and suggest remedies for them."[34] That awareness is to be celebrated according to Illich as it is the source of discursive openness. The threshold which is a limit is also an opening—the only real open space for epistemological *askesis*. For that reason, Illich invites us to remain in the limen, at the threshold where an authentic convivial existence can be momentarily sustained and where we can feel liberated from the discursive closure of modern systems. It is certainly clear that the objective world can provide permanence to thresholds in portals, ritual objects, and buildings but what about the evolving subject? For how long such a liminal experience can be sustained by an individual? What do we do when we have reached the threshold beyond which our individuality is erased to become the unquestioned character of a social script? What practices bring us back to that place of awareness and generative contention with the world? How can we instill a secular liturgical imagination for the sustenance of conviviality?

The practice of a pedagogics of liminality can be derived from Illich's multiple approaches to suspending a facile acceptance of the axioms by which systems survive. Each approach will in fact require a larger exposure not permitted by the brevity of this essay, yet they merit an introduction as they account for the uniqueness of Illich's proposal among many critics of growth-based social systems. The pedagogics of liminality proposed by Illich will require challenging the main epistemological tradition from which the rationale for modern systems is built—the Western-Christian discourse. Therefore, the pedagogics of liminality will privilege *intercultural exchanges* and the identification of convivial resources from various cultures. Illich himself built his critical theory using the best philosophical and linguistic frameworks from Latin American philosophy and experience, Asian linguistics, and the Islamic principle of Tawhid among other resources.

In addition, a pedagogics of liminality will require the recovery of *vernacular* resources to address the same challenges that systems and its institutions are trying to find solutions for. Acknowledging, for example, that people have traditional ways of educating their offspring, of displacing themselves geographically, and healing their sick is a good way to assess the benefits and limitations of institutions created to achieve the same objectives. In order to practice a pedagogics of liminality and discover those vernacular sources, we ought to develop, according to Illich, an undivided historical consciousness. This requires, as many Latin American historians have proposed, to look at history *desde el reverso*. To focus first on present reality, find the critical key that will shatter discursive closure, and look backward to the various openings in the past where the discourse was contingent or even nonexistent. Using Ludolf Kuchenbuch's parable of the "crab," Illich saw his work as a historian not as looking at the past with foresight but as knowing the present with crab-like hindsight so that one after the other our "certainties disappear from the landscape through which [we] move back."[35] This backward movement does not seek to perpetuate the ritualization of traditional social practices but to broaden the register of modes in which these practices can be engaged.

Finally, the pedagogics of liminality that resists discursive closure on social systems will reinstate the *transformative power of silence*. Silence, as antithesis to discourse, can be utilized to resist the univocal way in which communication interprets and renders the world to people. Illich suggests that silence, according to Western and Eastern traditions, is necessary for the emergence of personhood before it is encroached by the commodified language of the market where forms of speech are deemed as acceptable or deviant.[36] In *Celebration of Awareness*, Illich's most theologically oriented text, he adds that "silence too is threatened, not only by hurry and by desecration of multiplicity of action, but by the habit of verbal confection and mass production which has no time for it."[37]

As a critic of systems, Illich positions himself as a pedagogue of liminality living "in the fringes of institutions."[38] From there Illich wants to wake up his listeners to a liberating consciousness of their social captivity to systems so that they can break the spell that has enslaved them to institutionalized thinking and living. Only then can an authentic convivial community be fostered. In Illich's prescient words:

The celebration of man's humanity through joining together in the healing expression of one's relationships with others, and one's growing acceptance of one's own nature and needs, will clearly create major confrontations with existing values and systems. The expanding dignity of each man [*sic*] and each human relationship must necessarily challenge existing systems.[39]

In many ways, Illich's works become more relevant today as scholarly interest starts to germinate in fertile analytical fields he helped seed six decades ago. Illich is a required point of reference for current conversations regarding post-growth theories, emerging research in the formation of convivial societies, and the practical leveling of antagonist public discourse toward a sense of what he called "proportionality."[40] Through his comprehensive critical approach to modern institutional encroachment, Illich assisted the transition from the study of rites within bound societies to the analysis of the social rituals that constitute global systems. Illich's work is an invitation to celebrate such awareness in the threshold where the rituals that sacralize modern institutions become evident as well as their power for enchantment. In such a potential site of creative reconstruction, Illich can stand as a companion, a sage who holds a key for reengaging aging critical agendas anew.

NOTES

1. Y. N. Sushkova, "Lev Nikolayevich Tolstoy: Political and Legal Views and Protection of Religious Rights," *European Research Studies* XIX, no. 3, Part B (2016): 122.

2. See Hannah Arendt, *The Life of the Mind* (New York: Harcourt Brace, 1978).

3. Eric Davis, "Why Were the 1970's So Weird?" in *Literary Hub*. August 12, 2019. For a more systematic discussion of the significance of such transition in American culture, see Bruce J. Schulman, *The Seventies: The Great Shift in American Culture, Society and Politics* (New York: Free Press, 2001).

4. Illich's treatment of these three institutional formations can be found in a large number of his work and reiterated in his numerous essays and lecture notes. Yet, the emblematic texts where these topics are systematically analyzed are *De-Schooling Society* (New York: Harper & Row, 1971), *Medical Nemesis: The Exploration of Health* (New York: Random House, 1976), and *Energy and Equity* (New York: Harper & Row, 1974).

5. The critique of an applied social development theory is the framework for all historical analysis conducted by Illich. *De-Schooling Society* serves as the first attempt to offer a radiography of a system to prove the contingency of professionally managed development that grants legitimacy to the social arrangements of capitalist modernity. In doing so, Illich becomes a forerunner of current post-development theorists who use this framework to address matters of economics, globalization, and environmental sustainability. For a more comprehensive review of postdevelopmental theories, see Majid Rahnema and Victoria Bawtree, eds., *The Post-Development Reader* (London: Zed Books, 1997).

6. See James C. Conroy, *Betwixt and Between: The Liminal Imagination, Education and Democracy* (New York: Peter Lang, 2004).

7. For a methodical analysis of Illich's idea of convivial reconstruction in society, see Illich, *Tools for Conviviality* (New York: Harper & Row, 1973). In the conceptual framing of this analysis, Illich states that he choses the term "conviviality," *via negativa*, to designate the opposite of industrial productivity. Once this opposition is realized, autonomous interdependence between people and unmediated interactions of people with their environments is made once again possible.

8. Illich, *De-Schooling Society*, 71.

9. Illich, *Medical Nemesis*, 3.

10. Illich, *Medical Nemesis*, 3.

11. For a contemporary take on this critique, see Pete Conrad, *The Medicalization of Society* (Baltimore: John Hopkins University Press, 2007). See also Gilbert H. Welch, Lisa Schwartz, and Steven Woloshin, eds., *Over Diagnose: Making People Sick in the Pursuit of Health* (Boston: Beacon Press, 2011).

12. Illich, *Medical Nemesis*, 127–128.

13. This argument is the basis for a later treatment of the "commons" by Michael Hardt and Antonio Negri as interpreted by Jesse Bazzul and Sara Tolbert when they state that engagement with the commons is "an engagement with alterity, as the commons sets the stage for interactions with singularities and becoming. Encountering alterity begins a critique of what we have taken for granted as other or self as well as processes of becoming autonomous that arise from the production of a shared commons." See Alexander J. Means, Derek R. Ford, and Graham B. Slater, eds., *Educational Commons in Theory and Practice* (New York: Palgrave MacMillan, 2019), 61.

14. Illich, *Energy and Equity*, 45.

15. Illich, *Energy and Equity*, 9–12.

16. Illich, *Energy and Equity*, see 23–26.

17. Illich, *Energy and Equity*, 18.

18. Illich, *Energy and Equity*, 25.

19. Illich, *Energy and Equity*, 45.

20. See Karl Popper, *The Poverty of Historicism* (Boston: Beacon Press, 1957).

21. See Oswald Spengler, *The Decline of the West* (Oxford: Oxford University Press, 1991).

22. One example of the postmodern approach to the idea of progress can be found in Lyotard's critique of the grand narrative of emancipation that is promoted by the development theories of the so-called "Third World." See Jean-Francois Lyotard, *The Postmodern Condition* (Minneapolis: University of Minnesota Press, 1984). In the same way, Michael Foucault's *oeuvre* shows an overt skepticism of the idea that history is to be understood as the progressive realization of reason. See Michel Foucault, *Madness and Civilization*, trans. Richard Howard (New York: Pantheon, 1965) and *The Order of Things*, trans. Alan Sheridan (New York: Random House, 1970).

23. Giorgio Agamben, "Forward: Laughter and the Kingdom," in Ivan Illich's, *The Powerless Church and Other Selected Writings, 1955–1985* (University Park: Penn State University Press, 2018). A similar hypothesis alluding to the theological and even mystical basis for Illich's sociological work has been presented elsewhere by his biographer, interpreter, and personal friend David Caley. See David Caley, *Ivan Illich in Conversation* (Toronto: House of Anansi Press, 1992) and his most recent book *Ivan Illich: An Intellectual Journey* (University Park: Penn State University Press, 2021).

24. The social construction of institutional necessities is the focus of analysis in Illich's work *Toward a History of Needs* (New York: Random House, 1977).

25. Catherine Bell, *Ritual: Perspectives and Dimensions* (Oxford: Oxford University Press, 1997), 169.

26. In the field of ritual studies, the work of Throop and Laughlin advances the thesis that the individual consciousness formed by ritual practices (such as institutional rituals in this case) are more than social conventions, they build the conceptual frames by which we experience social living. In making this argument, the authors seek to explain this consciousness, utilizing the more contemporary approaches of neuroscience in the study of consciousness, as a form of "cultural neurophenomenology." See Charles Laughlin and C. Jason Throop, "Emotion: A View from Biogenetic Structuralism," in *Biocultural Approaches to the Emotions*, A. L. Hinton, ed. (Cambridge: Cambridge University Press, 1999), 329–361.

27. As quoted in Caley's *Ivan Illich in Conversation*, 50.

28. Victor Turner, *Ritual Process: Structure and Anti-Structure* (Chicago: Aldine Publishing, 1969). Second print 2008, 105.

29. See Jan Bengtsson, "The Many Identities of Pedagogics as a Challenge: Towards an Ontology of Pedagogical Research as Pedagogical Practice," in *Educational Philosophy and Theory* 38, no. 2 (Oxford: Blackwell Publishing, 2006), 115–118.

30. Chris Shilling, "Body Pedagogics: Embodiment, Cognition, and Cultural Transmission," *Sociology* 51, no. 6 (London: Sage, 2016), 1205–1221. More specifically, Turner's pedagogics may be closer to what Shilling refers to as the religious notion of pedagogics based on the ritual experience of individuals requiring them to make a conscious decision to accept or reject certain forms of socialization.

31. Turner, *Ritual Process*, Ibid.

32. Catherine Bell establishes a useful distinction between ritual and liturgy inferring the former is a more inclusive term of religious performativity while the latter refers to "high church" sacramental activity established by some type of canonicity. See Catherine Bell, *Ritual Theory, Ritual Practice* (Oxford: Oxford University Press, 1992). While aware of this important distinction, the "liturgical imagination" ascribed to Illich here, while informed by an ecclesiological mindset, is a formal approach to patterned social activity outside the confines of church tradition. In fact, it is more attune to Catherine Bell's understanding of ritual systemization where ritual performativity relates to other social and cultural phenomena while constituting them, making this performance a powerful force in politics, economics, social stratification, and intellectual discourse. See Bell, *Ritual: Perspectives and Dimensions*, 171–177.

33. See Augusto Boal, *The Rainbow of Desire: The Boal Method of Theater and Therapy* (London: Routledge, 1995).

34. Victor Turner, *Ritual to Theatre: The Human Seriousness of Play* (New York: PAJ Publications, 1982), 11.

35. Ivan Illich, *In the Mirror of the Past* (New York: Marion Boyars, 1991), 196.

36. See the chapter entitled "Silence Is a Commons," 47–54. In discussing liminal entities, Victor Turner also mentions that one of the characteristics of such liminal entity is silence. *Ritual Process*, 364.

37. Illich, *Celebration of Awareness* (New York: Doubleday, 1969), 48.

38. Illich, *Mirror of the Past*, 192.

39. Illich, *Celebration of Awareness*, 18.

40. Significant sample of the importance of Illich's work in the discussion of post-growth theories can be found in the collection *The Post-Development Reader*, Majid Rahnema and Victoria Bawtree, eds. (London: Zed Books, 1998). See also *An Anthropological Critique of Development: The Growth of Ignorance*, Hobart, Mark, ed. (London: Routledge, 1993). For a discussion on the impact of post-growth consciousness on social embodiment, see Milena Büchs and Max Koch, *Postgrowth and Wellbeing: Challenges to Sustainable Welfare* (London: Palgrave, 2017). For a sample of articles on conviviality see *Conviviality at the Crossroads: The Poetics and Politics of Everyday Encounters*, Oscar Hemer, Maja Povrzanović Frykman, and Per-Markku Ristilammi, eds. (London: Palgrave, 2020).

BIBLIOGRAPHY

Agamben, Giorgio. "Forward: Laughter and the Kingdom." In *The Powerless Church and Other Selected Writings, 1955–1985,* edited by Ivan Illich. University Park: Penn State University Press, 2018.

Arendt, Hannah. *The Life of the Mind.* New York: Harcourt Brace, 1978.

Bell, Catherine. *Ritual Theory, Ritual Practice.* Oxford: Oxford University Press, 1992.

Bell, Catherine. *Ritual: Perspectives and Dimensions.* Oxford: Oxford University Press, 1997.

Bengtsson, Jan. "The Many Identities of Pedagogics as a Challenge: Towards an Ontology of Pedagogical Research as Pedagogical Practice." *Educational Philosophy and Theory* 38, no. 2 (2006): 115–118.

Boal, Augusto. *The Rainbow of Desire: The Boal Method of Theater and Therapy.* London: Routledge, 1995.

Büchs, Milena and Max Koch. *Postgrowth and Wellbeing: Challenges to Sustainable Welfare.* Switzerland: Palgrave, 2017.

Caley, David. *Ivan Illich in Conversation.* Toronto: House of Anansi Press, 1992.

Caley, David. *Ivan Illich: An Intellectual Journey.* University Park: Penn State University Press, 2021.

Conrad, Pete. *The Medicalization of Society.* Baltimore: John Hopkins University Press, 2007.

Conroy, James C. *Betwixt and Between: The Liminal Imagination, Education and Democracy.* New York: Peter Lang, 2004.

Hemer, Oscar, Maja Povrzanović Frykman, and Per-Markku Ristilammi, eds. *Conviviality at the Crossroads: The Poetics and Politics of Everyday Encounters.* London: Palgrave, 2020.

Davis, Eric. "Why were the 1970's so weird?" *Literary Hub.* August 12, 2019.

Foucault, Michael. *Madness and Civilization*, trans. Richard Howard. New York: Pantheon, 1965.

Foucault, Michael. *The Order of Things.* Translated by Alan Sheridan. New York: Random House, 1970.

Hinton, Alexander L. *Biocultural Approaches to the Emotions*. Cambridge: Cambridge University Press, 1999.

Hobart, Mark, ed. *An Anthropological Critique of Development: The Growth of Ignorance*. London: Routledge, 1993.

Illich, Ivan. *The Powerless Church and Other Selected Writings, 1955–1985*. University Park: Penn State University Press, 2018.

Illich, Ivan. *Medical Nemesis: The Exploration of Health*. New York: Random House, 1976.

Illich, Ivan. *Celebration of Awareness*. New York: Doubleday,1969.

Illich, Ivan. *De-Schooling Society*. New York: Harper & Row, 1971.

Illich, Ivan. *Energy and Equity*. New York: Harper & Row, 1974.

Illich, Ivan. *In the Mirror of the Past*. New York: Marion Boyars, 1991.

Illich, Ivan. *Medical Nemesis: The Exploration of Health*. New York: Random House, 1976.

Illich, Ivan. *Tools for Conviviality*. New York: Harper & Row, 1973.

Illich, Ivan. *Toward a History of Needs*. New York: Random House, 1977.

Laughlin, Charles and C. Jason Throop. "Emotion: A View from Biogenetic Structuralism." In *Biocultural Approaches to the Emotions*, edited by A. L. Hinton, 329–361. Cambridge: Cambridge University Press, 1999.

Lyotard, Jean-Francois. *The Postmodern Condition*. Minneapolis: University of Minnesota Press, 1984.

Means, Alexander J., Derek R. Ford, and Graham B. Slater, eds. *Educational Commons in Theory and Practice*. New York: Palgrave MacMillan, 2019.

Popper, Karl. *The Poverty of Historicism*. Boston: Beacon Press, 1957.

Rahnema, Majid and Victoria Bawtree, eds. *The Post-Development Reader*. London: Zed Books, 1997.

Schulman, Bruce J. and William E. Huntington. *The Seventies: The Great Shift in American Culture, Society and Politics*. New York: Free Press, 2001.

Shilling, Chris. "Body Pedagogics: Embodiment, Cognition, and Cultural Transmission." *Sociology* 51, no. 6 (2016): 1205–1221.

Spengler, Oswald. *The Decline of the West*. Oxford: Oxford University Press, 1991.

Sushkova, Y. N. "Lev Nikolayevich Tolstoy: Political and Legal Views and Protection of Religious Rights." *European Research Studies* XIX, no. 3b (2016): 122.

The Post-Development Reader, edited by Majid Rahnema and Victoria Bawtree. London: Zed Books, 1998.

Turner, Victor. *Ritual Process: Structure and Anti-Structure*. Chicago: Aldine Publishing, 1969. Second print 2008.

Turner, Victor. *Ritual to Theatre: The Human Seriousness of Play*. New York: PAJ Publications, 1982.

Welch, H. Gilbert, Lisa Schwartz, and Steven Woloshin, eds. *Over Diagnose: Making People Sick in the Pursuit of Health*. Boston: Beacon Press, 2011.

Chapter 11

Agents of Conversion Agency of Women in Early Islam

Keren Abbou Hershkovits

I do not wish women to have power over men, but over themselves.
— Mary Wollstonecraft Shelley

Gender and the status of women in the Muslim world receive much attention from both scholars and the general public throughout the world. The scholarly interest in gender is traced back to at least the 1960s and has gone through several phases, methodological and conceptual.[1] Public interest is also evident. However, it seems that the past few years have seen a surge in this respect. It is indeed interesting, but why do Muslim women engage the curiosity of the public? Several reasons may come up. This interest can be explained partly due to Arab Spring rising, in which women were very much active and as a result demand various demands.[2] Another reason may be that Islam is the fastest-growing religion in the world or the immigration of millions from the Middle East to the rest of the world due to ISIS usurping various regions and the ongoing war in Syria and other places in the area. All these put Islam in a much more visible place, women wearing traditional attire may have become a source of interest as they become much more visible in everyday lives in new places. The unknown, the hidden, may have contributed to this interest. It may also relate to a general concept, according to which Muslim women are extremely marginalized, bound by social norms, tradition and religious commandments, and in need of a savior.

With interest also come questions and controversies. When reading contemporary studies, dealing with the status of women in early Islam, it seems that most answers repeat the medieval frame of the marginality of women, or alternatively, resonate with modern-day arguments concerning the status of women today. It is continuously debated whether most women were of very low status, mostly treated as a commodity to be enslaved, used, sold, or even killed when considered useless or shameful, or if there can be a different reading. The other point of view refers to strong rich women, starting with no other than Muhammad's first—and beloved—wife, Khadījah (d. 619), the rich, powerful, and older woman who hired Muhammad and later on proposed to him. Khadījah and women of similar riches or social standing, are at times juxtaposed with the "disenfranchised" point of view or considered as the exception proving the rule (i.e., that women lacked any kind of agency, and that they were nothing but property).[3]

These viewpoints are also used in an even larger debate concerning Islam—did it improve the status of women or worsen it? Do Muslim women need feminism? Or is equality inherently present at the root of Islamic belief? Let us stop here for a moment. None of these readings of early Islamic histories relate the story of those women as their story but rather as the story of a society, a community, and a religion. Is it possible that while trying to "save" women of early Islam, these women were actually forgotten? Anecdotes are used to build the "large picture" or the "narrative." In this process, women were collapsed into one single category, differences were flattened to serve the wish to answer big questions such as "what was/is the status of women" or the "did medieval Muslim women have agency?"

Therefore, I suggest we abandon, at least for a short while, the larger frameworks and consider the stories and women one may encounter in early Islamic texts. I will adopt Caroline Bynum's conception of liminality of women, she argues that for women, liminality is in the continued situation rather than in the reversed. Women stand in liminal status when they act according to the accepted and common rules not necessarily when they push away from them.[4] This chapter will focus on early Islamic community and on narratives of conversion to Islam and will argue that agency and liminality are categories that need to be unpacked and reexamined.

By looking at diverse methods and tools employed by women, when encouraging others to convert, we may also see that they were part of the society, that they were not necessarily bound to one single route, and that there may not be a category of "female conversion" clearly defined and distinguished from "male conversion." While their space was limited, women still exercised some assertiveness and some control over their lives. Such an approach will allow us to discuss questions of agency but from a different perspective not whether or not Islam changed the status of women but rather how are we to understand representation of gender relation against the background of conversion of people in early Islam, bearing in mind that early converts are also role models for later generations.

This chapter will start by discussing the sources pertaining to conversion stories, followed by an analysis of several such stories, depicting several cases in which women acted as (successful) agents of conversion. Last I will show how these stories may help us consider the above-mentioned questions, reframe them—by looking into sisterhood stories—and at times also answering them, and reconsider the category of agency in early Islam.

THE SOURCES

Narratives depicting the emergence of Islam were transmitted orally and only several decades after the events, were put into writing. The earliest texts available to us are from the late eighth and early ninth century. The chronological distance between events and their literary form were the basis for many critique and revisionist attempts to narrate the events leading to the establishment of the Muslim community and rulership. This mistrust is countered in the past decade with a wave of scholars calling for discarding this general suspicion in favor of other readings, arguing that the much sought-after label of *valid* or *historically proved* is a vain search and probably also the wrong one.[5]

Robert Hoyland, for instance, acknowledges some problematic aspects of Islamic historiography that might compromise their validity.[6] Yet he argues against reading medieval historical texts as depicting a particularly faulty narrative. Rather, he relates the importance scholars, patrons, and readers attributed to these narratives and the measures taken to verify and maintain narratives within the boundaries of what was considered "correct," "reliable," or "true."[7] Hoyland convincingly argues that the modern "obsession" for "facts" leads to some very problematic results. Hence he suggests to employ a different criteria for historicity: "Concentrate more on the manner and style of delivery, the apparent aim of the text and the nature of its intended audience."[8]

I will employ this approach in reading several anecdotes narrating a story of conversion. My main assumption would be that whether or not an actual event took place is secondary to the fact that the author and his readership considered it plausible. By plausible I mean, that such a story is told and retold and no reservations—available to us—are mentioned. When reservations are made, for instance, omissions, or comments, these reservations will be analyzed rather than accepted at face value.

Therefore, the following will not be tracing back historical figures but rather look into several stories of early converts and read the way their story is told and the possible values, norms, concepts, and expectations that construct the story.

I will now turn to several anecdotes narrating a story of conversion, in which the agent of conversion is a woman. By reflecting the story of agents of conversion, I also define the group of women addressed in this study—women who were part of the early Islamic community.

WOMEN WHO PREACHED FOR ISLAM

The first person to convert to Islam was Khadījah, Muhammad's first and beloved wife. Among the first wave of converts, one may find several women, some of them did not make do with their own conversion but also took trouble in persuading others to convert or took measures to ensure and encourage the conversion of others. For instance, the pattern of conversion with family members is abundantly found in Ibn Saʿd's (d. 845)[9] biographical dictionary: for example, Muhammad's daughters[10] converted with their mother. Also ʿUmayrah converted with her mother Laylā bint al-Khāṭīm.[11] ʿUmayrah's three daughters Ḥabība, al-Farīʿah, and Kabshah also converted with her.[12] An interesting case in point is Suʿād, who wished to give the oath of allegiance on behalf of her fetus.[13]

It is indeed a well-known fact that women were agents of conversion. It is usually argued that they did so by their female character: waiting patiently for their family to see the light, conducting religious life and introducing their family to their new religion, as well as good old emotional extortion, for example, Ruqayqa bint Ṣayfī bin Hāshim (d. c. 659), who, according to Ibn Saʿd, was "the harshest of people towards her son, Mukhāramah [bin Nawfal], before he became Muslim."[14]

Another form for encouraging people to convert was destroying idols. Al-Maqrīzī, a fifteenth-century historian (d. 1442), relates several short anecdotes describing how early believers smashed idols and proved their owners wrong, in one of these anecdotes, there is a woman who took part in smashing and explaining.[15] All in all it seems that women took part in general acts of persuasion to convert.

Some women did more than be present on the scene of conversion when another person converted but rather used more direct forms of persuasion. Preaching to Islam is an interesting category, though at times boundaries of what constituted "preaching" is not clear. One such activity can be part of the Quranic commandment: *al-amr bi-ʾlmaʿrūf wa-ʾlnahy ʿan al-munkar*—commanding good and forbidding the evil. There are several such women in early Islam, though not clear if they were actively doing so during the lifetime of Muhammad. Samrah bint Nāhik was a contemporary of the Prophet, who "used to command the good and forbid the wrong," but the information is, as always, very obscure and short. It is not clear why she did so or under what authority. Another figure mentioned calling people to do good is Shifāʿah al-Adaywāʾ. She was appointed by ʿUmar bin al-Khaṭṭāb as a market inspector.[16] Both women were active within the Islamic community, that is, they voiced boundaries to a community that has already accepted Islam.

Other women preached conversion to Islam among the pagans, some publicly, others in the confines of their home and family. One such woman is Umm Sharīk al-ʿĀmiriyyah,[17] who actively proselytized among Qurayshi women inviting them to Islam. It is told she used to go to the fields and call women to convert. Interestingly, her story does not appear in Ibn Saʿd's biographical dictionary and not in the early chronicles of al-Yaʿqūbī's (d. c. 897) *Tārīkh* and al-Ṭabarī's (d. 923) *kitāb al-rusul wa-l-mulūk*.[18] These authors are primarily concerned with whether or not she offered herself to the Prophet Muhammad, and if so, whether or not he accepted her offer. This is of course of great importance for her status as a *ḥadīth* transmitter and relates to the validity of information she transmitted. However, for our purposes, it is interesting that neither Ibn Saʿd, al-Yaʿqūbī nor al-Ṭabarī, who are usually the source of much information concerning early Islam (Ibn Saʿd's being the first biographical dictionary discussing early converts to Islam) do not mention her call—her *da ʿwah* to Islam.

Our informant concerning her *da ʿwah* is Ibn Ḥabīb in his *kitāb al-muḥabbar*.[19] Ibn Ḥabīb al-Baghdādī (d. c. 860 in Samarā), more or less of the same generation as al-Yaʿqūbī and Ibn Saʿd, was a prolific author, known for his knowledge of genealogy and of the times of the *Jāhiliyyah* (the period that preceded Muhammad's prophecies).

It is important to mention her *da ʿwah* is not mentioned, however, at least Ibn Saʿd mentioned that Umm Sharik was tortured for her belief in Muhammad and his prophecy but was rescued by divine help. The narratives differ as to the identity of torturer but agree that she was deprived of drinking water, and her thirst was quenched with the miraculous appearance of a vessel full of sweet liquid. Seeing that she was so rescued, her torturer realized she was following true religion and converted immediately to Islam.[20]

Both narrations, the one relating a miracle saving Umm Sharīk's life, and the one disclosing information concerning her preaching for Islam, portray her as an agent of conversion. The difference between the two narratives lies in the proactivity assigned to Umm Sharīk, one sees her as a passive figure, willing to suffer for her (true!) beliefs. The other portrays her as an active and assertive person, making her belief known in public and calling others to join her. Let us leave Umm Sharīk for now, we shall return to her later on.

Another case of conversion through preaching or introduction to Islamic basic principles is the story of Umm Sulaym. According to Ibn Saʿd:

Umm Sulaym believed in the Messenger of Allah, and Abū Anas came. He had been absent and he said: "Have you become a heretic?" she said, "I have not become a heretic, I have believed in this man." I have begun to teach Anas. I told him to say: "There is no god but Allah," and to say: "I testify that Muhammad is the Messenger of Allah." He did that. His father said to her, "Do not corrupt my son for me." She said, "I am not corrupting him."[21]

Abū Anas was not too happy with what his wife said, however, he soon died and Umm Sulaym swore to living alone until the right person makes his appearance. After a while, a man named Abū Ṭalḥah wished to marry her, but she refused.

> One day she said to him, "Do you think that a stone should be worshipped when it can neither harm nor benefit you? Or what about a piece of wood which you take to a carpenter who carved it for you? Does it help or harm you?"
> "What you said has had a profound effect on me." He believed. She said, "I will marry you and will not take any dower from you except that."[22]

Thus Umm Sulaym raised her son as a Muslim in defiance of her husband's instruction and in real danger to herself. Later on she motivated another man to consider his beliefs and contemplate Islam as a better concept. These anecdotes indicate that women, as well as men, were involved in acts of conversion, implementing various tools and methods. The women discussed here are not quiet women, they are not passive and they are not naïve. They make good claims for their choices and are ready to stand up for these choices.

CONVERSION USING REASON

In many anecdotes, women are portrayed as tools, a means to an end. For instance, women were forced to the battlefield to goad warriors to keep fighting.[23] Women were also used as leverage in persuasion of males to convert. For instance, when Muhammad wished to persuade Mālik ibn ʿAwf to convert to Islam, he took prisoner his family (no detail provided) among them his aunt, Umm ʿAbdallah bint Abī Umayyah—oddly enough, this detail is mentioned—and sent word to Mālik: "Inform him that if he becomes a Muslim I will return his family and property to him and give him a hundred camels."[24] Mālik got the message and decided to convert, the reason given by al-Wāqidī is quite intriguing: "Mālik feared the opposition of the Thaqīf against him, that they knew what the messenger of God said to him, and that they would, therefore, imprison him."[25]

The offer to free his family (including the above-mentioned aunt) can be understood as a demonstration of Muhammad's benevolence, or, as al-Wāqidī explains, as a clever maneuver. Mālik is tricked into submitting not for the love of his family (and aunt!) but for saving face, fearing his inability to protect those who rely on him will lead allies to disrespect him. Which should we believe? The text does not give any answer, but we are informed that the deal worked out great for both parties, Muhammad appointed Mālik to be responsible for those from his tribe who chose to convert, and Mālik, on his part, sent Muhammad a fifth from what he captured.[26]

Another version telling the circumstances of Mālik's conversion tell a different story, and once again, women are involved. According to al-Ya'qūbī, Muhammad won the battle, and Mālik left for Ṭayy, but then comes a much different set of event. When in camp, with hundreds of women and children held captive, Muhammad is approached by al-Shaymā' bint Ḥalīmah, Muhammad's foster-sister.[27] Al-Shaymā' asked Muhammad to release all female captives, convincingly arguing that they are all his foster-sisters or foster-aunts. Muhammad treats her with great respect and granted her wish. Then came an old woman and spoke to him about Mālik. We are not informed what she said, only that after her appeal Muhammad gave Mālik safe-conduct (amān), which was followed by Mālik's acceptance of Islam.[28]

So here once again, we have women at center stage not only as pawns. They are aware of their position, and the fact that in a way they are tools in a man's game, but they are not silent, nor are they passive. They take some control into their hands without changing the rules or outwardly attempting to appear in control.

We may look at this narrative as disclosing significant information about Muhammad: his generosity, his mild temper allowing even women to approach and address him, and his great compassion and loyalty to his kin. We can also learn about the way women are staged in this narrative, they could be silent and passive, but they could also be very strong, and, more importantly, they are portrayed as part of the community, they exercised their agency on behalf of tribe's women but also for its leader—Mālik.

Muhammad was well aware which tribe he was fighting against, and yet the narrative does not attribute him the initiative to release members of the tribe due to kinship relations. It takes al-Shaymā''s voice to make that happen. Her familiarity with Muhammad makes it plausible that she would approach him. Could other women approach Muhammad and ask for his help?

Bint Ḥātim is yet another woman who found herself in the hands of Muhammad with no rescue in sight; Muhammad waged war against the Ṭayy, the leader, 'Adī b. Ḥātim (d. c. 686) understanding his tribe is about to lose the war, took his family and fled.[29] His sister, Bint Ḥātim, was left behind and eventually was taken prisoner, along with many of her people. Realizing her brother left her behind, and no prospect of ransom in sight, she decided to take the situation into her own hand.

When she saw Muhammad she addressed him explain that the person that should have been responsible for her safety had fled and left her behind, hence she is obliged to address him herself, she added that she comes from an honorable family and needed Muhammad's assistance to set her free.

Muhammad enquired who was the one that should have been responsible and learned that it was ʿAdī b. Ḥātim, the very person he was fighting against, the one that fled the war as Muhammad's soldiers gained the upper hand on the battlefield, but other than that did not say a word.

On the second day, she tried once again to catch his attention, and once again failed to do so. On the third day, she didn't even try, but then a man approached and told her she should try once more to appeal to Muhammad. This was ʿAlī bin Abī Ṭālib (d. 660), Muhammad's cousin, son-in-law, and one of his closest companions. This time Muhammad heard her and agreed to let her go. Mind you, not talking about conversion, or about ransom, on the contrary, Muhammad encouraged her not to be hasty that she should take her time finding an appropriate escort.[30] Once she found a convoy of her people on their way to Bilād al-Shaʾm, where her brother was supposed to be, she informed so to Muhammad, who gave her allowance, and she left.

Once she arrived and met with her brother, she was furious! But also a woman of advice: "You should join Muhammad, because he is a man of honor!" ʿAdī b. Ḥātim converts and receives much respect,[31] for instance, al-Yaʿqubī mentions him several times as the person responsible of collecting the *zakāt* (the tax Muslim are required to pay) and participated, with great courage, in several important battles.[32]

These narratives, the ones illustrating Mālik's conversion and the one portraying ʿAdī b. Ḥātim's position women in a state of solitude and distress. Some are passive, others are assertive and do not despair, they work with what social norms and values allocate them. Al-Shaymāʾ refers to Muhammad's sense of kinship obligations, a significant emotion of the time.[33] Bint Ḥātim plays a different card, the one of honor and nobility, traits much valued and appreciated, none challenges gender relations. Both women improved their current situation, and along the way help the process of conversion of another person.

"HE IS A NOBLE MAN!"

As it turns out, the concept of honor and nobility works on both directions, Bint Ḥātim mentioned her father's nobility to evoke Muhammad's sympathy, and then used the same concept when consulting her brother to convert to Islam. She was not alone in her form of action.

Al-Ṭabarī informs us that, on the day of the conquest of Mecca in 629, ʿIkrimah bin Abī Jahl was among those whom Muhammad had sentenced to death on account of their opposition to himself and to Islam. ʿIkrimah's wife, Umm Ḥakīm bt. al-Ḥārith, who had already converted, asked for safe conduct on behalf of her husband. When Muhammad granted this protection,

Umm Ḥakīm sought her husband, finding him on a boat en route to Yemen. ʿIkrimah returned, pledged, and converted to Islam.[34]

Most germane to our investigation is Umm Ḥakīm's presentation of the news of safety to her husband: "O cousin, I come to you from the man who is the kindest toward his kin."[35] Hence, Muhammad's protection was read by Umm Ḥakīm as part of his kinship obligations. Notably, Muhammad and ʿIkrimah have no direct familial ties (indeed, al-Wāqidī's narrative neglects to mention such phrasing though the general story has more or less the same details).[36] The factual reality of such relations is of little importance here, though; what matters is that in the view of Umm Ḥakīm, Muhammad provided a stay of execution for her husband in the name of kinship.

We could ask ourselves what was Umm Ḥakīm's incentive to go after ʿIkrimah. A Muslim woman cannot be married to an idol worshipper, hence their marriage would be dissolved upon Umm Ḥakīm's conversion. It is possible that she was not interested in divorce or was worried that she would be forced to unwelcomed marriage.[37]

Umm Ḥakīm is not a pawn, she is proactive—she converted, she addressed Muhammad to her own benefits, and she went on a quest in search of her husband. Indeed, the reason she gave her husband to show him the right path, that is, to Islam and to the messenger of God, is that Muhammad is a trustworthy person. Why would she do that? Did it play in her behalf? We cannot tell that, however, we could tell that not all stories attribute her with any contribution to ʿIkrimah's conversion. Wāqidī and Ibn Saʿd as well as al-Ṭabarī referred to her actions, reiterating more or less the same general phases: Muhammad conquered Mecca, Umm Ḥakīm converted to Islam, whereas ʿIkrimah fled fearing Muhammad's wrath. Later on, Umm Ḥakīm's asked for safe conduct for her husband, upon accepting it, she traveled in his footsteps, persuaded him to return and then he finally converted to Islam.[38]

Ibn al-Jawzī (d. 1201), the Ḥanbalite jurist, who wrote more than two hundred years after the above-mentioned scholars, narrated a different story: ʿIkrimah encountered a sever storm on sea, which made it clear for him that God does not approve with his leaving Mecca. Hence he went back to Mecca and converted.[39]

In this narrative, only the first part is mentioned, the part of him leaving Mecca and going to sea. The interaction is between a man and his God, ʿIkrimah understood the message sent to him and returned to Mecca. Umm Ḥakīm remained unacknowledged and maybe also unimportant. This version conveys ʿIkrimah's conversion as an act of finding truth and belief rather than being persuaded.

Ibn al-Jawzī's book is very similar in its purposes to Ibn Saʿd's. Both books intend to tell the stories of early converts to Islam, however, as in many other cases, later author tend to erase female involvent and contributions, even in the cases of early converts who are usually perceived as a unique *ṭabaqah*, a special and particularly pious group.[40]

EXERCISING AGENCY

The clear distinction between men and women is very much present; as already mentioned, women were used as leverage to persuade their male relatives to convert, used as booty, sold, and exchanged hands with very little ability to assert themselves and change their lives. And in many cases, authors tended to disregard contributions recorded by earlier authors.[41] In other words, women are marginalized and in more examples than others are disregarded. In light of that, one should consider the concept of agency, what it actually means and what constitutes agency for medieval Muslim women.

So what is agency? Ahmed Rageb argues that female authority "usually involved a complicated socio-cultural process involving the presence of qualifying reasons and corroborating empirical evidence."[42] Truly, it is hard to come up with many examples of women exercising authority over men, but that does not mean women had no agency, and certainly does not mean women had no power at all. Finding influential women is easier than one may think, starting with Khadījah, and later wives of Muhammad, and continuing all the way through history.[43] Rather, it illuminates the need to redefine what agency means for medieval Muslim women and their contemporaries.[44] According to Joan Scott, a person's ability to navigate the world depends upon his or hers agency, that is, their ability to use force, execute authority, and the social meaning such actions are attributed with.[45] Scott's work and arguments opened up a whole new world for gender studies. It made gender into a historical category. However, Scott's work focused on case studies from European history, moreover, none of the scholars whose work she cites used Middle Eastern examples or societies for constructing their theories. Hence, rather than using acceptable theories or concepts, our first question should be whether or not the available definitions for agency and for examining agency are applicable for women of early Islam.

Traditional conception of agency assumes that agency is found only when women (or men) assert authority and actively resist patriarchal boundaries. That agency is found in places where women attempt at crossing boundaries set up in economic, governmental, or institutional spheres. Such definitions also draw a direct line between free choice and agency, assuming that agency is an action freely committed. Such conceptions of agency led to the inevitable conclusion that apart from a few exceptions, women of early Islam as a rule had no agency. They had very little choice and even less ability to exercise any free choice. They were forced into marriage, divorced at husbands' whim, and had very little public visibility. They were subordinate, powerless, and generally simply unseen. At this point one has two choices, first, close the book and go look for agency somewhere else. Second option, question these assumptions. In the past few years, several scholars have chosen the latter and suggested different approaches and definitions to agency. In the case of Muslim women there is much more to it. Many studies concerning women in the Muslim world focus on religious aspects and ask what contributions Islam had on women's social status. Such questions distance us from dealing with women as social objects and suggest that religion is by far the most critical criteria in setting social, economic institutional, and so forth categories. It also assumes that Islam is a one single category shared by almost 2 billion adherents of Islam.[46] But is Islam to blame[47] (or to applaud) an appropriate category for the study of gender relations? Is that a beneficial starting point? I would argue that it isn't. As already mentioned by Lila Abu-Lughod, religion is not to blame,[48] people are. Moreover, stressing the victimhood of women under Islam may contribute to giving them a voice and telling their story, but it also puts great emphasis on being victims, being marginal while instances or spaces where females were in a position of power are once again marginalized.[49]

Clare Hemmings and Amal Treacher Kabesh suggest that a search for women who break the rules will rule out many instances where women were very much active in defining their world and path. Such a search will be blind to women who act against other women (is that agency?) or men who empower women (is *that* agency?). It will also be blind to the huge differences between women, what is accessible to each and what may lead to a life-threatening situation. According to Hemmings and Treacher Kabesh, there are several basic assumptions it is best to rid of. For instance, agency should not be identified strictly with breaking the rules or with fighting authority. Nor should it be identified with a counter-response to oppression. Rather, they suggest one should begin by identifying a person's particular position, restrictions, and circumstances. The very attempt at negotiating one's life circumstance should be considered as a form of agency.[50]

Several studies have already demonstrated the need in different categories for agency, which is context dependent and even person dependent. Saba Mahmood[51] argues against the concepts that agency is inherently a free choice. Allen Fleischman defines feminist activity as an act aiming at alleviating the constraints set by gender definition and their affect on women, but not necessarily altering the gender dynamics.[52]

The stories discussed earlier indicate that women were active members of society, they were not only commodity and not only a tool. They exercised some agency, within the boundaries of what they considered useful. True, they never went out with full-fledged ambition to change gender relations or social structures. But given a set of norms and rules, they acted on their own behalf, harnessing those values and concepts of womanhood to their benefit.

SISTERHOOD ACROSS RELIGIOUS BOUNDARIES

Anecdote of conversion have an inherent value. The Islamic community benefitted from conversion and it is of importance for later generations to know who converted and when. Thus preserving anecdotes depicting conversion was important. The participation of women in scenes of conversion is not blatantly out of character for medieval community though, as mentioned, did not carry immense interest. However, close reading of medieval texts illuminate other scenes in which women were present and were proactive. They are featured not as followers but as initiators, at times at some risk. There are a handful of anecdotes depicting women offering help to other women, whereas the men featured in the same scene either ignored or refused to help.

Such instances of female comradery appeared across religious and social boundaries, where women reach out to other women, assisting them for the sole reason that they are women. A case in point is the help offered to Zaynab bint Muhammad.

Hind bint 'Utbah (d. c. mid-seventh century)[53] was a pagan not only that she was very much opposed to Muhammad, particularly after the death of her father, paternal uncle, brother, and son in the Battle of Badr (624). Zaynab, Muhammad's daughter, lived in Mecca with her pagan husband Rabī' ibn al-'Aṣṣ, and did not immigrate with Muhammad to Medina. However, after the battle of Badr, Muhammad asked for her to be allowed to join him. When Hind heard of the planned journey, she approached Zaynab and offered her any help she may need. Be it a riding beast, travel money, or any other need, stating that: "[M]en's quarrels are nothing to do with the women."[54] Though on opposite political and religious camps, Hind found it in her heart to be kind to Zaynab, seeing a shared interest between them—being women in a world of men, being marginalized, in need of comradery. Zaynab, by the way, did not take up Hind's offer. According to al-Ṭabarī, she was not convinced Hind was honest in her offer and worried it was a trap. Hence Zaynab preferred to hide her travel plans from her.[55]

Fāṭimah bt. Al-Aswad needed somebody to help her as well, Muhammad ordered her hand amputated, after she was caught stealing.[56] She tried evading punishment and asked Salama, one of Muhammad's wives to intercede on her behalf but to no avail.[57] After the execution of the punishment, Fāṭimah needed a place to rest and recuperate. This time she got help from the wife of Asyyad b. Hudayr, who is not mentioned by name. All we know is that she gave her food. Interestingly, Asyyad made a point in telling Muhammad that his wife was helping Fāṭimah, Ibn Saʿd does not inform us why Asyyad thought it required to inform Muhammad nor do we know what was Muhammad's reaction to that. We are only told that after some rest, Fāṭimah tried asking her father to let her come to his household, which he refused and told her that she was not welcomed in his house, saying that she should go to the ʿAbd al-ʿUzzā tribe, due to the great resemblance between them. Eventually Fātima's uncle—who was from that very tribe, took her in. The women who tried to help could not save her or offer long-term security. Nonetheless, they allowed for a short-term help—until male help arrived with a solution.[58]

It is not clear why the father thought Fātima should go with ʿAbd al-ʿUzzā. It is even less clear what this actually meant, as we cannot set clear chronology for these events, it is not clear whether the uncle, Ḥaṭīb bin ʿAbd al-ʿUzzā was pagan or have already converted. His conversion took place in 630 or 632, prior to that he was part of the opposition to Muhammad. Hence, not giving Fāṭimah a place to stay on part of the father might have also meant exclusion from the Muslim community and perhaps apostasy.

The agency exercised in these two cases is of great significance. They do not stand on the same ground as the above-mentioned cases of conversion, not only because no conversion is involved but also because in both cases the helper and the one being helped are on two sides of religious boundaries or status. In both cases, there is no obvious expectation for help, and probably some risk for the helper. Additionally, while conversion stories may relate to authors' wish to present the greatness of early Islamic community, and the moral and honorable qualities of early converts, these two stories are not to be read in that context. These are side stories, in one case we don't even have a name, just the name of the spouse. And yet, both woman *choose* to act, and set priorities to their values.

CONCLUSION

The status of women in late antiquity was, in general very different from their male counterpart's. Their circumstances were probably very much related to their social position, to family ties and blood relations, economic status and so forth very few of which were initiated by them, most were probably imposed upon them.[59] They were married to seal pacts, sent back home when political situation shifted, and in constant need of a male guardian. But even under such extreme constrains, some women found courage and means to alter their position. Some used conversion as a tool to assert themselves, other were deeply involved and committed to Muhammad's message that they made it a point to convert others.

This chapter focused on demonstrating that agency is not always the fight for equality or even a demand for particular rights. At times, agency is the steps a woman took in order to make her life a little easier within the boundaries of gender roles.

NOTES

1. Deniz Kandiyoiti, "Contemporary Feminist Scholarship," in *Gendering the Middle East: Emerging Perspectives*, ed. Deniz Kandiyoti (New York: Syracuse University Press, 1996), 127.

2. For instance, women in Sudan demand political rights claiming they have been marginalized for years and that time has come to acknowledge their importance and significant contribution to the society. Michael Atit, "Sudan's Women Demand Power in New Government," *Voice of America News,* https://www.voanews.com/africa/sudans-women-demand-power-new-government (last accessed July 21, 2019). Similarly, the declaration of the Saudi crown prince, Muhammad Ibn Salman, that "Women are absolutely equal" resonated throughout the international media and social networks. Ben Hubbard, "Saudi Crown Prince, in His Own Words: Women Are 'Absolutely' Equal," *The New York Times,* https://www.nytimes.com/2018/03/18/world/middleeast/mohammed-bin-salman-saudi-arabia-60-minutes.html (Last accessed July 21, 2019).

3. Aisha Geissinger, "Feminist Muslim (re) Interpretations of Early Islam," in *Routledge Handbook on Early Islam*, ed. Herbert Berg (London: Routledge, 2018 [2017]), 296–308.

4. Caroline Walker Bynum, *Fragmentation and Redemption: Essays on Gender and the Human Body in Medieval Religion* (New York: Zone Books, 1991), 27–50, esp. 50.

5. For a survey of the skeptic approach and its criticism, see Aziz Al Azmeh, *The Arabs and Islam in Late Antiquity: A Critique of Approaches to Arabic Sources* (Berlin: Gerlach Press, 2014).

6. Robert G. Hoyland, "History, Fiction and Authorship in the First Centuries of Islam," in *Writing and Representation in Medieval Islam*, ed. Julia Bray (London: Routledge, 2006), 18.

7. Another important point raised by Hoyland is the concept that by the late eighth century, history had a very particular role; the past had "come to acquire legitimating and normative value" for the political, economic, and theological of everyday life. Moreover, argues Hoyland, "history requires the mediation of fiction in its treatment of the past." See ibid., 16–18.

8. Ibid., 35. See also Robert G. Hoyland, "Writing the Biography of the Prophet Muhammad: Problems and Solutions," *History Compass* 5, no. 2 (2007): 581–602.

9. J. W. Fück, "Ibn Saʿd," in: *Encyclopaedia of Islam, Second Edition*, ed. P. Bearman, Th. Bianquis, C.E. Bosworth, E. van Donzel, W.P. Heinrichs, Consulted online on 14 August 2019, http://dx.doi.org/10.1163/1573-3912_islam_SIM_3343.

10. Ibn Saʿd (d. 845), *Kitāb al-ṭabaqāt al-kabīr*, ed. ʿAlī Muḥammad ʿAmr (Cairo: Maktabat al-Khangi, 2001), 10:33.

11. Ibn Saʿd, 10:319.

12. Ibn Saʿd, 10:415.

13. Ibn Saʿd, 10:378.

14. Ibn Saʿd, 10:211–212. Ruqayqah was ʿAbd al-Muttalib's niece, it is not clear when exactly she converted to Islam. From the little information available it seems she was among Muhammad's followers and a *ḥadith* transmitter. Mukharama converted on the day of the conquest of Mecca (630), like many of the inhabitants. For his conversion, see al-Ṭabarī, 39:42–43.

Interestingly, and to the point of this chapter, Ibn Saʿd adds that Ruqayqah warned Muhammad against the plans of the Quraysh to harm him. Hence, Muhammad asked ʿAlī bin Abī Ṭālib to sleep in his bed, and thus be saved. Ibn Isḥāq, the author of the earliest biography of the Prophet Muhammad, attributes the warning to the Angel Gabriel. This is a good example of the reading one should adopt to these texts. Ibn Isḥāq's narrative is a hagiography and accordingly is imbedded with miraculous events and divine guidance. See Alfred Guillaume, *The Life of Muhammad: A Translation of Ibn Ishaq's Sirat Rasul Allah* (Oxford: Oxford University Press, 1955), 222. Interestingly, Ṭabarī does not mention Ruqayqa's contribution either. Abū Jaʿfar Muḥammad bin Jarīr al-Ṭabarī (d. 923), *The History of al-Tabari, vol. 6: Muhammad at Mecca,* trans. and ann. W. Montgomery Watt and M. V. McDonald (New York: SUNY Press, 1998), 142–143. I will return to the difference between early and later sources in their narration of female's activism.

15. I wish to thank Prof. Michael Lecker for kindly sharing with me these anecdotes from a forthcoming edition of the manuscript. For a description of the manuscript, see Michael Lecker, "Idol Worshipping in North Arabia in the Jahillyya," in *The Gods of Yonder: Polytheism in the Land of Israel and Its Surrounding, from the Second Millennia till Islamic Period,* ed. Menachem Kister et al. (Jerusalem: Yad Ben Tzvi, 2008), 250–262 [HEB].

16. See Michael Cook for a legal discussion concerning the validity and permissibility of females as commanders of good. Michael Cook, *Commanding Right and Forbidding Wrong in Islamic Thought* (Cambridge: Cambridge University Press, 2001), 82–83.

17. Abū Jaʿfar Muhamad Ibn Ḥabīb (d. 860), *kitāb al-muḥabbar,* ed. Ilse Lichtenstädter, trans. Ella Landau-Tessaron (Beirut: Dar al-Afaq al-Jadida, 1942), 82–83. I thank Prof. Landau-Tessaron for pointing out this anecdote.

18. Ibn Saʿd, 10:148–149; Aḥmad bin Abī Yaʿqub al-Yaʿqūbī, *The Works of Ibn Waḍiḥ al-Yaʿqubī,* vo.1 3: "The History (Taʾrīkh) the Rise of Islam to the Reign of al-Muʿtamid," trans. Matthew Gordon, Chase F. Robinson, Everett K. Rowson, and Michael Fishbein (Leiden: Brill, 2018), 695–696; Abū Jaʿfar Muḥammad bin Jarīr al-Ṭabarī, (d. 923), *The History of al-Tabari, vol. 39: Biographies of the Prophet's Companions and Their Successors: al-Tabari's Supplement to His History,* trans. Ella Landau-Tasseron (New York: SUNY Press, 1998), 204, 287.

19. For Ibn Ḥabīb and his work, see Ilse Lichtenstädter, "Muhammad Ibn Ḥabīb and His Kitâb Al-Muḥabbar," *Journal of the Royal Asiatic Society of Great Britain and Ireland* 1 (1939): 1–27. See also Abed el-Rahman Tayyara, "Ibn Ḥabīb's Kitāb al-Muḥabbar and its Place in Early Islamic Historical Writing," *Journal of Islamic Studies* 29, no. 3 (2017): 392–416.

20. Ibn Saʿd, 10:149–152. See also Uriel Simonsohn, "Female Conversion to Islam: A Sample Analysis of Medieval Narratives of the Prophetic Age," *Mediterranean Historical Review* 35, no. 1 (2020): 9–25, esp. 13–14.

21. Ibn Saʿd, 10:395–404.

22. Ibid.

23. See H. Lammens, "Mālik B. ʿAwf," in *Encyclopaedia of Islam*, Second Edition, accessed October 31, 2021, doi: http://dx.doi.org.ezproxy.bgu.ac.il/10.1163/1573-3912_islam_SIM_4863.

24. Abū ʿAbd Allāh Muḥammad bin ʿUmar Al-Wāqidī (d. 823), *kitāb al-maghāzī*, ed. Marsden Jones (Beirut: Maṭbaʿat jāmiʿat al-Uxford, 1922), 2:972; Faizer Rizwi, *The Life of Muhammad: Al-Waqidi's Kitab Al-Maghazi* (London: Routledge, 2013), 467.

25. Ibid. See Lammens, "Mālik B. ʿAwf," in *Encyclopaedia of Islam*, doi: http://dx.doi.org.ezproxy.bgu.ac.il/10.1163/1573-3912_islam_SIM_4863.

26. Al-Wākidī, 2:955 (Ar.); Rizwi, 467–468 (ENG).

27. Ḥalīmah nursed Muhammad and hence her children as well as other infants she nursed are considered to be related. For breastfeeding brothers see J. Schacht, J. Burton, and J. Chelhod, "Raḍāʿ or Riḍāʿ," in: *Encyclopaedia of Islam, Second Edition*, ed. P. Bearman, Th. Bianquis, C.E. Bosworth, E. van Donzel, W.P. Heinrichs, consulted online on 9 August 2019, http://dx.doi.org.ezproxy.bgu.ac.il/10.1163/1573-3912_islam_COM_0896.

28. Aḥmad bin Abī Yaʿqūb al-Yaʿqūbī, *The Works of Ibn Wāḍiḥ Al-Yaʿqūbī*, trans. and ed. Matthew Gordon, Chase F. Robinson, Everett K. Rowson, and Michael Fishbein (Leiden: Brill, 2018), 3:665–666.

29. Ibn Hishām, *al-sīra al-nabawiyya* (Cairo: Muʾassasat ʿulūm al-Qurʾān, 1936), 2:579.

30. Ibn Hishām, 2: 80–582.

31. Ibid.

32. See al-Yaʿqūbī 3:683, 741, see also al-Ṭabarī 39:86.

33. Keren Abbou Hershkovits, "Kinship, Expectations, and God," *Hawwa* 15, no. 3 (2017): 293–314.

34. Al-Ṭabarī, 39:17–19.

35. Ibid., 39:17.

36. Al-Wāqidī, 2:850–851; Rizwi, 418–419.

37. It is not clear what were the options available to women of the time. Studying a much later period, Boaz Shushan demonstrates that for fifteenth-century Damascene women, being divorced was not better than unhappy marriage. He based his argument on diary of a local legalist, who described the cases he attended and heard. See Boaz Shushan, "From the Diary of a Muslim Notary, Damascus 1480-1500," *Jamaa* 22 (2016): 7–22.

38. Al-Ṭabarī, 39:17.

39. Jamāl al-Dīn bin al-Farāj Ibn al-Jawzī, *Ṣifat al-Ṣafwa*, ed. Khālid Muṣṭafā al-Ṭaṭūsī (Beirut: Dār al-Kitāb al-Arabi, 2012), 265.

40. For a study reflecting and comparing narratives from different phases, see Doris Decker, "Frauen zwischen Selbst- und Fremdbestimmung. Wandel weiblicher 45 Geschlechterkonstruktionen in religiosen Veranderungsprozessen am Beispiel

ruhislamischer Uberlieferungen," in *Doing Gender—Doing Religion Fallstudien zur Intersektionalitat im fruhen Judentum, Christentum und Islam*, ed. Eisen E. von Ute, Christine Gerber and Angela Standhartinger (Tubingen: Mohr Siebeck, 2013), 193–223.

41. To that one may also add the tendency of modern scholars, discussing medieval Islamic history not to question the narratives presented by medieval authors, when it comes to gender issues. See Maaike van Berkel, "The Young Caliph and his Wicked Advisors: Women and Power Politics under Caliph Al-Muqtadir (r. 295–320/908–932)," *Al Masaq: Islam and the Medieval Mediterranean* 19, no. 1 (2007): 3–15.

42. Ahmed Ragab, "Epistemic Authority of Women in the Medieval Middle East," *Hawwa* 8, no. 2 (2010): 181–216.

43. For instance, Ibn Saʻd mentions that people who wished to pass on information to Muhammad sent gifts and word to the rooms of his wives (the best bet would have been ʻĀiʼsha, Muhammad's favorite). See Ibn Saʻd, 10:157. When Abū Sufyān (d. 650), one of Muhammad's opponents wanted to ensure his safety, he asked his daughter, Umm Ḥabība, for her help. Umm Ḥabībah, who was one of Muhammad's wives, turned his request down, it is possible she did that in order to stir him into conversion. See Wāqidī, 2:792–793; Faizer, 390–391.

44. Ragab, "Epistemic Authority of Women in the Medieval Middle East," 181–216.

45. See Joan Wallach Scott, "Gender as a Useful Category of Historical Analysis," in *Culture, Society and Sexuality, Culture, Society and Sexuality a Reader*, ed. Richard G. Parker and Peter Aggleton (London and Philadelphia: UCL, 1999), 57–75, http://web.b.ebscohost.com.ezproxy.bgu.ac.il/ehost/ebookviewer/ebook/bmx lYmtfXzcwNzkxX19BTg2?sid=14c40763-b6ba-402b-88c7-ec32024cc32d@pdc-v -sessmgr02&vid=0&format=EK&lpid=6&rid=0.

46. Fatima Mernissi, *Women and Islam: An Historical and Theological Inquiry* (Oxford: Blackwell, 1991).

47. Abdellah Elboubekri, "Is Patriarchy an Islamic Legacy? A Reflection on Fatima Mernissi's Dreams of Trespass and Najat El Hachmi's the Last Patriarch," *Journal of Multicultural Discourses* 10, no. 1 (2015): 25–48.

48. Lila Abu-Lughod, *Do Muslim Women Need Saving?* (Cambridge, MA and London: Harvard University Press, 2013).

49. Lois McNay, *Gender and Agency: Reconfiguring the Subject in Feminist and Social Theory* (Cambridge: Polity Press, 2013).

50. Clare Hemmings and Amal Treacher Kabesh, "The Feminist Subject of Agency: Recognition and Affect in Encounters with 'the Other,'" in *Gender, Agency, and Coercion*, ed. S. Madhok, A. Phillips and K. Wilson, Asingstoke (New York: Palgrave Macmillan, 2013), 29–46.

51. Saba Mahmood, "Feminist Theory, Embodiment, and the Docile Agent: Some Reflections on the Egyptian Islamic Revival," *Cultural Anthropology* 16, no. 2 (2001): 202–236.

52. Ellen Fleischmann, "The Other 'Awakening': The Emergence of Women's Movements in the Modern Middle East, 1900–1940," in *A Social History of Women and Gender in the Modern Middle East*, ed. Margaret L. Meriwether and Judith E. Tucker (New York: Routledge, 1999), 89–134.

53. Fr. Buhl, "Hind Bint ʿUtba," in *Encyclopaedia of Islam*, Second Edition, accessed November 1, 2021, doi:http://dx.doi.org/10.1163/1573-3912_islam_SIM_2881.

54. Abū Jaʿfar Muḥammad bin Jarīr Al-Ṭabarī (d. 923), *The History of al-Tabari*, vol. 7: *The Foundation of a Community*, trans. and ann. W. Montgomery Watt and M. V. McDonald (New York: SUNY Press, 1987), 75.

55. Ibid.

56. Ruth Roded, *Women in Islamic Biographical Collections: From Ibn Saʿd to Who's Who* (Boulder: L. Rienner, 1996), 33; for the three versions of the punishment, see Gertrude H. Stern, "Muḥammad's Bond with the Women," *Bulletin of the School of Oriental and African Studies* 10, no. 1 (1940): 192–193.

57. Ibn Saʿd, 10:250.

58. Ibn Saʿd, 10:250–251.

59. Indeed, males were also confined to social norms and obligations, however, they had much more room to act on their own and were much less monitored or restricted to the private sphere.

BIBLIOGRAPHY

Abū Jaʿfar Muhamad Ibn Ḥabīb (d. 860). *kitāb al-muḥabbar*. Edited by Ilse Lichtenstädter. Beirut: Dar al-Afaq al-Jadida, 1942.

Abu-Lughod, Lila. *Do Muslim Women Need Saving?* Cambridge, MA and London: Harvard University Press, 2013.

Aḥmad ibn Abī Yaʿqub al-Yaʿqūbī, *The Works of Ibn Waḍiḥ al-Yaʿqūbī.* Translated by Matthew Gordon, Chase F. Robinson, Everett K. Rowson, and Michael Fishbein. Vol. 3: The History (Taʾrīkh) The Rise of Islam to the Reign of al-Muʿtamid. Leiden: Brill, 2018.

Al Azmeh, Aziz. *The Arabs and Islam in Late Antiquity: A Critique of Approaches to Arabic Sources.* Berlin: Gerlach Press, 2014.

Al-Ṭabarī, Abū Jaʿfar Muhammad bin Jarīr (d. 923). *The History of al-Tabari.* Vol. 39: *Biographies of the Prophet's Companions and Their Successors: al-Tabari's Supplement to His History.* Translated by Ella Landau-Tasseron. New York: SUNY Press, 1998.

Al-Ṭabarī, Abū Jaʿfar Muhammad bin Jarīr (d. 923). *The History of al-Tabari.* Vol. 6: *Muhammad at Mecca.* Translated and annotated by W. Montgomery Watt and M. V. McDonald. New York: SUNY Press, 1988.

Al-Ṭabarī, Abū Jaʿfar Muhammad bin Jarīr (d. 923). *The History of al-Tabar.* Vol. 7: *The Foundation of a Community.* Translated and annotated W. Montgomery Watt and M. V. McDonald. New York: SUNY Press, 1987.

Al-Wāqidī, Abū ʿAbd Allāh Muhammad bin ʿUmar (d. 823). *Kitāb al-maghāzī.* Edited by Marsden Jones. Beirut: Maṭbaʿat jāmiʿat al-Uxford, 1922.

Atit, Michael. "Sudan's Women Demand Power in New Government." *Voice of America News.* Accessed July 21, 2019. https://www.voanews.com/africa/sudans-women-demand-power-new-government.

Bynum, Caroline Walker. *Fragmentation and Redemption: Essays on Gender and the Human Body in Medieval Religion.* New York: Zone Books, 1991.

Cook, Michael. *Commanding Right and Forbidding Wrong in Islamic Thought.* Cambridge: Cambridge University Press, 2001.

Decker, Doris. "Frauen zwischen Selbst- und Fremdbestimmung. Wandel weiblicher 45 Geschlechterkonstruktionen in religiosen Veranderungsprozessen am Beispiel ruhislamischer Uberlieferungen." In *Doing Gender—Doing Religion Fallstudien zur Intersektionalitat im fruhen Judentum, Christentum und Islam,* edited by Ute E. Eisen, Christine Gerber, and Angela Standhartinger, 193–223. Tubingen: Mohr Siebeck, 2013.

Elboubekri, Abdellah. "Is Patriarchy an Islamic Legacy? A Reflection on Fatima Mernissi's Dreams of Trespass and Najat El Hachmi's the Last Patriarch." *Journal of Multicultural Discourses* 10, no. 1 (2015): 25–48.

El Cheikh, Nadia Maria. *Women, Islam, and Abbasid Identity.* Cambridge, MA and London: Harvard University Press, 2015.

El Shamsy, Ahmed. "The Social Construction of Orthodoxy." In *The Cambridge Companion to Classical Islamic Theology* 110, edited by Tim Winter, 97–117. Cambridge: Cambridge University Press, 2008.

El-Rahman Tayyara, Abed. "Ibn Ḥabīb's Kitāb al-Muḥabbar and its Place in Early Islamic Historical Writing." *Journal of Islamic Studies* 29, no. 3 (2017): 392–416.

Fleischmann, Ellen. "The Other 'Awakening': The Emergence of Women's Movements in the Modern Middle East, 1900–1940." In *A Social History of Women and Gender in the Modern Middle East,* edited by Margaret L. Meriwether and Judith E. Tucker, 89–134. New York: Routledge, 1999.

Fück, J. W. "Ibn Saʻd." In *Encyclopaedia of Islam, Second Edition.* Edited by P. Bearman, Th. Bianquis, C. E. Bosworth, E. van Donzel, W. P. Heinrichs. Consulted online on 14 August 2019. http://doi.org/10.1163/1573-3912_islam_SIM_3343.

Geissinger, Aisha. "Feminist Muslim (re) Interpretations of Early Islam." In *Routledge Handbook on Early Islam*, edited by Herbert Berg, 296–308. London: Routledge, 2018 [2017].

Guillaume, Alfred. *The Life of Muhammad: A Translation of Ibn Ishaq's Sirat Rasul Allah.* Oxford: Oxford University Press, 1955.

Hemmings, Clare and Amal Treacher Kabesh. "The Feminist Subject of Agency: Recognition and Affect in Encounters with 'the Other'." In *Gender, Agency, and Coercion,* edited by S. Madhok, A. Phillips, and K. Wilson, 29–46. New York: Palgrave Macmillan, 2013.

Hershkovits, Keren Abbou. "Kinship, Expectations, and God." *Hawwa* 15, no. 3 (2017): 293–314.

Hoyland, Robert G. "History, Fiction and Authorship in the First Centuries of Islam." In *Writing and Representation in Medieval Islam,* edited by Julia Bray, 30–60. London: Routledge, 2006.

Hoyland, Robert. "Writing the Biography of the Prophet Muhammad: Problems and Solutions." *History Compass* 5, no. 2 (2007): 581–602.

Hubbard, Ben. "Saudi Crown Prince, in His Own Words: Women Are 'Absolutely' Equal." *The New York Times.* Accessed July 21, 2019. https://www.nytimes.com /2018/03/18/world/middleeast/mohammed-bin-salman-saudi-arabia-60-minutes.html.

Ibn Hishām. *Al-sīra al-nabawiyya*. Cairo: Mu'assasat ʿulūm al-Qur'ān, 1936. 2 vols.

Ibn Saʿd (d. 845). *Kitāb al-ṭabaqāt al-kabīr*. Edited by ʿAlī Muhammad ʿAmr. Cairo: Maktabat al-Khangi, 2001.

Kandiyoiti, Deniz. "Contemporary Feminist Scholarship." In *Gendering the Middle East: Emerging Perspectives*, edited by Deniz Kandiyoti, 1–27. New York: Syracuse University Press, 1996.

Lammens, H. ʿMālik B. ʿAwf'. In *Encyclopaedia of Islam*, Second Edition. Edited by P. Bearman, Th. Bianquis, C. E. Bosworth, E. van Donzel, W. P. Heinrichs, P.J. Bearman (Volumes X, XI, XII), Th. Bianquis (Volumes X, XI, XII), et al. Accessed October 31, 2021. http://dx.doi.org.ezproxy.bgu.ac.il/10.1163/1573 -3912_islam_SIM_4863.

Lichtenstädter, Ilse. "Muhammad Ibn Ḥabîb and His Kitâb Al-Muḥabbar." *Journal of the Royal Asiatic Society of Great Britain and Ireland* 1 (1939): 1–27.

Mahmood, Saba. "Feminist Theory, Embodiment, and the Docile Agent: Some Reflections on the Egyptian Islamic Revival." *Cultural Anthropology* 16, no. 2 (2001): 202–236.

McNay, Lois. *Gender and Agency: Reconfiguring the Subject in Feminist and Social Theory*. Cambridge: Polity Press, 2013.

Mernissi, Fatima. *Women and Islam: An Historical and Theological Inquiry*. Oxford: Blackwell, 1991.

Rizwi Faizer. *The Life of Muhammad: Al-Waqidi's Kitab Al-Maghazi*. London: Routledge, 2013.

Roded, Ruth. *Women in Islamic Biographical Collections: From Ibn Saʿd to Who's Who*. Boulder: L. Rienner, 1996.

Schacht, J., Burton, J., and Chelhod, J. "Raḍāʿ or Riḍāʿ." In *Encyclopaedia of Islam, Second Edition,* edited by P. Bearman, Th. Bianquis, C. E. Bosworth, E. van Donzel, W. P. Heinrichs. Consulted online on 09 August 2019 http://dx.doi.org .ezproxy.bgu.ac.il/10.1163/1573-3912_islam_COM_0896.

Scott, Joan Wallach. "Gender as a Useful Category of Historical Analysis." In *Culture, Society and Sexuality a Reader,* edited by Richard G. Parker and Peter Aggleton. London and Philadelphia, PA: UCL, 1999. http://web.b.ebscohost.com.ezproxy.bgu .ac.il/ehost/ebookviewer/ebook/bmxlYmtfXzcwNzkxX19BTg2?sid=14c40763-b6ba -402b-88c7-ec32024cc32d@pdc-v-sessmgr02&vid=0&format=EK&lpid=6&rid=0.

Shushan, Boaz. "From the Diary of a Muslim Notary, Damascus 1480–1500." *Jamaa* 22 (2016): 7–22.

Stern, Gertrude H. "Muhammad's Bond with the Women." *Bulletin of the School of Oriental and African Studies* 10, no. 1 (1940): 185–197.

van Berkel, Maaike. "The Young Caliph and his Wicked Advisors: Women and Power Politics under Caliph Al-Muqtadir (r. 295–320/908–932)." *Al Masaq: Islam and the Medieval Mediterranean* 19, no. 1 (2007): 3–15.

Yaʿqūbī, Aḥmad bin Abī Yaʿqūb. *The Works of Ibn Wāḍiḥ Al-Yaʿqūbī.* Edited and translated by Matthew Gordon, Chase F. Robinson, Everett K. Rowson, and Michael Fishbein. Leiden: Brill, 2018.

Chapter 12

Wife and Leader

Khadījah as a First Follower

Zohar Hadromi-Allouche

Best known for being first wife of the prophet Muhammad, Khadījah bint Khuwaylid is concurrently portrayed in early Islamic literature as the first convert to Islam, first follower of Muhammad, and a distinctly liminal figure. Early Islamic sources (from the eighth to the tenth centuries) depict her as liminal on several levels. As a first follower, she had a crucial, leading, and liminal role in the emergence of the new religious movement, being posited between Muhammad and other followers. Several liminal traits apply to her, in particular, being a trickster figure. As she walks alongside Muhammad through the process of his transformation into a prophet and a leader, she also fills a liminal function for him. As a liminal character, Khadījah demonstrates agency, proactivity, and authority. Later medieval and modern scholarship, however, tends to deny her liminal qualities, leadership, and agency, replacing these with passivity and marginality.

The current study demonstrates the leadership and liminality of Khadījah through her role as a first follower, tracks the shift in the construction of her character, and discusses its causes and implications. The chapter consists of four parts and a summary.

Part one discusses Victor Turner's concept of social drama, Caroline Bynum's narrowing critique of it, and Arpad Szakolczai's argument for the broad applicability of liminality. It then presents Derek Sivers's theory of the "first follower" and highlights its liminal components. Part two establishes the applicability of these theories to Khadījah and her portrayals in early Islamic sources from the eighth to the tenth centuries. It indicates her several levels of liminality, in particular, as a trickster figure (in reference to Margaret A. Mills and Arpad Szakolczai's' works) and a first follower. The final section of this part discusses the underappreciated leadership of first followers and demonstrates how later Islamic medieval sources deny the liminality and leadership of Khadījah. Part three examines representations of Khadījah in modern works, both Islamic and Western academic, and demonstrates their tendency to further undermine and eliminate the agency and leadership of Khadījah, deny her liminality, and confine her to the domestic sphere.

Part four concludes by discussing the causes of this denial, considering the work done by Doris Decker, Haifaa G. Khalafallah, and Rahemtulla and Ababneh on women's roles in early Islam, and the backward projection of contemporary perception onto these. It is followed by the summary.

LIMINALITY, WOMEN, AND LEADERSHIP: THEORETICAL BACKGROUND

The term "liminality" was introduced by the French ethnographer and folk-lorist Arnold van Gennep in 1909.[1] He identified that rites of passage consist of three phases: segregation, liminality, and reaggregation. As of the 1960s, anthropologist Victor Turner adopted and adapted the term "liminiality." He expanded its use beyond the ritual into other realms of cultural expression, using liminality as a metaphor for describing human experience. Turner developed van Gennep's three stages into a four stages model, which he called "social drama."

Social drama, according to Turner, is characteristic of life crisis rites, such as puberty or election for leadership. It occurs in groups with shared values and interests, following the public breaking of a convention, practice, or a norm. This causes breach between social elements, which leads to a crisis and an open conflict. To limit the extent of this crisis, by way of redress or adjust-ment of the breach, a verbal or moral sacrifice is made, and leading members in the group sanction those perceived as causing the crisis. This is the liminal phase in the drama, which Turner regards crucial. It includes suspension of norms and roles and symbols of inversion such as men becoming women, strong becoming weak, rich becoming poor, the distinguished despised, and vice versa. Among other liminal symbols are the trickster figure and para-dox. The drama concludes by either reintegration into the social structure or acknowledgment that the breach is irreversible, leading, for example, to an exodus.[2]

Whereas Turner presents this model as universal, Caroline Bynum has shown that Turner's model does not typically apply to women. Following her study of women's stories in medieval Europe, she argues that when women narrate their stories, the themes are more about continuity, rather than conver-sion, liminality, inversion, or reintegration. For men, the inversion of images expresses liminality, with the main image being women, both factual and symbolic. Often, a man in a liminal moment, especially toward accepting administrative responsibility, is described as seeking comfort with an actual woman, as refuge from reintegrating into power and status. He would thereafter return to the world, "girded with information and consolation." Turner assumes symmetry between the inversion symbols between men and women, but Bynum notes that such a symmetry is rare. For women, there is no inversion rather than symbols and images of masculinity, prowess, or accession. The images of women continue, or empower, their ordinary experience. Rather than describe themselves as men, women maintain their feminine identity, on both the symbolic and practical levels. Their own liminality is marked by symbols of struggle and continuous feminine experience (bride, mother, lover; feeding; illness). There are dramatic moments but no breach or reintegration. Therefore, argues Bynum, Turner's expanded, metaphorical perception of liminality is only applicable to men. Only men's stories are full social dramas, and only their symbols are fully inverted.[3]

Bynum qualifies her criticism of Turner, noting that whereas her findings undermine the universality of the social drama, it should not in itself become an all-embracing generalization. Indeed, Massimiliano Carocci discusses the use by women of role inversion as well as images of manliness, power, and prowess, in the scalp dance rituals of the Plains Indians.[4] The work of Keren Abbou Hershkovits shows that women in early Islam had agency, however this was demonstrated through choice, initiative, decision, and actions rather than challenging norms.[5] Szakolczai argues that liminality is a widely applicable concept since "the sequential order of a rite of passage is the structure of lived experience" and "the appearance of new structures, identities, or ideas can be traced to liminal conditions." Liminality, therefore, helps understand situations where the existing order dissolves and new structures are formed—such as the emergence of Islam.[6]

The following discussion will demonstrate that liminality is highly effective in understanding the role of Khadījah in the emergence of Islam. Early Islamic texts depict Khadījah as liminal on several levels, such as her transition from Jahiliyyah to Islam, liminal characteristics, and her leadership function as a "first follower," a role that is liminal as of itself. And yet, seeing that Khadījah does not reach the final phase of Turner's social drama, indicates that Bynum's critique does apply to her in part.

Sivers and the First Follower Theory

Followership studies first emerged in the 1930s, as part of leadership studies. Initially, followers were regarded mostly as obedient, passive subordinates.[7] This approach began to change in the late twentieth century. In 1988, Robert E. Kelley published "In praise of followers," asserting that organizational success equally requires leadership and followership.[8] In *The Power of*

Followership (1992), he further expanded on the shared characteristics between effective leaders and effective followers.[9] Shortly after Ira Chaleff published *The Courageous Follower* (1995), which proclaims that followers are active participants in an organization.[10] Following these two works, followership studies became a discipline in its own right and scholars grew critical of the former leader-centric approach and more inclined to see followers as "active agents of leadership."[11]

Derek Sivers took this approach a step further. His 2010 short TED talk, "How to start a movement,"[12] introduces the "first follower" theory, which shifts the focus of attention away from the leader and demonstrates the crucial role of the first follower in the emergence of a movement. According to Szakolczai, too, once the focus is on the relationship between the two centers (leader and followers), the margin (occupied by the first follower) becomes liminal and even a new central.[13]

It is the first follower, argues Sivers, who transforms an individual with a unique idea from a "lone nut" into a leader.[14] The "first follower" theory was further supported and validated through a number of later studies in followership.[15]

Often discussed within the contexts of business, marketing or even pedagogy, the first follower theory is not usually applied to female leadership in early Islam. However, as Szakolczai notes, "Concepts are tools for research; they cannot be copyrighted by the discipline in which they were developed."[16] The first follower theory is overwhelmingly compatible with the portrayal of Khadījah in early Islamic literature, both in terms of her significance for the creation of Muhammad's new religious movement and her liminal position of underestimated leadership as a first follower.

Sivers characterizes the first followers through a number of traits, which ultimately define their leadership:

- Transforming a lone nut into a leader: Sivers depicts the first follower as "the spark that makes the fire."
- Being alongside the leader, who treats them as equal.
- Being imitated by other followers. This role is crucial, since by calling friends to join in, and publicly showing everyone how to follow, the first follower teaches others how to follow. New followers, notes Sivers, emulate the first follower rather than the leader. A movement, he concludes, must be public. The leadership aspect of imitation, especially in transition, liminal situations, is stressed by Szakolczai. As such situations involve the suspension of ordinary structures, the search for solution often involves imitation of an individual who can supply stability and guidance.[17]

- Sharing social risk. Similar to the leader, the first follower, too, risks ridicule, due to public exposure.[18]
- Providing an underappreciated form of leadership. Being a first follower, too, is a form of leadership. Through courageously following, the first follower transforms an idea into a movement. However, there are often misconceptions about the leading role of the first follower.[19]

Such misconceptions might derive from the ambiguous, liminal position of the first follower, between the leader and other followers. Notably, the aforementioned characteristics portray the first follower as occupying a middle, paradoxical position, being a follower (spatially behind), whom the leader (at front) treats as an equal (alongside); imitating the leader, while being imitated by others; and providing leadership that is concurrently underappreciated.

As the person who transforms an idea into a movement, a first follower accompanies the leader through the liminal stage between his former status (not a leader) into the new one (a leader). However, since the first follower does not achieve a full acknowledgment, the first follower never fully reaches the postliminal stage of reintegration. This characteristic is particularly applicable to Khadījah.

KHADĪJAH: LIMINALITY AND LEADERSHIP

All early Islamic sources agree that Khadījah bint Khuwaylid was born in the late sixth century in Mecca to a rich merchant from the tribe of Quraysh. She further cultivated her father's wealth through her own commercial activity. Before marrying Muhammad and becoming his first wife, Khadījah was married twice. She hired Muhammad to trade for her, and shortly after proposed to him. In response, Muhammad's uncle contacted Khadījah's father (or uncle), the marriage was agreed, and Muhammad moved to her house. Their marriage was monogamous (unlike the later marriages of Muhammad after her death) and lasted for twenty-four or twenty-five years. They had several children (at least four daughters and one or more sons, who died in childhood). Khadījah died a few years before the *hijrah* of Muhammad from Mecca to Medina, which is generally dated to 622 CE. Most importantly, all sources are unanimous that Khadījah fully supported Muhammad in his prophetic mission.[20]

Within this general biographical framework, details are blurred and often contradictory. For example, versus the prevailing view that upon their marriage Khadījah was forty years old and Muhammad was twenty-five, multiple reports suggest otherwise: for Muhammad, the ages of twenty-one, twenty-three, twenty-nine, thirty or thirty-seven are mentioned; for Khadījah, twenty-five, twenty-seven, twenty-eight, thirty, or forty-five. Since all sources agree that Khadījah had at least five children with Muhammad, and recognizing the typological nature of the number forty, M. J. Kister, Fatema Mernissi, Kecia Ali, and others indicate that "[i]n all probability, Khadījah was not forty years old" when she married Muhammad.[21] A much younger age seems more likely.

Forty as her age at marriage derives from the view that Khadījah was born fifteen years before the Year of the Elephant (often identified as 570 CE),[22] and that Muhammad was born on that year and married Khadījah when he was twenty-five. Other views, however, argue that Muhammad was born ten, twenty-three, thirty, forty, or seventy years *after* the Year of the Elephant;[23] the date of that Year is likewise much debated in Islamic sources.[24] Contradictory reports exist also concerning the identity of the first two husbands of Khadījah, the order in which she married them, whether she was twice a widow or a widow and then a divorcée and the number, gender, and names of her children from these marriages.[25] Finally, controversy prevails even the death of Khadījah, which is dated one, two, three, four, five, or six years before the *hijrah*.[26]

These multiple contradictions make it impossible to know when she (or Muhammad) was born, when they got married, or how many sons (and children) they had.[27] The tendency of classical and, particularly, modern authors to portray the story of Khadījah as a single-lined narrative is therefore questionable.[28] Rather, it seems advisable to read such biographical narratives as literary constructions, which result from the choice of specific details by the author, in order to characterize Khadījah in a particular way, for example, elevating or downplaying her leadership.

At the same time, of the few generally agreed details concerning Khadījah, most significant is her enduring support of Muhammad and his prophetic mission, starting with the very first revelation. The following discussion will demonstrate how the "first follower" model and its liminal aspects are helpful in highlighting the leadership, function, and agency of Khadījah in early Islamic biographical and historiographical sources, versus her portrayal in later accounts, Islamic and Western alike.

Transforming the Lone Nut into a Leader

According to Ibn Isḥāq's (d. 767 CE) biography of Muhammad as recorded in Ibn Hishām's (d. 834 CE) recension (henceforth, Ibn Isḥāq), the first revelation of angel Gabriel to Muhammad took place in a cave on mount Ḥirā', where Muhammad was staying by himself. Muhammad found this experience quite unsettling, and upon his return home shared it with Khadījah. In response, Khadījah said: "Rejoice, oh cousin, and rest assured, for I hope that you are to become the prophet of this nation."[29] Through her instant recognition, she preceded Muhammad himself in acknowledging his leadership and mission. This quick recognition, argues Nabia Abbot, was as important as the angel's words in convincing Muhammad that he was a prophet.[30] Indeed, according to Szakolczai, in liminal situations words not only describe reality, but form it. Following the first revelation, Muhammad is in a "stressful, emotive" liminal crisis, which prevents clear thinking.[31] Muhammad imitates Khadījah by accepting her statement that he is a prophet and thus is removed from unclarity into a new reality.

Writing somewhat later, Ibn Saʿd (d. 845 CE) and al-Ṭabarī (d. 923 CE) record a different course of events, omitting Khadījah's explicit recognition of Muhammad. Instead, these narrations relate that the Prophet was much shaken by the first revelation, and feared that he was being inspired, or even possessed, by an evil spirit. But Khadījah assured him that he was not possessed, saying that "God would never do that to you."[32] Khadījah literally transformed "the lone nut into a leader." She embodied for Muhammad the liminal phase, through which he was transformed from an ordinary person into a prophet. She constituted the safe place from which he would return into society having been transformed into a prophet.

All three sources agree that following this conversation, Khadījah went to consult her learned Christian cousin, Waraqah bin Nawfal. Waraqah repeated that which Khadījah has already observed—that this was the beginning of a prophetic revelation and indicated further that Muhammad has been visited by an angel. The phrasing used by each is very similar: according to Ibn Isḥāq, Khadījah has initially told the shaken Muhammad that "Rejoice, oh cousin, and *rest assured* for I hope that *you are to become the prophet of this nation*;" whereas Waraqah later told Khadījah that "if you tell me the truth, oh Khadījah, then the great angel who has come to Moses indeed came to him, and *he is the prophet of this nation*." Notably, whereas Khadījah has expressed a complete confidence in Muhammad, Waraqah—despite his scholarly and religious knowledge—cautiously preceded his statement with a qualifying phrase.[33] Yet his words are very similar to hers, and his imitating Khadījah demonstrates her leadership.[34]

Khadījah never questioned the integrity of Muhammad. Knowing that he was still in doubt, she sought to reassure him of his prophetic mission through a third form of confirmation, by testing the nature of his visitant. Khadījah asked Muhammad to inform her once angel Gabriel was present, upon which she became increasingly intimate with Muhammad. As this made Gabriel depart, Khadījah assured Muhammad that his visitor was not a demon but an angel.[35] She is portrayed here as having confidence, initiative, and knowledge of the nature and ways of supernatural beings. Notably, her tricking the angel also depicts Khadījah as a trickster figure, which is a major liminal symbol.

The relevance of tricksters for liminality is noted by Szakolczai. However, he considers their gaining power in liminal situations as highly dangerous, since they might take over and create an enduring roles–and values reversal. Rather than a temporary condition, liminality then becomes permanent. Such a condition, where previous social unity was broken, but the rival parties are forced to remain together, in a "truly miserable existence," rather than return to normality (separate or overcome the schism), Gregory Bateson calls Schismogenesis.[36] Margaret A. Mills, on the other hand, who studies female trickster figures in Muslim folklore, notes that trickery is a common trait of women in Islamic folktales. She finds that tricksters challenge, compromise, or change the social order and considers female trickster figures in Muslim narrations as prosocial.[37] Among the traits of the female trickster Mills counts mobility, liminality, ability to hide or change form, and paradoxical agency (where the outcome of an action is different, implicitly or explicitly, from what it seemed to aim at). Whereas the male trickster has physical mobility, the mobility of a woman trickster is cognitive (through redefining a stationary space). She uses her control of the familiar domestic space to assume moral agency and initiate a strategic action that the would-be male trickster, who illegitimately enters the feminine domestic space, would not be able to overcome. She is also a truth-teller and might act as an older wise sister or protector of a young innocent man. Paradoxically, her actions dismantle patriarchy, in order to protect it.[38]

All these characteristics are evident as typifying Khadījah. She clearly emerges as a trickster figure, however, not necessarily as negative, calculative, and cunning as Szakolczai would argue. Notably, as Szakolczai indicates, tricksters are ambivalent.[39] In the episode of her encounter with Gabriel, as the angel intrudes her home and unnerves Muhammad, Khadījah changes her appearance through covering and uncovering herself. She thus redefines the domestic space as intimate and forces Gabriel to reveal his true identity, as well as leave her home. Her authoritative behavior toward Muhammad is intended to protect him, and her driving away of the angel is paradoxically intended to enable the revelation to continue. Other expressions of Khadījah's trickery occur around their marriage as is discussed further. She does, however, represent Schismogenesis, too, as only after her death does Muhammad move from his liminal position in hostile Meccan society and performs the *hijrah* to Medina.

Being Alongside the Leader and Treated as an Equal by the Leader

Nurturing the first few followers as equals, says Sivers, is highly important.[40] This, as well as the first follower being alongside the leader, is clearly evident in the relationship of Muhammad and Khadījah.

According to Ibn Isḥāq, Muhammad used to consult Khadījah and share with her all his troubles and important moments as is also evident through his turning to her following the first revelation experience. Muhammad never defied Khadījah, and during their nearly twenty-five years of marriage, he never married an additional wife.[41] The striking contrast between this detail and the multiple marriages of Muhammad (the sources mention at least eleven additional wives)[42] after the death of Khadījah is evidence of its telling significance.

The sharing between the two was in terms of mission and politics as well. Ibn Isḥāq relates that when Gabriel taught Muhammad how to perform ablution and pray, Muhammad first taught this to Khadījah.[43] According to Ibn Saʿd, at this early stage the two of them would pray together secretly.[44]

Khadījah, too, received messages from God through the angel Gabriel, like Muhammad. Ibn Isḥāq relates that the angel Gabriel commanded Muhammad to announce Khadījah of a house of pearls awaiting her in Paradise. On another occasion, Gabriel instructed Muhammad to give Khadījah greeting of peace from God, to which she reciprocated: "God is peace, and peace is from him, and peace be upon Gabriel."[45] This anecdote posits Khadījah apart from the rest of the community and closer to the Prophet.

Ibn Isḥāq highlights the role of Khadījah as an important and honest supporter of Muhammad in regard to Islam, referring to her as a *wazīr ṣidq ʿalā al-Islām* (a faithful vizier in regards to Islam).[46] Literally, the word *wazīr* (origin of the anglicized form "vizier") means "one who bears a burden with, or helps, another." From this derives the prevalent meaning of vicegerent to a king, upon whose counsel the ruler relies.[47] Abbot notices that the phrase *wazīr ṣidq* is usually associated with Abū Bakr, but Ibn Isḥāq applies it to Khadījah, adding that Muhammad approached her at all times of internal doubts and external persecutions.[48] Khadījah thus emerges as a first follower, who supports and influences the leader[49] as well as functions as a safe, liminal zone for Muhammad, his "breakout room." The use of the word *wazīr*, with its political connotation, indicates that Khadījah was not just performing her "wifely duties," as modern scholars often argue,[50] but functioned as a first follower, committing herself to the cause of Islam. When describing her conversion, Ibn Isḥāq notes that Khadījah believed in Muhammad, "assisted and strengthened him on his prophetic mission."[51] Her support and advice were within the context of their relationship as leader and first follower of a new religious movement.

Being Imitated by Other Followers

A crucial role of the first follower is to call others to join in and publicly demonstrate how to follow. New followers emulate the existing ones, says

Sivers, hence publicity is important.[52] Several reports apply this aspect to Khadījah. This is a particularly liminal aspect of the first follower, who serves as a mediator between the leader the (future) community.

Ibn Isḥāq notes that upon the beginning of Muhammad's mission, not only did Khadījah accept Islam but so did her daughters.[53] She thus set a model for others. Similarly, the next female convert, Umm al-Faḍl, wife of the prophet's uncle al-ʿAbbās, who was the first woman convert after Khadījah, brought three of her sisters to the prophet to convert soon after her own conversion.[54] Abbot argues that thanks to Khadījah, Muhammad "sensed the great influence that women converts could exert in establishing and spreading the new faith."[55]

The public role of Khadījah as a first follower and her function as a role model are further demonstrated through a narration that is attributed to a Yemenite merchant named ʿAfīf, describing his first encounter of Islam:

> Said ʿAfīf: I was a merchant, and came to Mecca during the *ḥajj*, and stayed with al-ʿAbbās. While we were at his place, there came out a man and prayed, facing the Kaʿbah. Then came a woman, and stood praying with him. Then came a boy, and stood praying with him. I asked al-ʿAbbās about that religion, which I did not know, and he said that these were Muhammad, who has argued that God sent him [. . .] and his wife Khadījah who believed in him, and his cousin ʿAlī who believed in him.[56]

Khadījah is described as praying equally with the Prophet. They are then joined (and imitated) by ʿAlī bin Abū Ṭālib, cousin of Muhammad who later became the Prophet's son in law; fourth caliph; and leader of Shīʿite Islam.[57] Their order of appearance in public reflects the prevalent view that Khadījah was the first convert to Islam and ʿAlī was second.[58] This report depicts a public prayer (unlike the aforementioned report, which probably refers to an earlier period, when Muhammad and Khadījah used to pray in secret). Publicity is necessary for others to watch and learn as is evident from the questions of ʿAfīf. Indeed, the presence of Khadījah and ʿAlī turns Muhammad from a nutty loner, into the leader of a movement, which has its followers and shared practices.[59] Khadījah serves here as an agent of liminality. The distinctive public aspect of the first follower's leadership is also significant in that it contrasts with the domestic image that is often applied to women, especially married women.

Sharing the Social Risk

Yet publicity has its toll. Sivers observes that it exposes both leader and first follower to social risk and ridicule.[60] This too applies to Khadījah. Ibn Isḥāq notes that Khadījah bore with Muhammad the burden of hostile responses:

Khadījah [. . .] bore the burden with him [. . .] This way God relieved his prophet, who did not hear a thing of the hateful responses and rejections which made him sad, but God removed his sorrow through her: when he came back to her, she asserted him and relieved him, held him to be telling truth and made easy for him the affairs of the people. [61]

Khadījah concurrently shares with Muhammad these characteristics of the liminal phase before he is turned into a leader and constitutes his retreat from the world, to which he later returns with information and comfort.[62]

Social risk was not limited to sharing difficult moments with Muhammad. Khadījah suffered from the Qurashite rejection of Islam too. Upon the Qurashite boycott of Muhammad, she had to leave her home and move to the valley of Abū Ṭālib.[63] For Khadījah, this was a significant move of tangible liminality. She had to leave her former space in society, her matrilocal home, into which Muhammad has moved upon their marriage, for a marginalizing patrilocality. From providing home and support to Muhammad, she became dependent on shelter and support from his family; her central, distinguished social status is replaced for that of a refugee, of a no-status, as she is removed to an isolated space outside society. The richest woman of Quraysh became under threat of hunger; the woman who was desired for marriage by all men of her tribe became an outcast. Abū Jahl (d. 624 CE), a Meccan leader and prominent opponent of Muhammad, attempted to prevent the relatives of Khadījah from providing her with food.[64] Leila Ahmed notes that there is no reference to Khadījah as leaving an inheritance after her death for Muhammad or her daughters, meaning that throughout the Meccan persecutions she had lost all her fortune.[65] 'Utbah bin Abī Lahab, her non-Muslim son-in-law, divorced Muhammad and Khadījah's daughter Ruqayyah due to the prophetic mission of Muhammad.[66] Khadījah's son, al-Ḥārith b. Abū Hāla, who converted to Islam, was killed by a nonbeliever during prayer, or as he defended the Prophet against slander.[67] During this time of persecution, Khadījah fell ill (a feminine symbol of liminality, according to Bynum)[68] and died. In this context, it is also interesting to note that Mills follows Hyde in indicating that the fate of a trickster might be either domestication, neutralizing/extermination, or moving on to their next adventure.[69] Khadījah, who used to live in her own house, was domestic but not domesticated. The Quraysh boycott, which removed her from her house into the house of Muhammad's family functioned as a forced domestication, which led to neutralization and death. Due to her public support of Muhammad and Islam, Khadījah made a big sacrifice. This tragic aspect of Khadījah is part of her liminality and trickery. Whereas liminality contributes to creativity and renewal, it also causes anxiety to those going through it.[70] It was the death of Khadījah which enabled Muhammad to complete his social drama, move from liminal Mecca to victory in Medina whereas Khadījah remained permanently in this liminal phase.

Providing an Underappreciated Form of Leadership

Finally, by standing out and transforming the idea of the "lone nut" into a movement, the first follower exercises leadership. This leadership, however, is often underappreciated.[71]

Generally speaking, both biographical sources and authoritative *ḥadīth* (prophetic tradition) collections contain multiple praises of Khadījah, and her character and emphasize "her exclusive position among the wives of the Prophet."[72] Early biographies emphasize the moral excellence of Khadījah, and Muhammad's good fortune in marrying here. According to Ibn Isḥāq, she was "the most distinguished of the Quraysh women in lineage, the most highly honored, and the wealthiest" and "all the men of her tribe would have been eager to accept this proposal had it been made to them."[73]

She is portrayed as a charismatic, strong person, with evident leadership qualities. For example, she sends trading caravans to Syria and, in this context, hires Muhammad (thus demonstrating control of his spatial location);[74] proposes to him and arranges their marriage; initiates a search expedition when, following his encounter with angel Gabriel, he does not return home from mount Ḥirā';[75] and, after acknowledging his prophecy, Khadījah helps Muhammad overcome his internal doubts, by consulting her cousin Waraqah and testing angel Gabriel. In this affirmation, Khadījah demonstrates both her self-confidence and devotion to the greater cause. Furthermore, despite her own confidence that Muhammad is a true prophet, she knows that he still has doubts, which must be overcome. She therefore puts her ego to one side and applies for additional, external reassurances (Waraqah). Khadījah thus emerges as an active, effective agent of the leadership process. Tarif Khalidi describes her as being "honorable, strong-willed and intelligent"[76] and Ali observes that following the first revelation, "Khadija [. . .] became a key part of the story."[77] Her competence, self-management, commitment, and courage are, according to Robert E. Kelley, characteristics of an effective follower.[78]

Nevertheless, as is typically the case with first followers, the leadership of Khadījah, is often underappreciated,[79] even undermined. Her very status as a first follower is questioned, as her presence alongside Muhammad is dimmed irrelevant, secondary, or even negative. This is represented through the following episodes: Khadījah and Muhammad's marriage, the first revelation and first convert debate, the interval in the revelation, public prayer (the story of ʿAfīf), and Khadījah's death.

One of the few undisputed details in the biography of Khadījah is the monogamous marriage of her and Muhammad. Seeing his multiple marriages after her death, it is evidence of her unique status with Muhammad. Nevertheless, also this detail is being questioned on a number of levels. Ali notes that some classical authors relate a report which depicts Khadījah as fearing that her father would object her marriage to Muhammad. She thus got him drunk and received his approval through deception.[80] This report depicts Khadījah as a negative, opportunist, and morally vague trickster figure.[81] It associates her with the stereotypical trickster woman, Eve, who, according to a report recorded by al-Ṭabarī, intoxicated Adam so that he would agree to eat the forbidden fruit of paradise.[82] Khadījah's marital and seniority status are further undermined through a report arguing that in paradise she would become Muhammad's co-wife, together with Maryam mother of Jesus and Āsiya (wife of Pharaoh, who saved baby Moses according to the Qur'an).[83]

A more explicit dis-acknowledgment of Khadījah and her first follower status emerges from the context of the first revelation, and the events that followed soon after. Whereas Ibn Isḥaq and al-Ṭabarī are explicit that Khadījah designed the testing of Gabriel in order to assuage Muhammad's anxiety, Ibn Kathīr (d. 1373 CE) argues, quoting al-Bayhaqī (d. 1066 CE), that she was trying to calm her own doubts.[84] Moreover, although early Islamic literature generally agrees that Khadījah was the first convert to Islam,[85] following the explicit statement by Ibn Isḥaq,[86] this, too, is sometimes undermined, particularly in reports concerning the identity of the first male convert.[87]

The scholarly debate in early Islamic sources regarding this matter is surveyed by al-Ṭabarī.[88] A prevalent view is that the first male convert to Islam was 'Alī b. Abū Ṭālib, cousin of Muhammad, who is said to have been ten years old at the time.[89] Other identifications include Abū Bakr (d. 634 CE), Muhammad's close friend and father-in-law, who later became first caliph, or Zayd b. Ḥāritha (d. 629 CE), the adopted son of Muhammad, who passed away during Muhammad's lifetime. The main significance of this debate is political and religious. 'Alī and Abū Bakr represent, respectively, Shi'ah and Sunnah Islam. Therefore, reports asserting the primal conversion of either serve to validate the claim of the respective denomination to rule the Islamic nation.[90] Reports that identify the first male follower as Zayd, who passed away before Muhammad, offer an a-political midway. Whatever the underlying interest, such reports often elevate the respective male figure on account of Khadījah.

Al-Ṭabarī begins his survey of this debate by stating that some consider 'Alī as the first *male* convert. He then supports this view with several reports, which relate that 'Alī was the *first convert* to Islam. Another report argues that 'Alī was the first one to have performed prayer.[91] Such reports eliminate Khadījah and her role as first believer and first person to have performed prayer alongside Muhammad. Similarly, al-Mas'ūdī (d. 956 CE) relates that 'Alī was the first convert, and Abū Bakr converted next. Al-Mas'ūdī and al-Ya'qūbī (d. 897 CE) also record the view that Khadījah was the

first convert among women whereas ʿAlī was among men,[92] thus removing Khadījah from the "first follower" position. Another report recorded by
al-Yaʿqūbī relates that once prayer obligation was revealed to Muhammad, he
taught the ablution and prayer to Khadījah. She performed it like him. Then
ʿAlī saw Muhammad doing ablution and prayer and imitated him.[93] While
acknowledging the status of Khadījah as the first convert, this report removes
her from the role of a model of imitation. Instead, it puts ʿAlī in direct relation to Muhammad, creating a leader-first follower relationship between the
two men.

Abū Bakr, too, is described as the first convert. Both al-Ṭabarī and
al-Masʿūdī record reports which depict him as "the first person to have converted to Islam."[94] Al-Bukhārī (d. 870 CE) records a report which further
degrades Khadījah, as the companion ʿAmmār b. Yāsir states: "I saw the
messenger of God, with him but five slaves, two women and Abū Bakr."[95]

A report which relates explicitly that Zayd b. Ḥāritha was the first convert,
and Khadījah second, is recorded by al-Masʿūdī.[96] Al-Ṭabarī relates a more
implicit report, which depicts Zayd as the first convert; for comparison, a
similar report states that Zayd was the first *male* convert. Another report has
Khadījah as the first believer among women and Zayd among men,[97] thus
locating both on the same level.

Such reports, with their mild phrasing variants, deny Khadījah of her
chronological and qualitative precedence in Islam. By implicitly (or explicitly) acknowledging a male figure as the first convert, they remove Khadījah
from her liminal and leadership status as "first follower," confining her instead
to the marginalized group of women believers. By transferring Khadījah from
a leadership position into that of a follower, the sources furthermore try to
deprive Khadījah of the agency and liminality that the first follower position
entails. This removal becomes further evident in modern scholarship, as will
be discussed below.

Some medieval Islamic historiographers noted the implications of such
reports on the status of Khadījah. Al-Ṭabarī in his *Taʾrīkh* opens and concludes his discussion concerning the first male convert with a disambiguating
disclaimer, explicitly stating that this discussion only relates to the first *male*
follower whereas the first person to have believed in Muhammad and follow
him was Khadījah. To further support this, al-Ṭabarī quotes two early biographers of Muhammad, al-Wāqidī (d. 823 CE) and Ibn Saʿd.[98]

Another episode which serves to weaken Khadījah's status is the interval
in revelation. According to Ibn Isḥāq, Ibn Saʿd, and Al-Ṭabarī, after the first
revelation of the Qurʾan, revelation ceased for a while. During this interval
(*fatrah*), Muhammad was distressed. Al-Ṭabarī records several reports concerning how the enemies of Muhammad used this interval to mock him, saying that his Lord must hate him.[99] One of these identifies Khadījah as telling

Muhammad that his Lord must hate him, to cause him such sorrow. Such a statement is anything *but* support or followership.[100]

A more implicit underappreciation of Khadījah emerges from the afore-mentioned account of ʿAfīf. Two additional variants of this story question the status of Khadījah as a first follower, while promoting ʿAlī into that position. A variant recorded by al-Ṭabarī relates that ʿAfīf first saw Muhammad praying. Then came Khadījah and stood in prayer. Last came ʿAlī, and prayed alongside Muhammad. When ʿAfīf asked who those people were, al-ʿAbbās first mentioned Muhammad, then ʿAlī, then Khadījah.[101] This variant maintains the chronological precedence of Khadījah as the first convert, however, it pushes her backwards in terms of space and significance from her liminal, first follower position. Khadījah thus embodies the unification of the center and the margins through embodying the "in-between-ness." She is at once marginal, liminal, and central (between the prophet and ʿAlī).[102]

The other variant, recorded by Ibn Saʿd and al-Ṭabarī, relates that ʿAfīf first saw Muhammad coming out and praying. Then came ʿAlī and stood next to him. Last came Khadījah and stood behind them.[103] Here Khadījah is further marginalized, pushed back, literally and symbolically whereas ʿAlī takes the liminal space between prophet and believers, which implies his precedence as first follower. While the aforementioned variant of this story suggests an egalitarian prayer, the latter ones reflect gender hierarchy and seek retrospective support for later norms of gender segregation and locating women at the back during prayer.

Finally, an implicit degradation of Khadījah is found in references to her death. Ibn Hishām relates from Ibn Isḥāq that the death of Khadījah was particularly difficult for Muhammad, since she was his loyal support in Islam, and he used to share his trouble with her. Combined with the death of Muhammad's uncle Abū Ṭālib, it resulted in Muhammad losing protection from his opponents. Al-Ṭabarī, too, relates to Ibn Isḥāq; however, his narration concerning the death of Abū Ṭālib and Khadījah does not mention the death of Khadījah as causing a specific loss. Rather, he only mentions "a great affliction to the messenger of God. This is because after the death of Abū Ṭālib, Quraysh went to greater lengths in molesting him." Notably, Haifaa Khalafallah indicates that pagan Abū Ṭālib was protecting his nephew in line with pre-Islamic tribal norms, whereas Muslim Khadījah dedicated her material and emotional resources for the sake of Islam.[104]

Summary

The above discussion has demonstrated the applicability of the "first follower" theory to the character of Khadījah, as a major trait of her liminality. Early Islamic sources portray Khadījah as a first follower, whose ultimate support turns Muhammad from a lone nut into a leader. Located alongside Muhammad, who treats her as an equal, she is imitated by other followers, while sharing with Muhammad the burden and social risk of leadership. Other liminal traits of her include being a trickster, inversion, and a transition from mainstream society into indefinite space and status. Her very status as the first convert to Islam, as well as persecution, transition, and inversion, are characteristic of a social drama. However, Khadījah does not complete the process of reintegration/departure, as she dies during the liminal phase, having lost wealth, status, and her son. She embodies the sacrifice in this stage.

As a first follower, her leadership is underappreciated, and her character and traits undermined, sometimes in linkage with the promotion on her account of other, masculine, characters. Islamic sources as of the ninth century deny Khadījah her liminality, agency, and leadership as a first follower and a trickster, or present these as negative. Instead of liminal, she becomes marginalized. This process becomes further evident in modern scholarship.

KHADĪJAH: LIMINALITY AND LEADERSHIP DENIED

Despite such underappreciating reports as mentioned previously, Khadījah is generally remembered by Muslims, both Sunni and Shi'ite, in a highly positive manner, as a strong, independent and successful woman. In modern times, she is perceived as iconic businesswoman and leader.[105] One of the two "most influential women's institutions for entrepreneurship and finance in the Arabian Gulf region" is the Khadījah bint Khuwaylid Businesswomen's Centre in Jeddah.[106]

This iconic image is less prevalent in modern scholarship on Muhammad. Many such works eliminate the leadership of Khadījah and belittle her significance, sometimes with textual support.

Acknowledging the Prophetic Mission

A number of scholars transfer the role of "turning the lone nut into a leader" from Khadījah to her Christian cousin Waraqah. W. Montgomery Watt, for example, identifies Waraqah, not Khadījah, as initially and primarily acknowledging and supporting Muhammad. The belief, support, and initiative that Ibn Isḥāq attributes to Khadījah Watt transfers to Waraqah—despite that Waraqah never converted to Islam. Watt argues that it was Waraqah who influenced Khadījah to acknowledge that Muhammad had received divine revelation and supported Muhammad in believing this, whereas to Khadījah "Muhammad turned when in moments of desolation."[107] Also Michael Cook identifies Waraqah as the first person to have acknowledged Muhammad's prophethood, although he does credit Khadījah with having "established that his [Muhammad's] supernatural visitor was indeed an angel."[108] Martin Lings notes that the first revelation to Muhammad made Khadījah "alarmed" (i.e., seeing the nut rather than the leader). She thus consulted Waraqah, and only after his confirmation that Muhammad was a prophet, did she *repeat* his words to Muhammad.[109] In Ling's narration, Khadījah loses her first follower position. Rather, she imitates Waraqah. These descriptions stand in sheer contrast to the Ibn Isḥāq description of Khadījah as instantly acknowledging that Muhammad was a prophet whereas Waraqah demonstrated cautious skepticism.[110]

The First Convert

Jonathan E. Brockopp notes regarding the first follower that "All agree that she [Khadījah] was the first to believe in his [Muhammad's] mission, though there is a significant dispute about who among the men was first."[111] Similarly, Tarik Ramadan relates that Khadījah was "the first convert to Islam."[112] This conviction, which reflects the view of many classical Islamic scholars, is less evident for some other modern scholars.

Ali's observation that modern scholarship tends to create a single narrative of Islamic history, regardless of other alternatives available, is often evident in discussions concerning the first convert. Several works only mention Khadījah and ʿAlī as first converts, while ignoring Abū Bakr and Zayd. And yet, even with reduced competition, the leadership and first follower status of Khadījah are often overlooked. In his two-volume survey of Islamic history and thought, Andrew Rippin mentions Khadījah only once, describing her as Muhammad's wife who converted early, "like ʿAlī and others." The conversion of Khadījah thus becomes casual, its importance unnoticed. Moreover, versus the lack of details about Khadījah ("his wife Khadījah"), Rippin gives multiple details concerning ʿAlī ("ʿAlī, his cousin, future son-in-law, fourth Caliph and figurehead of the Shiʿite movement in Islam").[113]

Malise Ruthven does acknowledge to some extent the precedence of Khadījah; however, this extent is rather limited. He refers to her as "the first Muslim," only to confine this precedence to the physical domestic sphere, going on to depict Khadījah as "the first in Muhammad's household to accept that Muhammad's message came from God."[114] This confinement implies that outside the household of Muhammad there were others who preceded Khadījah in converting to Islam. In another statement, Ruthven presents the conversions of Khadījah and ʿAlī as equivalent, stating that "Khadija accepted Muhammad's message as did his uncle's son ʿAli".[115] Also Michael Cook presents the conversion of Khadījah, ʿAlī and Zayd as equivalent: "At first [. . .] converts were confined to his immediate family: Khadija, his wife;

'Ali, a young son of Abu Talib whom Muhammad had taken into his household at the time of a famine; and Zayd, a slave whom he had manumitted."[116]
For comparison, Ziauddin Sardar communicates the same information while
maintaining Khadījah's status: "Khadija was the first convert. She was followed by his [Muhammad's] teenage cousin and ward, Ali, and his adopted
son, Zaid."[117]

David Waines argues that following the first revelation, Muhammad feared
that he was being possessed, but then he was "[c]omforted by Khadījah
and supported by ʿAlī."[118] Waines identifies ʿAlī (who reportedly was ten-
year-old at the time) as the first supporter of Muhammad, while confining
Khadījah to the domestic, wifely role of comforting, and removing her from
the public, leadership role of the first follower.

Marriage: The Comforting Loving Wife

Muslim tradition clearly depicts Khadījah as the dominant side in her and
Muhammad's marriage, being his senior in terms of age, marital experience,
status, and finances. It is Khadījah who contacts Muhammad and offers him
a job. Later, she proposes marriage, following which he moves in with her
(a matrilocal union). Some modern authors, however, are uncomfortable
with this early Islamic narrative. Syed A. A. Razwy, for example, insists that
Khadījah was not married before she married Muhammad. He also insists
that rather than Khadījah proposing to Muhammad, it was her friend, Nafīsah,
who initiated this union and went ahead to discuss it with Muhammad, without informing Khadījah—who remains completely passive. Furthermore, he
argues that after marrying Muhammad, Khadījah withdrew from running her
business. No textual evidence supports these arguments. Conversely, Kecia
Ali notes that it was Khadījah's wealth that allowed Muhammad to take
extended periods of meditation in the mountains, that is, she was the provider
in this marriage.[119]

Throughout their marriage, Khadījah provided Muhammad with support
and comfort in times of crisis.[120] Chris Cillizza, CNN Politics Reporter and
Editor-at-Large, regards comforting and reassurance an important role of
political leaders. According to Cillizza, "in moments of crisis [. . .] people
look to politicians for comfort and reassurance [. . .] leaders in our community [. . .] are responsible for bringing the community together in moments of
tragedy or catastrophe."[121] Modern biographies of Muhammad, however, both
Western and Islamic, choose to frame the comforting role of Khadījah within
the domestic sphere, defining it as a wifely duty, part of her portrayal as "the
perfect wife."[122] Carole Hillenbrand, for example, maintains that whenever
Muhammad has had doubts, Khadījah would "bolster" him with "loving
comfort and encouragement."[123]

Several Islamic authors depict Khadījah as "an angel of hope and con-solation," a Victorian phrase probably adopted from a nineteenth-century Western work on Muhammad. This phrase removes Khadījah from the context of actual revelation, confining her to the domestic sphere instead.[124] Barbara Stowasser notes the general tendency in modern religious Islamic literature to depict the wives of Muhammad, and especially Khadījah, as ideal wives and mothers, who were his domestic helpmates as well participated in the struggle for his cause. The term *wazīr* is interpreted in this context as a deputy.[125]

This tendency is evident among Western scholars as well. Watt depicts Khadījah as a "faithful wife and helpmate,"[126] with evident association to Genesis 2:18, that is indicative of a subordinate status of Khadījah. Kister holds that "[t]radition emphasizes Khadīja's virtues, her piety, her dedication to the cause of the Prophet, her care and affection for him and her firm belief." He interprets the term *wazīr ṣidq* as evidence of this dedication.[127] Ruthven defines Khadījah as "devoted wife and confidante."[128]Ali suggests that such depictions of Khadījah as Muhammad's beloved companion, domestic com-forter, and mother of his children derive from the modern emphasis on mar-riage as the focus of one's emotional life.[129]

Wife and Mother

The motherly image of Khadījah reoccurs in multiple works. Lings, while describing her as the wise advisor of Muhammad, also depicts Khadījah as his intimate friend and mother of all his household. Ali notes the implied patriar-chal view (*his* household).[130] This is particularly remarkable since, according to Rahemtullah and Ababneh, after their marriage, it was Muhammad who moved into Khadījah's house.[131] ʿĀʾishah ʿAbd al-Raḥmān (Bint al-Shāṭiʾ) calls her chapter on Khadījah "The mother and housewife." She and Maʾmūn Gharīb both describe the relationship of Khadījah with Muhammad as "sub-stitute mother." Khadījah's reaction to Muhammad following the first revela-tion she describes as "the deepest feeling of motherhood."[132] In this context, it is interesting to note Bynum's discernment that men authors tend to perceive the female images of a virgin, a bride, or a mother, as expressive of the male self-image, as it escapes the existing social structure. By depicting Khadījah as a mother in relation to Muhammad, modern scholars relate to her as an image, rather than a person in her own right.[133]

Ali notes that almost all modern biographers of Muhammad, Western and Islamic alike, give the age of Khadījah at marrying Muhammad as forty, tak-ing as factual this probably symbolic age. This in turn leads to the assumption that their marriage was based on companionship, and results in condescend-ing descriptions of Khadījah as an elderly comforting helpmate, a motherly wife who takes interest in her young husband's career. The implication is that Muhammad was doing her a favor by marrying her, seeing that she was old and unattractive. This approach is absent in medieval sources—perhaps, Ali suggests, since they realized that forty was a symbolic number. Abbot indicates that these condescending descriptions diminish the dominant character of Khadījah, and Muhammad's acceptance of her as his companion and advisor.[134]

Personal Traits

Some scholars go as far as undermining the personal traits of Khadījah. Versus the early Islamic depiction of Khadījah as an independent woman, running her own business and proposing to Muhammad, modern authors Yahia Emerick and Deepak Chopra depict her as insecure, doubtful that Muhammad might reject her. Emerick emphasizes the kindness of Muhammad in treating her as a "loving life-partner" despite her lack of youth and virginity.[135] Rahemtullah and Ababneh note that all of Muhammad's wives, except ʿĀʾishah, were not virgins at the time of marrying him. Unlike the contemporary sources, none of the early sources finds this unusual, nor uses Khadījah's former marriages to undermine her status.[136]

Furthermore, the aforementioned depiction of Khadījah in the early Islamic sources as "the richest woman of Quraysh in her time," who further cultivated her father's wealth through her own commercial activity, was reinterpreted by some early Western scholars to suggest that much of Khadījah's wealth derived from "frequent contracts of a loose form of marriage."[137] Versus the explicit classical references to Khadījah as morally excellent and "most distinguished of the Quraysh women in lineage, the most highly honored," these scholars chose to portray her as a prostitute.

Liminality Acknowledged

Some scholars, however, do acknowledge the liminal position of Khadījah as concurrently a first follower and comforting wife.

Mernissi emphasizes the initiative of Khadījah in her private and public life alike.[138] Ali holds that following the first revelation, Khadījah had "a key part" in the story of the emergence of Islam. This part was combined of the comfort and reassurance with which Khadījah provided the Prophet; her confidence that God was with him; and her active initiatives to provide Muhammad with additional reassurance (Waraqah; testing Gabriel).[139] Similarly, Khalidi depicts Khadījah as being concurrently "the great comforter of Muhammad" and "honorable, strong-willed and intelligent."[140] Ramadan depicts her as a first follower and faithful companion, who turned Muhammad into a leader, walked the path with him, stood by him, and "underwent with him rejection by his kin, persecution, and isolation." At the same time, Ramadan describes her also as a loving wife, who comforted Muhammad and "wrapped him with her love."[141] Sardar describes Khadījah as the first convert and "beloved wife, friend and councilor," who served as a role model for other followers.[142] Muhammad Anis-ur-Rahman highlights the political and religious activity of Khadījah, alongside her companionship to Muhammad, calling her "the right hand of the Holy prophet." While emphasizing her wealth, as evidence of her success as businesswoman, he also praises her as a wife, who gave Muhammad solace and comfort.[143]

Finally, Marshall G. S. Hodgson acknowledges the liminal position of Khadījah as a wife and first follower, who encouraged Muhammad to accept "the summons as coming from God himself." Hodgson concludes that Khadījah "had been a major spiritual support for [Muhammad]."[144]

Summary

The above mentioned discussion illustrates Khadījah as a liminal figure, who goes through a social drama: a breach (emergence of Islam), a crisis (open conflict with Meccan leadership), and a liminal phase (Quraysh boycott of the Muslims). Following her conversion, she is depicted as having diverse liminal characteristics. As a first follower (a liminal position), she transforms a lone nut into a leader; serves alongside the leader; shares social risk with him; is imitated by other followers; and her leadership is underappreciated. Khadījah is also a trickster figure and experiences inversion (e.g., rich to poor, honorable status to exclusion, matrilocal marriage to patrilocal). She hence does not conform with Bynum's assertion that social drama only applies to men. Indeed, one might argue that Khadījah is an untypical female figure, being Muhammad's senior, employer, and financial supporter. As such, the model of social drama might be more applicable to her than to weaker women, whose stories Bynum has studied.

Social drama, however, applies to Khadījah only partially. This becomes particularly evident when comparing her with Muhammad. Muhammad, for whom Khadījah has served as a liminal space, completed his social drama by reintegration and victory, as he conquered Mecca and married the daughter of his former head opponent, Abū Sufyān.[145] Khadījah, contrarily, did not complete the liminal phase. She died during the persecutions period in Mecca. Her inversion, therefore, was not symbolic and temporal, but irreversible and actual. A tragic trickster character, she is caught in the liminal stage through her death—which simultaneously allowed Muhammad to proceed. Furthermore, later sources deny her liminality and agency and portray her as passive and domestic. Instead of reintegration, she goes through marginalization. This is particularly evident in later medieval Islamic sources and modern scholarship.

KHADĪJAH, LIMINALITY, AND THE RECONSTRUCTION OF EARLY FEMALE CHARACTERS IN ISLAM

To an extent, the origins of this underappreciation can be traced back to Khadījah's status as a first follower. Sivers identifies underappreciated leadership as characteristic of this paradoxical, liminal, position. However, the case of Khadījah goes beyond that. The level of underappreciating and undermining her status reflects a broader, gender-related process. The impact of gender in followership is yet to be explored; however, evidence from leadership studies suggests that women face greater challenges than men in this respect.[146]

Khadījah was one of many Muslim women who were publically active in the early seventh century. Abbot, Denise Spellberg, Doris Decker, and Khalafallah have analyzed texts from the eighth to tenth century, which discuss the emergence of Islam. These texts present women as autonomous, religiously educated, and active in various aspects of public life, such as religion, education, politics, and military. However, the perception of women has gradually changed and became more restrictive during the eighth and ninth centuries, until in the tenth century, women were completely excluded from public life. Texts from this period reject female public activities and depict as passive women of earlier centuries, which earlier sources portray as active.[147] The underappreciation of Khadījah and her leadership can be interpreted in light of this development. Whereas the *sīrah* of Ibn Isḥāq (d. 767 CE), as preserved by Ibn Hishām (d. 834 CE), presents her as having agency and initiative, the chapter on Khadījah in the work of Ibn Saʿd (d. 845 CE) includes no direct speech by her.[148]

Khalafallah and Rahemtullah and Ababneh note that modern scholars, too, project later concepts and social norms unto early Islamic narratives. Applying Foucault's "history of the present," Rahemtullah and Ababneh demonstrate how later medieval Islamic sources, as well as modern Islamic and Western texts, reconstruct seventh-century Arabia so as to validate and legitimize social norms of their authors' present. Such sources exclude narratives that do not fit with their author's perceptions of what was supposedly adequate for Arab/Muslim women in seventh-century Arabia. Ali and Decker, too, observe the inclination of both Islamic sources as of the tenth century, and modern scholarship, to create an unequivocal, linear history of the origins of Islam, ignoring that the earliest Islamic sources include multiple, often contradictory, versions of specific episodes.[149] In order to legitimize and validate hegemonic practices of present day, such as patriarchal power relations in marriage, Khadījah's portrayal as a woman of agency and financial independence, whose marriage to Muhammad was matrimonial, is reframed into that of a passive, domestic(ated) woman, who married as a virgin, and quit her career upon marriage. Other wives of Muhammad, too, became a model of patriarchy and polygamy. Their significant involvement in the public, military, religious, and educational spheres was completely suppressed, until its manifestation by recent scholarship.[150]

Notably, Elaine Pagels has shown that a similar process took place during the emergence period of Christianity. Whereas early Christian women (particularly gnostic) fulfilled official roles in public and religious life (preachers, prophets, and priests), such activities were gradually repressed, and by 200 CE women were denied authority.[151] From the point of view of Turner's social drama, this process can be interpreted as the resolution of the transitional, liminal period between the emergence of a new religious movement, and its institutionalization. The agency and public activity of Khadījah and other women in seventh-century Arabia were part of the liminal context of transition from pre-Islamic to Islamic era.[152]

Liminality, however, does not have to result in removal and confinement. Sivers and Szakolczai suggest to redirect the focus from the leader to the first follower, thus making the liminal central; Bynum goes further, as she suggests to stand *with* (Khadījah), rather than look *at* her.

Early and modern sources alike acknowledge the story of Khadījah and her continuous liminality as wife and leader, who as first follower had a crucial role in the emergence of Islam.

SUMMARY

This study demonstrated that the portrayal of Khadījah in early Islamic sources corresponds fully with the "first follower" paradigm. Concurrently the first wife and first believer of Muhammad, Khadījah had a crucial role in turning the "lone nut" into a leader of a world religion. Through acknowledging Muhammad's mission; standing by him as an equal; setting a model for followership; sharing the social risk; and providing leadership, she emerged as an active, interdependent, and effective agent of the leadership process, as defined by Robert E. Kelley. By courageously following and showing others how to follow, she exercised "the best way to make a movement," according to Sivers.[153]

Indeed, the earliest Islamic sources portray Khadījah as a leader, a trickster, and a liminal character, who participated with Muhammad in the social drama of the emergence of Islam. However, unlike him, she did not see it through. Rather than reintegration, she went through marginalization. Later sources denied her liminal traits, agency, and leadership and depicted her as passive and confined to the domestic realm.

Misconceptions about one's leadership is a typical trait of the "first follower," probably deriving from the liminal nature of this position; however, in the case of Khadījah, underappreciation seems to go further beyond and reflects a gender-related bias. As of the tenth century, more restrictive gender norms came to prevail Muslim society, which collided with the earlier depictions of Khadījah as exercising agency and leadership. Similarly, certain modern works would project unto women of seventh-century Arabia norms and practices of their authors' lifetime, as a means of validating these norms. The unequivocal voice that later sources use in narrating the story of Muhammad further contributes to marginalizing Khadījah and confining her activity to the domestic sphere, thus transforming her from a first follower and an equal leadership partner of Muhammad, into a motherly figure at best, and a spiteful wife at worst.

Research has shown that other women in early Islam, and early Christianity, have gone through a similar process. The agency of these women during the emergence period of a religious movement, versus their later marginalization, can be explained through Turner's social drama. Whereas the liminal phase of the new religious movement included the removal of social norms and allowed for more freedom, following the reintegration and victory of the movement, restrictions were reapplied. Women participate in the social drama as far as breach, crisis, and liminality are concerned, but are then marginalized rather than reintegrated.

Bynum is therefore correct that social drama is not universal. However, neither is Bynum's own conviction, that social drama does not apply to women. In the case of Khadījah, it does, albeit partially. As first follower, Khadījah is a liminal, pro-active, leader figure, who is crucial for the social drama to take place. As Sivers concludes, "There is no movement without the first follower."[154]

NOTES

1. Arnold van Gennep, *The Rites of Passage*, trans. Monika B. Vizedom and Gabrielle L. Caffee (London and Henley: Routlege and Kegan Paul, 1977 [1960]).

2. Victor Turner, *The Ritual Process: Structure and Anti-Structure* (London & New York: Routledge, 2017 [1969]), 166–203. Victor Turner, "Social Dramas and

Stories about Them," *Critical Inquiry* 7, no. 1 (1980): 141–168 (149–161). Caroline Walker Bynum, "Women's Stories, Women's Symbols: A Critique of Victor Turner's Theory of Liminality," in *Fragmentation and Redemption: Essays on Gender and the Human Body in Medieval Religion*, ed. Caroline Walker Bynum (New York: Zone Books, 1992), 27–52 (29–38).

3. Bynum, 29–50.

4. Massimiliano Carocci, "Women, Temporary Liminality and Two-spirits: The Staging of Community in the Plains Indians Scalp Dance's Masquerade," *Journal of Ritual Studies* 13, no. 2 (1999): 12–25.

5. Keren Abbou Hershkovits, "Agency as Seen through the Lenses of Conversion," *The New East: Special Edition* (2018): 17–34 (34).

6. Arpad Szakolczai, "Liminality and Experience," *International Political Anthropology* 2, no. 1 (2009): 141–172 (147, 159, 165).

7. Brian Crossman and Joanna Crossman, "Conceptualizing Followership – A Review of the Literature," *Leadership* 7, no. 4 (2011): 481–497 (486), https://doi.org /10.1177/1742715011416891, retrieved 23 February 2021. Sajjad Nawaz Khan, Abdul Halim Busari, and Siti Mariam Abdullah, "The Essence of Followership: Review of the Literature and Future Research Directions," in *Servant Leadership Styles and Strategic Decision Making,* ed. Yasir Hayat and Shahid Kamal, IGI global, 2019, 148–170 (151), https://doi.org/10.4018/978-1-5225-4996-3.ch006, retrieved 19 January 2021.

8. R. E. Kelley, "In Praise of Followers," *Harvard Business Review* 66, no. 6 (1988): 142–148. Khan *et al.*, 149–151.

9. R. E. Kelley, *The Power of Followership: How to Create Leaders People Want to Follow, and Followers Who Lead Themselves* (Doubleday, 1992).

10. I. Chaleff, *The Courageous Follower: Standing Up to and for Our Leaders* (San Francisco, CA: Berrett-Koehler Publishers, 1995). Khan *et al.*, 149.

11. Khan *et al.*, 151, 158. Crossman and Crossman, 481–482.

12. Derek Sivers, "First Follower: Leadership Lessons from a Dancing Guy," https://sivers.org/ff. uploaded 2010-02-11, retrieved 29 January 2019.

13. Szakolczai, 152.

14. Sivers, "First Follower."

15. Jeffrey Inman, Is the Follower the Leader? How the First Follower Establishes the Social Norm in Sequential Behavior, Seminar Presentation, University of Melbourne, 11.02.2019, 33. Available from: https://foster.uw.edu/wp-content /uploads/2019/01/Inman_JMR-Main-Document-First-Follower.pdf, retrieved 19 January 2021. Edward J. Cartwright, Denise Lovett and Anna Stepanova, First Follower Effect in a Public Good Game Presentation, Presentation at the PET17 conference in Paris, 2017. Available from: https://pet2017paris2.sciencesconf.org /141978/document, retrieved: 23 February 2021.

16. Szakolczai, 165.

17. Szakolczai, 156.

18. Sivers mentions this trait as part of point 3; however, since the two points are not identical, here they are treated separately. As will be shown below, sharing social risk is a significant trait of the first follower, and stands in its own right.

19. Sivers, "First Follower."

20. "Abd al-Mālik Abū Muḥammd Ibn Hishām (d. 834 CE)," *Al-Sīra al-Nabawi-yya li-Ibn Hishām*, ed. Muṣṭafā al-Siqā, Ibrāhīm al-Abyārī and ʿAbd al-Ḥafīẓ Shalbī, Beirut: Dār al-Maʿrifa, n.d., 1:187–190. M. J. Kister, "The Sons of Khadīja," *JSAI* 16 (1993): 59–95 (59–61, 67, 69, 80–81, 83–84). Michael Lecker, "The Monotheistic Cousins of Muḥammad's Wife Khadīja," *Der Islam* 94, no. 2 (2017): 363–384 (363–364). Haifaa G. Khalafallah, "Precedent and Perception: Muslim Records That Contradict Narratives on Women," *Hawwa* 11 (2013): 108–132 (126–129). Barbara Stowasser, "Khadijah," *Encyclopaedia of the Qurʾan* 3:80–81. Barbara Stowasser, "The Mothers of Believers in the *Ḥadīth*," *The Muslim World* 82, no. 1–2 (1992): 1–36 (17). Shadaab Rahemtulla and Sara Ababneh, "Reclaiming Khadija's and Muhammad's Marriage as an Islamic Paradigm: Towards a New History of the Muslim Present," *Journal of Feminist Studies in Religion* 37, no. 2 (2021): 83–102 (92).

21. Kister, 68–69, 85; Naseeha S. Hussain, "Khadīja and ʿĀʾisha: A Study of Premodern and Modern Scholarly Portrayals" (master's thesis, University of Illinois at Urbana-Champaign, 2015), 51. Lecker, 364; Lawrence I. Conrad, "Abraha and Muḥammad: Some Observations Apropos of Chronology and Literary 'topoi' in the Early Arabic Historical Tradition," *BSOAS* 50, no. 2 (1987): 225–240 (236). Kecia Ali, *The Lives of Muhammad* (Cambridge; London: Harvard University Press, 2014), 119–120. Tariq Ramadan, *The Messenger: The Meanings of the Life of Muhammad* (London: Penguin Books, 2008 [first published by Oxford University Press, 2007]), 23. Other reports argue that Khadījah and Muhammad parented five, six, seven, eight, ten or thirteen children. Kister, 70–73.

22. The term "Year of the Elephant" refers to an Abyssinian expedition into the Hejaz. Conrad, 225.

23. Conrad notes that "well into the second century A.H. scholarly opinion on the birth date of the Prophet displayed a range of variance of 85 years." Conrad, 239.

24. Conrad demonstrates the likelihood of its dating to 552CE. Conrad, 225–240 (esp. pp. 227, 237). Kister, 80–81.

25. Kister, 59–66.

26. Kister, 83–84.

27. Kister, 83.

28. Ali, 232–237. Doris Decker, "The Love of Prophet Muḥammad for the Jewish Woman Rayḥāna bint Zayd: Transformation and Continuity in Gender Conceptions in Classical Islamic Historiography and Aḥādīth Literature," in *Islamic Interpretive Tradition and Gender Justice*, ed. Nevin Reda and Yasmin Amin (McGill-Queen's University Press, 2020), 209–258 (241).

29. Ibn Hishām, 1:236–238. Ibn Jarīr al-Ṭabarī (d. 923 CE), *Taʾrīkh al-Ṭabarī*, ed. Ṣudqī Jamīl al-ʿAṭṭār (Beirut: Dār al-Fikr, 1998), 218–219.

30. Nabia Abbot, "Women and the State in Early Isla," *Journal of Near Eastern Studies* 1, no. 1 (1942): 106–126 (122).

31. Szakolczai, 152, 154.

32. Muḥammad b. Manīʾ al-Hāshimī al-Baṣrī Ibn Saʿd (d. 845 CE), *Al-Ṭabaqāt al-Kubrā*, ed. Muḥammad ʿAbd al-Qādir ʿAṭāʾ (Beirut: Dār al-Kutub al-ʿIlmiyya, 1997), 1:153. Al-Ṭabarī, *Taʾrīkh*, 2:217.

33. Ibn Hishām, 1:238. Ibn Saʿd, 1:153. Al-Ṭabarī, *Taʾrīkh*, 2:218.

34. Szakolczai, 154–156.

35. Ibn Hishām, 1:238–239. Al-Ṭabarī, *Taʾrīkh*, 2:219–220.

36. Szakolczai, 155.

37. Margaret A. Mills, "Afghano-Persian Trickster Women: Definitions, Liminalities, and Gender," *Marvels & Tales: Journal of Fairy-Tale Studies* 32, no. 1 (2018): 33–58.

38. Ibid.

39. Szakolczai, 154.

40. Sivers, "First Follower."

41. Ibn Hishām, 1:190.

42. Denise Spellberg, "Political Action and Public Example: ʿĀʾishah and the Battle of the Camel," in *Women in Middle Eastern History*, ed. Nikki R. Keddie and Beth Baron (New Haven and London: Yale University Press, 1991), 45–57 (47).

43. Ibn Hishām, 1:244. Al-Ṭabarī, *Taʾrīkh*, 2:222.

44. Ibn Saʿd, 8:14.

45. Ibn Hishām, 1:241.

46. Ibn Hishām, 1:416.

47. Edward William Lane, *Arabic-English Lexicon* (London: Willams & Norgate, 1863), root *w–z–r*.

48. Abbot, 122.

49. Todd J. Foley, "Followership and Student Leadership: Exploring the Relationship," *Journal of Leadership, Accountability and Ethics* 12, no. 4 (2015): 11–23. Susan D. Baker, "Followership: The Theoretical Foundation of a Contemporary Construct," *Journal of Leadership & Organizational Studies* 14, no. 1 (2007): 50–60.

50. See part three below.

51. Ibn Hishām, 1:240.

52. Sivers, "First Follower."

53. Ibn Hishām, 1:652.

54. Martin Lings, *Muhammad: His Life Based on the Earliest Sources* (Cambridge: The Islamic Texts Society, 1991 Originally published by George Allen and Unwin, 1983), 51.

55. Abbot, 108.

56. Al-Ṭabarī, *Taʾrīkh*, 2:224.

57. Ibn Hishām, 1:245.

58. See discussion in what follows.

59. Sivers, "First Follower." Al-Ṭabarī, *Taʾrīkh*, 2:224.

60. Sivers, "First Follower."

61. Ibn Hishām, 1:240.

62. Bynum, 37.

63. Hussain, 42.

64. Ibn Hishām, 1:353–354.

65. Rahemtulla and Ababneh, 99. Leila Ahmed, *Women and Gender in Islam* (New Haven and London: Yale University Press, 1992), 48.

66. Ibn Hishām, 1:652.

67. Kister, 64, quoting al-Balādhurī (d. c. 892 CE).

68. Bynum, 48.

69. Mills, 41.

70. Szakolczai, 166.

71. Sivers, "First Follower."

72. Kister, 80. Hussain, 9.

73. Ibn Hishām, 1:189. Ali, 151.

74. Mills, 53.

75. Ibn Hishām, 1:236–237. Al-Ṭabarī, Ta'rīkh, 2:218–219.

76. Tarif Khalidi, *Images of Muhammad: Narratives of the Prophet in Islam Across the Centuries* (New York: Doubleday, 2009), 75.

77. Ali, 120.

78. Foley, 144–146. Baker, 55, 57.

79. Sivers, "First Follower."

80. Ali, 118–119.

81. Mills, 38.

82. Al-Ṭabarī, Ta'rīkh, 1:78.

83. Kister, 80

84. Rahemtulla and Ababneh, 98.

85. E.g., Ibn Hishām, 1:238–240; Ibn Saʿd, 8:13–14. See also, Jonathan E. Brockopp, "Introduction," in *The Cambridge Companion to Muhammad*, ed. Jonathan E. Brockopp (Cambridge University Press, 2010), 1–18 (p. 6).

86. "She was the first one to have believed in God and his messenger, and who held whatever he brought to be true." Ibn Hishām, 1:240.

87. Al-Ṭabarī, Ta'rīkh, 2:223.

88. Al-Ṭabarī, Ta'rīkh, 2:223.

89. Ibn Hishām, 1:245.

90. Similarly, Bukhārī records two variants of the same report, according to which Muhammad was attacked by a nonbeliever, and either his daughter Fāṭimah (later wife of ʿAlī) helped him, or Abū Bakr. Al-Yaʿqūbī relates another narration of this incident, where Abū Ṭālib father of ʿAlī helps Muhammad. Muḥammad b. Ismāʿīl al-Bukhārī (d. 870 CE), *Ṣaḥīḥ al-Bukhārī* (Beirut: Dār al-Jīl, n.d.), 5:57–58 (section of the persecution toward Muhammad and the Muslims in Mecca). Aḥmad b. Isḥāq al-Yaʿqūbī (d. 897 CE), *Ta'rīkh al-Yaʿqūbī* (Beirut: Dār al-Kutub al-ʿIlmiyya, 1999), 2:17.

91. Al-Ṭabarī, Ta'rīkh, 2:222–227.

92. ʿAlī b. al-Ḥusayn al-Masʿūdī (d. 956 CE), *Murūj al-Dhahab wa-maʿādin al-Jawhar*, ed. Saʿīd Muḥammad al-Laḥḥām (Beirut: Dār al-Fikr, 1997), 2:279–280; al-Yaʿqūbī, 2:16.

93. Al-Yaʿqūbī, 2:16.

94. Al-Masʿūdī, 2:279–280. Al-Ṭabarī, Ta'rīkh, 2:226–227.

95. Al-Bukhārī, 5:58 (section of Abū Bakr's conversion).

96. Al-Masʿūdī, 2:279–280.

97. Al-Ṭabarī, Ta'rīkh, 2:226–227.

98. Al-Ṭabarī, Ta'rīkh, 2:222–227.

99. Ibn Hishām, 1:241. Ibn Saʿd, 1:154. Al-Ṭabarī, *Taʾrīkh*, 2:221. Ibn Jarīr al-Ṭabarī (d. 923 CE), *Jāmiʿ al-bayān fī tafsīr al-Qurʾān* (Beirut: Dār al-Jīl, 1987), 30:147–148.

100. Al-Ṭabarī, *Taʾrīkh*, 2:218. Al-Ṭabarī, *Tafsīr*, 30:147.

101. Al-Ṭabarī, *Taʾrīkh*, 2:224.

102. Szakolczai, 153.

103. Ibn Saʿd, 8:14. Al-Ṭabarī, *Taʾrīkh*, 2:224.

104. Khalafallah, 127.

105. Abirami Devi Sivakumar and Siddhartha Sarkar, "Women Entrepreneurs in Small and Medium Scale Businesses in Saudi Arabia," *International Journal of Finance & Policy Analysis* 4, no. 1 (2012): 25–32 (27). Mark Nearl, Gh. Alexndru Catana, Jim L. Finlay and Foina Catana, "A Comparison of Leadership Prototypes of Arab and European Females," *International Journal of Cross Cultural Management* 7, no. 3 (2007): 291–316 (311, n. 4).

106. Sivakumar and Sarkar, 26.

107. W. Montgomery Watt, *Muhammad: Prophet and Statesman* (London: Oxford University Press, 1961), 12, 22, 34.

108. Michael Cook, *Muhammad* (Oxford and New York: Oxford University Press, 1983), 15.

109. Lings, 44.

110. Lings, 45. Rahemtulla and Ababneh, 98.

111. Brockopp, 6.

112. Ramadan, 37.

113. Andrew Rippin, *Muslims: Their Religious Beliefs and Practices,* Vol. 1: *The Formative Period,* 4th edition (Oxon: Routledge, 2012), 44.

114. Malise Ruthven, *Islam: A Very Short Introduction* (Oxford and New York: Oxford University Press, 1997), 35, 115–116.

115. Ruthven, 35.

116. Cook, 16

117. Ziauddin Sardar, *Muhammad,* All that matters series (London: Hodder Education, 2012), 45–46.

118. David Waines, *An Introduction to Islam* (New York: Cambridge University Press, 1995), 12.

119. Rahemtulla and Ababneh, 95–96. Ali, 114.

120. Ali, 121–122.

121. Chris Cillizza, CNN Editor-at-large, "Ted Cruz's Cancun Trip Violates the First Rule of Politics," https://edition.cnn.com/2021/02/18/politics/cruz-cancun -texas/index.html?iid=ob_lockedrail_topeditorial. Updated 2157 GMT (0557 HKT) February 18, 2021.

122. Ali, 121–122.

123. Carole Hillenbrand, *Islam: A New Historical Introduction* (London: Thames and Hudson, 2015), 31.

124. Ali, 122.

125. Stowasser, "Mothers," 34.

126. Watt, 79. Ali, 131–132.

127. Kister, 80; n. 96.

128. Ruthven, 36.

129. Ali, 123–124, 173.

130. Ali, 128–129.

131. Rahemtulla and Ababneh, 92

132. Barbara Stowasser, "Wives of the Prophet," *Encyclopaedia of the Qur'an* 5: 509–521 (520). Stowasser, "Mothers," 29. Hussain, 39–43.

133. Bynum, 36.

134. Abbot, 123. Ali, 119, 126, 150, 152, 173.

135. Ali, 151.

136. Rahemtulla and Ababneh, 91.

137. Abbot, 121.

138. Hussain, 50.

139. Ali, 120–121.

140. Khalidi, 75.

141. Ramadan, 9–30, 34, 35, 37.

142. Sardar, 43, 45–46, 52.

143. Ali, 126.

144. Marshall G. S. Hodgson, *The Venture of Islam: Conscience and History in a World Civilization,* Vol. 1: *The Classical Age of Islam* (Chicago and London: The University of Chicago Press, 1974), 160, 162, 171.

145. Rahemtulla and Ababneh, 84.

146. Baker, 58; See for example, Alice A. H. Eagly, "Achieving Relational Authenticity in Leadership: Does Gender Matter?," *The Leadership Quarterly* 16 (2005): 459–474.

147. Abbot, 107–108, 123. Spellberg, 46–55. Khalafallah, 127–131. Decker, "The Love," 240, 242. Doris Decker, "Frauen zwischen Selbst- und Fremdbestimmung. Wandel weiblicher Geschlechterkonstruktionen in religiösen Veränderungsprozessen am Beispiel frühislamischer Überlieferungen," in *Doing Gender—Doing Religion Fallstudien zur Intersektionalität im frühen Judentum, Christentum und Islam,* ed. Ute E. Eisen, Christine Gerber und Angela Standhartinger (Tübingen: Mohr Siebeck, 2013), 193–223 (205). Doris Decker, "Religious Educated Women in Early Islam: Conceptions of Women's Images in Arab-Islamic Texts until the Tenth Century," in *Muslim Women and Gender Justice: Concepts, Sources, and Histories,* ed. Dina El Omari, Juliane Hammer, and Mouhanad Khorchide (London and New York: Routledge, 2020), 204–220 (204–205, 215–216).

148. Hussain, 7. Decker, "The Love," 240, 242. Khalafallah, 127–131.

149. Ali, 237. Decker, "The Love," 211, 241.

150. Rahemtulla and Ababneh, 85–95. Khalafallah, 132. Decker, "Religious Educated Women," 204–220.

151. Elaine Pagels, *The Gnostic Gospels* (London: Weidenfeld & Nicholson, 1980), 49–66.

152. Abbou Hershkovits, 34. Decker, "Frauen," 219.

153. Sivers, "First Follower."

154. Abbot, 123. Sivers, "First Follower."

BIBLIOGRAPHY

Abbot, Nabia. "Women and the State in Early Islam." *Journal of Near Eastern Studies* 1, no. 1 (1942): 106–126.

Abbou Hershkovits, Keren. "*Agency as Seen through the lenses of Conversion.*" *The New East: Special Edition* (2018): 17–34.

Ahmed, Leila. *Women and Gender in Islam.* New Haven and London: Yale University Press, 1992.

Al-Bukhārī, Muḥammad b. Ismāʿīl (d. 870 CE). *Ṣaḥīḥ al-Bukhārī,* Beirut: Dār al-Jīl, n.d.

Al-Masʿūdī, ʿAlī b. al-Ḥusayn (d. 956 CE). *Murūj al-Dhahab wa-maʿādin al-Jawhar.* Edited by Saʿīd Muḥammad al-Laḥḥām. Beirut: Dār al-Fikr, 1997.

Al-Ṭabarī, Ibn Jarīr (d. 923 CE). *Jāmiʿ al-bayān fī tafsīr al-Qurʾān.* Beirut: Dār al-Jīl, 1987.

Al-Ṭabarī, Ibn Jarīr (d. 923 CE). *Taʾrīkh al-Ṭabarī.* Edited by Ṣudqī Jamīl al-ʿAṭṭār. Beirut: Dār al-Fikr, 1998.

Al-Yaʿqūbī, Aḥmad b. Isḥāq (d. 897 CE). *Taʾrīkh al-Yaʿqūbī.* Beirut: Dār al-Kutub al-ʿIlmiyya, 1999.

Ali, Kecia. *The Lives of Muhammad.* Cambridge and London: Harvard University Press, 2014.

Baker, Susan D. "Followership: The Theoretical Foundation of a Contemporary Construct." *Journal of Leadership & Organizational Studies* 14, no. 1 (2007): 50–60.

Brockopp, Jonathan E. "Introduction." In *The Cambridge Companion to Muhammad,* edited by Jonathan E. Brockopp. Cambridge University Press, 2010, 1–18 .

Bynum, Caroline Walker. "Women's Stories, Women's Symbols: A Critique of Victor Turner's Theory of Liminality." In *Fragmentation and Redemption: Essays on Gender and the Human Body in Medieval Religion,* edited by Caroline Walker Bynum, 27–52. New York: Zone Books, 1992.

Cartwright Edward J., Denise Lovett, and Anna Stepanova. "First Follower Effect in a Public Good Game Presentation." Presentation at the PET17 conference in Paris, 2017. Accessed February 23, 2021. https://pet2017paris2.sciencesconf.org/141978/document.

Chaleff, I. *The Courageous Follower: Standing Up to and for Our Leaders.* San Francisco, CA: Berrett-Koehler Publishers, 1995.

Cillizza, Chris. "Ted Cruz's Cancun Trip Violates the First Rule of Politics." https://edition.cnn.com/2021/02/18/politics/cruz-cancun-texas/index.html?iid=ob_locke-drail_topeditorial. Updated 2157 GMT (0557 HKT). Accessed February 18, 2021.

Conrad, Lawrence I. "Abraha and Muḥammad: Some Observations Apropos of Chronology and Literary 'Topoi' in the Early Arabic Historical Tradition." *BSOAS.* 50, no. 2 (1987): 225–240.

Cook, Michael. *Muhammad.* Oxford and New York: Oxford University Press, 1983.

Crossman, Brian, Joanna Crossman. "Conceptualising Followership – A Review of the Literature." *Leadership* 7, no. 4 (2011): 481–497. https://doi.org/10.1177/1742715011416891. Accessed February 23, 2021.

Decker, Doris. "Frauen zwischen Selbst- und Fremdbestimmung. Wandel weiblicher Geschlechterkonstruktionen in religiösen Veränderungsprozessen am Beispiel frühislamischer Überlieferungen." In *Doing Gender—Doing Religion Fallstudien zur Intersektionalität im frühen Judentum, Christentum und Islam*, edited by Ute E. Eisen, Christine Gerber, und Angela Standhartinger, 193–223. Tübingen: Mohr Siebeck, 2013.

Decker, Doris. "Religious Educated Women in Early Islam: Conceptions of Women's Images in Arab-Islamic Texts until the Tenth Century." In *Muslim Women and Gender Justice: Concepts, Sources, and Histories*, edited by Dina El Omari, Juliane Hammer, and Mouhanad Khorchide, 204–220. London and New York: Routledge, 2020.

Decker, Doris. "The Love of Prophet Muḥammad for the Jewish Woman Rayḥāna bint Zayd: Transformation and Continuity in Gender Conceptions in Classical Islamic Historiography and Aḥādīth Literature." In *Islamic Interpretive Tradition and Gender Justice*, edited by Reda Nevin and Yasmin Amin, 209–258. McGill-Queen's University Press, 2020.

Eagly, A. H. "Achieving Relational Authenticity in Leadership: Does Gender Matter?" *The Leadership Quarterly* 16 (2005): 459–474.

Foley, Todd J. "Followership and Student Leadership: Exploring the Relationship." *Journal of Leadership, Accountability and Ethics* 12, no. 4 (2015): 11–23.

Hillenbrand, Carole. *Islam: A New Historical Introduction.* London: Thames and Hudson, 2015.

Hodgson, Marshall G. S. *The Venture of Islam: Conscience and History in a World civilization.* Vol. 1: The classical age of Islam. Chicago and London: The University of Chicago Press, 1974.

Hussain, Naseeha S. "Khadīja and ʿĀʾisha: A Study of Premodern and Modern Scholarly Portrayals." Master's thesis, University of Illinois at Urbana-Champaign, 2015.

Ibn Hishām, ʿAbd al-Mālik Abū Muḥammd (d. 834 CE). *Al-Sīra al-Nabawiyya li-Ibn Hishām.* Muṣṭafā al-Siqā, Ibrāhīm al-Abyārī and ʿAbd al-Ḥafīẓ Shalbī, eds. Beirut: Dār al-Maʿrifa, n.d.

Ibn Saʿd, Muḥammad b. Manīʾ al-Hāshimī al-Baṣrī (d. 845 CE). *Al-Ṭabaqāt al-Kubrā.* Muḥammad ʿAbd al-Qādir ʿAṭṭāʾ, ed. Beirut: Dār al-Kutub al-ʿIlmiyya, 1997.

Inman, Jeffrey. Is the Follower the Leader? How the First Follower Establishes the Social Norm in Sequential Behavior. Seminar Presentation, University of Melbourne. February 11, 2019. Accessed January 19, 2021. https://foster.uw.edu/wp-content/uploads/2019/01/Inman_JMR-Main-Document-First-Follower.pdf.

Kelley, R. E. "In Praise of Followers." *Harvard Business Review* 66, no. 6 (1988): 142–148.

Kelley, R. E. *The Power of Followership: How to Create Leaders People Want to Follow, and Followers Who Lead Themselves.* Doubleday, 1992.

Khalafallah, Haifaa G. "Precedent and Perception: Muslim Records That Contradict Narratives on Women." *Hawwa* 11 (2013): 108–132.

Khalidi, Tarif. *Images of Muhammad: Narratives of the Prophet in Islam Across the Centuries.* New York: Doubleday, 2009.

Khan, Sajjad Nawaz, Abdul Halim Busari, and Siti Mariam Abdullah. "The Essence of Followership: Review of the Literature and Future Research Directions." In *Servant Leadership Styles and Strategic Decision Making*, edited by Yasir Hayat and Shahid Kamal, 148–170. IGI global, 2019. https://doi.org/10.4018/978-1-5225 -4996-3.ch006.

Kister, M.J. "The Sons of Khadīja." *JSAI* 16 (1993): 59–95.

Lane, Edward William. *Arabic-English Lexicon*. London: Willams & Norgate, 1863.

Lecker, Michael. "The Monotheistic Cousins of Muḥammad's Wife Khadīja." *Der Islam* 94, no. 2 (2017): 363–384.

Lings, Martin. *Muhammad: His Life Based on the Earliest Sources*. Cambridge: The Islamic Texts Society, 1991 [Originally published by George Allen and Unwin, 1983].

Mills, Margaret A. "Afghano-Persian Trickster Women: Definitions, Liminalities, and Gender." *Marvels & Tales: Journal of Fairy-Tale Studies* 32, no. 1 (2018): 33–58.

Neal, Mark, Jim L. Finlay, Gh. Alexandru Catana, and Doina Catana. "A Comparison of Leadership Prototypes of Arab and European Females." *International Journal of Cross Cultural Management*, 7, no. 3 (2007): 291–316.

Rahemtulla, Shadaab and Sara Ababneh. "Reclaiming Khadija's and Muhammad's Marriage as an Islamic Paradigm: Towards a New History of the Muslim Present." *Journal of Feminist Studies in Religion* 37, no. 2 (2021): 83–102.

Ramadan, Tariq. *The Messenger: The Meanings of the Life of Muhammad*. London: Penguin Books, 2008 [first published by Oxford University Press, 2007].

Rippin, Andrew. *Muslims: Their Religious Beliefs and Practices*. Vol. 1: The Formative Period. 4th edition. Oxon: Routledge, 2012.

Ruthven, Malise. *Islam: A Very Short Introduction*. Oxford and New York: Oxford University Press, 1997.

Sardar, Ziauddin. *Muhammad*. All that matters series. London: Hodder Education, 2012.

Sivakumar, Abirami Devi and Siddhartha Sarkar. "Women Entrepreneurs in Small and Medium Scale Businesses in Saudi Arabia." *International Journal of Finance & Policy Analysis* 4, no. 1 (2012): 25–32.

Sivers, Derek. "First Follower: Leadership Lessons from a Dancing Guy." Accessed January 29, 2019. https://sivers.org/ff. Uploaded 2010-02-11. .

Spellberg, Denise. "Political Action and Public Example: ʿAʾisha and the Battle of the Camel." In *Women in Middle Eastern History*, edited by Nikki R. Keddie and Beth Baron, 45–57. New Haven and London: Yale University Press, 1991.

Stowasser, Barbara. "Wives of the Prophet." *Encyclopaedia of the Qurʾan* 5: 509–521.

Stowasser, Barbara. "Khadijah." *Encyclopaedia of the Qurʾan* 3: 80–81.

Stowasser, Barbara. "The Mothers of Believers in the *Ḥadīth*." *The Muslim World* 82, no. 1–2 (1992): 1–36.

Szakolczai, Arpad. "Liminality and Experience." *International Political Anthropology* 2, no. 1 (2009): 141–172.

Turner, Victor. *The Ritual Process: Structure and Anti-Structure*. London and New York: Routledge, 2017 [1969].

Turner, Victor. "Social Dramas and Stories About Them." *Critical* Inquiry 7, no. 1 (1980): 141–168.

van Gennep, Arnold. *The Rites of Passage*. Translated by Monika B. Vizedom and Gabrielle L. Caffee. London and Henley: Routlege and Kegan Paul, 1977 [1960].

Waines, David. *An Introduction to Islam*. New York: Cambridge University Press, 1995.

Watt, W. Montgomery. *Muhammad: Prophet and Statesman*. London: Oxford University Press, 1961.

Conclusion

Michael Hubbard MacKay and
Zohar Hadromi-Allouche

This volume does little to highlight the intensive fieldwork that led to Victor Turner's theories of liminality and communitas, but it celebrates the junctures and possibilities that emerged from his scholarship that are still relevant today. Though the structural functionalism that built his ideas is no longer in vogue, scholars are still interested in the processes of change, conflict, ritual, drama, society, and normativity. His obsession with structure leading to process is calculable and patterned, set for use and re-use, while his recognition of the possibility for historical change also still makes practical sense for scholars researching society. This volume makes four broad contributions organized by each section. It first takes hold of Turner's creativity and applies it broadly to a world setting to see how liminality can be a tool for examining society across cultures, nations, world religions, and migration. Second, it challenges the way we might use liminality to understand society within a defined group whether it be through graffiti, contingent agency, dance, or ritual polygamy. Third, this volume stretches liminality to examine the power of the imaginative in Christian/Jewish relationship in literature and the liminal space of the visceral and virtual in dance and choreography. Finally, this volume adds to the idea of change by juxtaposing liminality with Illich's hope to garner a kind of maintenance of a threshold in society in a benevolent attempt to challenge systems. Also, it recognizes the patriarchal emphasis of social change by finding the way women act as liminal figures without status in society and without the ritual process of maturation and hierarchy. In conclusion, this volume praises and questions Turner's ideas of liminality, all the while celebrating the development of gaps and changes in the human experience.

When work, like Victor Turner's, expands beyond the boundaries of the narrow discipline they were developed within, it is worth pausing to contemplate its significance and its ability goes beyond the historically contingent environment it was first articulated within. Scholars may find it outdated or irrelevant, but it may help develop new horizons too. Disciplinary work is easily critiqued from another discipline that maintains different perspectives and dissimilar world views. This volume demonstrates that an interdisciplinary approach to Turner's work gives it depth and shapes its more universal value. It also demands that theories like Turner's are used in malleable ways to avoid the dogmatism of theory, especially when it is used across disciplines and fields of study. On the other hand, liminality or a liminal condition is an important idea in general to explain the human experience in dance, dialogue, religion, and space. The moment when we are "betwixt and between" evokes a perpetual, ambivalent, and challenging state of social reality, not to mention its relationship to the processes of change.

LIMINALITY WITHOUT

In the first section, liminality and its relationship with marginalized people and religions illuminate the social realities and tensions of expatriate black Americans in Israel, marks the margins of East and West and the particular and the universal Algerian Christian experience from within a Muslim culture, and the psychological and emotional states splitting the minds of immigrants between home and host countries. This section captures a world of liminality marking itself across contemporary borders and betwixt and between world religions. It's a world that the Ndembu could never exhibit, a world of wandering souls, marginalized world groups, and distressed immigrants. This section demonstrates that liminality and marginalization multiply as the world becomes more accessible. It also demonstrates that if we are to use Turner's work on liminality more broadly it will need new tools and new ways of using those tools, from the carefully written novel to new ways of thinking about theology and how it collides with modern governments and breaches political borders.

LIMINALITY WITHIN

Section II returns to liminality within a group, rather than focusing on the transgression of groups and borders to focus on the importance of liminal space and communication. It does all this by examining graffiti, apprenticeship, dance, and ritual polygamy. Graffiti of all things exhibits evidence of liminality in the medieval church porch. The porch gathers and prepares and separates and divides the religious and nonreligious worlds. The graffiti itself is the language of how that space became ritual, it is the practice of ritual liminality. This section uses Turner's founding work in performance theory to springboard into a detailed examination of apprenticeship relationships. Coppersmiths are caught in a liminal space yet find their way to agential moments under the tensions of contingency. It enables the creative agency to be an important part of liminality, acknowledging "the creativity of perception and knowing-in-doing." This section asks how liminality emerges when the choreographer of the Taipei Dance Circle dies, and the dance becomes collaborative and impromptu. Bodies, movements, space, and time become liminal as the dance changes between individuals and institutions. Finally, it challenges Turner's theories to account for reaggregation by developing the relationship between secularism and religion in the lives of nineteenth-century Mormon polygamists. This section not only gives examples of how to use Turner's theories to expand liminality, but it also challenges his work to open doors to contemporary theory. It does this by examining groups changing and vetting themselves in social and cultural reproduction, all the while, finding agential creativity in the way individuals shape society.

WITHIN AND WITHOUT

The third section argues that liminality is dialogical. Focusing on the dialogue of the wise Jew called in to court to a foreign Christian or Muslim king, this section develops the precariousness of liminality in ritual drama. This reveals the relationship between ritual pattern found in Turnerian ritual process and narrative structure, and while the narrative and ritual gave maintenance to the process, it "was later dashed repeatedly by cruel realities of history." Creatively exploring liminality, this section is juxtaposed with an investigation of technology and dance through and exploration of Falling which includes live performance and digital images moving in and out of the stage area. The dancers themselves interact with their own digital projections in a visceral yet undeniable virtual performance. This intermediality deals not with the social reality of a group, like Ndembu, but rather with the possibility of liminality and its potential thresholds and worlds. These dialogical representations move us away from the ethnography of nature towards the visceral interaction with the wildly imaginative and virtual possibilities of liminality.

LIMINALITY AND CHANGE

The final section contributes to the perception or actual change that happens in the world through liminality. Using the work of Ivan Illich, this section challenges modernity and professionalization in the way that they monopolize thresholds and progression. Liminality is used to examine industrial and technological culture but challenges whether the professionalization of schooling is beneficial to learning or whether technology impedes communication. Rather, this section asks the question of whether liminality could be maintained in "a status of recurrent permanence" instead of ritual process or practice and reintegration. Living at the threshold would avoid systems and conspicuous consumption of systems in a pedagogy of liminality. Conversely this section also explores change and liminality by examining women's roles in conversion and transition in early Islam. Women could be agents of change and conversion. As such, they became relevant to change and conversion in early Islamic society. Khadījah, in particular, as the first follower of The Prophet Muhammad, became a decisive character in the new religious movement's founding. Liminality, which serves as an important way of understanding Khadījah's role as first follower, is essential also to describing perceived gendered roles in classical and modern sources about her.

Index

Page references for figures are italicized

313

About the Contributors

Keren Abbou Hershkovits teaches at the Open University and Ben Gurion University(Israel). Her PhD research in Middle Eastern Studies (Ben Gurion University, 2008) examined "'The Transmission of Science to the Muslim World, eighth–fourteenth Century," and she published several articles on the history of medicine and history of spectacles in the Muslim world. Her current research focuses on gender and conversion to Islam in the seventh to the tenth centuries and agency within the early Islamic community. She is currently a coeditor of *Scriptural Sexuality*, a volume on sexuality in sacred texts from Ugarit to Islam (with Nirmal Fernando and Zohar Hadromi-Allouche).

Patrick Brittenden is research associate at the Centre for Religion and Culture, Regents Park College, Oxford, and a member of the Advisory Board of the Centre for Muslim-Christian Studies, Oxford. He is also associate lecturer and faculty member of the Institute Chretien d'Algerie (ICA) and director of the Hikma Research Partnership.

Pauline Brooks (B.A., P.G.C.E., M.F.A, Ph.D.) is a Visiting Research Fellow at Liverpool John Moores University (UK) and an independent choreographer. Her research is practice-led and involves dance performance, technology, and pedagogy. For over fifteen years her research has involved collaboration in intermedial and telematic performance with colleagues in dance and music in the UK, United States, and Europe. She received the LJMU Vice Chancellor's Medal for Excellence for Teaching Innovation and served as Associate Dean (Quality and Assurance). Prior to lecturing at LJMU, she performed with *Nexus Dance Theatre* (Scotland), *Springs Dance Company* (England), *Ann Vachon/Dance Conduit,* and *Sybil Dance*

Company (USA). She has choreographed and taught extensively in the UK and overseas, and lectured in dance in Scotland, England, and the United States.

Yu-Chun Chen was born in Taipei city, Taiwan. She graduated from a Ph.D. program at the University of Roehampton in 2019, with the thesis "*'Become and becoming a dancer'': an ethnography of the Taipei Dance Circle.* From 2020 to 2022, three publications: "To the end of a dance troupe: On and Off the stage of Floating Horizons," Performances as Rituals," and "To Move 'the Technologies of the Self': the Embodiment of Somaesthetics in Dance Improvisation" had been published from her research in *Taipei Theatre Journal, Introducing Anthropology* and *Taiwan Dance Research Journal.* Currently, Dr. Chen has a full manuscript under consideration with Berghahn Publications.

Michele Avis Feder-Nadoff is an artist and anthropologist, PhD in Social Sciences, El Colegio de Michoacán, Mexico, M.F.A and B.F.A., School of the Art Institute of Chicago. She is assistant editor of the *Journal of Embodied Research*, a Fulbright Scholar (2010--2011), editor of *Rhythm of Fire: The Art & Artisans of Santa Clara del Cobre* (2004), and director-producer of the accompanying video *Huele de Noche/Night-Blooming Jasmine.* Feder-Nadoff founded Cuentos Foundation, an arts and culture non-profit in 1998 which she directed until 2009. The forthcoming monograph *Presence of Absence: An Anthropology of Making in Santa Clara del Cobre, Michoacán* is a meditation on her long-term mentorship to the coppersmith, Maestro Jesús Pérez Ornelas (1926–2014) in his family forge. *Performing Crafts in Mexico: Artisans, Aesthetics, and the Power of Translation.*

Zohar Hadromi-Allouche is assistant professor in Classical Islamic Religious Thought and Dialogue in Trinity College Dublin. Her research examines transitional themes, elements, and characters in Islamic religious texts, and in interreligious context, such as divine-human relations, gendered and fallen characters, and demonology. She is the editor of *Fall Narratives: An Interdisciplinary Perspective* (with Áine Larkin; 2016) and *Fallen Animals: Art, Religion, Literature* (2017), and currently coedits a volume on *Scriptural Sexuality* in neareastern religions (with Keren Abbou Hershkovitz and Nirmal Fernando). She is the author of articles, chapters, and encyclopedic entries on Satan in the Islamic tradition; Eve in Islamic art and tradition; and intertextual encounters between the Qur'an and the Hebrew Bible.

Jamie Ingram has recently completed his doctorate in Medieval Archaeology at the University of Southampton, focusing on lay activity and practice during personal worship. He has an interest in theoretical archaeology and ethnography and the integration of material culture and historical texts into theoretical debate, specifically the application of theory to aid in the understanding of social and cultural action in the past.

Jose R. Irizarry teaches in the field of Theology and Culture at Villanova University in Pennsylvania. A former president of the Religious Education Association in the United States and Canada, his research focuses on the intersections of intercultural practices and the pedagogy of religious institutions. Irizarry is native of the island of Puerto Rico and publishes in Spanish and English on topics that inform the emerging field of practical theology. He currently serves as newly appointed president of Austin Presbyterian Theological Seminary.

Michael Hubbard MacKay is associate professor of religion at Brigham Young University. His research focuses on religious authority, ritual studies, and religious studies. He the author of several monographs including *Prophetic Authority: Democratic Authority and the Mormon Priesthood* and an editor of several volumes including *Producing Ancient Scripture: Joseph Smith's Translation Projects in the Development of Mormon Christianity.*

Michael T. Miller works in Jewish Studies, initially in Jewish mysticism and philosophy, but more recently in Black Judaism. He is pursuing a major project on the African Hebrew Israelite community, for the new monograph (Bloomsbury 2023) on the thought and theology of Ben Ammi Ben Israel. His previous monograph was on the *Name of God in Jewish Thought* (2016). He taught Jewish Studies at Liverpool Hope University for three years and is currently based in Poland, where he works at the Polish Institute of Advanced Studies.

Maria Antonietta Struzziero is an independent scholar. She completed her PhD in Linguistic and Literary Studies at the University of Salerno with a doctoral dissertation on Jeanette Winterson and the love discourses in some of her novels. She has published several articles and book chapters on different topics and authors and given papers at Italian and international conferences. Her main fields of study include modernism, post-modernism, gender studies, auto/biographical writing, feminist theories, and trauma studies. She is currently working on experimental life-writing in two contemporary memoirs by Hilary Mantel and Maggie O'Farrell, as well as on the rereading of mythology in some recent novels. She has coedited "Voci ed echi: Quaderni di letteratura comparata" and translated two novels.

Eric Ziolkowski is H. P. Manson Professor of Bible, Head of the Department of Religious Studies, Co-coordinator of the Medieval, Renaissance, and

Early Modern Studies Program, and co-leader of the Humanities Center at Lafayette College in Easton, PA. He is author of numerous books, articles, and essays in the comparative study of religion and literature and main editor of the prospective thirty-volume *Encyclopedia of the Bible and Its Reception* (2009–) twenty-two volumes published to date. He also coedits two book series, Studies in Religion and the Arts (Brill) and Studies of the Bible and Its Reception (De Gruyter), and is coeditor of Bloomsbury's in-progress six-volume *Cultural History of Western Myth.*

Milton Keynes UK
Ingram Content Group UK Ltd.
UKHW042041120224
437713UK00004B/36